GANDHIGIRI

SATYAGRAHA AFTER HUNDRED YEARS

Books by the Author

Tradition and Innovation in Indian Political Thought

Political Theory : Interrogations and Interventions

Critical Theory : The Marx-Marcuse Encounter

Liberalism and the Communitarian Challenge

John Rawls and the Agenda of Social Justice

C.B. Macpherson and Liberalism

Contemporary Political Thinking

Nietzsche After Hundred Years

Citizenship in a Globalising World

GANDHIGIRI

SATYAGRAHA AFTER HUNDRED YEARS

B.N. Ray
Vice Principal
Ramjas College, University of Delhi

2008
Kaveri Books
New Delhi - 110 002

First Published in 2008

ISBN-10 : 81-7479-090-X
ISBN-13 : 978-81-7479-090-3

Published by
Kaveri Books
4697/ 5-21 A, Ansari Road,
New Delhi - 110 002 (India).
Ph.: 011-2328 8140, 2324 5799
E-mail: kaveribooks@vsnl.com

Laser Typesetting by
Aarati Computers, Delhi - 110 009

PRINTED IN INDIA

For

Ashok Das
who practises Gandhigiri
in an un-Gandhian way

Preface

In a time ravaged by large scale violence and unending terror where nothing seems more promising and urgent than to be reminded of another possibility: the path of non-violent struggle for justice exemplified by Mahatma Gandhi. Gandhi continues to be the subject of enduring relevance and interest as it is evident in the interest and passion generated by popular movie, *Lage Raho Munnabhai*. Gandhigiri is gradually entering into popular imagination and academic discourses. His writings, running into more than one hundred volumes contains wide range of views on different issues. In the nearly six decades since his death a large and diverse range of writings – comparative, expository, biographical, hagiographical and dialogical – has appeared on Gandhi.

Mohandas Karamchand Gandhi, described variously as the 'father of the nation', 'Mahatma', 'apostle of non-violence", and then disparagingly by his detractors as 'the half-naked fakir", Mr. Gandhi as Jinnah insisted and later 'Maulana Gandhi' as the Hindu right sneeringly called him instead of Mahatma, was quite simply addressed as 'Bapu' by his followers. He devoted his life to truth, non-violence and the promotion of communal harmony. Ironically, he fell to the bullet of an assassin – a violent death at the hands of a Hindu Fundamentalist man who harboured hatred and malice.

The life of Mahatma Gandhi is abundantly documented; perhaps no life in any period has been more so. Certainly it was an extraordinary life, fusing, as it did, ancient Hindu religion and culture and modern revolutionary ideas about politics and society. There are at present about four hundred biographies of Gandhi, yet, as Jawaharlal Nehru once observed "no man can write a real life of Gandhi, unless he is as big as Gandhi."[1] In Nehru's view, the best that anyone could hope to do was to conjure up some pictures of that life: "Many pictures rise in my mind of this man, whose eyes were often full of laughter and yet were pools of infinite sadness. But the picture that is dominant and most significant is as I saw him marching, staff in hand, to Dandi on the salt march in 1930; here was the pilgrim on his quest of truth, quiet, peaceful, determined and fearless, who would continue the quest and pilgrimage, regardless of consequences." Leaving aside the riddle of who but Gandhi could write his "real life," the writer's task would have to be to discover and truthfully portray the heroic but human pilgrim amid the myths that began proliferating around him when he started his quest and that have inevitably become more numerous because the quest ended in martyrdom. In fact, the very core of Gandhi's thought, presented and developed in tens of thousands of his writings and speeches—his search for God through celibacy and cleanliness, through mastery of all human needs and functions, mental and bodily, and through insistence on personal hygiene and public sanitation—has been obscured by mythologies fearful of debasing and sensationalizing their martyred hero. Perhaps because Indians rely for information more on the spoken than on the written word, and because they still live close to the soil.

The leitmotif of the book promises and promotes a fruitful dialogue with a creative and original thinker whose ideas and practices deserve more than either adoration or dismissal.

The periodic reassessment and reappraisal of the value of what we have inherited from thinkers living and dead is always undertaken from the vantage-point of our own time and circumstance. We reappraise in the light of problems we encounter or choose to emphasize. And we do so with some sense of where we, as students of political theory, have been and hope to go.

To supply any sort of forecast for the future direction and condition of political theory is always dangerous, if only because predictions about changing human thoughts, actions, and practices are notoriously unreliable and almost always precarious. One need not be a Hegelian to appreciate the point of Hegel's warning about the dangers inherent in attempting to go beyond the world one knows and inhabits. Whatever happens, every individual is a child of his time; so philosophy too is its own time apprehended in thoughts. It is just as absurd to fancy that a philosophy can transcend its contemporary world as it is to fancy that an individual can overleap his own age, jump over Rhodes. If his theory really goes beyond the world as it is and he builds an ideal one as it ought to be, that world exists indeed, but only in his opinions, an unsubstantial element where anything may, in fancy, be built.

In this book I want to explore the contemporary meaning of Gandhi's life and work – both his stupendous contributions in terms of making and remaking the world he lived in and his own strong sense of tragedy and trauma where he found he had failed to live up to his own expectations on matters that were close to his heart and to his sense of purpose and meaning in life. These are to be seen not merely as events or encounters during his own lifetime but also in the context of today's challenges and failures of the human enterprise, both building on what he has left behind and building a new edifice, struggling our way through the maze of ambivalences that seem to be out now and in the years and decades that lie ahead.

For we do face, as individuals and peoples and the world at large, as a planet and a cosmos, now and in the years and decades to come beyond which it is difficult to prognosticate, a highly uncertain future, in many ways going downhill yet somehow trying to keep hope alive while knowing fully well the depth of the crisis facing humanity. For, it is only through a major act of imagination backed by sustained experimentation through which new stirrings of both conscience and consciousness take place that the proverbial candle of hope can be generated. As the French philosopher and ecologist, Jacques Ellul has said, it is only at a time of abandonment and anguish that the need for hope arises, indeed becomes imperative. In Gandhi's life there were many moments of abandonment, both by his colleagues and compatriots but more by the high expectations that he had set out for himself and for those who cared to journey with him in search for truth and steadfastness. But while at some points he was full of remorse and a deep sense of failure, at no point did he give up putting up a valiant struggle for the values he stood for.

It was through this combination of transparency about one's travails, trials, and turbulations as well as of interventions through ceaseless "experiments" and by sharing them with one's fellow-beings through a unique style of communication that Gandhi was able to relate to the world he lived in and in the process seek to remake it that his singular contribution lay, and it is precisely in this respect that the world we are contemporaneously placed in is found to be deeply lacking. Hence the crisis of accountability on the one hand and a deep sense of alienation and anomie on the other. The world we live in is one characterized by an all–round decline in the democratic spirit and its moral basis – even while so many nations adopt an apparently democratic form of government – and one in which national and international elites are increasingly living in fear and insecurity, surrounding themselves with a massive apparatus of security, separating them from their own peoples, sharply reducing a sense of identity and community with them, not to speak of love for one's fellow beings and service of them based on love on which Gandhi laid so much stress.

Gandhi was and remains a communicator par excellance, making his presence felt far and wide, in his own country and beyond, a kind of village bard writ large over the expanse of the whole of human civilization, utilizing an idiom and a language that he himself created, cutting across the divides of cultures, of tradition and modernity, reinterpreting both and producing a new cross – fertilization across them. And he has not ceased to do so almost half a century after he physically left us, and today also in a language and idiom that is unique and characteristically his own which many of us are still trying to decipher and deconstruct, especially of late when he seems to be looking once again at us with his uncanny, piercing eyes, from behind his daunting pair of spectacles.

Whereas Gandhi himself strove, both in his fundamental thinking and in his activist encounters with reality, to wrestle simultaneously with larger civilizational and cosmic challenges and the here-and-now issues that were crying out for response and resolution, I think it would be a mistake on our part to accept or dismiss him merely on the basis of the immediate issues he faced, sought his best to deal with and, as with many other great men and women, ultimately failed to resolve. Perhaps the real task lies elsewhere: trying to grapple with the immediate both in the present and at same time by seeking to change the contours of the same at large, of the cultural and civilizational encounters engulfing its journey through time, through which alone, in the final analysis, the mundane and the immediate issues could be effectively dealt with. Without changing the former, the handling of the latter would remain too adhocism and unable to hold against the diverse currents sweeping humanity. Even if these latter temporarily produce "solutions," these cannot last for long and will recur once again, perhaps in more vicious forms. This was the import of Gandhi's holistic and unified approach. Towards the end, he felt he failed to carry through his mission in life.

But, then, that is the whole charm and meaning of the great moulders of the modern world – as indeed was in the ages gone by and especially of those who do not accept the world as it existed and were seeking ways of refashioning it after a new yearning for both comprehension and change and a new vision and idea of the world as it should be. If in the process they "fail" to solve problems of an immediate kind, it only underscores tenacity of certain kinds of problems, reflecting the persisting paradoxes and traumas that inform the human enterprise even while struggling to keep hope alive as was mentioned at the start of this essay and straining one's utmost to face up the many tests and trials that continue to beseech that enterprise – then, now, and in the times that lie ahead.

In the years to come, and may be right into the next millennium – as it unfolds this state of affairs is likely to continue – a litany of unresolved problems because of the failure to deal with the deeper social and intellectual causes to many of which Gandhi tried to draw the attention of his fellowmen at home and in the world at large. His overall effort was at once as a thinker and as an activist and through that combination as one trying to change the world.

For me Gandhi – and what he thought and taught and debated with his contemporaries – were at bottom intellectual and philosophical matters. He dwelt deep into the human enterprise and on that basis transcended categories of time, space, and various other divides. It is for this reason that he today once again gaining in resonance after having been forgotten for so long. It is in the context of this timelessness of Gandhi that we have to understand his relevance for all times and ages. He himself suffered from a deep sense of guilt and anguish for having "failed" on matters he had identified himself with during his life's journey for "truth". While we too can and must pass judgements on this journey of his – which still continues in our own time and is still available like an open book to us all – and while we should chart our own path suited to the call of our own time, and the times that lie ahead, we could also, in so doing, benefit from the thoughts and lessons left behind from his journey in his own time. As in many ways those lessons have a bearing on the challenges emerging before us, we could think of joining him on his unfinished journey.

Perhaps, the best way of explaining what this book does is by explaining what it does not. It does not, like Erikson's celebrated psychological reconstruction of Mahatma Gandhi, explore the subconscious reservoirs from which his theory of militant non-violence sprung. It is not, like Louis Fischer's hugely popular account, a brisk and breezy overview of Gandhi's ideas and his impact on the world. It is, in comparison to Joseph Doke's deeply personal recollection, much more than a portrait of a specific period in the great man's life.

There are no grand theories here, no sweeping generalisations, no too-clever-by-half conjectures. By and large, I am content to stay out of sight, emerging here and there to make a cautious interjection or a circumspect explanation. One of the very few places I depart from this approach is when I passionately defend Gandhi's approach against the criticism that he used religion and religious metaphors in the struggle for freedom. Between a politics that pretended religion was absent from India and a politics that squarely faced religion's hold," Gandhi's choice of the latter was the right one. The riots following the Partition, I argue, were not a result of religion being brought into politics; rather, I argue, they occurred despite Gandhi's efforts to persuade people that all religions "taught goodwill", because of the hate and fear many a Indians nursed and spread at the time.

The portrait of Gandhi painted here emerges slowly from the timid and somewhat cowardly Kathiawari childhood, the awkward years as a student in England, the growing confidence as a lawyer in South Africa, a self-assurance that ironically emerged from his humiliation, and his emergence as a leader in India..

Many books have been written at a time when the Mahatma has already been repeatedly put through the biographical wringer. His life has been scrutinised from every conceivable perspective. He has been praised and derided, his contradictions laid bare and reconciled, his ideas psychoanalysed, his motives demystified, his charisma deconstructed. In the face of such a daunting biographical history, it is something of a challenge to embark on another Gandhi project.

The library at Mani Bhavan already has 50,000 books on Gandhi that provide a measure of the man in every possible facet. Why would anyone wish to write the 50,001st book? One may be asked that question frequently. Some of the best biographies on Gandhi —by B R Nanda, Louis Fischer, Geoffrey Ashe, Tendulkar, Pyarelal — were written immediately after the assassination and therefore do not have access to many illuminating documents on his life that were discovered later.

Writing this book was a daunting task, and reading it may not be a very comfortable experience. After all Gandhi is our only serving national icon, even though our reverence for him is confined mainly to the ritualistic celebration of the birth and death anniversaries. Many idolize Gandhi even today and consider him as one of the tallest men to have visited this earth. But it is a historical necessity to reappraise, reinterpret and reevaluate once in a while every great movement, every great leader, to assess their contemporary relevance. And this book is a modest endeavour in that regard.

I hope that this portrayal of Gandhi's ideas will be useful for those who would like to explore his tactics, experiment with them, perhaps adopt them as their own. I hope it might also be valuable to those who want to compare Gandhi's ideas with other forms of conflict resolution and social action. Perhaps it will also be useful to those who are determined to rebuke Gandhi and prove him wrong.

I believe that Gandhi would have approved of all of these purposes, even the last. For if one follows Gandhi's own advice, nothing should go unchallenged—not even Gandhian concepts. In order to understand Gandhi's way of fighting, therefore, we will eventually have to fight a bit with him ourselves.

Gandhians, as well as non-Gandhians, are divided on what constitutes "the true Gandhi" and the true Gandhian approach to political reality. Both proponents and opponents often appeal to an essential decontextualized Gandhi, usually identified with a rather clear, static, and rigid political approach, and then disagree on whether this essential Gandhi is relevant or irrelevant to contemporary political development.

By contrast, I maintain that there is not one true, decontextualized political thought of Gandhi. Not only was Gandhi's political thinking flexible, eclectic, and at times contradictory, but our attempts at relating Gandhi's approach to contemporary political thinking always involve a dynamic process of contestation with the reinterpretation, reconstruction, and development of diverse Gandhian positions.

Was he a politician or a saint? Was he, as critics have alleged, someone who broke a pledge that he would rather die than accept Partition? Was he not an unfeeling husband and father? A man who did strange things in the name of chastity? Or emasculated India in the name of non-violence? Or patronised Dalits without empowering them?

It is, therefore, quite easy to prove that there are many Gandhis by selecting a set of his quotes which best serve one's purpose. And this was the greatest challenge facing me in writing this book. I have meticulously tried to overcome this temptation by applying two tests to my selections: one, how aptly a particular quote or event faithfully reflects the mood of the moment and is true to its context; and two, to what extent it is in consonance with Gandhi's overall worldview.

I have examined major aspects of Gandhigiri in this book. In each case, I have tried to first state his own version of the matter, and in his own words to the extent possible. I have attempted a critical appraisal of that aspect supported by Gandhi's own observations as far as possible. This approach may, at times, appear to construct the narrative with too many quotations, yet I have taken this risk so as to lend greater credibility to the conclusions drawn. For the same reason, I have mostly relied on primary sources in presenting my case.

Looking to the nature and vastness of the Gandhian crusade, it may seem inappropriate to describe it as a 'failure' despite all its shortcomings. Rabindranath Tagore may have been right in his comments that Gandhi will not succeed. Perhaps he will fail as the Buddha failed and as Christ failed to wean men from their inequities, but he will always be remembered as one who made his life a lesson for all ages to come.

Gandhi is not a preacher, but a doer. He engaged in political activity with the objective of achieving specific goals. He believed that every age has its *yugadharma*, and the dharma of his age was politics. His singular aim in life was to attain moksha, and he firmly believed that his moksha lay in the practice of politics. He did not attach any importance to his speeches and sermons, and said, 'As a mater of fact my writings shall be cremated with my body. What I have done will endures, not what I have said or written.' Gandhi stands in a category very different from that of the Buddha and Christ, and has to be appraised very differently. When he said, 'My life is my message,' he meant that he had delivered his message through his praxis.

The unexpected resurgence of interest in Gandhi in recent days thanks to the exposition of 'Gandhigiri" by Bollywood has seen a rise in the sales of books on the Mahatma. There has also been a renaissance of sorts over the last year of books of Gandhi which are not ephemeral, but contribute to modify and renew our knowledge of Gandhi and the forces that drove him.

The field of Gandhigiri is vast, and Gandhi's life and ideas explored so minutely that any new book needs to justify itself. I have taken Gandhi's insistence that his life was his message by collapsing the divide between the political and the religious. For this, I have Gandhi's own authority: "My struggle is not merely political. It is religious and therefore quite pure."

The appeal of writing about only a part of Gandhi's life and ideas is that it spares me from having to explore those aspects of Gandhi with which they feel uncomfortable, usually dismissed as his fads - vegetarianism, nature therapy, religious outlook, fasts, goat's milk - or that which they find embarrassing and unable to explicate - his comments on the Bihar earth-quake above all, his strange sexual experiments, which led even an admirer such as J.B.Kripalani to castigate him privately. In biographical writing, there is a thin line dividing hagiography and demonisation. The detachment that a biographer needs is difficult to achieve. Mine is critical, not hagiographical, but fair and balanced - and very readable.

The story in its outlines is a familiar one, but still with the capacity to surprise, not always pleasantly. I differ from the most biographers by examining Gandhi's formative life in England, the shock of failure on his return home, and his phenomenal transformation in South Africa. Disinclined to take Gandhi at his word that when he dropped his western dress for that of an Indian peasant, he also served all ideational links with the West, show how deeply influenced he was by the theosophists, esoteric Christians, vegetarians, to name just a few and how he carried their imprint to the end. Recreate the manner in which Gandhi controlled the Congress and led the nationalist movement, achieved huge triumphs and made equally big blunders, such the alienation of M.A. Jinnah.

Every generation reexamines the past, trying to understand it anew. It may be a difference in perspective, or the knowledge of new facts which alter the picture -sometimes superficially, sometimes totally. India today is clearly reassessing the legacy of Gandhi, and his continuing relevance. That is as it should be. My narrative is one of the markers in this undertaking, with both sunlight and shadow.

11.9.2007

Prof. B.N. Ray
Vice Principal
Ramjas College

Contents

1

The Birth of Satyagraha

The vow made by the resisters on 11 September, 1906 at the Empire Theatre of Johannesburg, did not have to be followed up by immediate action, because the registration act was not yet on the statute book and sanction could be refused to it by the imperial authorities in London. Gandhi and a Muslim merchant, H. O. Ali, were sent to London in order to protest against the bill on behalf of the Indian community. Initially they succeeded, the King vetoed the bill, but a year later Transvaal attained self-government and immediately put the registration act on the statute book as the King had no right to interfere with this any longer. The act stipulated that all Indians should get themselves registered within the month of July 1907. Led by Gandhi, the Indian community refused to do so. The boycott was very effective and the government extended the period of registration until the end of November, but even then only 511 Indians got themselves registered, the great majority remaining steadfast. Gandhi was hauled up before the High Court which ruled that he should leave Transvaal within a fortnight. He resisted this order and was sentenced to two months imprisonment. This was his first experience of going to jail. While he was there he read Henry Thoreau's essay on civil disobedience and was thrilled by it. Thoreau defended the right of the citizen to disobey unjust laws and to give expression to this by refusing to pay taxes. Thoreau had gone to jail in 1845 for doing that, because he wanted to protest against slavery which had not yet been abolished in the United States.

Thoreau had called his action resistance to civil government, but the more general term used for such action was "passive resistance". Gandhi felt that there was nothing "passive" about this kind of resistance and looked for a better term. He wrote about it in *Indian Opinion* and promised a prize to anybody who could suggest a more suitable Indian term. Maganlal Gandhi won the prize for suggesting "sadagraha" (holding on to the good), but then Gandhi himself improved upon it by creating the word "satyagraha".

It is very interesting to note that the concept of truth as expressed in the term "satya", had a special meaning for him which was very different from the meaning of truth in Western thought. But this special meaning became clear to him only in the course of political action and not as a consequence of philosophical reflection. Once he had found the proper expression for what he was doing, he was able to clarify his objection to "untrue" Machiavellian means in political life. Obviously all means such as secrecy, subterfuge and deceit were incompatible with satyagraha. Playing with open cards became the first principle of Gandhi's political actions. Another implication of this approach was that the adversary should always be given the benefit of doubt. Taking the adversary's promises to be true, put the burden of proof on him. If he did not keep his word, he put himself in the wrong.

General Smuts who emerged as Gandhi's adversary in Transvaal was to find out to his dismay how the rules of this game worked against him. He promised to Gandhi that the registration act would be abolished if the Indians registered themselves voluntarily. Gandhi relied on Smut's word and asked the Indians to register. It was not easy for him to do this and he was assaulted for it by a tough Pathan who thought that Gandhi had turned a traitor to the Indian cause. After the Indians had registered voluntarily, Smuts broke his word and even pretended that he had never given it. Thereupon the Indians requested the authorities to return their registration documents, but the High Court ruled that the government was not obliged to return those documents. Gandhi then organised a mass meeting where Indians publicly burnt their registration cards. But the government took no notice of this and did not prosecute those who were found without registration cards.

Smuts had tricked Gandhi all along the line and had got away with it. This left Gandhi only the option to attack him in a different field. The immigration laws which prohibited Indians to enter Transvaal offered a suitable opportunity. Gandhi organised parties of illegal immigrants whom the authorities had to arrest. Gandhi landed in jail once more in this context, this time he was sentenced to hard labour which he had to do in the company of ordinary criminals. This did not break him though the Indian community was harassed in every possible way, British creditors ruined their Indian debtors, residence permits were terminated etc. Moreover, there were no funds for continuing the campaign, having given up his practice, Gandhi had no private means any longer. Finally he returned to the old ways of the petitioner once more and proceeded to London where the constitution of the Union of South Africa was under consideration at that time.

Gandhi's visit of London in 1909 proved to be futile as far as the immediate purpose of his journey was concerned, but he met young Indian extremists there and also had intensive discussions with his old friend, Dr. Pranjivan Mehta. It seems that the radical turn in his view of Western civilisation owed much to his talks with Mehta who challenged him to present his arguments in a coherent text. This is what he did on the voyage back to South Africa, when he completed the writing of his manifesto *Hind Swaraj* within two weeks. The verdict on doctors and lawyers at which he arrived in *Hind Swaraj* was particularly striking in view of the fact that only a year earlier he had called them the arms of the community, when he had criticised the immigration policy of the government which tended to deprive the Indian community of these essential limbs. Now they were no longer essential, but even positively harmful to the community. In this respect Gandhi was obviously tempted to go too far in pursuing his basic argument. But in other passages of *Hind Swaraj* he was providing an excellent analysis of the foundation of British rule in India which rested on the cooperation of numerous Indians which could be easily withdrawn and thus bring the entire machinery of British rule to a grinding halt. His programme of non-cooperation was clearly delineated in *Hind Swaraj* ten years before he tried to practise it in India. *Hind Swaraj* was first serialised in its Gujarati version in *Indian Opinion* in 1909, the English text was published in 1910 only. The British in India had proscribed the Gujarati text *Hind Swaraj* as well as Gandhi's account of the trial of Socrates as seditious literature.

When Gandhi returned to Johannesburg after his frustrating trip to England, he began a new phase of his life. He could not retire to the Phoenix Farm in Natal, because that would have meant giving up his campaign against the Transvaal authorities and General

Smuts who had betrayed his trust. At this juncture help came from a German friend, Hermann Kallenbach, who bought land near Johannesburg and helped Gandhi to establish the *Tolstoy Farm* as another experiment in communal living. Gandhi had admired Tolstoy for a long time and had also corresponded with him. Naming the farm after him was not a whim but a conscious tribute to the life and thought of this great man. *Tolstoy Farm* also served a practical purpose in the context of the resumed satyagraha campaign. The families of imprisoned satyagrahis found shelter in the *Tolstoy Farm* and Gandhi served as a teacher for their children. There were some Tamil women among those living at the farm and Gandhi even taught their children in Tamil. He was only a few lessons ahead of his pupils in this subject, but this made him an even more attentive teacher. This contact with the Tamil women proved of crucial significance at the end of the satyagraha campaign in South Africa. Once more Gandhi was going to derive unexpected benefits from a relationship established without this end in view.

In 1912 Gandhi could welcome a prominent guest on the *Tolstoy Farm*: Gokhale had come to South Africa to study the problems of the Indian community. Touring with his friend, Gandhi learned a great deal about making political speeches based on a meticulous analysis of the facts. Gokhale also impressed the South African government and specific assurances were given to him that compulsory registration would be abolished and even the hated poll tax to be paid by the free coolies would be removed. Once more this promise was broken, and since now the interests of the coolies were also at stake, the campaign attained new dimensions. Smuts explicitly mentioned that the removal of the poll tax had been vetoed by the Natal authorities. Tensions increased when an awkward judgement practically annulled all Indian marriages as only Christian marriages were considered legally.

This incensed all Indian women and the Tamil women of Tolstoy Farm now volunteered to join the satyagraha campaign. Gandhi sent them to Newcastle where many Tamil coolies were working in the coal mines. The women incited them to go on strike. Since they had no quarters of their own but lived on the compound of the mines, they lost their shelter and their work at the same time. Local Indian families could not cope with thousands of strikers and therefore Gandhi decided to lead them all across the border into Transvaal where the authorities refrained from arresting them. Only when they were close to Johannesburg were they hauled up and deported by train back to the mines which were declared to be emergency prisons in which they had to do hard labour under duress. The coolies refused to do this, but they were maltreated by their supervisors, this news reached India where the Viceroy, Lord Hardinge, protested against these measures, but it also reached the plantations where the coolies then struck work in sympathy with the miners. Troops were called out, they shot at the coolies and arrested many of them. In the meantime Gandhi was kept in a distant prison at Bloemfontain in Orange Free State and could not interfere with the course of events. Gokhale sent C. F. Andrews, a young British clergyman whom he had met at Lahore, to South Africa in order to help Gandhi who met him soon after he had been released from prison.

In the meantime Smuts had realized that the government could no longer cope with the situation by sheer repression and had seen to it that a commission of enquiry was appointed. This was supposed to be a face-saving device which would help the government to arrive at a compromise. But because the commission consisted of white members only, Gandhi refused to cooperate and insisted that the satyagraha campaign should continue. At this point the white railway workers went on strike for altogether different reasons. Gandhi announced that a satyagrahi could not make use of a calamity which had befallen his adversary and suspended the satyagraha campaign for the duration of that strike. Smuts appreciated this but, of course, he realized that he was caught on the horns of a dilemma and should better try to get out of this by arriving at a compromise with Gandhi. In an exchange of letters Smuts finally granted the concessions to the Indian community which it had been demanding for such a long time. The poll tax for coolies was abolished. Indian marriages were recognized and Indian immigration was permitted subject to certain educational qualifications. Gandhi had won and could finally think of returning to India in 1915 after 21 years of service in South Africa which determined his approach to political affairs for the rest of his life.

2

Philosophical Foundations of Satyagraha

Everyone is influenced by his or her parents and peers, close relatives and friends, their culture; their religion, their education, and the time in which they live. This is the background from which we all emerge. In the case of Gandhi, this has been written about in numerous sources. To know the Mahatma well enough to attempt to pass judgement on why he did what he did, besides the above, one must understand the social and religious traditions of Kathiawad, his native region, know the folk tales of peninsular Gujarat and read the *Bhagavad Gita* and some of the key Upanishads (especially the short *Isha Upanishad)* which may have been crucial in determining his make-up. Of course there are other more immediate influences on all our lives which can be later seen to have been watershed events. We cross paths with someone, or pick up a book, or attend a lecture, or become involved with some event that alters the direction of our lives. The same, naturally, is true for Gandhi.

While there will always be some debate on just how strong an influence a particular text or close associate has had on another individual, it is revealing to see, for example, how often themes and phrases from the Western texts that Gandhi read, especially during the time of his early philosophical and intellectual explorations in London and South Africa crop up in his speeches and writings even decades later. Reading To story's *The Kingdom of God is Within You,* Ruskin's *Unto this Last,* Thorea's *On the Duty of Civil Disobedience*, or Plato's dialogues of Socrates (especially the *Apology* and *Crito)* are genuine eye-openers in this regard—many of Gandhi's favourite sayings or examples, and even whole areas of his philosophy, have been taken almost verbatim from these sources.

In the final analysis, because of his voluminous preserved writings, Gandhi himself would appear to be of great assistance in determining the influence of others on him. However, given the perhaps surprising lack of insight in much autobiographical writing, how much weight should be put on Gandhi's own words, especially when he never set out to write a comprehensive autobiography at all, merely instructive snippets for the readers of his newspapers that were later bound together as *An Autobiography*? And what do we make of the claim by George Woodcock, for example, that the influences of Tolstoy and Ruskin on Gandhi can be exaggerated, and indeed that Gandhi himself was inclined to do so because of his humility, and that these authors merely-strengthened concepts he had held into convictions, and the claims of others who have gone so far as to call Tolstoy the "founder of Gandhism"?

Some well-known influences upon Gandhi, such as Ruskin and Tolstoy, as well as Thoreau, various South African Christian missionaries, and Raychand, are discussed in his own writings. Others are more ephemeral. Erik Erikson and Victor Wolfenstein have written about the psychological influences that have gone into constructing Gandhi's non-violent philosophy and revolutionary personality, Sudhir Kakar about the psycho-sexual determinants of his behaviour, and some new scholarship, for example, the writings of Martin Green, looks at the influence of New Age intellectuals who helped to shape the Mahatma's persona. Here I will examine three examples of non-violent resistance of which Gandhi became aware at about the time that he was commencing his own political struggles in South Africa. One of them is well known and often credited for providing Gandhi with his political methodology. The other two may have been jusf as important in this regard but have not received similar attention.

Gandhi is usually taken as a symbol of the Orient's protest against modern Western civilization, apparently, perhaps, because of his very simple living, especially his dress-a mere loin-cloth. This is rather an over-simplification of his real stand. He is indeed, a critic of all that is dehumanizing in the modern Western civilization. But he is no less a relentless enemy of all the rot that he found in the

Indian cultural tradition. He is essentially an experimenter, with an open mind. He tries things on himself and if satisfied, accepts them whole-heartedly, without minding from where they come. If his European well-wishers were disappointed by his failure to embrace Christianity, he could not help. He maintained that all he needed as a human being, thirsting for religion, for Truth, he found in Hinduism. But this did not deter him from drinking deep at the frontiers of inspiration of other religions. His attitude is very aptly and beautiflly summed up in these words of his:

> I want the cultures of all the lands to be blown about my house as freely as possible. But I refuse to be blown off my feet by any.

The main Western influences that are generally discussed are those of the Bible, Ruskin, Thoreau and Tolstoy. The Bible only reinfoced what he had already imbibed from Hinduism. As to Ruskin's influence, he himself has said while referring to the exciting experience of reading *Unto This Last* that it emphasized only what was already within him. It remains to be seen whether Thoreau's essay on *Civil Disobedience* he read after or before he had already evolved the technique of Satyagraha. Thoreau's 'The Duty of Civil Disobedience' was rendered by Gandhi in Gujarati under the title 'The Duty of Disobeying Laws' and published in the *Indian Opinion'* issues of 7-9-1907 and 14-7-1907 and later as a pamphlet. The oath not to obey the unjust law was taken by the Indian community at a meetings held in Johannesburg on 11th September, 1906 by passing resoultion No. 4. Tolstoy also provided him with a verification of the truths he was culling from his experience as the leader of the oppressed Indian community in South Africa. While he did not fail to benefit immensely from all the great things that come his way, he could have grown into what he ultimatiely became, even without coming under their sway.

Gandhi and Socrates

There is one great Western influence on Gandhi's life-that of Socrates. One who takes a close view of the lives of both these great men cannot fail to observe certain common things. It should not surprise anybody if there is a close parallelism between the lives of these two teachers, because of their unquenchable thirst for Truth and their readiness to die for it. But there are some things in Gandhi's life which can be traced to that of Socrates and are evidently as result of the influence of the ancient sage on Gandhi. Gandhi not only read Plato's dialogues relating to Socrates's fundamental teaching especially *Apology*, *Crito*, *Phadeo*, etc. but also took into his head to give a Gujarati rendering of *Apology* to the readers of *The Indian Opinion* in 1908 and shared the noble sentiments expressed in it with them. He wrote an introduction to it on April 4, 1908. At the end of the translation was appended a small note in brackets by 'The Editor, Indian Opinion' written on May 5, 1908.

The specific influence of Socrates on Gandhi did not become like other Western influences a subject of discussion, as the fact of Gandhi's translation was little known to non-Gujarati readers. Now that the English version of the translation along with the introduction and the postscript is avaliable in the *Collected Works*, it will help all readers to assess the full impact of the influence.

Gandhi mentions in 'My Experiences of the Jail' on March 28, 1908 that he had with him in jail some of his own books, including writings of Socrates (evidently he means Plato's Dialogues), which he "read or re-read" there.

In fact he was in jail from January 10, 1908 to January 30, 1908. This was his first experience even of jaillife. On Febuary 10, Gandhi was attacked by Mir Alam and others while on his way to the government office where he was to give his fingerprints against their protest. He convalesced for ten days at Dr. Doke's house and then shifted to Phoenix. During March 1908 he wrote 'My Experiences of the Jail'. Till May 13, 1908, when General Smuts went back on his word, Gandhi was comparatively free and he serialized in *The Indian Opinion* the Gujarati translation of Plato's dialogue, *Apology*. The translation was done, either when he was in jail, or between April 4, 1908 and May 9, 1908, the respective dates of the introduction and the postscript.

The choice of *Apology* for translation during that critical period of his life is no accident. With Gandhi word is a deed, an action, *Apology* mirrors much of what was brewing in his own mind in those days. It emphasizes the affinity he has with the Greek. As we shall see later the affinity continued asserting itself, also in the years that follow.

The title in Gujarati speaks volumes. It is "The Story of a Truth Warrior or Socrates's Defence." He uses of Socrates the epithet 'Satya-Vira' (Truth Warrior, one who fights heroically for Truth), a new coinage. And this epithet 'Satya-Vira' brings out what according to Gandhi is the core significance of the heroic life and still more heroic death of Socrates.

In the introduction he calls him "a great Satyagrahi". The word Satyagraha was freshly coined by him (from Maganlal's Sadagraha) and in an article written on February 22, 1908 he gave instances of four Satygrahis, Thoreau, Luther, Galileo and Columbus, who offered satyagraha against their own people. About Socrates also he says: "Socrates was a Satyagrahi against his own people. The Greeks became a great people because of that."

Gandhi's mind is full of recent happenings. Again and again he underlines the strength to stand against one's own people for the sake of Truth even at the peril of one's life, after the attack by Mir Alam. Out of the five Westerners he referred to within six weeks, it seems he found Socrates to be the most kindred soul and concentrated on him. While the others were heroic souls struggling and fighling against even their own people for what they thought to be truth, perhaps the epithet 'Truth-Warrior' carries a much fuller significance when applied to Socrates. And so it is in the case of Gandhi also.

Both Socrates and Gandhi were rational. They argue reason tirelessly. They want to convince their associates rationally. Socrates says, "For I am and always have been one of those natures who must be guided by reason, whatever the reason may be which upon reflection appears to me to be the best". But both of them, at some crucial moment in their life, depend solely on something irrational, something which they refer to as 'humming' or 'the inner voice'.

Socrates gives a full description of 'the internal oracle':

> This, dear Crito, is the voice which I seem to hear murmuring in my ears, like the sound of the flute in the ears of the mystic; that voice, I say, is humming in my ears, and prevents me from hearing any other.
>
> You have heard me speak at sundry times and in diverse places of an oracle or sign which comes to me, and is the divinity which Meletus ridicules in the indictment. This sign, which is a kind of voice, first

> began to come to me when I was a child; it always forbids but never commends me to do any thing which I am goings to do.
>
> "Hitherto the divine faculty of which the internal oracle is the source, has constantly been in the habit of opposing me even about trifles, if I was going to make a slip or error in any matter; and now as you see there has come upon me that which may be thought and is generally belived to be, the last and worst evil. But the oracle made no sign of opposition, either when I was leaving my house in the morning, or when I was on my way to the court, or while I was speaking at anythings which I was goings to say; and yet I have often been stopped in the middle of a speech, but now in nothing I either said or did touching the matter in hand has the oracle opposed me. What do I take to the explanation of this silence? I will tell you. It is an intimation that what has ahppened to me is a good, and that those of us who think that death is an evil are in error."

With Socrates it was a voice saying 'no, don't do that.' As the inner voice had not intervened during the defence and thereafter Socrates took the silence as a proof of the good in all that had happered to him.

Socrates says he began to hear the voice when he was a child. Gandhi does not say when it began in his case. There is no mention of it in his South African days. But may be what emboldened the little boy Mohan to confess his theft to his father was this irrepressible voice, though not yet known to him as such.

One of the 'don'ts' that the internal oracle prescribed to Socrates was to remain aloof form politics.

> "And this is what deters me from being a politician. And rightly, as I think. For I am certain, O men of Athens, that if I had engaged in politics, I should have perished long ago, and done no good either to you or to myself. He who will fight for the right, if he would have even for a brief space, must have a private station and not a public one.
>
> The only office of State which I ever held, O men of Athens, was that of a senator. I was the only one who was opposed to the illegality and I gave my vote aginst you.
>
> The oligarchy of the Thirty, ordered to fetch Leon. 'But I went quietly home', might have lost life had not the power of the thirty shortly afterwards come to an end.

Gandhi is primarily a man of action. He led a stormy life. He took out marches, launched gigantic movements, activized and enthused a whole passive people. And yet he sought neither power nor any position. He ceased to be even a four-anna member of the Congress. Even as he seemed to be neck-deep in politics, he was non-attached. One is reminded of Shri Krishna who occupied no position of power and ceaselessly worked for achieving a harmonious pattern of social behaviour.

Gandhi eschewed any executive responsibility. Some Indian associates have held this up against him. They ask, why Gandhi did not take up a position in the central cabinet after independence. J. Bandopadhyaya begins the examination of the dynamics of Gandhian thought by stating:

> so far as the social and political thought of Gandhi is concerned (as distinguished from his private metaphysical beliefs), it is possible to divide his views on the social structure into two levels or orders, one of which can be regarded as an ultimate ideal and the other as an approximation (to Gandhi's own mind) to it-the first representing the maximum practicable consummation of the ultimate values of non-violence, freedom and equality and the second representing only a relative consummation of these values.

He ends up by saying,

> These is, to Gandhi's own mind, a vast temporal interregnum between this ideal and the absolute or first-order idea-an interregnum which is logically bridgable through successive approximation, but which Gandhi has deliberately chosen not to fill up with practical details.

It is fair to note that Gandhi was not so much bent upon achieving Utopia as upon articulating the grammar of socio-political behaviour for the use of mankind. He was shrewd enough to know that mankind was used to varieties of violent behaviour-patterns and it was to be patiently and progressively weaned away from them. What he, therefore, personified in himself was the feasibility of a marriage between religion and politics, i e. spiritualizing politics or, say, politicizing spirituality.

And here it is that he goes a step ahead of Socrates, or for that matter any spritual leader before him. And, of course, he does not care for the cost. After Gandhi mankind is bound to expect every spiritual leader worth his salt to get involved in politics. Indeed, his involvement in public affairs will be taken as a test of his spirituality.

No two trials in the whole of human history are more akin to each other than those of Socrates and Gandhi. The two cases are dissimilar in some ways though. There is, all the same, a basic similarity. Both Socrates and Gandhi are the most law-abiding persons, and if they appear to break the law of the land, something is wrong with law and not with them. Both operate from the plane of Law, which is far above that of law which the judges interpret and administer with the result that it is the judges who are judged and not they.

Both consider themsleves absolutely innocent. Socrates does not mince matters: "O men of Athens, I say to you, either aquit me or not but whichever you do, understand that I shall never alter my ways, not even if I have to die many times." Gandhi almost repeats the words of Socrates: "I knew that I was playing with fire. I ran the risk and if I was set free I would still do the same."

The trial ends in the punishment to the respective great man, but when each of the accused refers to the impending punishment,we have a feeling that there is an indictment against the judges themselves. Socrates asks rather for a reward, for the grant of free meals at the public mess:

> What would be a reward suitable to a poor man who is your benefactor; and who desires leisure that he may instruct you? There can be no reward so fitting as maintenance in the Prytaneum, O men of Athens, a reward which he deserves far more than the citizen who has won the prize at Olympia in the horse or chariot race.

Gandhi makes an appeal to the conscience of the judge and the assessors and shown them the way how they can save themselves from evil by resigning their posts:

> The only course open to you, the judges and the assessors, is either to resign your posts and thus disassociate yourselves from evil, if you feel that the law you are called upon to administer is an evil and that in reality I am innocent, or to inflict on me the severest penalty, if you believe that the system and the law you are assisting to administer are good for the people of this country, and that my activity is, therefore, injurious to the common weal."

Both Socrates and Gandhi were always prepared to lay down their life for Truth. In the postscript to the translation of *Apology* Gandhi says: "Just as Socrates followed the moral law till the end and met death as even a lover meets a beloved, may our readers and we as well attain that moral strangth. This we pray of God Almight.

This wooing of death Gandhi practised even at an early age. It was Gandhi's belief that God would choose him for martyrdom if He found him pure enough. And God did choose him. The purity was attained as a result of a life which followed the vows of truth, non-violence, celibacy, non-possession. Socrates says:

> In this present life, I reckon that we make the nearest approach to knowledge when we have the least possible intercourse or communion with the body, and are not surfeited with the bodily nature, but keep ourselves pure until the hour when God himself is pleased to release us.

Such a man is dead even before death has claimed him. Says Socrates: 'There would be a ridiculous contradiction in men studying to live as nearly as they can in a state of death, and yet repining when it comes upon them.'

Ramdas, Gandhi's third son, describes an incident that occurred in Johannesburg. Curfew was clamped down on a part of the city on account of a Zulu riot. Paragajibhai, one of Gandhi's associates, slipped away from the area under curfew and reached Kallenbach's house on the outkirts of the city where Gandhi was staying. Gandhi, disapproving Paragajibhai's action, asked him to return to his post immediately: "You want to live in the city and do not want to share its woes! You want remain where you are stationed."

This reminds one of the very touching dialogue of *Crito* in which Socrates convinces his disciple Crito that it would be unbecoming of him to escape from the prison, as he wanted him to do, and thereby let down the laws of Athens, which had made him what he was-the wisest man in Greece.

The laws appear as it were, before Socrates and tell him: "He who has experience of the manner in which we order justice and adminsiter the state, and still remains, has entered into an implied contract that he will do as we command. He has made an agreement with us that he will duly obey our commands." Then the laws remind Socrates: "And now you run away and forsake your agreements. Gandhi's advice to Paragajibhai is reminiscent of this sublime piece of Socratic wisdom.

Gandhi writes in the introduction to the translation of *Apology*, "We will give the main substance rather than a verbatim translation." His translation is very readable. It is couched in simple language, which can be followed by the semi-illiterate Gujarati-speaking community in South Africa, which again was composed of Hindus, Muslim and Parsis. But what is important is his style, reflecting the greatness and clarity of his soul.

There would be no end to piling up passages, showing similarity, from both, on important subjects. But a few similarities may be noted, and some of them may very well be influences. For example, in his first full-fledged address on 'A few important points concerining our education', given in Broach in 1917, we find Gandhi dwelling at length on music and gymnastics. I see that there is no place for music any where.' Indigenous games and gymnastics and Western-style drill need to be introduced in our schools. It would not be far-fetched to refer to what Socrates was told by the Laws of Athens while reminding him that it was they who were gymnastic.'

Gandhi must have had corroboration from Socrates, as from other teachers of mankind, about the supremacy of non-violent behaviour. To quote a few observations from Socrates:

> "Not life, but a good life, is to be chiefly valued."
>
> "Then we ought not to retaliate or render evil for evil to any one, whatever the evil we may have suffered from him."
>
> "Tell me, then, whether you agree with and assent to my first principle, that neither injury, nor retaliation nor warding off evil by evil is ever right."

At the end of *Symposium*, while describing personal traits-physical, moral and spiritual of Socrates, Alcibiades refers, among other things, to 'Socrates with his bare feet on the ice', his fortitude in enduring the rigours of weather. When Gandhi, during the Satyagraha movement in South Africa, gave up his European-style dress and put on a shirt and lungi and decided to walk bare-foot, emulating his poor Tamilian associates, he had surely before his eyes the figure of Socrates stalking bare-foot amongst the ancient Greeks.

In that very peroration before the august gathering Alcibiades refers to his having taken into his arms "this wonderful monster" and adds, "This again, Socrates, will not be denied by you. And yet, notwithstanding all, he was so superior to my solicitations, so contemptuous and derisive and disdainful of my beauty which really, as I fancied, had some attractions-hear, O Judges; for judges you shall be of the haughty virtue of Socrates-nothing more happened, but in the morning when I awoke (let all the gods and goddesses by my witnesses) I arose as from the couch of a father or an elder brother." I leave it to the readers to decide if at all, or how far an incident like this could have an influence on "the haughty virtue" of Gandhi as evinched in his experiments in sharing a bed, with a female, one may call it 'haughtier virtue' because in Gandhi's case it was a voluntary experimenting.

After the sixth and final part of the translation of *Apology* was published in *The Indian Opinion* of May 9, 1908, Gandhi serialized the translation of Ruskin's *Unto This Last* from the very next issue of May 16, 1908, under the title *Sarvodaya*.

It begins with an introduction, in which Gandhi, whose mind is full of the world of Socratic ideas, says: "Socrates showed a little that man should do. He acted upon his word. It can be said that Ruskin's ideas are an elaboration of his (Socrates's) ideas. Ruskin has vividly shown how every man, who wants to live according to the ideas of Socrates, should function in different professions."

At the end of 'Essay II' Ruskin imagines that some day in future "She (England), as a Christian mother, may at least attain to the virtues and the treasures of a Heathen one, and be able to lead forth her Sons, saying,-'There are my jewels'." Gandhi in his rendering refers to the Heathen mother as 'the eminent man from Greece'. It would not be rash to guess that this 'eminent man from Greece' was to his mind Socrates. In fact Ruskin refers to the proud utterance of the mother of the twin Gracchi, Tiberius and Caius, Roman patriots, pointing to her sons.

Unto This Last, one thought, was looking to the title references like 'she, a Christian' etc., and the general content and tone of argument, laden with Christiantiy. But Gandhi, disregardful of all such things, reaches the core of Ruskin's argument and finds it to be a redelivery of Socrates's ideas, so much so that he refers to 'the eminent man from Greece' even where another person, a non-Christian mother was meant. The reference to the Greek, say, Socrates, instead of the mother of the Gracchi, whom Ruskin meant, fits in and the argument does not suffer, though it might be on Gandhi's part in all probability, an error. But the main assessment of Ruskin's work, in the introduction, that *Unto This Last* is Socrates made easy, is very bold and perhaps daring. May be the true indebtedness of Ruskin to Socrates struck Gandhi, because he was dealing with the worlds of ideas of both of them during the same period, not only as a mere translator, but as one who was trying to live up to such ideas, in a period of extraordinary trials and tribulations in his life. One wonders if critics have emphasized this fact as Gandhi has done.

Not that Ruskin himself is unaware of this indebtedness. He actually acknowledges it in the Preface: "The real gist of these papers, their central meaning and aim, is to give, as I believe for the first time in plain English,- it has often been incidentally given in good Greek by Plato and Xenophon, and good Latin by Cicero and Horace,-a logical difinition of WEALTH". But Gandhi does not see a mere incidental but very substantial likeness of Ruskin's ideas with those of Socrates as presented by Plato.

One is simply overwhelmed to observe the affinity that Gandhi, even at the age of thirty-seven, had with Socrates. If Socrates were introduced to Gandhi, as Tolstoy was through Rev. Doke's biography of Gandhi, he too, would have uttered as even Tolstoy did that Gandhi was "a person very close to us, to me."

Tolstoy and Gandhi

The great influence that Leo Tolstoy exercised on Gandhi's life and thought was acknowledged by Gandhi himself several times, but a review of this theme is eminently warranted at the present juncture by a number of factors. The publication of the current series of *The Collected Works* of Mahatma Gandhi is a major event from the view-point of the Gandhian studies. We are now in possession of a most authentic source-material on the whole subject of Gandhi, and his life-work. And this material is much more extensive today than at any other time in the past. It is especially true in the case of a subject like Tolstoy's impact on Gandhi.

Recent evaluations of Gandhi are also notable for their penetrating study of this aspect of his thought. The topic of Gandhi's indebtedness to Tolstoy has been rigorously examined by the Gandhian scholars of both the East and the West. For this reason, we have again the advantage of a more comprehensive framework at present as we seek to discuss the profound nature of Tolstoy's unfluence on Gandhi's technique and thought.

In the first place, Gandhi's important references to Tolstoy will be briefly mentioned. The impact of the Tolstoyan philosophy on the Gandhian technique may be discussed next. Finally, the specific sources of the Gandhian thought that owe their development to the Tolstoyan influence will have to be identified. This will give us an integrated perspective to rightly assess the nature and extent of Gandhi's indebttedness to Tolstoy.

Gandhi must have been acquainted, even as a young student at London, with the works of Tolstoy. In 1890, when Gandhi visited the Eiffel Tower in Paris, he was reminded of Tolstoy's disparaging remark. This was perhaps the beginning of a long process in which the influence of Tolstoy's ideals on Gandhi was increasingly in evidence.

The early years of Gandhi's stay in South Africa were of greater singificance in this respect. It was at this period of Gandhi's life when he was deeply absorbed in the cultivation of the religious spirit that he studied the works of Tolstoy with a profound interest. Gandhi referred to it in his *Autobiography* as a religious ferment. In 1894, a year after his coming to South Africa, Gandhi read, among other religious works, *The Kingdom of God is Within You* by Tolstoy; and wrote:

> Tolstoy's *The Kingdom of God is Within You* overwhelmed me. It left an abiding impression on me. Before the independent thinking, profound morality, and the truthfulness of this book, all the books given to me seemed to pale into insignificance.

This impression that Tolstoy's book left on Gandhi was greatly strengthened in the subsequent years of Gandhi's sojourn in South Africa. One of the potential factors that was largely responsible for this development was Gandhi's close association with Herman Kallenback (1871-1945), a German Jew in Johannesburg. Kallenbach, like Gandhi, was an ardent Tolstoyan. By the time Gandhi came to know Kallenbach intimately, Satyagraha of the Indian settlers was already in progress in South Africa. The relevance of the Tolstoyan philosophy to the passive resistance movement under Gandhi's leadership was unmistakable.

Tolstoy was uppermost in Gandhi's mind when he was in prison for resisting the laws of racial discrimination. While serving a sentence in Pretoria prison in Transvaal, Gandhi wrote a letter on March 25, 1909, addressed to his cousion, Maganlal Gandhi:

> Please tell Maganlabhai that he should also try to read Tolstoy's *Kingdom of God is Within You*. It is a most logical book, what is more, Tolstoy practises what he preaches.

Gandhi's reference to the relationship between the precept and practice in Tolstoy is striking. In fact, it is no less true of Gandhi himself. Gandhi undoubtedly put into practice what Tolstoy preached. The establishment of *Tolstoy Farm* by Gandhi near Johannesburg on May 10, 1910 was another notable event. In this, Gandhi was greatly assisted by Kallenbach who actually owned the property of the Farm but offered it to Gandhi for the use of the Satyagrahis. The working of the Tolstoy Farm was completely based on the Tolstoyan principles.

Gandhi also, like Romain Rolland the other Tolstoyan, corresponded with Tolstoy. But Gandhi's problem was the passive resistance in South Africa. In his letter on October 1, 1909 Gandhi brought to the notice of Tolstoy the character and the significance of the passive resistance movement of the Indians. Tolstoy, in his moving reply to Gandhi on October 7, 1909 observed:

> I have just received your most interesting letter, which has given me great pleasure. God help our dear brothers and co-workers in the Transvaal.

Gandhi sent later on a copy of his booklet *Hind Swaraj or Indian Home Rule* to Tolstoy along with a letter, for his comment. In the course of that letter to Tolstoy on April 4, 1910, Gandhi described himself as "a humble follower" of his. Tolstoy acknowledged both of them with great appreciation. Writing to Gandhi on May 8, 1910

Tolstoy observed:

> I read your book with great interest because I think that the question you treat in it- the passive resistance-is a question of the greatest imprtance not only for India but for the whole humanity.

Tolstoy voiced the same conviciton in his last letter to Gandhi. Commenting on the relevance of Satyagraha, Tolstoy wrote to Gandhi on September 7, 1910.

> The more I live the more I feel inclined to express to other the feelings which so strongly move my being, and which according to my opinon, are of great importance. That is, what one calls non-resistance, is in reality nothing else but the discipline of love. Christ knew that the employment of violence is incompatible with love which is the fundamental law of life. Once violence is admitted, the law of love is thererby rendered futile.

Tolstoy's rejection of violence as the very negation of violence was of great consequence to Gandhi. It was of greatest value for Gandhi in his own repudiation of violence. And Gandhi's non-violence was positively sustained by Tolstoy's Gospel.

It was only natural that when Tolstoy died on November 20, 1910, Gandhi should have paid a memorial tribute to his master. In his journal, *Indian Opinion* of November 26, 1910 Gandhi dwelt on the message of Tolstoy's life, and wrote:

> We believe Tolstoy's teaching will win increasing appreciation with the passage of time. Its foundation was religion. What Tolstoy believed with special conviction was that in essence all religious soul force to be superior to brute force and taught that evil should be requited with good, not evil. It is no small encouragement to us that we have the blessings of a great man like Tolstoy in our task.

Gandhi recalled the great support that Tolstoy gave to the cause of the satyagrahis in South Africa. It was a source of perennial inspiration for Gandhi as the leader of satyagraha movement. The birth centenary celebrations of Tolstoy in 1928 provided an opportunity for Gandhi to reiterate the influence he derived from his works. He acknowledged it in a message he delivered on that occasion. Recalling his earlier reading of Tolstoy, Gandhi observed:

> It was forty years back when I was passing through a severe crisis of scepticism and doubt, that I came across Tolstoy's book, *The Kingdom*

of God is Within You, and was deeply impressed by it. I was at that time a believer in violence. Its reading cured me of my scepticism and made me a firm believer in Ahimsa. He was the greatest apostle of non-violence that the present age has produced.

Gandhi contrasted the unshakable conviction of Tolstoy in non-violence with the wavering belief of his own contemporaries in India in the same. He also defended Tolstoy against the prevalent ciritcism that Tolstoy's life was full of inconisistencies and contiadictions.

It is interesting to recall here the remarks of Mr. Vincent Sheean in his biorgraphy of Gandhi fathoming the impact of Tolstoy on Gandhi's thought. Mr. Sheean reveals, rather poignantly, that he was scheduled to discuss precisely this subject with Gandhi on January 30, 1948. This could not take place for the tragic-incidant of Gandhi's assassination. It is well known that the *The Kingdom of God Within You* undoubtedly influenced Gandhi, especially in his formative years in South Africa. Mr. Sheean wanted to know what Gandhi thought of this work of Tolstoy in the later years. While this particular issue remains largely a hypothetical question, the general influence of Tolstoy on the techniques and thoughts of Gandhi is no longer in doubt.

As the general impact of Tolstoy on the non-violent technique of Gandhi is already acknowledged, what needs to be examined now is the specific relationship between the Tolstoyan doctrine and the Gandhian method. Apparently the Gandhian technique of non-violent direct action is derived from the Tolstoyan principle of non-resistance. Gandhi's contribution to the Tolstoyan concept of non-resistance consists in his integrating it with non-violence. It is for this reason that Gandhi characterises his technique as 'non-violent resistance'.

Tolstoy spoke of 'love' as the central basis of his teaching. He insisted on the constant application of love in all walks of life for resolving its conflicts. It is, nevertheless, true that Satyagraha is primarily rooted in the spirit of Tolstoy's teaching of love. The Gandhian technique of non-violent resistances is primarily an extension of the Tolstoyan doctrine. There is considerable ideological continutiy in Gandhi claiming Tolstoy as an exponent of non-violence. Whatever Tolstoy preached as a prophet was put into invaluable practice by Gandhi in the social order. Gandhi's satyagraha embodies the spirit of Tolstoy's message of universal love.

Tolstoy's influence on the Gandhian thought is unmistakable. Among the list of books Gandhi included at the end in his book *Hind Swaraj,* are Tolstoy's famous works. And Tolstoy, in turn, warmly commended Gandhi's ideas in *Hindi Swaraj.* It was no wonder that Gandhi's contemporaries used to refer to him as a "Tolstoyan". Gandhi once answered a number of questions when the non-violent non-cooperation movement was at its zenith. His answer were reproduced in *Young India* of October 27, 1921. One of the questions was concerning the relationship between Tolstoy and Gandhi. In his answer, Gandhi said that he was a "devoted admirer" of Tolstoy and he owed much in his life to Tolstoy.

In this connection it is not enough to trace the influence of Tolstoy on Gandhi. What is more noteworthy is the manner in which Gandhi absorbed the Tolstoyan influence. Tolstoy's principal work in question, *The Kingdom of God is Within You* is based on the teaching of Jesus and the practice of Christianity. It is a challenging interpretaiton of the *Sermon on the Mount.* And the unique point of Tolstoy in this is his insistence to apply the Gospel for repudiating State and its all coercive institutions. The spirit of Tolstoy's strictures on violence are unmistakable in the work, but his references to non-violence as such are only implied, and not specified.

If we consider Gandhi's claim that he found non-violence in Tolstoy's *The Kingdom of God is Within You,* it is obvious that he was particularly susceptible to that part of Tolstoy's message which appealed to him most. In this case, Tolstoy's condemnation of violence, which is writ large throughout this book, must have captivated Gandhi's mind. This element of Tolstoy's philosophy, which Gandhi adopted for his own purposes, was considerably supplemented by the like factors in the Gospel as they were interpreted by Tolstoy. The result was altogether a creative absorption of the Tolstoyan teaching by Gandhi in his formulation of non-violence.

Gandhi's basic approach to Tolstoy was not that of a critical inquirer, who was interested in the examination of the minutest details of his works for the purposes of his academic study. His outlook was more like a seeker's in receiving the necessary enlightenment from a teacher. Gandhi's instinct for action was even more overwhelming. Therefore, whenever Gandhi studied the religious works of Tolstoy, he did it mostly with a view to practising it in his life. Writing in *Harijan* of November, 17, 1946 on his attitude to his great teachers, Gandhi stated:

> It was a habit with me to forget what I did not like and to carry out in practice whatever I liked.

This serves as a significant cannon for understanding Gandhi's attitude to the teaching of Tolstoy. It is equally applicable for other thinkers like Thoreau and Ruskin, who had similarly influenced Gandhi's thought.

In the case of Tolstoy, however, Gandhi found little to forget, and nothing to discard; and he also found a great deal to appreciate in Tolstoy for a number of reasons. Gandhi cherished the cardinal doctrines of Tolstoy as a reiteration of the beliefs he inherited from the indigenous sources in India. He discovered or rediscovered the innate 'truth' in the articulate writings of Tolstoy. For instance, the message of non-violence which Gandhi attributes to Tolstoy is a part of his own heritage. This profound conviction in non-violence as it is taken by Gandhi earlier from the indigenous tradition of India. The uniqueness of Gandhi was that he strengthened this indigenous idea of non-violence with the corresponding ideas in other philosophies and religions of the world.

Thus, Gandhi's thought owed much to Tolstoy for its growth and develpment. The writings of Tolstoy provided Gandhi with a philosophic confirmation of his own idea of non-violence. The theory and practice of Gandhian non-violence reflect the legacy of Tolstoy. It is chiefly notable in the two concepts of great significance in Gandhian thought which may be briefly discussed here in this connection.

Philosophical Anarchism

Tolstoy's anarchism was the. most predominant note in his *The Kingdom of God is Within You.* He condemned the State on several grounds but the religious (Christian in this case) ground was a formidable argument in Tolstoy's book. On the topic of State, Tolstoy writes :

> Christianity in its true sense puts an e.nd to the State.

The profession of true Christianity not only excludes the possibility of requiring the State, but even destroys its foundations. But Tolstoy's .anarchism was not violent. It was rooted in the Christian doctrine of non-resistance.

The philosophical anarchism of Tolstoy, found an eminent exponent in Gandhi. The main argument of Gandhi's *Hind Swaraj* essentially belongs to the school of philosophical anarchism. In a famous speech in February 6, at Benaras, Gandhi observed :

> India of to-day in her impatience has produced an army of anarchists. I myself-am an anarchist, but of another type.

Gandhi wanted to differentiate his anarchism from the anarchism of the terrorists. His anarchism, like Tolstoy's, was non-violent, while the terrorists' anarchism was violent. It is interesting to review the controversy that raged at that time in India about the philosophical anarchism of Gandhi. Annie Besant was notable among Gandhi's contemporaries for taking exception to this expression by Gandhi. The historic speech of Gandhi on February 6, 1916 at Benares roused a great deal of comment in the public. Referring to Gandhi's controversial speech, Annie Besant wrote in *New India* of February 19, 1916.:

> Now Mr. Gandhi is a ' philosophic anarchist', like Tolstoy, whom he closely resembles. The *Madras Mail* was annoyed that Mr. Gandhi was, apparently, compared to Tolstoy. Both are men of the prophet type.

Annie Besant's testimony was all the more significant as she differed from Gandhi on this particular point of Tolstoyan anarchism. Gandhi was not only a preacher of anarchism, but he was also a great practitioner.of the anarchist ideal. His non-violent movement for Indian independence rested on. the grounds of philosophical anarchism. Gandhi's opposition to the State was often expressed by him several times in the course of his leadership of the

Indian nationalist movement. The Indian National Congress, under the leadership of Gandhi, adopted the technique of non-violent non-co-operation in 1920, of civil disobedience in 1930 and again of individual civil disobedience in 1940. These techniques of Gandhi are all variants of the basic idea of non-violent resistance to the State. It was the distinctive contribution of Gandhi to the Tolstoyan heritage that he made the central doctrine of philosophic anarchism most practicable in the Indian nationalist struggle.

In the application and the justification of philosophical anarchism in the Indian context, Gandhi drew great inspiration from the cumulative experience of the Indian civilization through the ages. He had given his interpretation of the Indian history briefly in his *Hind Swaraj* which he considered as his credo. Gandhi's picture of the Indian social order as containing the genesis of an anarchist society was poignantly described in this book. Gandhian thought achieves a remarkable synthesis between the philosophical anarchism of Tolstoy and the Swadeshi anarchism of India. It is the creative genius of Gandhi that has rendered this union in political thought a practical reality.

Vicarious Responsibility

Another concept in the thought of Gandhi that can be attributed to the teaching of Tolstoy is the individual's responsibility to the society. That the cult of the lone solitary individual has been sufficiently disproved as a myth is evident in recent political theory. Nor can the total claim of the *Leviathan* remain unchallenged. Both individualism and collectivism have stated the residual issue of the political theory with an amazing unreality. The issue that still remains to be explored is the true relationship between an individual and the social order.

Tolstoy's teaching postulates a vicarious responsibility on the part of the individual to the society. The individual is an integral part of the social life, and he cannot escape from the reality of social living at any time. In one of his essay's Tolstoy writes:

> Everything now being done in Russia is done in the name of the general welfare, in the name of the protection and tranquility of the people of Russia. And if this is so, then it is also done for me who lives

> in Russia. For me, therefore, exists the destitution of the people, for me exists this terrible embitterment of man against his fellowmen.

And Tolstoy's article was entitled "lern not be silent". He expresses in this article his profound concern for the moral degeneration of his fellowmen. As the theme is developed in this essay, Tolstoy establishes the notion of an individual's responsibility for the social order. This responsibility is a vicarious one which the individual cannot disown. Tolstoy writes:

> Strange as it seems to say that all this is done for me, and that I am a participator in these terrible deeds, I cannot but feel that there is an indubitable interdependence between me and the terrible crimes.

Here the teaching of Tolstoy presupposes the working of a conscience in an individual which will arouse in him a moral awarness of his duties to the society. It is this awarness of the individual of other individuals that results in one's vicarious identification with others.

The relevance of this theory which is implicit in Tolstoy's thought.to the Gandhian thoughts lies in its suggestive explanation of the fasts. That "fasts" played a memorable role in Gandhi's life is beyond doubt. And Gandhi's fasts, unlike those of his followers to-day, are not political, but solely religious in nature. Gandhi's fasts are based on the assumption that an individual has a moral responsibility for his fellowmen. In his fasts Gandhi brings to life the ancient notion of the vicarious responsibility of the individual.

And a consideration of the vicarious theory may also offer an explanation to the often repeated question whether fasts are not coercive. Dr. E. Stanley Jones asked Gandhi if his fasts did not contain a coercive element. Gandhi says in answer :

> If it is agreed that my fast sprang from love then it was coercion, only if love of parents for their children was ' coercion, of the latter for the former. or to take a sweeping illusitration, love of Jesus for those who own him as their all, is coercion . And if all this love could be regarded as coercion, then the love that prompted my.fast and therefore my fast was coercion but it was in no other sense.

It was this ennobling principle of lovs that was the chief motive for the fasts of Gandhi. The underlying assumption is the vicarious responsibility of the individual for others in society. Its sanctions are religious, and not political.

If the 'fast' has recently become a 'technique' for the political purposes, it is chiefly because the fast is now bereft of the religious spirit. It was never a bargaining principle with Gandhi. Nor did Gandhi use the fast for political pressure. The criteria of a fast are different from those of a political technique. If the Gandhian concept of fast is more abused to-day, it is not the fault of Gandhi, but of his followers only. Gandhi's fasts are an embodiment of the Tolstoyan principle of the vicarious responsibility of a moral individual. Significantly enough, even in this respect, Gandhi could derive much inspiration from the indigenous sources in philosophy and religion.

In retrospect, Tolstoy's impact on Gandhi's ideas is altogether creative. It is also more positive as the main teaching of Tolstoy is most congenial to Gandhi's outlook. It had offered no room for any divergence, the like of which was partly evident in the impact of thinkers like Ruskin. and Thoreau on Gandhi. In the case of Tolstoy and Gandhi, it was only a natural affinity that existed between them.

In reviewing the relationship between Tolstoy and Gandhi, the differences that exist between them are not of vital significance. The differences are nominal, but the unity amidst the two is notable. If Tolstoy had the vision of a more civilized law of love, it was Gandhi who translated it into action as non-violence. Gandhi was the Evangelist of Tolstoy. The legacy of Tolstoy was inherited by Gandhi, but the legacy of Gandhi seems to travel again westward. It was Martin Luther King jr.who applied the Gandhian technique in America, that must be regarded as the Evangelist of Gandhi in recent times. Even if the influence of Martin Luther King jr.could be traced to Gandhi, it must ultimately be traced back to Tolstoy through Gandhi.

Thoreau and Gandhi

In the annals of non-violence, there are many historical examples that are included as precedents for Gandhi's own celebrated campaigns. The most often quoted is Thoreau's defiance of the American government and his essay on civil disobedience which followed it.

Many writers, particularly Americans, claim that Henry David 'Thoreau, anti-slavery and anti-war protestor and withholder of taxes from a government he saw as unjust, and of course the author of the authoritative essay "Civil Disobedience," had a formative influence in the development of the Mahatma. Gandhi himself has claimed that "the persons who have influenced my life as a whole in a general way are Tolstoy, Ruskin, Thoreau, and Raychandbhai, then quickly added, "perhaps I should drop Thoreau from this list.

It has often been assumed that Gandhi's commencement of civil disobedience in South Africa was inspired by his reading of Thoreau's essay. However, although it is possible that Gandhi knew of Thoreau since his London days, it appears that Gandhi in fact did not read the essay until almost a year after his key speech at the Empire Theatre in Johannesburg on 11 September 1906. On that day, 3,000 Indians had gathered to protest against the discriminatory Indian Registration Ordinance which required them to be registered, fingerprinted, and to carry registration cards at all times under fear of heavy punishment for a breach! During the meeting a resolution was passed calling all present to defy the provisions of the legislation. This meeting is seen in the Gandhian saga as the "birth of Satyagraha," where Gandhi first set the course for his campaigns of civil disobedience. The confusion seems to stem from some authors placing the Empire Theatre meeting in 1907, a year later than when it actually took place and others repeating the mistake so as to reverse the order of the events of the commencement of Satyagraha and Gandhi's reading of Thoreau's essay. Hunt, the most thorough scholar of this period of Gandhi's life, notes that Gandhi "would have published his knowledge of Thoreau earlier if he had it" because at this time "he was searching the world over for models and precedents for the new kind of action being undertaken by the Indians of Transvaal." Therefore, "it is safe to assume that his readers heard about Thoreau within a few days of Gandhi's discovery of him.

In his essay "Civil Disobedience," Thoreau reminds his readers that "Unjust laws exist" and then asks: "shall we be content to obey them, or shall we endeavour to amend them, and obey them until we have succeeded, or shall we transgress them at once?" His answer to the question is surely one that had great appeal to Gandhi:

> If the injustice is part of the necessary friction of the machine of government, let it go, let it go: perchance it will wear smooth, but if it is of such a nature that it requires you to be the agent of injustice to

> another, then, I say, break the law. Let your life be a counter-friction to stop the machine. What I have to do is to see, at any rate, that I do not lend myself to the wrong which I condemn.

And, again, in words that would have undoubtedly received Gandhi's enthusiastic approval when he read them, Thoreau instructs his reader to "cast your whole vote, not a strip of paper merely, but your whole influence," and proclaims that "under a government which imprisons any unjustly, the true place for a just man is also in prison." Gandhi published extracts from the essay in his paper *Indian Opinion* on 7 and 14 September 1907 and a week later the two extracts were combined and printed as a pamphlet. On 9 November the paper announced an essay contest on "The Ethics of Passive Resistance" for which submitted papers had to contain an examination of Thoreau's essay, Tolstoy's book and "also the application of the 'Apology of Socrates' to the question." However, as Gandhi pointed out in 1935:

> The statement that I had derived my idea of Civil Disobedience from the . writings of Thoreau is wrong. The resistance to authority in South Africa was well-advanced before I got the essay of Thoreau on Civil Disobedience. But the movement was then known as passive resistance. As it was incomplete, I had coined the word *Satyagraha* for the Gujarati readers. When I saw the title of Thoreau's great essay, I began to use his phrase to explain our struggle to the English readers.

Henry Polak, who not only introduced Gandhi to Ruskin but also was probably the person who gave him a copy of Thoreau's essay, wrote to the American press:

> I cannot recall whether, early in 1907, he [Gandhi] or I first came across the volume of Thoreau's Essays but we were both of us enormously impressed by the confirmation of the tightness of the principle of passive resistance and civil disobedience that had already been started against the objectionable laws, contained in the essay "On the Duty of Civil Disobedience."

By way of summary, Seshachari points out that although satyagraha was well-advanced when Gandhi came across Thoreau's writings, "Thoreau helped Gandhi gain greater insight into the tremendous potential of non-payment of taxes and non-cooperation." He continues by pointing out that Thoreau did more than merely provide "intellectual sustenance to Gandhi's beliefs," but possibly directly inspired Gandhi's tactic of boycotting government institutions such as schools and law courts, and the tactic of making bonfires of registration cards and later foreign cloth.[1] It should be noted that the careful scholar James Hunt doubts even this. He points out that both these tactics were well known in India in Gandhi's time and did not have to be imported from the West.

In short, it appears that the purported influence of Thoreau on Gandhi is nowhere near as great as is often claimed. However, the words of the title of the printed version of Thoreau's lecture, "civil disobedience," certainly were a boon to Gandhi who had come to reject the phrase "passive resistance" (there was nothing passive about what he was doing) and understood that "Satyagraha" was going to be a little mystifying for his Western audience.

The celebrated essay by a well-respected American and kindred spirit, certainly seemed to legitimise what Gandhi was doing and he was to go on mentioning Thoreau's dictum about the imprisonment of the just under unjust governments, for the rest of his life. This, however, was backing support and Thoreau's essay cannot be regarded as a causal influence of Gandhi's actions.

In the realm of thought there is little room for plagiarism; that great men think alike is a common saying but it carries an element of truth. Henry David Thoreau and Mahatma Gandhi share a community of thought. Both were brought up on the wisdom of the ancient scriptures of India. Thoreau declared, "The pure Walden water is mingled with the sacred water of the Ganges". The New Englander was temperamentally *en rapport* with Indian thinking. He made an open admission that he was a "Modern Hindoo". The picture he gives of what he would most like to be is flattering to an Indian :

> The descendant of the religious devotee who dwelt at the roots of trees, with his crust of bread and water jug, cools his water today with ice from my well. If I am not a *Modern Hindoo* we are near neighbous—and by the vehicle of commerce we quench our thirst and cool our lips at the same well.

Thoreau's transcendentalism enabled him to be receptive to influences from the East. He came to the Indian scriptures after he had read Confucius and Lao-tze. The *Bhagavad Gita*, which was also a favourite of Mahatma Gandhi, became his constant companion. He said "in the morning I bathe my intellect in the stupendous and cosmogonal philosophy of the *Bhagavad Gita*, since whose composition years of the Gods have elapsed, and in comparison with which our modern world and its literature seem puny and trivial". The *Bhagavad Gita*, besides other holy scriptures, formed the spiritual nourishment of the Mahatma. Thoreau's idea of a philosopher is in concord with the Indian idea of a philosopher, one given to the perpetual acquisition of wisdom. Thoreau says : "The philosopher is in advance of his age even in the outward form of his life. Hs is not fed, sheltered, clothed, warmed like his contemporaries". He knew that the ancient philosophers, Chinese, Hindu, Persian and Greek, all cared for the acquisition of knowledge. He declared, "None can be an impartial or wise observer of human life but from the vantage ground of what we should call voluntary poverty. Of a life of luxury the fruit is luxury, whether in agriculture or commerce or literature or art". This fits the description of an Indian *Sanyasi* who divests himself of all material comfort. This image of the *Sanyasi* is dear to the author of *Walden or Life in the Woods.* He is fascinated : "I lay down the book and go to my well for water and lo ! there I meet the servant of the Brahmin priest of Brahma and Vishnu and Indra, who still sits in this temple on the Ganges reading the Vedas or dwells at the root of a tree with his crust and water jug. I meet his servant come to draw water for his master and our buckets as it were grate together, in the same well". The buckets of Thoreau and Gandhi grate together 'like the grating roar of pebbles'. Gandhi in 1942 in an appeal "To American Friends", wrote: "you have given me a teacher in Thoreau, who furnished me through his essay, 'On the Duty of Civil Disobedience', scientific confirmation of what I was doing in South Africa". This statement is the result of having mused on Thoreau's sayings for about four decades. There are echoes of Indian thought which were very dear to Thoreau and also dear to Gandhi.

As Webb Miller pointed out, Thoreau's philosophy, essentially Indian in spirit, was taken back by Gandhi after it was distilled and crystallised in the mind of Thoreau. Thoreau lived like Spartan-hated luxuries as positive hindrances to elevation of mind, considered vegetarianism and abstemiousness necessary for the higher life. He says, "A command over our passions and over the external senses of the body, and good acts, are declared by the Veda to be indispensable in the mind's apiroximation. to God". His views on

Asvada, *Ahimsa* and *Aparigraha*, temperance, non-violence and non-possession, have echoes in the Indian system of life. He journeyed to the Walden Pond, not as many think to flee from life, but, in the act of apparent withdrawal, to find life. This kind of attitude is common to Christ, the Buddha and Gandhi and many teachers of mankind who insisted on the spirit of self-denial, and work for discovering 'something divine and immortal in man." Thoreau and Gandhi start from a similar premise as the basis of non-resistance ; the secret of worth-while living is in the wisdom of discovering oneself.

The study of Thoreau excited Gandhi, who was already soaked in the Indian spirit of living a selfless, disinterested life in the midst of material possessions. In 1931, when Gandhi was travelling in a train with Roger Baldwin of the American Civil Liberties Union, he was carrying Thoreau's *Civil Disobedience*. Roger Baldwin became very curious and asked him about the relevance of Thoreau's theory. Gandhi replied that the essay "contained the essence of political philosophy, not only as to India's struggle related to the British, but as to his own views of the relation of citizens to Government ". Gandhi had read Thoreau very early in his career as a non-violent fighter. He confided this to Webb Miller in London :

> I read *Walden* first in Johannesburg in South Africa in 1907 and his ideas influenced me greatly. I adopted some of them and recommended the study of Thoreau to all my friends who were helping me in the cause of Indian independence. Why, I actually took the name of my movement from Thoreau's essay, " On the Duty of Civil Disobedience " ,until I read that essay I never found a suitable English translation for my Indian word, *Satyagraha*.

Thoreau's refusal to pay his poll tax as a protest against the United States government and his going to jail willingly for what he believed to be a just cause, appealed to Gandhi.

One is not sure when exactly Gandhi came across Thoreau's essay. Henry S.L. Polak, one of the close associates of Gandhi in South Africa, in a letter to the *New York Evening Post* says.

> "I cannot recall whether early in 1906 or 1907, he or I first came across the volume of Thoreau's essays (published, I believe, in Scott's library), but we were both of us enormously impressed by the confirmation of the tightness of the principles of passive resistance and civil disobedience that had been started against objectionable laws contained in the eassy *On the Duty of Civil Disobedience*.

> "After consultation with Gandhi I reproduced the essay in the columns of *Indian Opinion* and it was translated into the Gujarati language, in which, as well as in English, the paper was published, and the essay was subsequently circulated in pamphlet form. Later in the same year *Indian Opinion* organised an essay competition on 'The Ethics of Passive Resistance', with special reference to Thoreau's essay and Socrates writings that had already come to Gandhi's notice."

Polak has not said the last **word** on the indebtedness of Gandhi to Thoreau. Henry S. Salt, the biographer of Thoreau, wanted to write a biography of Gandhi as well, but he seems to have been discouraged by Bernard Shaw on the plea that there was nothing more to be said about the saints after his play, *Saint Joan*. Salt, however, had met Gandhi in 1890 in London, and in the 1920s wrote to him to explain how much he owed to Thoreau in his use of non-violent resistance. Gandhi replied that he was greatly influenced and said:

> The essay seemed to be so convincing and truthful that I felt the need of knowing more of Thoreau, and I came across your life of him, his *Walden* and other essays, all of which I read with great pleasure and equal profit.

In *Indian Opinion* Gandhi printed extracts from Thoreau mixed with extracts from Tolstoy, under the heading "For Passive Resisters". The quotation from *The Kingdom of God is Within You*, which also made an indelible impression on Gandhi, begins thus:

> "The principle of State necessity can bind only those who disobey God's law, who for the sake of worldly advantage try to reconcile the irreconcilable, but a Christian who sincerely believes that the fulfilment of Jesus's teaching shall bring him salvation cannot attach any importance to this principle".

The essential principles quoted in *Indian Opinion* are reflected in the gentle alembic of Mahatma Gandhi. He quotes from Thoreau :

> Under a government which imprisons any unjustly, the true place for a just man is also a prison. If they think that their influence would be lost there, and their voices no longer afflict the ear of the State, that they would not be as an enemy within its walls, they do not know by how much truth is stronger than error, nor how much more eloquently and effectively he can combat injustice who has experienced a little in his own person. Cast your whole vote, not a strip of paper merely, but your whole influence. A minority is powerless while it conforms to the majority; it is not even a minority then; but it is

> irresistible when it clogs by its whole weight. If the alternative is to keep all just men in prison or give up war and slavery, the State will not hesitate which .to choose. If a thousand men were not to pay their tax bills this year, that would not be a violent-and bloody measure, as it would be to pay them and enable the State to commit violence and shed innocent blood.

These essential principles, thought out quite independently, guided the man who organised the Dandi March and Salt Satyagraha in India during the fourth decade of the 20th century. Before he had heard of Thoreau, he had begun the preparation for his later compaigns of civil disobedience. In 1906 he led a campaign involving civil breach of the law in the Transvaal; a decisive step in the struggle of the Indian patriots for their rights in South Africa. It was a fight "between gentleness and brutality, between humility and love, pride and violence," as Gandhi put it in his letter to Tolstoy.

Indian Opinion, possessing a name that speaks for itself, had spread the word of Gandhi against the inhuman acts of the South Africans against Indians. In 1906, in Johannesburg, about 13,000 Indians met and one of the resolutions passed was that the Indians should not submit to the Ordinance which they called the 'Black Act', and should defy it at all costs. Seth Haji Habib, seconding the resolution, wanted it to be passed with God as witness. Gandhi says that this reference to God awakened him to the significance of the vow he had asked them to take ; a vow in the name of God cannot be broken, even to save one's life. He set forth his new insight in a speech moving the hearts of his listeners. He extracted a pledge from them and warned them:

> We are going to take the pledge in a body, no one should imagine that default on the part of one or many can absolve the rest from their obligation.

The meeting was described as the advent of Satyagraha. 'Civil Disobedience ' was in the mind of Gandhi, although this significant meeting was held thirteen months before the publication of the extracts. While ruminating on the shape of Satyagraha, Gandhi constantly referred to Thoreau. A few days before the meeting where Satyagraha was born, *Indian Opinion* had printed an unsigned letter referring to the Archbishop of Canterbury's appeal to the clergy not to solemnise marriages with a man's deceased wife's sister even when such marriages have the force of English law. The letter commented that the Archbishop has recognised what Thoreau had said, that we should be men before we are subjects, and that there was no obligation imposed upon us by our conscience to give blind submission to any law, no matter what force or majority backs it. Further on in the letter, the anonymous writer, who is no other than Gandhi (as is clear from the style), quotes Thoreau, while making clear the distinction between the doctrine of passive resistance and the doctrine of obedience to the law. "We cannot give the dividing line in words more appropriate than those of Thoreau when, speaking of the American Government, he says :

> If one were to tell me that this was a bad Government because it taxed certain foreign commodities brought to its ports, it is most probable that I should not make an ado about it, for I can do without them. All machines have their friction, and possibly this does enough good to counterbalance the evil. At any rate, it is a great evil to make a stir about it. But when the friction comes to have its machine, and oppression and robbery are paramount, I say let us not have such a machine any longer. In the Asiatic Registration Act, British Indians have not only a law which has some evil in it, that is to say, using Thoreau's words, a machine wiih friction in it, but it is evil legalised, or it represents friction with machinery provided for it.

Thoreau like Gandhi did not preach what he did not practise himself. In the terms of the *Gita*, which was a tremendous influence on them, they both cared for means conforming to ends. The incompatibility of means to achieve an end is not honourable to a satyagrahi. Thoreau who lived in communion with nature in a log cabin in the woods outside Concord emphasised self-help:

> "I went lo the woods because I wished to live deliberately, to front only the essential facts of life, and see if I could not learn what it had to teach and not, when I came to die, discover that I had not lived— I wanted to live deep and suck out all the marrow of life, to live so sturdily and Spartan-like as to put to rout all that was not life—to drive life into a corner, and reduce it to its lowest terms, and, if it proved to be mean, why then to get the whole and genuine meanness of it, and publish its meanness to the world ; or if it were sublime, to know it by experience and be able to give a true account of it in my next excursion.

Gandhi became self-sufficient in the daily chores. He did away with scavengers and coolies and tried to do away with the help of machines, and thus proved to himself that slavery and bondage are unnecessary. Gandhi does not discuss the influence of *Walden*. However, he speaks of Thoreau going to jail for the sake of his principles and for suffering humanity, which confirmed Gandhi's faith in non-resistance and achieving victory through suffering. Gandhi hated slavery, either in India or in any part of the world. He and his followers defied the Registration Act in South Africa and in an announcement in *Indian Opinion* on giving a prize of ten guineas for the best essay on " The Ethics of Passive Resistance ", he says, "The doctrine, religiously construed, means a fulfilment of Jesus's fomous saying Resist not evil '. As such, it is of eternal and universal application, and if it were practised largely, it would replace, to a great extent, if not entirely brute force and other kindred methods for securing redress of grievances or inauguration of reforms ". It required that the essayist should show an intimate knowledge of Thoreau's *On the Duty of Civil Disobedience*, Tolstoy's *The Kingdom of God is Within You*, and the *Apology* of Socrates. The names of these writers suggest the universality of the doctrine. Gandhi had written articles on Socrates, as he had read of him during his jail term in 1908, and he published *The Defence and Death of Socrates* under the title *The Story of a Satyagrahi* in Gujarati. This pamphlet was banned in India. Socrates and Thoreau followed their conscience or 'inner voice', in the words of Gandhi, who wrote " Socrates as Passive Resister ", which reflects the views of Thoreau and the importance of following one's conscience. The overtones from Thoreau are pretty clear :

> For (Socrates) when there was to be a choice between his conscience—what he knew to be good—and what the government of the day had ordered and what he knew to be wrong, there was no hesitation even though it might lose him his life. Indeed, his trial was a brilliant example of passive resistance.

After having defended Socrates' preference of the poison-bowl to a life of servile and superstitious obedience to human authority, Gandhi says:

> The essence of Socrates' teaching and practice was that it is lawful to disregard a law or order when it is against one's conscience, i.e., the higher law, but it is not lawful to try to escape the punishment that the law imposes for such disregard.

He applies the principle to the Indians in Transvaal, who were prepared to suffer all penalties that the law they refused to respect might provide for them. He lays down that "acquiescence in a law which is repugnant to one's notion of right is nothing but rank cowardice, for it shows disinclination to submit to physical inconvenience".

> For this he has the support of Thoreau, who said, "There are nine hundred and ninety-nine patrons of virtue to one virtuous man. But it is easier to deal with the real possessor of a thing than with the temporary guardians of it".

The prison term gave Gandhi an opportunity to read all those masters with whom he found himself in agreement. He had read the *Gita* while studying law in England, on the suggestion of two brothers who were Theosophists who wanted his help in studying Edwin Arnold's *Song Celestial.* Forty years after this, he translated the *Gita* into Gujarati under the title *Anasakti Yoga*, and in the introduction he emphasised *'Karma-phala tyaga'*, renunciation of the fruits of action, as the *Gita's* central doctrine. The battle on the field of Kurukshetra is a description not of a war between cousins but between the two natures in us—the good and the evil. Thoreau in his essay on the *Gita* in *A Week on the Concord and Merrimack Rivers,* had disapproved of the justification of violence. Gandhi was aware of Thoreau's creacive interpretation and says, "Under the guise of physical warfare, it described the duel that perpetually went on in the hearts of mankind,and physical warfare was brought in merely to make the description of the internal duel more alluring ". To him Duryodhana and his party represented the baser impulses, while the Pandavas stood for the higher impulses. Gandhi was aware of Thoreau's interest in the *Gita* through his study of *Walden.*

But while Thoreau was a lone protestant who could afford to think abstractly and insist on the ideal, Gandhi was a polilical leader who had to consider all the circumstances in which he was asking people to act. He knew from his own life experience that virtue of any kind can seldombe improvised but must be built up by prolonged effort. Non-violence needs training, he said, even more than a soldier's courage does. He was aware, moreover, that the doctrine of ahimsa can be used as an excuse for shirking unpleasant duties, and he often pointed out this possibility and declared that violence may be better than non-violence inspired by cowardice. "If our *ahimsa* is not of the brave but of the weak and if it will bend the knee before *himsa,* Gardhism deserves to be destroyed." Gandhi further says "Where there is only a choice between cowardice and violence, I would advise violence." Thus in some circumstances non-violence can be put in a backseat. He argues : "Suppose a man runs amuck and runs furiously about, sword in hand and killing anyone that comes in his way from the point of view of *ahimsa* it is the plain duty of everyone to kill such a man." Similar cases occur in politics. In October 1947 he approved of the despatch of troops to protect Kashmir against the tribal invaders, and this apparent relaxation of his principle was not an unforeseen departure. He had long anticipated that free India would need armed forces, because the people had not been trained to the point of being able to defend the country non-violently. Many years before, at the Round Table Conference in 1931, he had suggested that after Independence, British troops should remain in India to initiate Indiansoldiers into modern techniques of war. "Having clipped our wings," he said, "it is their duty to give us wings wherewith to fly."

The domain of Gandhi's activities in South Africa widened and gave occasion for the use of passive resistance with General Smuts's refusal to keep his promise and repeal the Compulsory Registration Act after the Indians had voluntarily registered. Gandhi was annoyed at Smuts's breach of faith and declared that if the Asiatic Act were not repealed, he would ask his followers to burn the registration certificates. This corresponds to Thoreau's act referred to in Salt's biography. Thoreau's essay on ' Slavery in Massachusetts' was delivered as an address at the anti-slavery celebration at Birmingham in 1854, on which occasion the Constitution of the United States was publicly burned by Lloyd Garrison, an incident which may explain the passionate tone of Thoreau's paper. On August 16, 1908 the registration certificates issued by the Smuts's Government were burnt, and as a consequence Gandhi was put in prison. During the prison term he read Ruskin, the essays of Thoreau, those of Bacon, and the Bible, and he declared 'From Thoreau and Ruskin, I could find out arguments in favour of our fight". Like a true satyagrahi, he braved the conditions of prison in South Africa and in India. Many people wrote to Gandhi to ask why he should submit to humiliation and live on a non-nutritious and semi-starvation diet, and live a life of isolation inside the four walls of the prison. His answer was that he was not a cowardand that he was prepared to do everything for the sake of justice. He wrote that it was the "height of one's good fortune to be in jail in the interest and good name of one's country and religion. In jail the necessities of life were provided and the soul was left free; the body was restrained, but not the soul. A malevolent warden merely taught self-control to the prisoner". He claimed that his experiences of suffering and privation in the Transvaal jail were in the interest of justice. For this kind of austere attitude he found support and solace in Thoreau, who refused to pay his poll-tax in 1849 and expressed similar thoughts about prison life. Gandhi quotes these lines approvingly :

> I saw that, if there was a wall of stone between me and my townsmen, there was a still more difficult one to climb or break through before they could get to be as free as I was. I did not for a moment feel confined, and the walls seemed a great waste of stone and mortar. I felt as if I alone of all my townsmen had paid my tax. They plainly did not know how to treat me, but behaved like persons who are underbred. In every threat and in every compliment there was a blunder ; for they thought that my chief desire was to stand on the other side of that stone wall. I could not but smile to see how industriously they locked the door on my meditations, which followed them out again without let or hindrance, and they were really all that was dangerous. As they could not reach me, they had resolved to punish my body ; just as boys, if they cannot come at some person against whom they have a spite, will abuse his dog. I saw that the state was half-witted, that it was as timid as a lone woman with her silver spoons, and that it did not know its friends from its foes, and I lost all my remaining respect for it and pitied it.

These sentiments of Thoreau made a great impression on Gandhi, who by now had become a political leader and had practised passive resistance on a number of occasions. A passive resister had to pursue truth, and act according to the dictates of his conscience. A satyagrahi abjures physical force as a matter of principle. About 1908, Gandhi practised civil disobedience for the first time. The extracts from " Civil Disobedience", printed in *Indian Opinion*, were appreciated by the Indian passive resistors. When Gandhi became an ardent advocate of Hind Swaraj or Indian Home Rule 'in order to demonstrate the sublimity of Satyagraha, he spoke in terms reminiscent of Thoreau and Tolstoy, who were critical of Western industrialism. About 1909, he felt that the railways, machinery and the corresponding increase of self-indulgence, are the badge of slavery of the Indian people as they are of Europeans. Hind Swaraj, in dialogue form, aimed at demonstrating that the European civilization was turning away from God and emphasising material values, while the Indian civilization stressed the importance of spiritual values. This booklet showed Gandhi as an idealist first and a politician afterwards. In 1910, he published excerpts from Hind Swaraj in *Indian Opinion* under the heading, 'Thoughts from Thoreau.' They denounced many activities of the Government directed against members of the public.

Thoreau had his own meaning of freedom and liberty; he never difined them. To him they were synonymous. He felt most nineteenth-century Americans were not free men and were not conscious of their deprivation. "The American", he lamented, "has dwindled into an Odd Fellow, one who may be known by the development of his organ of gregariousness and a manifest lack of intellect and cheerful self-reliance" . Thoreau doubted that the Americans were a free nation. He hated moral enslavement. He quipped, "What is it to be free from King George and continue to be the slaves of King's prejudice?" Gandhi likewise was uncommonly free from the ordinary man's slavery to the conventional values of his community. The comment in which Gandhi chided Mrs. Millie Polak for buying curtains has echoes in Thoreau. When she said that the curtains would be a substitute for the poor upkeep of a cheap house, he said, "Why do you want to cumber yourself with things that will only need more time to be spent upon them? You say you want beauty. You have it around you. God has given you the reality; why, then, worry about things made by man ?" It is interesting that the transcendentalist philosopher Thoreau too did not want men and women to be slaves of custom, habit and prejudice. He wrote to H.G.O. Blake, "Circumstances are not rigid and unyielding, but only habits are rigid".

> Thoreau makes the simple life appealing and charming. Gandhi after reading Thoreau went to Emerson, and he advised his nephew Maganlalbhai to read Emerson's essays, which he characterised as the teaching of Indian wisdom by a Western guru.

Gandhi was aware of Emerson's views on 'The Over-Soul'. But Emerson was an idealist and a thinker. "He was a thinker ; Mohamed and Jesus were through and through men of action in a sense Emerson would never be ". Emerson and Thoreau differed in their attitudes to Nature ; to Emerson, Nature was a mere abstraction, to him, it was something to be learned *about* rather than something to be learned *from*. To Thoreau appreciation of Nature meant identification, a kind of Wordsworthian mystical experience. Nature even in her most fearful aspects whispered to him. His search for what he called ' wildness ' in the surroundings of the Walden Pond and to indicate the right road to humanity was dear to Gandhi who founded his Sabarmati Ashram on the bank of the river Sabarmati.

Thoreau studied the best natural man, the woodchopper; while Gandhi studied the manual worker. Thoreau, the apostle of civil disobedience, was both a thinker and a man of action. He and his work in Walden interested Gandhi and he followed it. The instrument of passive resistance formulated by Gandhi has again travelled to the West. Martin Luther King used it effectively in getting redress for Negro wrongs. Many, even in Communist countries, have believed in the efficacy and righteousness of Satyagraha. It has become one of the dominant realities of the twentieth century. It is a doctrine, whether borrowed or invented, which if practised sincerely can cure no small part of "all that human hearts endure".

The influence of Henry Thoreau upon Gandhi, now universally recognized, is generally treated perfunctorily; almost all popular articles on Thoreau usually devote at least one sentence to Gandhi's indebtedness to "Civil Disobedience." Since *Indian Opinion,* the South African newspaper published by Gandhi from 1903 to 1914, is now available for study, much new material on Gandhi's knowledge of Thoreau has come to light. Before *Indian Opinion* could be studied, information about Gandhi's indebtedness to Thoreau was scattered and fragmentary. For example, Gandhi, in his 1942 appeal "To American Friends," wrote, "You have given me a teacher in Thoreau, who furnished me through his essay on the 'Duty of Civil Disobedience' scientific confirmation of what I was doing in South Africa."

Similarly, Gandhi had written to Franklin Roosevelt in 1942, "I have profited greatly by the writings of Thoreau and Emerson." Roger Baldwin, chairman of the American Civil Liberties Union, rode with Gandhi on a train trip through France in 1931 and noticed that the only visible book was Thoreau's "Civil Disobedience."

Baldwin remarked on the extremeness of Thoreau's doctrine, and Gandhi replied that the essay "contained the essence of his political philosophy, not only as India's struggle related to the British, but as to his own views of the relation of citizens to government."

At the Second Round Table Conference in London that same year, the American reporter Webb Miller, a long-time admirer of Thoreau, asked Gandhi, "Did you ever read an American named Henry D. Thoreau?" Gandhi replied,

> Why, of course I read Thoreau. I read *Walden* first in Johannesburg in South Africa in 1906 and his ideas influenced me greatly. I adopted some of them and recommended the study of Thoreau to all my friends who were helping me in the cause of Indian independence. Why, I actually took the name of my movement from Thoreau's essay, 'On the Duty of Civil Disobedience,' written about eighty years ago.

Miller noticed that Gandhi, a "Hindu mystic," adopted from Thoreau the philosophy which was to affect millions of Indians and inspire them to defy and shake the powerful British Empire. "It would seem," Miller concluded, "that Gandhi received back from America what was fundamentally the philosophy of India after it had been distilled and crystallized in the mind of Thoreau."

Because of lack of information, however, inaccuracies have been perpetuated. Henry Seidel Canby wrote in the *Yale Review* that "Civil Disobedience" came to Gandhi's attention while he was studying law in London in 1907." *The New York Evening Post* used this information in an editorial and then received a letter of correction and amplification from Henry S. L. Polak, Gandhi's co-worker in South Africa.

There can be no doubt about the appeal of Thoreau's essay which Gandhi read at a crucial phase of his life. He was then fighting the Asiatic Registration Act ("Black Act") which required all Asiatics over eight years of age residing in the Transvaal to register and, as if they were criminals, give their fingerprints. Failure to register would result in a fine, a prison term, or deportation. "I have never known legislation of this nature," Gandhi wrote, "being directed against free men in any part of the world."

If Gandhi did not write all of the articles which mention Thoreau, he certainly read them, as his newspaper received his constant attention. "During ten years," he wrote, "that is, until 1914,. there was hardly an issue of *Indian Opinion* without an article from me."

Gandhi may well have read *Walden* as early as 1906; before the first Satyagraha movement, he dispensed with servants, acted as his own scavenger, and attempted to be independent of machinery. His views were seemingly influenced by *Walden*, but since lie was using the *London Times* as a pattern for *Indian Opinion*, his journalistic endeavors did not reflect his personal interests as his later papers in India did, and his reactions to *Walden* were not discussed in the paper. It was rather the Thoreau who went to jail "for the sake of his principles and suffering humanity" who was emphasized in *Indian Opinion* because he confirmed the non-cooperation campaign.

Readers of *Indian Opinion* were frequently reminded of Thoreau's essay on civil disobedience. Thoreau had opposed the enslavement of man; Indians, being enslaved themselves, needed encouragement in their struggle. The Indian community was openly defying the registration act, and the resistances of Thoreau, Tolstoy, Jesus, and Socrates seemed vital confirmations to Gandhi.

A settlement calling for voluntary rather than compulsory registration for Indians was arrived at, and Gandhi's days of reading were cut short. Thoreau's essay on civil disobedience was again brought to the attention of *Indian Opinion* readers when on April 18, 1908, the prize essay, "The Ethics of Passive Resistance," was printed. Reverend J. J. Doke read the first four essays submitted, and awarded the first prize to M. S. Maurice. *Indian Opinion* carefully pointed out that the essay which won did not reach the level which they had anticipated; it was indeed a pedestrian production; the section on Thoreau was largely a reproduction of the extracts which *Indian Opinion* had printed, and the sections on Tolstoy, Ruskin, and Jesus were uninspired.

Gandhi's transformation from a respectable lawyer to a radical political leader was completed. Thoreau was not ignored during the years after Satyagraha was first tried; for several years after 1908 passive resistance was offered on a small scale, and Gandhi himself did not court arrest. Two years after *Indian Opinion* had 'printed extracts from "Civil Disobedience," it printed selections from Mazzini with the comment: "We believe that when the first stage of passive resistance was at its height, the extracts we gave from Thoreau's essay 'On the Duty of Civil Disobedience' were very greatly appreciated by Indian passive resisters." Gandhi himself was still reading Thoreau; by 1909 he considered that "railways, machineries, and the corresponding increase of indulgent habits are the true badge of slavery of the Indian people, as they are of Europeans." Thoreau and Tolstoy had said the same thing, and their influence is particularly strong in Gandhi's *Hind Swaraj*, a severe castigation of the evils of Western imperialism which enslaved colonial peoples and brought material prosperity to the governing nations. Works by Tolstoy, Ruskin, Edward Carpenter, and Thoreau's "On the Duty of Civil Disobedience" and "Life Without Principle" were among the sources listed in the bibliography; and in a Preface to raj printed in *Indian Opinion*, Gandhi stated, "Whilst the views expressed in *'Hind Swaraj'* are held by me, I have but endeavoured humbly to follow Tolstoy, Ruskin, Thoreau, Emerson and other writers, besides the masters of Indian philosphy." *Hind Swaraj*, banned in India, was a call for individual, Thoreauvian regeneration shows that in 1909, six years before he was to leave South Africa, Gandhi was beginning to think of Indian affairs. One year after the publication of *Hind Swaraj*, *Indian Opinion* published excerpts from "Life Without Principle," under the title "Thoughts from Thoreau."

These extracts, condemning commerce, government, and intellectual stagnation, must have delighted Gandhi. The middle-class lawyer Gandhi underwent a conversion in South Africa which made him discard almost all aspects of his old life and beliefs and made him turn to writers who probed the meaning of civilization. Once Gandhi adopted and modified Thoreauvian-Tolstoyan-Ruskinian principles, he acted without hesitation and with determination.

Gandhi found in Thoreau a practical man willing to practice his beliefs. It is a mistake, however, to overestimate Thoreau's influence upon Gandhi and the satyagraha movement—to maintain that Gandhi did nothing original and merely applied Thoreauvian teachings. Gandhi himself protested to P. Kodanda Rao in 1935, "The statement that I derived my idea of Civil Disobedience from the writings of Thoreau is wrong. The resistance to authority was well advanced before I got the essay." The Passive Resistance movement, however, had not been tested when Gandhi first read "Civil Disobedience," and the essay offered confirmation of the effectiveness of deliberate resistance to unjust laws. There can be no doubt that Gandhi was deeply indebted to the Thoreau who defied society and government to follow his conscience.

Ruskin and Gandhi

Ruskin is another philosopher who had a great impact on the ideas of Gandhi. The influence of Ruskin's book *Unto This Last* on Gandhi's views on the economic system he advocated, his theory of trusteeship, economic equality, relationship between the employers and. the employees and the use of modern technology is well documented by schotars.

Ruskin's and Gandhi's views, both moral and intellectual, and particularly Gandhi's averment that after reading *Unto This Last* he determined to change his life in accordance with the ideals of the book. The impact of Ruskin on Gandhi can be know form Gandhi's own statement. "Out of the few books I read, the one which brought about an instantaneous and practical transformation in my life was .*Unto This Last*". At another place Gandhi says: "I stand by what is implied in the phrase 'Unto This Last'. I saw clearly that if mankind was to progress and realise the ideal of equality and brotherhood, it must adopt and act on the principle of 'Unto This Last"

The textbook of Gide and Rist brackets Ruskin,Tolstoy and in some respects Thomas Carlyle, who preceded both, in a special category, strangely termed as "The Mystics'. It would be interesting to deduce the influence of this trio on Gandhi's thought.

All the three along with Gandhi shared the disapproval and denunciation of the dominant economic thought and practice as represented by the classical economists. Both Ruskin and Tolstoy condemn the hedonistic principle and denounce money as an instrument of tyranny which they felt had resulted in setting up a new system of slavery, hence they both advocate a return to manual labour as the only power that can free the individual and regenerate social life. They, however, differ in their perception of the future society. To Ruskin the future society should be 'aristocratic, chivalrous and heroic' besides being aesthetic, to Tolstoy it was to be 'egalitarian, communal and above all ethical'. Thus Gandhi's stress on manual labour (charkha) owes its inspiration to both Ruskin and Tolstoy his strong and all pervasive accent on ethics, truth and non-violence seems to be derived from Tolstoy. Ruskin's programme of social regeneration can be summarised as follows:

(1) Manual labour should be compulsory for everybody, to live upon the fruits of dead labour of others is surely absurd and contradictory. Machinery of all kinds must be renounced, except that which may be driven by wind and water - natural forces which, unlike coal, do not defile, buj purify. Ruskin wanted labour to be artistic, and he' longed to see that the artisan again became an artist. Tolstoy, on the other hand, does not strive for artistic effect. His heart is set on rural work, which he magnificently describes as 'bread work' and which seemed to him sufficiently noble without any embellishment of any kind.

(2) Gandhi adopted the essence of the above from both Ruskin and Tolstoy and synthesised the two in the Indian context, Work for everyone is the natural complement and the necessary corrective of the preceding rule of no idleness and no unemployment. In society as at present organised everybody is not obliged to work while some individuals are obliged to be idle. This monstrous inequality must be remedied.

(3) Labour would no longer be paid according to the exigencies of demand and supply, which tend to reduce manual work to the level of a mere commodity. It would be remunerated according to the eternal principles of justice, which would not of necessity imply an appeal to any written law. Ruskin elsewhere elaborates what he considers as just payment.

(4) Natural sources of wealth - land, mines and waterfalls - and the means of communication should be nationalised. Ruskin speaks of himself as an out-and-out communist, but with a touch of the aristocrat and the aesthete. Tolstoy is a much more thoroughgoing communist and was violently opposed to that low bestial instinct which men call the right to private property. His cry was 'back to the land' and the practice of co-operation.

Everyone ought to produce his own food. In between the aristocratic and aesthetic communism of Ruskin and the Spartan communism of Tolstoy where should we place Gandhi? Gandhi claims: "I' was a socialist long before those I know in India had avowed their creed".

(5) A social hierarchy graded according to the character of services rendered should be established. Chivalry is as necessary in an industrial as in a military service.

(6) Above all else must come education - not mere instruction. What is needed above everything is a sense of greatness, a love of beauty, respect for authority, and a passion for self-sacrifice. Carlyle's economic ideas are akin to Ruskin's. He was possibly the strongest adversary of the old classical school. It was he who spoke of political eonomy as the 'dismal science'. He is equally fierce in his denunciation *of laissez-faire* as a social philosophy.

Proceeding further from Ruskin's academic status in the history of economic thought, we come specifically to his *Unto This Last*. We shall discuss here only two issues which figure prominently both in Ruskin's and Gandhi' s thoughts; justice to which Gandhi added non-violence as a foundation of a civil society and rejection of machinery or industrialisation in general. Justice is universally accepted as a basic value encompassing all human activities, yet perceptions as to what constitutes justice differ. Under capitalism, free market is upheld as the most just and competent arbitrator in this matter. Its motto is 'each according to his ability and the devil take the hindmost'. Ruskin and Gandhi accept the importance of ability in acquiring wealth, but not in its use which should be governed by the principle of 'each according to his need'. Hence the principle of trusteeship evolved by Ruskin and perfected by Gandhi. Communism, on the other hand, propounds that emergence of inequality should be nipped in its bud through socialisation of all means of production and abolition of private property. By adopting the 'middle path', Ruskin partially and Gandhi wholly, rejected both the amoral acquisitive and possessive base of capitalism and the communist's usurpation of individual freedom, initiative and creativity by the state which virtually meant political dictatorship with bureaucracy as its tool. With the collapse of communism, capitalism with its aggressive acquisitiveness remains the only dominant ideology today. In this context, Ruskin's and Gandhi's ideology which leaves scope for individual entrepreneurship and hence acquisition of wealth but social use is perhaps the only alternative. It is true that under the prevailing etlhos of consumerism, such a radical change in the value system is not possible, yet ideals like 'satya', 'ahimsa', asvad and 'aparigraha' are too precious for the health and survival of the civilisation and should not be discarded as a lost dream.

But it is on the question of equality that we see some difference in emphasis in Ruskin's and Gandhi's writings. While Ruskin along with his insistence that the rich and the wise should use their richness and wisdom for the good of all, also emphasised 'the impossibility of equality'. Gandhi's statements on equality and inequality are apparently confusing. For example, his advice to the rich was "Earn your crores by all means but understand that your .wealth is not yours, it belongs to the people". But thereafter he states: "Strictly speaking all amassing or hoarding of wealth, above and beyond one's legitimate requirement is theft". And the gulf that separates the rich and the poor today is appalling. It has to be bridged. He was equally aware of the exploitation involved in accumulation of wealth. When served milk and fruit in gold bowls and plates by a zamindar host, Gandhi .expressed his reaction, in following words: "Where did he get these golden plates from?" At the same time he says: "I do not grudge the prince his palace and the millionaire his mansion, but it is my earnest request to them to do something to bridge the gulf that separates them from the peasant". Gandhi in his trusteeship formula emphasised that a limit should be fixed for maximum income that could be allowed to any person. The difference between the minimum decent living wage and maximum income should be reasonable and equitable and variable from time to time so much so that the tendency would be towards obliteration of the difference. Economic equality constitutes an integral part of his constructive programme.

This last is the master key to non-violent independence. Working for economic equality means abolishing the eternal conflict between capital and labour. It means the levelling down of the few rich in whose hands is concentrated the bulk of the nation's wealth on the one hand, and the levelling up of the semi-starved naked millions on the other. A non-violent system of government is clearly an impossibility so long as the wide gulf between the rich and the hungry millions persists. The contrast between the palaces of New Delhi and the miserable slums of the poor labouring class nearby cannot last for one day in a free India in which the poor will enjoy the same power as the richest in the land. A violent and bloody revolution is a certainty one day unless there is a voluntary abdication of riches and the power that riches give and sharing them for the common good.

Why is one man richer than the other? Ruskin's answer is, "Because he is more industrious, more persevering and more sagacious". He further added: "My continuing aim has been to show the eternal superiority of some men to other. Sometimes even of one man to all others; and to show also the advisability of appointing such persons to guide, to lead, or on occasion even to compel and subdue their inferiors according to their better knowledge and wiser will". To the poor, an employee, for example, he preached 'loyalty and duty, obedience and submission'. He told the poor "claim your crumbs from the table, if you will but claim them as children not as dogs, claim your right to be fed but claim more loudly your right to be holy, perfect and pure."

Gandhi was sometimes equally paternalistic, yet as the above passage indicates, he did not subscribe to submission of some to the 'eternal superiorities of some'. "Millionaires no less than other business and commercial firms ought to take a parental interest in the welfare of their employees. The relations between the employer and employee have been upto now merely of the master and servant; they should be father and children". The employer should become father to the employees working under him. A touch of feudalism or romantic medievalism!

According to Ruskin, since the industrialists have acquired wealth and possess organising power, it is their responsibility to guide labour. He exhorted the wealthy people of England that by the strength of their possession they should.direct the acts, command the energies, inform the ignorance. Ruskin and Gandhi wanted the rich men to use their capital and wisdom as a trust for the good of all. Ruskin's emphasis was on just payment to the worker and elaborates what he meant by just payment of wages. Gandhi was more strict on the behaviour of the trustee. He did not rule out state regulation to ensure that the trustee "does not hold or use his wealth for selfish satisfaction or disregard the interest of the society".

Ruskin's and Gandhi's views on machine and technology needs to be more elaborate and forthwith. On Ruskin's part it is a reaction to the egregious excesses of adolescent industrialisation:

> Spinners at the age of seven worked in worsted factories from five in the morning until eight in the night with only one break of thirty minutes at noon under overseers who strapped them when they grew tired, young girls in mills at the busy season slaved from three in the morning until ten at night and arrived home so exhausted that they fell asleep with their poor food unmasticated in their mouth.

For Ruskin and Gandhi more importantly, industrialisation was the culprit who destroyed their idyll of peaceful self-sufficient rural society, in which workers bought their own raw materials spun and wove them and sold their finished good to the rural community, it destroyed craftsmanship and dignity of labour. They shrank from the idea of skilled craftsmen turning into 'hands in factory'. For Gandhi there was an additional factor. To us in India industrialisation was associated with imperialism. India was encouraged and forced to cultivate raw cotton in preference to foodgrains which was our dire need, railways were built to transport cotton from the hinterland to port-towns for export to Great Britain, which was spun and woven in the factories in Manchester and Lancashire and the cloth so made was exported back to India. This process not only destroyed India's dispersed spinning and weaving industry, the charkha and the handloom, but the very source of livelihood of millions of craftsmen drove them back to agriculture as landless labourers.

Yet, this revulsion towards the ugliness of industrialisation and machineries was contextual, their total rejection is to raise it to an inalienable principle. The latter propostion is unacceptable to us. Could India have sustained her rapidly rising population with a wooden plough and rainfed agriculture or defended herself against a modern war? Historically the civilisation has evolved from the stone age till say Ruskin's and Gandhi's era through initially slow but persistent improvement in technology. Like time, technology cannot be stopped or frozen at a point of history.

Several kinds of refutations can be advanced against this poser. One can say, do not mix up technology with machinery and industrialisation. Bio-technology for example, can be used for development. Besides no one is against machinery, it is its craze to which Gandhi was opposed. We can pick and choose appropriate technology. To which we can ask: where does desirability stop and craze begin! One can cite examples, such as destruction of environment or unrestricted pollution as unacceptable. But it is difficult to fix a border line. We can pin-point what is inappropriate but cannot precisely define what is appropriate, under fast changing situations.

Frankly, we ourselves cannot provide any convincing answers. All that we can say is that in several fields we have no choice. A glaring case is that of defence equipment. Can we reject the radar or missile technology, tanks and fighter planes, or do without satellites and remote sensing, fax machines, if you want to be a global partner? One can retort, we do not want to be global, we demand swadeshi, self-reliance if not self-sufficiency. Most of us may fully accept the principle of self-reliance in regard to essential commodities like foodgrains. But even in this regard, we had to compromise even with almost stagnant foodgrains production. We had to import large quantities of foodgrains till the high-yielding varieties of wheat and rice seeds - initially imported from Mexico and the Philippines - boosted our food production, and enabled us to discontinue imports. This is what one scholar has termed as "dependency to end dependency' through indigenisation. As a mater of fact our entire industrial development from the early textile factories, and steel mills right up to automobile industry, communication technology, is derived from initial imports and technology but gradually we are becoming self-reliant in all these areas of economy.

In the mid-1960s domestic food production was stagnant creating an acute food scarcity. Rapid and fast growth of food production was the essence and hence the need of the time. With food self-sufficiency, we can opt for a different technology, environment friendly. Likewise if the whole world accepts Gandhi's non-violence as a governing principle of the polity, we can dispense with armaments. We too would prefer organic and natural farming over the current practice. But we are convinced that for at least a decade or two it will not be able to fully replace the current farming technology and feed our galloping population with organic farming, which should be our ultimate aim. We are unable to resolve the dilemma of the compulsion of hi-tech for defence and food security and the charm of a simple life, unpolluted rivers and green mountains.

Is it possible to synthesise hi~tiech with the simplicity of tradtiional technology? Alvin Toffler, the author of *Future Shock* and the *Third* Wave mises question. Most recent technological developments in energy, agriculture, for example, bio-technology, and micro-chips suggest the possibility of whole new societies based on the fusion of the past and the future, of the First Wave (industrialisation) and the Third Wave. "One can begin to picture a transformation strategy based on the development of both low-stream village oriented and certain carefully selected high-stream technologies, with an economy zone to protect and promote both". "Indeed linking of the two economic activities (the market and producers sectors) more intelligently to one another may be the missing key to the survival of the millions. Toffler gives one of his chapters the title 'Gandhi with Satellites'. The quintessence of Ruskin's and Gandhi's thought is fully reflected in the title of Ruskin's *Unto This Last.* The empathy for the most disadvantaged individuals and groups should mould our economic and social philosophy, politics, social behaviour and provide the basic values for their formulation. The major flaw of the capitalistic system and its economic policies is its value neutrality. The market, guided by the quest for profitability, determines the fate of the people. The excesses of the early rugged capitalism are vividly narrated in *Unto This Last.* In due course capitalism realised the imperfections of the market, and misery it inflicted on a large section of the population. It took some steps to correct the distortions; enact labour laws and introduce several 'welfare' measures. The capitalist West now talks of development with a human face, after having built its own prosperity on the most inhuman exploitation of its own native population and conquest of colonies through unspeakable brutality, in addition to the plunder of the environment.

The fact that there is less poverty and deprivation in capitalist economies than in less developed countries and ex-communist regimes is no proof of any basic change in its value system - 'The devil take the hindmost'.

Karl Marx launched a severe attack on capitalism, and communism charmed the intellectuals all over the world with its egalitarian appeal. But that appeal did not emanate from the empathy for the disadvantaged. In fact, sentiments like love, compassion, charity were shunned as bourgeois morality. It was this amoral attitude of its philosophy which provided a fertile ground for the emergence of Stalinism -tyranny, suppression of freedom of the individual and scant respect for his dignity. Ultimately, it was this total disregard of human values that led to its economic and political policies which culminated the collapse of communism in spite of its good record in the field of literacy, health, employment and removal of brutal poverty.

It is this concern for the downtrodden, the *daridranarayan* that gives Ruskin's and Gandhi's thought its universal relevance in all climes and climate. Add to this Gandhi's emphasis on non-violence. Other aspects of their thought are contextual and should be revised and re-designed to syncrhonise with the ongoing technological revolution.

Sooner or later, perhaps much later, the mankind will realise that whatever the technological progress, there is no alternative to *Unto This Last*, in which non-violence, limitations of wants and sharing, constitute the ethos of a civilised society.

The Suffragettes

Gandhi also had encounters with the English suffragettes in London just weeks after the Empire Theatre meeting, and wrote at length about them and their tactics. Hunt notes that Gandhi had admiration for the English and their women and that he received "significant assistance from a contemporary women's movement at a point when he was formulating his own philosophy of non-violent action" and that this "yielded valuable results which assisted considerably in the maturing and development of his work."

In late 1906 Gandhi's movement for the rights of South African Indians had been announced but had not yet commenced. In a final act of constitutional lobbying before commencing the campaign of active resistance, Gandhi spent six weeks in London to present his case to the British authorities. During this visit the women's suffrage movement reached new heights of militancy "employing tactics and seeking goals strikingly similar to his own."

Three days after his arrival, the Women's Social and Political Union held a demonstration in the House of Commons, resulting in the arrest of eleven of their numbers. After refusing to pay their fines, the women were sentenced to three months' imprisonment. This was the largest number arrested in the year-long increasingly militant campaign. This was not lost on Gandhi who wrote an article for *Indian Opinion* a few days later. He has one of the main protesters announcing "I shall never obey any law in the making of which I have had no hand; I will not accept the authority of the court executing those laws; if you send me to gaol, I will go there, but I shall on no account pay a fine. I will not furnish any security either."

He then ties this determination to inevitable success, success that the South African Indians could also achieve with the adoption of similar tactics;

> Today the who'e country is laughing at them, and they have only a few people on their side. But undaunted, those women work on steadfast in their cause. They are bound to succeed and gain the franchise, for the simple reason that deeds are better than words. Even those who laughed at them would be left wondering. If even women display such courage, will the Transvaal Indians fail hi their duty and be afraid of gaol? Or would they rather consider the gaol a palace and readily, go there? When the time comes, India's bonds will snap off themselves.

Following his return to South Africa in December, Gandhi kept up to date with the suffragette campaigns in London and continued to write about them. Following large-scale arrests during marches to Parliament in March 1907, Gandhi wrote that "we have to follow the example of the women referred to above. They go to gaol, though they are few in number, and thus draw the attention of the world to their cause." He used the example of the sacrifice of the suffragettes to shame his followers into courageous action: "While English women do manly deeds, shall we, though men, behave like women? In a few days our mettle will be tested.

In 1909, the now long-standing civilly disobedient Gandhi was again in London pushing the cause of the South African Indians. During the 18 weeks he spent there, he finally met members of the women's movement and attended their rallies at a time when the movement was taking a more violent turn with the resisting of arrest, stone throwing, window breaking, hunger strikes in prison and even arson. Gandhi lauded the commitment and actions of the English suffragettes as examples for satyagraha, however their violence now made them problematic as a model. To get around this problem, in his earlier writings he did not inform his audience of everything they may have done, omitting references to their destruction of property: "The systematic way in which they set about their work and their skill deserve the highest commendation," and "when we consider the suffering and the courage of these women, how can the Indian satyagrahis stand comparison with them?"

Later, he voiced his concern at what he saw as the impatience of some of the women, noting that it will prove self-defeating in the long-run:

> Some of these women have grown impatient. It is, of course, an admirable thing that they should go to goal. No one can have anything. to say against their inviting suffering on themselves. If the British women mean to fight in the spirit of satyagraha, they cannot adopt tactics (such as breaking windows). There is no room for impatience in Satyagraha. Those who want the franchise are in a minority, whereas the majority of women oppose the demand; so the minority has no option but to suffer for a long time. If demoralized by suffering, they take to extreme measures and resort to violence, they will lose whatever sympathy they have and set the people against themselves.

Eventually he was to realise that the violence was not merely the action of a few who had grown impatient but that it had become part of the strategy of the campaigning for some of the leading suffragettes. He noted that as the English respected violence, these tactics may in fact succeed in a limited way but could never bring about any meaningful transformation and may even endanger the whole social fabric.

Although on the question of violence he parted company with them, as Hunt points out, the suffragettes provided Gandhi with an important precedent to cite and a political model to examine. "It was a living example of the organization of a campaign for rights. "He studied their tactics and methods with interest, first, in 1906 when he needed inspirational examples, he emphasised their courage and faith as a moral model, Later, in 1909 when he was in the midst of his own campaign of civil disobedience, he became more concerned with operational aspects of the suffragettes struggle-fund-raising, organisation, and publications.

Hunt notes that Gandhi's debt to the suffragettes has never been fully appreciated. He points out that while neither the women activists Gandhi came to know about and observe in London, nor indeed any other Western model, can claim to be the immediate and direct author of what became known as satyagraha, Gandhi often talked about the example of the suffragettes to encourage his South African Indian followers-and was doing so more than a year before he discovered Thoreau's "Civil Disobedience".

Ferenc Deak

Another possibly influential example of what was then called "passive resistance" of which Gandhi became aware at the time he first read Thoreau, and referred to with favour, was the movement, led by Ferenc (Francis) Deak, of non-violent resistance by the Hungarians to despotic Austrian rule' in the 1850s and 60s. Although this movement is mentioned in the early classics of non-violence literature, and even hailed as the "first mass or corporate form of non-violent resistance," the possible influence it had on Gandhi's own thinking seems to have escaped attention.

When Gandhi was still at the beginning of his life as a political activist, having moved beyond mere lobbying and legal petitioning, he attempted to put the case for what would become known as satyagraha (his method of creed rather than mere policy-based nonviolent activism) before his constituents, the Transvaal Indians. In a 1907 article in his South African newspaper *Indian Opinion,* he wrote on "The Benefits of Passive Resistance" pointing out some notable instances. He explained how the Irish Sinn Fein movement was organising a peaceful campaign of self-suffering that would see Irish members withdrawing from the British parliament and a boycotting of British courts and goods. He believed that through such measures "without any violent struggle taking place the British would ultimately be obliged, or might agree, to grant Home Rule to Ireland, or would quit Ireland, and the Irish people would have an absolutely independent government."

The Irish struggle (as he saw it unfolding then) was a prototype of Gandhi's later campaign to free India from the British yoke. The Irish movement, in turn, had its antecedents in Hungary:

> This movement had its roots in Austria-Hungary in the south of Europe. Austria and Hungary were two separate countries. But Hungary was under the rule of Austria and was always exploited by it. To discomfit Austria, a Hungarian named Dick taught the people that they should not pay any taxes to Austria, should not serve any Austrian officers, and even forget the very name of Austria. Though the Hungarians were very weak, this kind of spirit enabled them in the end to assert themselves against Austria. Now Hungary is not regarded as subject to Austria, but claims parity with it.

During his visit to London in October and November of 1906, Gandhi was honing his political philosophy. He met with old friends, including vegetarians and theosophists, and studied the actions of the idealist rational Ethical Society and, the suffragettes.[1]If he was not aware of it already, it may be a fair assumption that Gandhi came to know of Hungary's non-violent resistance campaign at this time through discussing the political situation in Ireland. By the time of his London visit, the Irish Sinn Fein party had been formed to wrest independence, or at least home rule, from Britain. In 1904, one of the founders of the party and leading Irish nationalist, Arthur Griffith had published an influential little book on the Hungarian passive resistance movement and how it could serve as a model for the Irish struggle. While there is no direct evidence that Gandhi had read Griffith's book, the tone of the above quote and the fact that it is coupled with his note on Sinn Fein tends to indicate that he at least knew of the main arguments that it contained. His article on Deak and Hungary's resistance to Austria appeared a year after this visit. We do not know how soon before the publication of the article was originally written or when or if the book had come into his possession. It is possible that he only learned about the Hungarian passive resistance campaign shortly before the article went to press. Guesses as to the timing or immediate source of this knowledge are mere speculation. Nevertheless it can be assumed that the Irish question, and the possible direction the "Home Rulers" could take given the Hungarian example, was discussed in the circles in which he moved in London. Later, many of the early Gandhi-following writers on non-violence were to make much of Griffith's book and the Hungarian example.

The campaign is summarised by Griffith in a way that with a few minor changes could easily have characterised Gandhi's major Indian civil disobedience campaigns:

> When the Austrian tax collector came to gather the taxes the people did not beat him or hoot him-they declined to pay him, assuring him he was a wholly illegal person. The tax collector thereupon called in the police and the police seized the man's goods. Then the Hungarian auctioneer declined to auction them, and an Austrian of his profession had to be brought down. When he arrived he discovered he would have to bring bidders from Austria also. The Austrian government found in time that it was costing more to fail to collect the taxes than the taxes, if they were collected. In the hope of breaking the spirit of the Hungarians, the Austrians decreed that soldiers should be billeted upon them. The Hungarians did not resist the decree but the Austrian soldier, after a little experience of the misery of living in the house of a man who despises you, very strongly resisted it.
>
> Austria strove to encounter the Passive Resistance of Hungary by ordaining, "exclusive trading" illegal. The Hungarians despised the ordinance and pursued their policy, occasioning much filling of jails with "village ruffians," "demagogues," and other disreputable people who disturb the peace of a country which a stronger country desires to rob. Yet a few .months of the jail-filling process, Austria found herself in another cul-de-sac.

The Resurrection of Hungary was a propaganda piece rather than a scholarly historical work. It was written to inspire Irish non-violent resistance to the British, but was equally useful for others, like Gandhi, who were engaged in their own civil disobedience struggles, and eventually to those wanting to popularise Gandhian-style nonviolent resistance generally. It provided a lineage, an incorruptible and humble hero, many quotable quotes, and, most importantly, a story of success.

In Griffith's account Deak, who had retired from overt political activity following the revolt against Austria in 1848-49 and who from the tnid-1850s was living in the Queen of England hotel in Pest, was an annoyance to the Austrians by his mere presence and his continual statements that he was loyal to the Hungarian Constitution which had not legally been abolished. His simple presence seemed to give the populace hope and fanned their nationalist feelings. He was the spokesman of the country which kept hotter heads in check, conducted negotiations with the emperor, and authored the declarations by the Hungarian parliament and to whom the Hungarian people turned to for advice. When Austria was threatened by wars for which it needed Hungarian support, it made concessionary moves. When the threat of war receded, repression resumed. Throughout, the message of Deak was the same: the lawful Hungarian Constitution of 1848 is still in force and as soon as the Austrians recognised this and allowed Hungarians to run their own affairs in line with the Constitution, they would receive Hungarian friendship and loyalty. In this account, Deak, while smoking his pipe and talking with friends in his hotel room, not only makes proclamations very reminiscent of Gandhi's statements fifty years in the future, but seems to be almost a prototype Mahatma.

When the boycotting Hungarians refused to take their place in the "Imperial Parliament", according to Griffith, the parliament becomes "a topic for laughter throughout Europe," and Austria was forced "into the humiliating position of a butt for Europe's jests." Further, The *Times* noted that "passive resistance can be so organised as to become more troublesome than armed rebellion." In 1866, when Austria faced defeat at the hands of the Prussians, a "pale and haggard" emperor Franz Josef sent for Deak in another attempt to ensure the loyalty of his Hüngarian subjects:

> What am I to do now Deak, the monarch asked of his opponent. peak's laconic reply is celebrated in Austrian history, "Make peace, and restore Hungary her rights." "If I restore Hungary her Constitution now, will Hungary help me to carry on the war?" the Emperor inquired. The reply of Deak exhibits the fearless and uncompromising character of the great leader. It was in one word, "No." He would not make the restoration ot his country's rights a matter of barter.

By the following February the Austrians had to capitulate. In the Compromise of 1867, the Habsburg emperor was crowned monarch of Hungary, which became an equal partner in the Austro-Hunganan Dual Monarchy. Eighteen years after the uprising to defend the constitution, eighteen years of oppression and appeasement, and passive resistance, Deak had triumphed and the emperor came to Pest to restore the Constitution of 1848 "and pledge himself as King of Hungary to defend it with his life." Deak refused public office but consented to stay on in parliament as a simple member. He declined any honour from the new king, requesting only that on his death Franz Josef would say "Francis Deak was an honest man." The Hungarian resistance, as portrayed by Griffith, was the very type of example Gandhi was looking for as he was forging his own methodology of struggle. And Griffith's story of Deak, like the example of the jail-going Thoreau, must have made an impression on one who in childhood was so deeply touched by the story of the mythical hero Harishchandra who suffered many ordeals in his total commitment to the principle of-honesty.

Conclusion

Of course there were outside influences on Gandhi-they play on everyone. Perhaps to the degree that Gandhi did build on historical examples he was aware of the London Suffragettes and Deak and the Hungarian example, through the writing of Griffith, had as much influence on his earliest campaigns as Thoreau had. It would appear that Gandhi came across the history of Hungarian resistance at about the same time as he read Thoreau-he writes about them both for the first time in the same issue of his paper—but the Hungarian forerunner, in particular, has simply not been caught up in the evolution of the Gandhi story.

While Thoreau may have furnished backing theory for resistance to the state and a practical personal example of carrying it out, the Deak-inspired Hungarians provided a mass popular example. Although Gandhi does not mention the Hungarian resistance again in his writings, there does not appear to be much more reason for the claim that Thoreau was instrumental in molding Gandhi the nonviolent activist than Hungarians could claim for the influence of their history of resistance if they were so inclined. It also seems that the feminists have riot had as strong a need to stake a claim to having helped shape the Mahatma as some Thoreau supporters did. As with the Hungarians, if they were so inclined, they could mount just as strong a case for claiming credit for Gandhi.

3

Truth

> Since satyagraha is one of the most powerful methods of direct action, a satyagrahi exhausts all other means before he resorts to satyagraha. He will, therefore, constantly and continually approach the constituted authority, he will appeal to public opinion, educate public opinion, state his case calmly and coolly before every body who wants to listen to him; and only after he has exhausted all these avenues will he resort to satyagraha.

The concept of satyagraha is an important component of Gandhi's theory of spiritual politics. It has generally been argued that satyagraha, Gandhi's method of non-violent resistance, is a method of conflict resolution. Rather than merely examining satyagraha's applicability to the dynamics of group conflict, satyagraha is brought back to the micro level, that is back to the individual within larger conflicts and is examined from the Gandhian perspective. Unlike conflict resolution literature, which generally tends to focus on strategic and tactical considerations to the exclusion of psychological, philosophical and, especially, ethical ones, conflict and its resolution are here examined in the light of Gandhi's moral and ethical thought.

The practice of satyagraha has become the most potent weapon used by the Gandhians against the British in India, from its first use in Bihar in 1917 until 1947, when Indian independence was finally granted.

Satyagraha, as developed by Gandhi, is composed of four essential elements. First, civil disobedience must be offered to unjust laws. The Gandhians believe that if the law injures human dignity or causes unwarranted suffering to the human community, then one must choose to disobey the law by intentionally courting jail, physical injury, imprisonment or death. The satyagrahi, as the Gandhian follower of satyagraha came to be called, must be prepared for the physical, the legal, and the moral consequences of the act of civil disobedience. Civil disobedience to unjust laws is important because it attracts and marshals public attention, that is, the attention of those who support the unjust law, those who are against it, as well as those who are indifferent to it.

Second, the disobedience must be carried out with an attitude of non-violence and love. The satyagrahis, after fasting and prayer, must conduct themselves in a morally exemplary fashion so as not to hurt or harm those who would attempt to prevent their disobedience.

Third, Gandhi exhorted his stragrahis to look upon the act of disobedience as an offering of their bodies, souls and lives to God. Thus an element of what Hindus call bhakti yoga, the way of loving devotion to God, enters into satyagraha. The business of disobedience becomes a sacrifice, a spiritual act, a religious rite within a social or political environment, where the consequences of the act, through what Hindus call karma yoga, the way of selfless action, are renounced by the satyagrahi.

The fourth and final element of satyagraha followed hard upon the second and third. Gandhi felt that it was more important to change people than to change laws, hence, the aim of satyagraha ought to be to change the hearts and minds of the oppressor rather than the laws through which they oppressed. Only when those who had previously supported and defended the unjust law had been turned around, only then could one say that satyagraha had been successful; even the oppressor can be a member of the community. These four elements of satyagraha were to become the essential ingredients of Gandhi's later philosophy, a philosophy that he used in solving the day-to-day problems of human existence within, as well as outside, the community.

Gandhi first used the technique of satyagraha during the resistance of the Indian workers of South Africa against the Asiatic Law Amendment Ordinance of 1906. At that time, the movement was called "passive resistance", which later on was changed to satyagraha. In India, Gandhi led many satyagraha or campaigns, some notable ones being those of Champaran, Ahmedabad, Vaikom, Barodoli and Kheda.

The term satyagraha means "holding fast to truth", "adherence to truth". Explaining why he chose satyagraha as the name for his resistance movement in South Africa, Gandhi wrote, "Truth (Satya) implies love, and firmness (agraha) engenders a force which is born of truth and love or non-violence. Gandhi gives his concept of truth a basis in classical Hindu metaphysics. He claims :

> I am an Advaitist [believer in non-dual subsistent reality underlying all diversity] and yet I can support Dvaitism [dualism]. This world is changing every moment and is, therefore, unreal; it has no permanent existence. But though it is constantly changing, it has something about it which persists and it is, therefore, to that extent real. I have no objection to calling it real and unreal and being called an Anekantavadi (Jaina term for one who takes all logical conclusions to be non-final) or a Syadvadi, Jain term for one who believes truth can be seen only through its many facets, and specifically by synthesis of seven logical vantage points very much like this doctrine of the manyness of Reality.

Thus Gandhi accepts "manyness of viewpoints" on a single impartible reality, but for him the dual viewpoint of the practical/ spiritual distinction has an inherent moral qualification, a tinge that in facts all action and activity as these stand in opposition to the one changeless reality. Gandhi writes:

> I believe in Advaita (non-dualism). I believe in the essential unity of man and for that matter of all that lives. When we descend to the empirical level, we descend to the world of duality. In God there is no duality. But as soon as we descend to the empirical level, we get two forces—God and Satan.

Gandhi identifies God with "What Is" and calls this totality "Truth". This connects his metaphysics of Truth with his spiritual ideal, and these together give his religion-based moral ideology. He identifies the force of non-violence ultimately with God, or Truth and he believes that since "man's ultimate aim is the realization of God, all his activities, social, political, religious, have to be guided by the ultimate aim.

Combining his metaphysics of existence and of God, Gandhi gives us his metaphysics of morals. The central aim of Gandhi's moral ideology and metaphysics of non-violence is the realization of God. He believes that though God is one, and though God is all Goodness, it is God who also creates in this world evil, and we as moral beings, actively struggle against it. Though the evil is ultimately imaginary, it is not unreal, because the moral imagination which creates it follows its own laws. Gandhi writes that "the distinction between Good and Evil is not unimportant. Nor do these thoughts come haphazard. They follow some law, which the scriptures have tried to enunciate. I say the distinction is imaginary. God is one, without a second. He alone is." And he continues, "In reality, there is no God who is at war with Satan; but we have imagined that war. It is we who entertain thoughts and again it is we ourselves who repulse. We have thus to strive against ourselves. This duel is imaginary, not real. We can, however, sustain ourselves in the world only by assuming the existence of the imaginary duel to be real." God creates this evil in mental consciousness to induce the activity, virtues and discrimination that are prerequisite to self or god-realization.

With Gandhi it can be said that the operative core of all struggle for truth and justice is self-sacrifice and renunciation or self-purification. But this needn't bear the puritan and ascetic interpretation that Gandhi gives them. His refined and forceful puritanism leads him to a wrong theory of karma, a fundamentally punitive and "miserly" theory of reality that is sparse and ungiving.

Gandhi's entire translation in the practical sphere of non-violence as non-exploitation, rests on the proposition that " Divine Law gives to man from day to day his daily bread and no more," –exactly the opposite of the conception of God and reality as creative and abundant, full and gracious.

Also, though Gandhi believes in an all good, loving and gracious God, his theory identifies divinity with law and punishment. In the logic of Gandhi's concepts God figures as a punitive meter of just deserts, and "just" has a hard negative tone. One must beware what one sows because one will have to reap its consequences, or one should not complain because one is only receiving the fruits of one's own actions. These are negative readings of moral and practical law connecting action and reaction, fruits and actions.

Gandhi's negative valuation of life and consequent determination that the aim of life is its negation in a supra-empirical concept of liberation and salvation, moksa, and his negative conception of the conditions of spiritual growth as a process of moral austerity, all overemphasize evil and its evasion.

In *Hind Swaraj,* Gandhi distinguished between body-force—brute force—the force of arms and soul-force—love-force—truth-force. He referred to the former as the method of violence, which he said, is celebrated in and by modern civilization. Satyagraha, he said, relies on soul-force or truth-force and is appropriate to Swaraj. He wrote in *Hind Swaraj* as follows:

> Satyagraha is referred to in English as passive resistance. Passive resistance is a method of securing rights by personal suffering: it is the reverse of resistance by arms. When I refuse to do a thing that is repugnant to my conscience, I use soul-force. For instance, the Government of the day has passed a law which is applicable to me. I do not like it. If by using violence I force the Government to repeal the law, I am employing what may be termed body-force. If I do not obey the law and accept the penalty for its breach, I use soul-force. It involves sacrifice of self.

Satyagraha, Gandhi said, was both a practically necessary and morally desirable mode of political action for Indian Swaraj.

Principles of the Satyagraha

Satyagraha is based on the principles of Satya (truth), Ahimsa (non-violence) and Tapas (self-suffering). Gandhi clarified this in his oral submission before the Disorder Inquiry Committee, presided over by Lord Hunter at Ahmedabad on 9 January 1920. The relevant question and answer are reproduced below:

> It is a movement intended to replace methods of violence and a movement based entirely upon Truth. It is, as I have conceived it, an extension of the domestic law on the political field and my experience has led me to the conclusion that movement and that alone can rid India of the possibility of violence spreading throughout the length and breadth of the land, for the redress of grievances. People differ as to the justice or injustice of particular laws. This is the main reason why violence is eliminated and a satyagrahi gives his opponent the same right of independence and feeling of liberty that he reserves to himself and he will fight by inflicting injuries on his person.

Gandhi believed in *Dharmasastra* tradition according to which dharma, derived from dhr (to be firm, to sustain or uphold), refers to the moral law governing the cosmos. Its essence is satya (truth), the root of which is sat (being, reality, right, what is and what will be). Gandhi writes:

> The word satya (truth) is derived from sat, which means 'being'. And nothing is or exists in reality except truth. That is why sat or Truth is perhaps the most important name of God. In fact, it is more correct to say that Truth is God than to say that God is truth. It will be realized that sat or satya is the only correct and fully significant name for God.

Since "nothing is or exists in reality excepts Truth", the practico-political field too, says Gandhi, must partake of it. For Gandhi, the dissociation of politics from truth or morality is untenable. He said:

> Some friends have told me that truth and non-violence have no place in politics and worldly affairs. I do not agree. I have no use for them as a means of individual salvation. Their introduction and application in every-day life has been my experiment all along.

Gandhi's satyagraha is an experiment for the introduction of truth and non-violence into political conduct. According to Gandhi, although Truth is absolute, our knowledge and experience of it is relative and partial. What we take to be truth, may be untruth for others. In fact, the satyagrahi assumes that his opponents or oppressors are also truth-seekers, acting on the basis of what they perceive to be truth. It is for this reason that ahimsa (non-violence) is the means to the discovery of truth. Gandhi writes:

> It appears that the impossibility of full realization of truth in this mortal body led ancient seeker after truth to the appreciation of ahimsa. The question which confronted him was shall I bear with those who created difficulties for me, or shall I destroy them? The seeker realized that he who went on destroying other did not make heady way but simply stayed where he was, while the man who suffered those who created difficulties marched ahead, and at time even took the other with him. The more he took to violence, the more he receded from truth. For, in fighting the imagined enemy without, he neglected the enemy within.

Satyagraha uses truth-force or love-force not to eliminate the opponents or oppressors but to bring about a restructuring of the total conflictual or oppressive relationship so that both parties to the initial conflict can realize a heightened mutually or moral interdependence. Through satyagraha, the victims of oppression seek to liberate themselves by aiding in the emancipation of their oppressors from their self-deceptive, truth-denying beliefs and actions. Satyagraha, Gandhi wrote in *Hindi Swaraj*, "blesses him who uses it and him against whom it is used."

The two central features of Gandhi's theory of satyagraha are non-violence and truth. Of the two terms, non-violence is a relatively straightforward concept, but truth represents special problems of interpretation. For Gandhi, violence meant exploitation, which, he insisted, represented a denial of individual integrity. As moral beings, we have a right to expect our integrity to be respected by others and also a responsibility to respect the integrity and freedom of others. Such a moral posture meant that individuals must be treated as ends in themselves even if we judge their actions as immoral, unethical or unjust. Violence, Gandhi said, treated other people as means and we are willing to excuse violence as justified because of some higher end. Our opponents are seen as impediments to the good, the just, the virtuous and, therefore, could be approached violently to force them to change their own perspective and to accept our standards. Such a position makes us arrogant, think that we have discovered the absolute truth, a position Gandhi is unwilling to accept, and that our claims of having discovered justice or equality are superior to the actual freedom and dignity of others. Such a stance is antithetical to Gandhi, who holds that only in respecting the moral worth of ourselves and others, could we achieve justice. In this respect, he argued that "means are after all everything. As the means, so the end. There is no wall of separation between means and end."

Violence not only treats others instrumentally and degrades them, it also makes the users of violence less human. The violent person is at war with the world and believes the world is 'at war with him and he has to live in perpetual fear of the world.' But such violence leads to helplessness, isolation, and incompleteness and builds barriers to a full social life.

Not all violence is personal, with one individual inflicting physical coercion on others. Much of it is institutional, negating the autonomy of others. Gross poverty, unemployment, and discrimination are recurring themes in Gandhi's writing that are presented as destructive to free choice and result in violence, either directly or indirectly, to control others. Unfortunately, these institutional forces are often incomprehensible and uncontrollable; many 'hugged the chains that bound them'. And so it would become necessary, Gandhi argued, to look at new institutional arrangements that would promote non-violence, truth and freedom.

Gandhi's notion of truth echoes the Hindu understanding of truth as an all pervading force of divine consciousness that holds the universe together. "This truth," Gandhi claims, "is the Absolute Truth, the Eternal Principle, that is God". Following the Hindu tradition of advaita, or non-duality, Gandhi sees the cosmos as a divine whole within which human beings participate. The task of human perfectibility is regarded as the ultimate reunification with this divine consciousness, through which one comes to know the Absolute Truth or God. Ontologically, then, man can potentially experience the infinitude of his own being, transcending the limitations of worldliness and participating in a divine whole greater than himself.

This enterprise, however, is complicated by the pluralistic nature of this Absolute Truth toward which humans aspire. "There are," Gandhi claims, "innumerable definitions of god because His manifestations are innumerable." Gandhi famously claimed that truth was much like the story of seven blind men who touched various parts of an elephant: "They were all true from their points of view, and yet each appeared to be untrue from the points of view of the rest. The truth was beyond all seven." Thus, "what may appear as truth to one person will often appear as untruth to another." Gandhi distinguishes between Absolute Truth and what he calls "relative truth": "Beyond the limited truth, however, there is one Absolute Truth, which is total and all-embracing. But it is indescribable, because it is God. Other things, therefore, can be true only in a relative sense." For Gandhi, the truth is such that each relative claims to truth or each particular element of a moral project—contains only some fragment of the Absolute Truth.

Notice that these relative truths are not necessarily false: they can all be true, but only in some limited sense that implies a lack of complete understanding. "What appear to be different truths are like the countless and apparently different leaves of the same tree."

The problem is that Absolute Truth is so multifaceted that it cannot adequately be captured by any one mind or manifested entirely in any given human life. The task of worldly action is doubly difficult. Not only are human beings attempting to transcend worldly limitations by finding the totality of truth, this endeavor is further complicated by the fluid and pluralistic nature of the truth they seek. Most human beings are, in practice, deeply limited in their capacity to see the Absolute Truth, and any one person's grasp of moral knowledge is necessarily incomplete. In keeping with the Hindu tradition, Gandhi holds on to the possibility of ultimate realization of the Absolute Truth; although lofty, this ideal is something that all should aspire to through their "ceaseless striving." Despite this perfectionism, Gandhi maintains in a somewhat Platonic vein that most of us spend the better part of our lives in a cave, and that it takes significant effort for us to see life beyond the cave. "Human beings shall never know in its fullness truth which is in itself infinite."

Human capacity to know the truth is not only deeply limited but also fallible and subject to constant revision. "Man is a creature full of errors." But man is a self-governing being, and self-government. Gandhi subtitled his autobiography *The Story of My Experiments With Truth*. The notion of experimentation emphasizes the corrigibility of individual epistemological enterprise: "Far be it from me to claim any degree of perfection for these experiments. I claim for them nothing more than does a scientist who never claims any finality about his conclusions, but keeps an open mind regarding them at every step I have carried out the process of acceptance and rejection." Thus, Gandhi holds out the possibility of something approximating eventual knowledge of the totality of truth but finds this path subject to the constant possibility of error. The task of human life for Gandhi is the very progress from human limitation toward the state of perfection, through "ceaseless striving." These limitations are the framework within which human action including political action must take place.

Gandhi's response to these challenges lies in his concept of non-violence. Although this may not have been the primary role that Gandhi assigned to the concept, non-violence can provide a solution to the moral and political dilemmas engendered by this framework. Minimally, non-violence arises as a constraint on human behavior in the political world because of epistemological deficit. Violence in politics is unjustified "because man is not capable of knowing the absolute truth and therefore not competent to punish." For Gandhi, the problem of moral authority is need to that of knowledge—it is because of our difficulty in coming to know the truth that certain kinds of political action become unjustifiable. However, Gandhian politics goes far beyond the simple prohibition of violence, or "abstention from causing physical hurt." Simply disavowing violence hardly guarantees access to truth in the moral world. Even in its broadest sense, non-violence is not used as an all-encompassing prohibition on violence: "You would not understand me to mean that I regard all taking of life as wrong in every possible circumstance; for I do not think that there is any ethical principle that can be regarded as absolute and admitting of no exception whatever." In fact, there are several instances in which Gandhi condones violence as the dutiful action for that particular case.

There is a more comprehensive sense in which Gandhi uses the term "non-violence". Beyond the negative constraint, non-violence is also a total ethical system that tells us what kinds of political actions are in accordance with truth, and, therefore, justifiable. In a more robust sense, Gandhi uses the term to refer to the cultivation of certain virtues. The general term for Gandhian non-violence is ahimsa, which he translates alternatively as non-violence or love. Himsa is Sanskrit word for violence, while prefix 'a' denotes the negative. Thus, minimally ahimsa means a refusal to do harm. "In its negative form," Gandhi acknowledges, "it means not injuring any living being, whether be body or mind."

In the more expansive interpretation that Gandhi gives it, however, ahimsa means more than simply non-injury. "In its positive form, ahimsa means the largest love, the greatest charity." Here, ahimsa denotes the highest and most Absolute Truth, the supreme moral principle within which all other virtues are contained. Gandhi claims that "non-violence implies love, compassion, forgiveness." Ahimsa, in the widest sense, means the willingness to treat all beings as one's self, a complete absence of ill-will, and goodwill toward all life. Moreover, ahimsa and truth, Gandhi claims, "are the obverse and reverse of the same coin. Ahimsa is my God, and Truth is my God." In this sense, ahimsa is a moral principle equivalent to

Absolute Truth, but it is also a means for attaining this principle. Gandhi states that truth is the end, and ahimsa the means: "Without ahimsa, it is not possible to seek and find truth." In this formulation, non-violence is identical to the principle of Absolute Truth and the means for its realization through the complete fulfillment of all moral virtues. For Gandhi, the pursuit of total ahimsa is a way of life wherein constant self-examination and rigorous discipline are combined with virtues such as humility, sincerity, and selfless service to others. Ahimsa, Gandhi claims, "is a great vow; it is more difficult than walking on the edge of a sword. Complete adherence to it is almost impossible for one who has a physical form. Severe penance is required for its practice." In the pursuit of such rigorous penance, Gandhi believes, human beings are truly able to access the truth.

Thus, the practice of ahimsa involves the systematic cultivation of various virtues in daily life, accompanied by self-examination and self-regulation. The list of vows and rules established at Gandhi's Sabarmati ashram included, for instance, truth, non-violence, celibacy, and control of the palate, non-thieving, non-possession, self-reliance, and fearlessness. Of these, truth and non-violence were foundational virtues that served as the basis for practicing the rest. Such vows, observed through daily practice, become the manifestation of ahimsa in its various forms. Gandhi's own life style was an exemplar of this rigorous practice of ahimsa. Total ahimsa, then, is the way to cultivate right action by seeking truth in the most comprehensive sense. Gandhi envisions it as an enlightened state of perfected virtue in which the moral or political agent approaches the greatest possible union with Absolute Truth. There appears to be no contradiction between the cultivation of total moral virtue and the idea that goodness is arrived at through the practice of everyday, relative, practical truths. Because Gandhi sees all worldly, practical action as directed towards the search for Absolute Truth, non-violence, as a state of perfected virtue, is the sum of a series of relative moral and political truths achieved in the course of worldly life.

But how does this commitment to total non-violence purport to solve the dilemmas we have highlighted? For Gandhi, strict adherence to total ahimsa constitutes a systematic training of the individual will, leading to a transformation of the mind. This transformative effort works primarily on the individual conscience which, for Gandhi, is "the voice of God., of Truth, or the inner voice. (all are) one and the same thing." Despite his scathing indictment elsewhere of the individualism of modern society, Gandhi emphasizes the "call of the individual conscience" as the main vehicle for accessing truth. The key here is that conscience "has to be awakened." Once aroused from its thoughtless adherence to either convention or self-interest, it acquires the capacity of the conscience to arbitrate among various political choices and it arises from his belief that an awakened conscience is significantly different from one that is driven by narrow self proper for everyone to claim to hear the voice of conscience. There are rules and observances for the purpose of awakening the conscience. Not everyone can be said to have his conscience awakened. Emotions which are stimulated by unconscious social and environmental pressures cannot count as conscience. The awakened conscience is the "ripe fruit of the strictest discipline." Nonviolence becomes a method that arbitrates among truth claims because the rigorous discipline involved in living the life of total non-violence constitutes a training of the political actor's interior consciousness, and consequently provides access to truths about the moral and political world. In this awakening, the Gandhian conscience is moved by recognizing its obligations to others as well as to morality itself. Like the Kantian conscience, it must be motivated by duty rather than by self-interest, and it must achieve moral autonomy. For Gandhi, the key lies in distinguishing between an awakened and an unthinking conscience—non-violence is the method for that awakening.

Ahimsa can be seen as a method of right action for cultivating greater access to the truth, achieved through intensive training of the conscience. Ahimsa method carries with it the possibility of moral or political arbitration. The term "arbitration" in the sense of mediating a conflict but rather as an internal adjudication that allows people to use their own judgment to make moral and political choices in consonance with the truth. Because the problem of political action for Gandhi is mainly one of knowledge about the moral universe, adherence to the non-violence method would allow a political agent to take the right kind of political action and provide the justification for that action as the one closer to approximating truth than that of the adversary. In this sense, ahimsa arbitrates—it allows one to pass judgment upon the worthiness of an action.

Notice also that the adjudicatory role of non-violence applies to practical or relative truth claims rather than to claim about truth. A Gandhian position should not simply imply that the virtues cultivated through non-violence are a tool of some mystical insight into absolute truth. Rather, non-violence is a guide to practical judgment in the search for everyday, relative truths of the political world. Rather than allowing one simply to contemplate theories about nature of human beings, or of the good life, ahimsa would assist us in making daily decisions about relative truths within political life. Broad, overarching truths may not provide guidance for the ways in which the truth may be specified in practical action. Here, non-violence is a guide to such specification.

Arbitration among conflicting truth claims, then, pertains to the sorts of truths involved in the practice of satyagraha. Satyagraha is Gandhi's doctrine of political action, and political companion to the right-living prescriptions of ahimsa. Literally, the term satyagraha means "holding firm to the truth," "truth-force," or "soul-force." As the practical corollary of the theory of ahimsa, satyagraha refers to the political tactics of resistance, such as civil disobedience and active non-cooperation in the form of strikes, fasts, sit-ins, and deliberate law-breaking, along with the strict commitment to the disavowal of violence for gaining advantage. Arbitration among truth claims is possible with this Gandhian view because the moral authority of political action in any given instance is begotten by the epistemological work done by the requirements of comprehensive non-violence. Truth claims involved in the practice of politics receive their moral justification from the underlying commitment to the lifelong pursuit of right action.

Political actins such as strikes, boycotts, or protest movements all gain moral justification because of the background assumption that an activist's grasp of truth has already been tested by the call of his own conscience through the requirements of ahimsa. Thus, his truth claim can withstand the challenge—both epistemological as well as moral—from the position of his adversary. Ahimsa is, therefore, an arbiter among competing truth claims: when partial or relative moral truths conflict, he whose conscience is said to be awakened by the rigorous discipline of ahimsa is considered more successful than his adversary in overcoming certain epistemological limitations. Here relative or partial grasp of the truth is keener or more complete than that of his adversary. It is important to note that the possibility of epistemological arbitration does not imply that the problem of knowledge can be resolved entirely. On the contrary, Gandhian metaphysics and epistemology retain a commitment to the complexity of moral reality, the continued fallibility of the individual moral project, and the ongoing contestability of one's grasp of the truth. The work of arbitration simply suggests that in specific instances of political conflict, the awakened conscience is able to see more clearly than another, such that its grasp of a specific political matter is the clearest possible one.

Violence has many sides. It can be spontaneous or planned, it can be individual or institutional, it can be physical or psychological, it can be delinquent or adult, it can be revolutionary or authoritarian. A great deal has been written on violence: on its psychology, on its possible philosophical justifications under certain circumstances, and of course on its long career in military history. Non-violence has no sides at all. Being negatively defined, it is indivisible. It began to be a subject of study much more recently and there is much less written on it, not merely because it is defined in negative terms but because until it became a self-constituted as or in something else. It was studied under different names, first usually as part of religious or contemplative ways of life remote from the public affairs of men and state, and later with the coming of romantic thought in Europe, under the rubric of critiques of industrial civilization.

For Gandhi, both these contexts were absolutely essential to his conception of non-violence. Non-violence was central in his nationalist mobilization against the British rule in India. But the concept is also situated in an essentially religious temperament as well as in a thoroughgoing critique of ideas and ideologies of the Enlightenment and of an intellectual paradigm of perhaps a century earlier than the Enlightenment. This as a paradigm in science became set on a path, which seemed destined to cumulative results, building to a progressively complete understanding of the world in which we lived, a world which we could as a result control. It is a familiar point that there can be no understanding of Gandhi, the anti-colonial nationalist, without situating him in these larger trajectories of his thought.

The strategy of non-violence resistance was first introduced by him as so as to bring into the nationalist efforts against the British, an element beyond making only constitutional demands. On the face of it, for those reared on western political ideas, this seemed very odd. Constitutional demands, as they are understood in liberal political theory, is the essence of non-violent politics: as is well known the great early propounders of liberal democratic thought conceived and still conceived of constitutions and their constraints on human public action as a constraint against tendencies toward violence in the form of coercion of individuals by states and other collectivities, no to mention by other individuals. So why did Gandhi, the prophet of non-violence, think that the Indian people, in their demands for greater self-determination, needed more than constitutional demands? And why did he think that this is best called 'non-violent' action? The obvious answer is the instrumental and strategic one: he knew that making demands for constitutional change had not been particularly effective or swift in the first two decades of this century, and that since the conventionally conceived alternative was violent revolutionary action – which found advocates on the fringes of nationalist sentiment in India – he instead introduced his own strategy of civil disobedience, at once a non-violent and yet a non or extra-constitutional strategy. But, of course, he had more in mind than this obvious motive.

First, Gandhi wanted all of India to be involved in the movement, in particular the vast mass of its peasant population. He did not want the nationalist achievement to be the effort of a group of elite, legally and constitutionally trained, upper-middle class Indian men ('Macaulay's bastards'), who argued in assemblies and round-table conferences. He almost single-handedly transformed a movement conceived and promoted along those lines by the Congress Party into a mass movement of enormous scale, and he did so within a few years of arriving from South Africa on Indian soil. Non-violent action was the central idea of this vast mobilization.

Second, he knew that violent revolutionary action could not possibly carry the mass of people with it. Revolutionary action was mostly conceived hunger-mugger in underground cells and took the form of isolated subversive terrorist action against key focal points of government power and interest, it was not conceived as a mass movement. He was not unaware that there existed in the West ideologies of revolutionary violence which were geared to mass movements, but he was not unaware either, that these were conceived in terms of middle class leadership vanguards that were the fonts of authority. Peasant consciousness mattered very little to them. In Gandhi there was not a trace of this vanguard mentality of a Lenin. He did indeed think that his 'satyagrahis' – the non-violent activists whom he described, with that term, as 'seekers of truth' – would provide leadership which the masses would follow, but it was absolutely crucial to him that these were not to be the vanguard of a revolutionary party along Leninist lines. They were to be thought of along entirely different lines, they were to be moral exemplars, not ideologues who claimed to know history and its forward movement better than the peasants to whom they were giving the lead.

Third, Gandhi chose his version of non-violent civil disobedience instead of the constitutional demands of the Congress leadership because he thought that the Indian people should not merely ask the British to leave their soil. It was important that they should do so by means that were not dependent and derivative of ideas and institutions that the British had imposed on them. Otherwise, even if the British left, the Indian populations would remain a subject people. This went very deep in Gandhi and his book *Hind Swaraj*, is full of a detailed anxiety about the cognitive enslavement even of the nationalist and anti-colonial Indian mind, which might, even after independence, never recover from that enslavement and collective aminesia.

The idea that non-violence was of a piece with the search for the truth was central to his integrity. Gandhi was explicit about this, even in the terminology he adopted, linking ahimsa (non-violence) with satyagraha literally, 'truth-force', or more liberally, a tenacity in the pursuit of truth. There is a standard and entrenched reading of Gandhi which understands the link as follows from the most widely read textbook of modern Indian history, Sumit Sarkar's, *Modern India*:

> Non-violence or ahimsa and satyagraha to Gandhi personally constituted a deeply-felt and worked-out philosophy owing something to Emerson, Thoreau and Tolstoy but also revealing considerable originality. The search for truth was the goal of human

life, and as no one could ever be sure of having attained the truth, used of violence to enforce one's own view of its was sinful.

There is no doubt that Gandhi says things that could lead to such a reading, and for years, that it was more or less uncontroversially, what he had in mind. After scrutiny of his writings however, especially his many dispatches to *Young India*, it seems now a spectacular misreading. It fails to cohere with his most fundamental thinking.

Notice that according to this reading, or misreading, his view is no different from one of the most celebrated liberal argument for tolerance – the meta-inductive argument of Mill's *On Liberty*. Mill contends that since much that we have thought to be true in the past has turned out to be wrong, this in itself suggests that what we presently think true might also be wrong. We should therefore tolerate not repress dissent from our present convictions just in case they are not true. According to Mill, and according to Gandhi on this widespread misreading of him, truth is never something we are sure we have attained. We must therefore be made modest in the way we hold our present opinions, and we must not impose our own conceptions of the truth on others. To do so would be a form of violence, especially if it was enforced by the apparatus of the state.

The modesty would appeal to Gandhi, but he would find something very alien in Mill's argument for it. There is no echo in Gandhi of the idea that the source of this modesty is that however much we seek truth, we cannot attain it, which is what many scholars contend is the ground of his non-violence. In fact, it make little sense to say that truth is something we should seek, even if we can never attain it. How can we intend to attain what we know we cannot attain? It would be bootless to protest that Gandhi and Mill are not saying that we can never attain the truth, only that we cannot know if we have attained it –so there is still point in the search for truth.

In any case, there is something rather odd in Mill's argument for tolerance. There is an unsettling tension between the argument's first two premises. The first premise is that our past beliefs have often turned out to be wrong. The second premise is that our present opinions might be wrong. And the conclusion is that we should therefore be tolerant of dissent from current opinion. But the fact is that when past opinions are said to be wrong, that is a judgment made from the present point of view, and we cannot make that judgment unless we have the conviction in the present opinions which Mill is asking us not to have. It is all right to be asked to be different about our present opinions, but then we should, at least to that extent, be different about our judgment made on their basis, viz, that our past opinions are wrong.

The pervasive diffidence and lack of conviction in our opinions which is the character of the epistemology that Mill's argument presupposes, is entirely alien to Gandhi; and though he is in favour of the modesty with which we should be holding our opinions, that modesty does not have its source in such an epistemology and such a conception of unattainable truth. It is quite elsewhere located its source is to be found in his conception of the very nature of moral response and moral judgment. The satyagrahi or non-violent activist has to show a certain kind of self-restraint, in which it was not enough simply not to commit violence. It is equally important not to bear hostility to others or even to criticize them; it is only required that one does not follow these others, if conscience doesn't permit it. To show hostility and contempt, to speak or even to think negatively and critically, would be to give in to the spiritual flaws that underlie violence, to have the wrong conception of moral judgment. For it is not the point of moral judgment to criticize. In 'Ashram Vows' of his book *Hindu Dharma*, he says "Ahimsa is not the crude thing it has been made to appear. Not to hurt any living thing is no doubt part of ahimsa. But it is its least expression. It is hurt by hatered of any kind, by wishing ill of anybody, by making negative criticisms of others'. This entails the modesty with which one must hold one's moral opinions, and which Mill sought in a quite different source: in a notion of truth which we are never sure we have attained and therefore from Gandhi's point of view it is a quite untenable epistemology. The alternative source of the modesty in Gandhi has less to do with issues about truth, and more to do with the way we must hold our moral values.

Despite the modesty, one could, of course, resist those with whom one disagrees, and Gandhi made an art out of refusal and resistance and disobedience. But resistance is not the same as criticism. It can be done with a 'pure heart'. Criticism reflects an impurity of heart, and is easily corrupted to breed hostility and, eventually, violence. With an impure heart one could still indulge in non-violent political activism, but that activism would be strategic, merely a means to a political end. In the long run it would, just as surely as violence, land one in a midden. Even the following sensible sounding argument for his own conclusions, often given by many of his political colleagues who found his moral attitudes obscure, did not satisfy Gandhi: "Let us adopt non-violent and passive resistance instead of criticizing the British colonial government. Because to assert a criticism of one's oppressor would usually have the effect of getting his back up, or of making him defensive, it would end up making things harder for oneself." Gandhi himself did occasionally say things of that sort, but he thought that colleagues who wanted to rest with such arguments as the foundation of non-violence were viewing it too much as an instrument and they were not going deep enough into the spiritual nature of the moral sense required of the satyagraha. One did not go deep enough until one served the assumed theoretical connection between moral judgment and moral criticism, the connection which, in our analytical terms, we would describe by saying that if one judges that 'x is good', then we are obliged to find morally wrong those who in relevant circumstances, judge otherwise or fail to act on x. For Gandhi this does not follow. The right moral sense, the morally pure-hearted satyagrahi, sees no such connection between moral judgment and moral criticism. Of course, we cannot and must not cease to be moral subjects: we cannot stop judging morally about what is and is not worthy, cannot fail to have moral values. But none of that requires us to be critical of others who disagree with our values or who fail to act in accord with them. That is the relevant modesty which Mill sought to justify by a different argument.

This view of the moral sense might well seem frustratingly namby-pamby now as it certainly did to those around him at that time. The fact is that his view of moral sense is of considerable philosophical interest, and is intended entirely earnestly by its author. It is given a fascinating theoretical consolidation in his writing which may be lost on his readers because it is "buried in a porridge of saintly rhetoric of 'purity of heart'."

Gandhi has not presented truth as a cognitive notion at all. It is an experiential notion. It is not propositions purporting to describe the world of which truth is predicated. It is only our own moral experience which is capable of being true. This was of the utmost importance for him. It is what in the end underlies his opposition to the Enlightenment, despite the undeniably Enlightenment elements in his thought including his humanism and the concern that our moral judgments be relevant to all people. Those who have seen him as an anti-Enlightenment thinker usually point to the fact that he is opposed to the political and technological developments which, he insist, issue inevitably from the very conception of reason as it is understood in scientific terms. So understood, some time in the 17th century, with the rise of the scientific method in Europe, all the predispositions to modern government and technology came into place. All that was needed for those predispositions to be triggered in our sustained efforts to organize and control our physical and social environment, was for the Enlightenment to articulate the idea of Reason as it affects social life and the polity. But this familiar understanding of his view of the Enlightenment does not take in his 'final and audacious integrating' philosophical move. This conception which set in sometime in the 17th century itself owns much to a more abstract element in our thinking, which is that truth is a cognitive notion, not a moral one. Only if truth is so conceived can science become the paradigmatic pursuit of our culture, without it the scientific outlook lacks its deepest theoretical source. And it is a mark of his intellectual ambition that by making it an exclusively and exhaustively moral and experiential notion instead. Gandhi was attempting to repudiate the paradigm at the deepest possible conceptual level.

Truth as a cognitive notion is that it is a property of sentences or propositions that describe the world. Thus when we have reason to think that the sentences to which we give assent exhibit this property, then we have knowledge of the world, a knowledge that can then be progressively accumulated and put to use through continuing inquiry building on past knowledge. His recoil from such a notion of truth, which intellectualizes our relations to the world, is that it views the world as the object of study, study that makes it alien to our moral experience of it, to our most everyday practical relations to it. He symbolically conveyed this by his own daily act of spinning cotton. This idea of truth, unlike our quotidian practical relations to nature, makes nature out to be the sort of distant thing to be studied by scientific methods. Reality will then not be the reality of moral experience. It will become something alien to that experience, wholly external and objectified. It is no surprise then that we will look upon reality as something to be mastered and conquered, an attitude that leads directly to the technological frame of mind that governs modern societies, and which in turn takes us away from our communal localities where moral experience and our practical relations to the world flourish. It takes us towards increasingly abstract places and structures such as nations and eventually global economies. In such places and such forms of life, there is no scope for exemplary actin to take hold, and no basis, possible for a moral vision in which value is not linked to 'imperative' and 'principle', and then, inevitably, to the attitudes of criticism and the entire moral psychology which ultimately underlies violence in our social relations. To find a basis for tolerance and non-violence under circumstances such as these, we are compelled to turn to arguments of the sort Mill tried to provide in which modesty and tolerance are supposed to be derived from a notion of truth which is always elusive, never something which we can be confident of having achieved because it is not given in our moral experience, but is predicated of propositions that purport to describe a reality which is distant from our own practical and moral experience of it.

All these various elements of his opposition to Mill and his own alternative conception of tolerance and non-violence were laid open by Gandhi and systematically integrated by these arguments implicit in his many scattered writings. There remains the question whether such an integrated position is at all plausible. It should be a matter of some intellectual urgency to ask whether our interests in politics, moral philosophy, and notions of truth and epistemology, are not more fragmented or more miscellaneous than his integrations propose. It is not a wiser and more illuminating mythological stance sometimes to recognize that there is often a lack of connection in our ideas and our interests and that to register that lack is sometimes more important and revealing than to seek a strained connection.

If Gandhi is right and if truth is an exclusively moral notion, then when we seek truth, we are pursuing only a moral value. Actually Gandhi's writings leave it a little unclear whether he is making the steepest claim that truth is not a cognitive notion at all, or the more cautious one that even if there is such a notion, it yields no special value of its own for us, a specifically cognitive value. The texts don't decide this matter, but it is obviously more sympathetic to read him as making the latter claim. This leaves a great deal out of our normative interest in truth, which as we have seen, Gandhi is perfectly willing to do. He is quite happy to discard as illusory our tendency to think that apart from the moral virtues involving truth there is also in some sense a value or virtue in getting things rights about the world and discovering the general principles that explain its varied phenomena. This latter is not a moral virtue, it is a cognitive virtue, and for Gandhi, cognitive virtues are a chimera.

The Status of Truth

It quit logical to admit that as we do not know the absolute truth, we cannot impose our partial vision of the truth on others. Gandhi's approach to the subject of truth must be understood in this light. He attempted to provide a direction to approaching answers rather than to produce solutions that admit of no change. For Gandhi, Truth may be absolute, but knowledge of it is relative. In this regard, he observes:

> It has been my experience that I am always true from my point of view and often wrong from the point of view of honest critics. I know that we are both right from our respective points of views. And this knowledge saves me from attributing motives to my opponents or critics. I very much like the doctrine of the manyness of reality. It is this doctrine that has taught me to judge a Mussulman from his own standpoint and a Christian from his.

A relativity about knowledge and respect for different points of view restraints claims to absolute power. Like Camus's existential stance about absolute power corrupting liberating ideas in violent revolutions, Gandhi argues that absolutism destroys the truth we try to reach. Any insistency by someone that he possesses absolute truth gives that person, in his mind at least, the justification to impose that truth on others, to force other to be free. Gandhi's theory is opposed to Rousseau's fanciful doctrine of "forced to be free". In Gandhi's opinion even that exercise of such power negated any recognition of the integrity of those who would be hurt in the quest for truth. Power-holders who think they own the truth, see no need to enter into a dialogue to convince others and close themselves from the possibility of learning more.

One reason for which we cannot justify violence is that we can never absolutely justify any project as solving all problems one and for all and liberate everyone now and forever. Moreover, we must recognize our own inevitable fallibility and egoism. No one, Gandhi claims, can attain perfect detachment from his own ego, 'for the simple reason that the ideal state is impossible so long as one completely overcomes his ego, and ego cannot be wholly gotten rid of'.

Because we cannot be absolutely sure about our actions, we need to act in ways which are true to or honest with our best intentions and knowledge without forcing our solutions on others. Indeed, Gandhi holds that our humanity comes from trying to improve ourselves morally and from respecting the worth of others, even though we know we cannot be completely successful in this task. According to Gandhi, we should hold our ideal firm even if we shall ever fail to realize it, but never cease to strive for it. According to Gandhi, we should hold our ideal firm even if we shall ever fail to realize it, but never cease to strive for it. According to him that constant striving, that ceaseless quest after the ideal, represents the best of the human condition.

Gandhi's political theory and politics emphasized dialogue as a way of discovering truth. Dialogue implies an openness between moral equals. In hierarchical power relations, openness is difficult to achieve and superiors are unlikely to see their inferiors as equals. Dialogue opens the possibility that others might be converted to our position rather than coerced. In this regard, Gandhi insisted: "We must try patiently to convert our opponents. If we wish to evolve the spirit of democracy out of slavery, we must be scrupulously exact in our dealings with opponents. We must concede to our opponents the freedom we claim for ourselves."

Gandhi's position about the relativity of knowledge gives rise to the need for tolerance, a civic virtue that virtually all theories of democracy hold as essential. Tolerance implies a mutual respect for other; and if it is missing, the dialogue of the democratic process is diminished, if not destroyed. Gandhi like John Dewey considers dialogue as necessary to both individual growth and to the democratic prospect. Indeed, democracy receives one of its primary justifications from Dewey because it promotes tolerance and fosters development. Dewey holds that open communication enlarges and changes experience. 'One shares in what another has thought and felt and insofar, meagerly or amply, has his own attitude modified.' Dewey demands that our position 'requires getting outside of it, seeing it as another would see it, considering what points of contract it has with the life of another so that it may be got into such form that he can appreciate its meaning.' Through open dialogue, people not only test their own ideas, they also learn, and in the process, advance tolerance and non-violence. Intolerance' writes Gandhi, 'is itself a form of violence and obstacle to the growth of a true democratic spirit'.

Satyagraha

But how did Gandhi expect this mode of conflict resolution to work? What were the intended dynamics of satyagraha? Firstly, he saw satyagraha not in terms of a right to resist but rather as the fulfillment of a duty to resist perceived wrong. It was designed at a deep moral and spiritual level to set in motion radical processes of moral transformation—not by coercion but by conversion, by changing the moral perceptions of all those involved in the conflict concerned. It was thus aimed at altering the total dynamics of a situation, and at opening the way to a broader vision of right and wrong, to the possibility of compromise on non-essentials, and to an attitude of mutual understanding and forgiveness between former opponents. It was in part for this reason that Gandhi was always anxious for "talks" with officials of the Raj before contemplated civil disobedience movements and at strategic points during movements. Most notable were his famous talks with the then-current Viceroy, Lord Irwin, in 1931, which ended civil disobedience temporarily and paved the way for Gandhi's presence at the Round Table Conference in London in 1931.

It was also because of this sense of satyagraha as means to enable mutual moral growth that Gandhi was not greatly concerned with the number of satyagrahis. His intention was never to make the life and work of the opponent impossible, or in the case of the Raj to bring government to a halt: in this way satyagraha was very different from passive resistance. He was much more concerned with the quality of the satyagrahis and their reliability in the face of temptations to abandon non-violence—hence his emphasis on strict discipline, as in the case of the 1930 march to Dandi to make salt on the seashore, or in the most Gandhian of satyagrahas, the "individual civil disobedience" movement of protest against the war in 1940-1941. In this movement he quite literally handpicked those individuals and categories of people who would be permitted to make the protest, gave detailed instructions on protesters' appropriate behavior, and was evidently conscious that he was making a unique experiment in non-violent action. His belief was that even one genuine satyagrahi could begin the process of moral transformation that satyagraha would inevitably bring about, if properly undertaken. Large number of untrained and uncontrollable activists were worse than useless and would indeed negate the moral dynamic of any campaign. This was the reasoning behind his abandonment of the first great all-India non-cooperation campaign in 1922 after the massacre of policemen at Chauri Chaura, and behind his disillusion with the "Quit India" campaign of 1942. It was also the rationale behind his attempts in 1946 to prove that his personal purity and self-control in sexual matters was such that he at least had the strength to be a sole satyagrhi in the situation of escalating communal violence.

The historian of Indian politics has of course to weigh the political efficacy of Gandhi's non-violent campaigns, in ways that would have been quite alien to Gandhi himself. To him the action of true satyagrahi on circumstances of conflict was a matter of theological faith, and he was only making an affirmation of its inevitable moral consequence, giving his understanding of it and of human nature. Even when confronted in 1938 by the plight of the Jews in Nazi Germany he argued that true satyagraha would transform the situation: to him even their death in large numbers would not be a sign of satyagraha's defeat. Moreover, when confronted by the "failure" of the 1942 Quit India movement and the subsequent outbreak of internecine violence within the sub-continent, he asserted that his compatriots had never offered true satyagraha. An understanding of satyagraha as a theory and practice of moral growth rather than as a strategy for exerting pressure on the opponent does suggest that Gandhi placed it in the context of an understanding of human duties and the duty to follow after Truth rather than in the context of human rights and the grasping of such rights.

Gandhi was often asked whether he was a saint or a politician. On one occasion, Gandhi replied that the world "saint" is too sacred to be lightly applied to someone like him," a humble searcher after truth, who knows him limitations, makes mistakes." But then Gandhi continued to say: "The politician in me has never dominated a single decision of mine. If I seem to take part in politics, it is only because encircles us like the coil of a snake from which one cannot get out. I wish to wrestle with the snake." This humble seeker after truth would call his life story as The Story of My experiments with Truth as experiments in the spiritual field. As he explains in his Autobiography,

> My experiments in the political field are now known not only in India but to a certain extent to the "civilized" world. For me they have not much value. But I should certainly like to narrate my experiments in the spiritual field, which are known only to myself and from which I have derived such power as I possess for working in the political field.

Even as a young boy, little Mohandas was averse to telling lies or resorting to unfair methods. When he was a student at the Rajkot High School, the Education Inspector was visiting the institution. In an English test on spelling given by the teacher, Mohandas was the one to fail, just for misspelling the world "kettle." The teacher had tried to prompt the twelve year old Mohandas to copy from a nearby student, but it did not work out. When the teacher called him after the inspector had left, and berated him for disgracing the school and the teacher himself, Mohandas had no answer to give him, except to tell his inner self that he could never learn the art of copying. "One thing took deep root in me," Gandhi would write in his *Autobiography*, "the conviction that morality is the basis of things and that truth is the substance of all morality. Truth became my sole object."

By the time Gandhi returned to India in 1915, the Indian National Congress had been active in their quest for national independence. There were several occasions for Gandhi, however, to test out his principle of satyagraha in the Indian context. The Rowlatt Bills with their powers of arbitrary arrest and detention without trial was the first occasion. But it led to the infamous order of General Dyer to shoot into a crowd at Amristar. This event came to be a great and symbolic punctuation mark in Indio-British relations. A shock wave went through the entire country and Gandhi never truly trusted the Raj again. In 1930 came Gandhi's famous Salt march to the sea, publicly to violate the salt monopoly of the British Government. From then on, the story of the Mahatma was one of recurrent campaigns, arrests, imprisonments, and releases. But Gandhi was not alone. There were some intellectuals who made considerable sacrifices in following Gandhi. There was Vallabhai Patel, the prosperous Ahmedabad lawyer, Rajendra Prasad from Bihar, Rajagopalachari from Madras, and the aristocrat Nehru from Allahabad. Gandhi, also for the first time, brought different sections of Indian society into the forefront of politics. Gandhi's moral influence on these people coming from different stratas of Indian society, was indeed astonishing.

Gandhi saw in the Indian freedom struggle the greatest experiment with truth. It is not sure whether Gandhi expected political success through religious interventions as Martin Buber claims in his critique of Gandhi's introduction of religion into politics. In his political endeavour, Gandhi was immensely influenced by the *Bhagavadgita's* emphasis on anasaktiyoga, the principle of engaging oneself in activity without any expectation of or attachment to the fruit of the action. While describing the ideals significant in Gandhi's philosophy, Paul Power includes the "devotion to anasaktiyoga as the best way to pursue the ultimate." But, then, Gandhi believed that political success would be an outward expression of an inner transformation. In fact, Gandhi would not have wanted any political success without an inner change. He often advised people to practice satyagraha as an expression of their inner conviction. Further, Gandhi was insistent that if the method of satyagraha was to be in accordance with the demands of truth, it had to be effective and practical. Further, "if any action of mine claimed to be spiritual is proved to be unpractical, it must be pronounced as a failure. I do believe that the most spiritual act is the most practical in the true sense of the term."

On the day India achevied its independence, Gandhi did not participate in the celebrations. At the time of the glorious climax of his struggle, Gandhi was in deep agony seeing the bloodshed which the partitioning of India had caused. The Hindu-Muslim unity was the one issue that engaged Gandhi all his life. Some highly-strong orthodox Hindu youth saw Hinduism menaced by its contact with Islam. It was one such person, Nathuram Godse, a journalist from Pune, who shot Gandhi, as he was going to the usual prayer meeting on the evening of 30 January 1948. Gandhi's last words were "Hey Ram" (O God). Reporting on Gandhi's death the *New York Times* wrote: "Gandhi has left as his heritage a spiritual force that must in God's time prevail over arms and armaments and dark doctrines of violence. The rest remains for history's inexorable hand to write down."

Satyagraha as Dialogue

The term satyagraha as a combination of the Sanskrit words satya and agraha stands for the firmness that results in insisting on truth. In Gandhi's word's "Satyagraha then is literally holding on the truth and it means therefore Truth force. Truth is soul or spirit. It is therefore known as soul force." Although satyagraha was used to describe the civil disobedience and non-cooperation, Gandhi soon made it into a whole philosophy of life. In Gandhi's thinking, satyagraha was also dharmayuddha which demands of its adherents, courage, sincerity, depth of purpose, and faith in God. Satyagraha was also an ideology of action, to be used effectively in the political and social arena. As a way of life, satyagraha encompasses both truth and non-violence.

Because of his philosophy of satyagraha, Gandhi always differentiated between people and institutions. If the British empire was an enemy because of its colonial rule, it did not mean that Gandhi could not love the people of Britain. In fact, many English persons were his close colleagues and friends. Even in his first visit to London, he made friends with members of the vegetarian and theosophical societies. During the freedom struggle, two of his closest friends were Charles Andrews and Madeleine Slade. Thus Gandhi was able to transform the political situation of a conflict between these two nations into a dialogue. For all the outward struggle during the Indian independence movement, the result was a harmonious transformation of relationship between England and India.

Lokmanya Tilak told Gandhi in 1918: "Truth has no place in politics." Further, in a letter to *Young India*, he wrote "politics is a game of worldly people and not of Sadhus." The question is whether politics can be pursued by religious persons. And is it possible to introduce religious and ethical values into politics? Both Gandhi and Buber seem to have struggled with these questions. Buber was forthright in saying that if religion enters politics, "it is threatened by evaporation in the rapid fire of political activity." In Buber's view, politics cannot be avoided, but we must deal with it without inflexible principles, Buber sees an inflexibility of principle in Gandhi, and this is the tragedy that he is referring to. Although Buber is emphatic that the tragedy be honourd, Buber himself does not want to follow Gandhi.

According to Buber, the meeting of morality and politics depends on each situation. We need to determine the limit of the ethical command in that particular context. The line of demarcation will mark the maximal possibility of truth and justice in that situation. Thus the line of demarcation has to be drawn anew in each case. For Gandhi, the answer lies in recognizing that absolute truth is not available to the human person and that one had to depend on relative truth. What Gandhi would do is to keep on holding on to the relative truth, all the while keeping in mind that life is still informed by the spirit of the unrealizable absolute truth.

It looks as though neither Gandhi nor Buber gives us any clear-cut answer to the problem of the politics-morality combination. Any method of reconciling religion and politics looks very fragile in the light of the hard realities of the political and social life. There is still a wide gap between politics and morality. However, both Buber and Gandhi seem to be conscious of some spiritual current, flowing underneath the apparent contradiction. While recognizing a moral dilemma in their attempt to relate religion to politics, precisely at that point, Buber and Gandhi see a divine response. The readers participate in this response.

Ahimsa as Policy, Not Creed

Questions have been asked and doubts have been raised about the issue whether Gandhi's mode of political action, one might object, would be far too dependent on the stringent requirements of right-living. Precisely because Gandhi sees no separation of the almost saintly aspirations of spiritual seeking from worldly political concerns, it may be that his method demands an intensity of spiritual commitment that seems impractical. The idealization of the satyagraha makes this mode of political action the exclusive privilege of some unavailable to those who subscribe to neither its metaphysical commitments or its teleological requirements. In fact, it would be argued, Gandhi's insistene on total ahimsa can only be derived from the presuppositions he takes from Hindu cosmology. The emphasis on the potential unity of human and divine and the possibility of achieving this state through human action gives Gandhi the confidence that the achievement of complete virtue through ahimsa will be an adequate response to the problem of moral and political conflict. Moreover, the concept of arbitration suggests the capacity to be impartial among competing truth claims, a possibility that looks remote if non-violence itself is shown to be based upon a particular truth system or comprehensive moral word-view.

For these reasons, we can extract from the Gandhian mode a secular doctrine of political action that performs the same functions of arbitration and political justification without depending on the metaphysical assumptions of Hinduism, as Gandhi does. Thus, we go beyond the limits of the virtue based model that Gandhi has provided by excavating a model of moral and political arbitration shorn of the Mahatma's religious/metaphysical framework. We use his political vision as a theoretical foundation, building upon it to address the contemporary problem of conflicting moral claims. However, we first need to make the crucial distinction between ahimsa as creed and ahimsa as civic virtue. While this may not be a distinction Gandhi himself would have made, it is useful for the purposes of applying Gandhi's thought to contemporary political life.

Non-violence thus far described as total moral virtue resembles what Gandhi calls a "creed" or a "religion." He also refers to non-violence as a "law of life," or a life-force, emphasizing its spiritual components. However, Gandhi also makes the following distinction between a creed, and a policy: "A particular practice is a policy when its application is limited to time and space. Highest policy is therefore fullest practice." Gandhi sometimes suggests that non-violence can only be practiced in this manner, as a creed or a way of life: "Non-violence to be a creed has to be all-pervasive. I cannot be non-violent about one activity of mine and violent about others. That would be a policy, not a life-force." Yet, Gandhi also accepts the possibility of something less than the fullest pursuit of non-violence: "To expect a whole mass of men and women to obey that law of ahimsa all at once is not to know its working, the limited measure of its application can be realized in respect of masses of people within a short time."

Can non-violence as a civic virtue be isolated from the creed-like elements of ahimsa? Gandhi's views on this are inconsistent. On the one hand, his metaphysical posture commits him to rejecting any separation of the public/private, politics/religion, moral/civic realms. Accordingly, in many instances, he disavows any moves toward a lesser form of ahimsa that would lower moral and political standards in order to make it more accessible. He considers this a pragmatic mode of political action that does not live up to the fullest expression of ahimsa. Yet, Gandhi occasionally wavers. Raghavan Iyer cites various instances in which Gandhi acknowledges that the standard of ahimsa may need to be adjusted for certain situations, that ahimsa as policy was the "next best thing" to ahimsa as creed, and that ahimsa often demands compromises.

Parel remarks on this distinction, clarifying that non-violence as a creed remains a private virtue, while as a policy it is a public or civic virtue—one may think of it as the virtue of the monk versus that of the citizen. Ahimsa as a way of life plays what Parel calls a "private, monastic role," for it is based in the quest for an overarching spiritual truth. As a mode of political action, however, satyagraha may be seen as the civic virtue of the citizen or the statesman, appropriate for political life, with no basis in any particular metaphysics. As such, the moral logic or non-violent action need not depend on the spiritual or metaphysical elements of right living through total ahimsa. Even if we abstract away from the activity of seeking Absolute Truth, three components of non-violence as a civic virtue still allow us to arrive at relative political truths. Extracting these three elements from the creed of ahimsa will provide a model for non-violent political action that contains a persuasive force independent of Hindu cosmology.

First, Gandhi places great emphasis on humility or recognition of one's fallibility. Like Socrates who connected humility and recognition of fallibility with possession of the truth in the *Apology*, Gandhi famously claimed: "Truth is not to be found by anybody who has not got an abundant sense of humility." This recognition of fallibility acknowledges that we may err in our own grasp of the truth, and that our commitments may require adjustment, recognizing precisely the epistemological dilemma that characterizes the human condition. The unshakeable conviction that one is in possession of some ultimate wisdom can be damaging to one's search for truth.

This requirement also implies the possibility that one's adversary may, in fact, be right. Without fully endorsing Hindu cosmology as Gandhi did, human beings who maintain a basic sense of humility about their finitude recognize that the totality of truths may be too complicated to grasp in its entirety. One's own partial, relative grasp of it may be mistaken. Always present is the possibility that one's adversary could have a better-although not necessarily complete—grasp of truth in any given situation. The idea is not that we are aware of the tenuous and ever-changing nature of our grasp of the truth. Rather, even as we are campaigning for the establishment of our own truth, by acting non-violently, we maintain our awareness that we could be mistaken. For this reason, Gandhi also demanded the greatest courtesy on the part of satyagrahis toward their opponents. Because one always acknowledges the possibility of error, one treats opponents with love and respect, as people engaged in their own search for truth, who could be further long this path than we.

The second element of the Gandhian model is a capacity for self-examination and correction. A seeker, Gandhi claims, "must always hold himself open to correction, and whenever he discovers himself to be wrong he must confess it at all costs." The truth is not merely the product of a mysterious inner voice or awakened conscience but rather of numerous experiments through which the seeker tests his partial or relative understanding to ensure that it is on the appropriate path. Grasping the truth is the result of rigorous effort and capacity to confront persistent Cartesian doubt. This is tied directly to the issue of fallibility: if I acknowledge that I could be mistaken and that my adversary could be more in tune with the truth of a matter, then what may seem truthful to me today could be false tomorrow. More radically, my opponent's truth today could be my own tomorrow. Gandhi's secretary Pyarelal writes of Gandhi's "wholehearted acceptance on his part of his opponents' standpoint as their truth, which might one day become also his truth."

The requirement of self-correction implies, in turn, the seeker's ability to withstand challenges from two different sources—self-scrutiny and discursive rationality. The notion of experimentation requires that the seeker continually conducts an internal dialogue in which he subjects himself, his own beliefs, and his actions to scrutiny. Gandhi's autobiography is full of confessional stories in which he revises his beliefs after self-examination. However, Gandhi's truth-seeking is also open to challenges from others, wherein his assertions are subject to the imperatives of rational discourse. Despite his strong spirituality, Gandhi's faith was not immune to the requirements of reason, and he often called for faith and reason to work in tandem. This was most often the case in the realm of truth-seeking, where Gandhi claimed, sacred writings "were never intended to supplant reason but to supplement it." Truths for Gandhi were not to be held in arbitrary or dogmatic fashion. Considered speech, deliberation, and rational persuasion in dialogue with the self and with others—were always considered to be important elements of moral and political life. Meanwhile, rational persuasion also works to convert the opponent to one's own position, reinforcing the idea of political action as a means to seek and spread truth on any given matter. Convincing the adversary of the correctness of one's moral position, rather than simply gaining one's own interest, is the goal of political action. Furthermore, by subjecting our own conscience to scrutiny and experimentation, we strengthen the epistemological warrant of our deeply held beliefs, for they are now the product of a humble conscience that has tested them and subjected them to the challenges of rational discourse.

Third, the epistemological warrant of the individual conscience is strengthened by the component of conscious, disciplined self-suffering. There is evidence that Gandhi relied on the classical Hindu understanding of suffering as a tool of connection with the truth. This, of course, derives from the Vedic emphasis (most directly in Patanjali's Yogasutraṣ) on tapas (sufferings) as a spiritual tool that purifies consciousness and moral vision. In the yogic branches of

Hindu thought, tapas literally means "the heat of disciplined, austerity, which burns the impurities between the seeker and his truth." This language of self-cleansing and clarifying is prominent in Gandhi's notion of self-suffering. However, non-violence as a civic virtue relies on suffering in a purely political sense, as a tool of political action not attached to any metaphysical assumptions. Suffering mitigates the problem of epistemological limitation, for it allows the activist to demonstrate the strength of his conviction while simultaneously acknowledging the potential fallibility of his moral position. If it turns out that our grasp of the truth is wrong, we alone suffer the consequences of our mistakes.

Suffering also serves to supplement the call of reason: "If you want something really important to be done," Gandhi claims, "you must not merely satisfy the reason, you must move the heart also." It functions as an alternative or subsequent step to persuasion by reason. In a strategy of non-violent political action, suffering operates to break through the rational defenses of the opponent when the appeal of reason has failed by dramatizing the satyagrahis's position through a sort of shock treatment, demonstrating the activist's strength of conviction, representing his sincerity by the willingness to suffer for his moral position. In taking politics beyond merely a matter of reasoned deliberation and speech, Gandhian non-violence turns the body into an instrument of non-rational, , emotive persuasion. Gandhian non-violence does not see any broad proscription against the use of the body as a political instrument or infliction of pain on the body: the key is that the person inflicting the pain also be the one suffering it, such that self-injury is not within Gandhi's definition of violence. To refuse to fear for the flesh in the course of fighting for a cause—indeed, actively to mortify the flesh-is to demonstrate one's strength of conviction. As a civic virtue, non-violence relies upon this capacity for persuasion through means that are entirely other than rational.

Finally, self-suffering in satyagraha also attempts to achieve the moral conversion of the adversary. Satyagraha, Gandhi claims, "postulates the conquest of the adversary by suffering in one's own person." By acting nonviolently and accepting the often dire consequences of his actions, the satyagrahis "meekly and willingly submit to the penalty of disobedience and cheerfully accepts its attendant hardships." In this sense, satyagrahi serves to bolster the claim of politics as an effort to seek the truth. Through his suffering, the satyagrahi hopes to engage his adversary in a joint examination of their respective truth claims. This recalls the earlier claim that one's adversary is not simply someone whose own moral or political truth is mistaken, and, therefore to be overthrown by force. Because we keep ourselves open to the possibility that her truth may be valid, we treat his as a partner in the search for truth and demonstrate to his own conviction in terms that do not threaten him.

As a civic virtue, then, non-violence relies on the requirements of fallibility, self-examination, self-correction, and self-suffering in refining moral judgment. Because one has tested one's conscience by subjecting convictions to scrutiny, remaining epistemologically humble, and consciously suffering for one's beliefs, one gains the moral authority to engage in certain actions. One has chosen this particular action or position after sustained effort, rather than simply due to convention or self-interest. One is more qualified to pass moral judgment on its worth because one's faculty of moral judgment has been subjected to rigorous labours. One is able to see the moral/political world more clearly because of these efforts. As a policy or a civic virtue, non-violence is a doctrine of political action that relies on truth-seeking in a practical or relative sense and on the possibility of choosing well among such truths.

The larger purpose of truth-seeking in the comprehensive sense remains open for the virtuous non-violent citizen. This model of political action may still require a minimal belief in the necessity of truth as the basis for justifying political action. However, this commitment is only to truth in the practical or relative sense, therefore detaching non-violence as a policy from non-violence as a creed or way of life. Non-violence as a policy retains the commitment of politics as a realm of truth-seeking without requiring the disciplinary constraints of total ahimsa for which the Gandhian life calls. One need not live in an ashram, take vows of celibacy, non-possession, and control of the palate to engage in non-violent political action. Rather, one has to adhere to the requirements of epistemological humility, self-examination, reasoned persuasion and conscious, disciplined self-suffering, so that one's moral judgment in a particular instance can be as close to the truth of the matter as possible.

Finally, the activist must be wiling to suffer non-violently, undergo punishment, and invite legal sanction, if necessary, without harming others. The final step of undergoing suffering serves as the test of truth conviction. It allows the activist to draw on his fundamental convictions regarding the ultimate meaning and purpose of life.

An individual who believes strongly in the validity of a truth as the basis of a political position should be willing to suffer for it, but in a way that harms only oneself. In so doing, one has acknowledged the potential fallibility of one's own position yet has dramatized that position by suffering alone the consequences. Such action could take the form of civil disobedience, long marches in harsh conditions, deliberate law-breaking with intent to invite the full sanction of the law, or simply a dramatic act such as fasting publicly, sitting-in or other prolonged discomfort to gain attention/empathy. Notice also that his dramatization would be means of last resort, used only after genuine moral persuasion through discourse had been exhausted. Non-violent suffering is not trivialized as a mere political stunt; that is, those who simply strike, boycott, fast, or break the law without having engaged in moral discourse would not be granted validity.

The non-rational, emotive elements of Gandhian political action represented in the act of suffering are by no means separable from the rest of his thought. In this sense, he presents a far more real assessment of the political world than one which always assumes pure rationality on the part of all actors. The appeal to emotion suffuses Gandhi's entire notion of political action, rather than simply the step of self-suffering. Certainly, self-suffering is to be undertaken subsequent to attempts at moral persuasion through discourse, which must always be the first strategy of the satyagrahi. However, the satyagrahi does not appeal first to reason and then to emotion, as though the two were entirely separate. Rather, the appeal to emotion always underlies the various steps in Gandhian political action, even in the initial steps of self-scrutiny and of moral persuasion.

It is also important to make several distinctions among kinds and degrees of suffering and to consider how use of each of these different kinds of suffering may be appropriate under different circumstances. The first distinction is between active and passive self-suffering, the second is between self-suffering and self-destruction, and the third is a distinction among levels of non-violence. To begin, non-violence should not ever be considered an act of passivity or, as Gandhi called it, a "weapon of the weak". Bondurant reminds us that non-violence is a "technique of action" that seeks to effect change by "employing force." Non-violent suffering is to be active, deliberate, and purposive: it is to be done in conjunction with actions such as agitation, marching, slogan-shouting, issuing of ultimatums, and acts of civil disobedience, such as law-breaking and non-cooperation. Political suffering should be undertaken in a purposeful manner, with specific goals and demands to be met, and with careful planning to dramatize a position and invite certain reactions. Such acts of conscious suffering should also be governed by a code of discipline and are, therefore, to be distinguished from extreme acts of self-torture such as self-mutilation and self-immolation, which, while technically falling under the rubric of self-suffering, and not acts of conscious self-suffering. Gandhian self-suffering focuses on the consistent, prolonged, and disciplined infliction of suffering on the self so as to demonstrate the strength and continued commitment of individual conviction. Extreme acts of self-destruction (suicide, self-amputation, or self-immolation) achieve only a single destructive blow to the self. While all non-violent activists should in theory be prepared to make the ultimate sacrifice of life, this should only be seen as a last resort rather than the immediate goal of non-violent action. The logic of non-violent suffering, then, is not a call for acts of mass self-destruction, such as suicide. It stands on more than simply the willingness to die. In this, it differs from martyrdom as a test of strength of belief. Death can only be the final test of confidence in one's grasp of the truth when it is preceded by a disciplined, sustained self-suffering, without which the willingness to die has no relationship to moral authority.

It is also important to note that there are different levels of self-suffering, and that the most rigorous kinds of self-suffering (such as law-breaking with intent to be imprisoned or fasting unto death) need not be expected in all instances of conflict. It may be reasonable to expect that people demonstrate their conviction in, say, the selection of certain kinds of textbooks in public schools, by participating in a sit-in or a protest march. It is however, quite unreasonable to expect that they be wiling to fast unto death—or even go to jail, for that matter—for such a conviction, no matter how strong. On the other hand, if the moral conflict is over something as fundamental as say, slavery or civil rights, we may reasonably require people to move up the chain of self-suffering act and be prepared to make the ultimate sacrifice. In such cases, it is appropriate to expect that adherents to these causes suffer nonviolently by sitting-in, fasting, being prepared to be forcibly removed, or even jailed and tried. These are, no doubt, high prices to pay for their convictions. No one should think less of them, or of their convictions, should they decide to undertake no political challenge. However, if they do decide to undertake rigorous self-suffering then, under the criteria of the non-violent method, their actions should be granted an extremely high level of moral credibility. What is crucial and should be common to all cases of disagreement is that the parties to the conflict abstain rigorously from violence against others. This abstention, we might say, is the minimal requirement of non-violent suffering. Beyond this, we should make sure that our expectation of the kind of self-suffering in each case is proportional to the truth at stake, and accordingly, so is the approbation and legitimacy granted to such actions.

Gandhi insisted that moral agent was to lead the life of truth, that is, constantly to examine and be true to one's sincerely held beliefs in thought, word and deed. Such an integrated life involoved not only eliminating all traces of hypocrisy from one's way of life but also fighting against untruth when one felt strongly and was in a positon to do something about it. This raised two important questions. First, since different men perecived truth differently, it was not only possible but an inescapable feature of human life that 'what appeared to be truth to the one may appear false to the other'. Even as a moral agent did not wish to live with untruth himself, he could not consistently ask other to do so either. The question therefore arises as to how they should resolve their differences or, as Gandhi perferred to put it, co-operatively search for truth.

Second, a moral agent had no alternative but to take a stand and fight when his opponent either refused to talk or to do what they both agreed to be right or true thing to do in a given situation. The method of fighting for a goal was not external to it but an integral part of it. The goal did not exist at the end of a series of actions designed to achieve it. Gandhi contanded that the distinction between means and ends ignored this fundamental fact and was untenable. The so-called means were ends in an embryonic stage and they represented the two sides of the same coin. Since this was so, the fight for truth had to be conducted by truthful means, raising the obvious question as to what mode of action was truthful.

Gandhi's theory of satyagraha was intended to answer these two questions. The term itself was suggestive. Satya means truth, and agraha which, contrarty to what almost all his commentators have said, Gandhi used in its ordinary Gujarati and not the classical Sanskrit sense, means insisting on something without becoming obstinate or uncompromising. When the two terms are combined there is a beautiful duality of meaning implying both insistence on and for turth. A moral agent insists on truth as he sees it, but acknowledges that he might be wrong or only partially right and invites his opponent to join him in a co-operative search for truth. When the invitation is declined, he insists on it in a truthful manner and continues to do so until his opponent is ready to talk. Insofar as it is concerned to discover truth, Gandhi's theory of satyagraha is an integral part of his theory of truth; insofar as it is an attempt to insist on and realise truth, it is an inseparable part of his theory of non-violence. Gandhi's theory of satyagraha is at once both epistemological and political, a theory of both knowledge and action, and much misunderstood when seen as either alone.

Gandhi insisted discusion and persuassion were the best ways to deal with a situation of conflict. Since each individual was uniquely constituted, his perecption of truth necessarily differed from and even conflicted with those of others. The point of rational discussion was to step into each other's shoes, look at the subjects in question from each other's point of view, appreciate the force of each other's arguments and arrive at a view based on the insights of both and acceptable to both. For Gandhi it was necessarily based on three assumptions.

First, since neither party was in possession of the Absolute Truth, each should enter the discussion in a spirit of humility and with an open mind.

Second, since each saw truth differently, he should make a sincere effort to enter into the other's world of thought-and appreciate why he saw the matter differently. He might ultimately disagree with another, but only after making every possible effort to understand his position in its own terms. For Gandhi rational discussion entailed the duty of sincerity, and its purpose was defeated if each party could not count on trust or the other to make a genuine attempt to look at the dispute from his point of view.

Third, rational discussion was of no avail if the parties concerned were selfish and ill-disposed towards or hated each other. Selfishness, hatred and ill-will led to emotional and moral rigidity and clouded the processes of sympathetic understanding and critical self-reflection indispensable for all rational discussion. Objectivity required an open mind, and an open mind presupposed an open heart. When the heart rejected someone, that is, when he did not come within one's range of sympathy and form part of one's emotional and moral universe, reason tended to reject him too and did not take due account of his feelings and interests. Sympathy, love or good-will was a necessary precondition of rationality, and only universal love guaranteed total objectivity.

In Gandhi's view, the basic preconditions of rational discussion did not generally obtain in practice. Self-righteousness, dogmatism, insincerity, prejudice, ill-will, self-interest, limited sympathies, moral inertia and sheer obstinacy often distorted and hindered the operations of reason. He claimed to have discovered this painful truth after a series of unpleasant experiences in South Africa. He had led there several movements against the laws subjecting Asians to the most offensive forms of racial discrimination. For years he wrote open letters, circulars, leaflets, letters to newspapers and editorials in his weekly paper refuting the arguments and correcting the misinformation on which white racism was based. The Whites said that Asians were an uncivilised and aboriginal people the litany of whose defects included low intelligence, lack of morality, bad habits, want of personal hygiene, mendacity, sharp business practices, miserliness, the practices of untouchability, lack of family loyalty and the tendency to live in overcrowded and ugly surroundings. In two remarkeble documents Gandhi assumed the role of a judge, distanced himself from his own people and impartially analysed the charges against those men. He agreed that they lived in insanitary and overcrowded houses, used their shops as bedrooms, lacked personal hygiene and practised untouchability.

He admitted some of the other criticisms, but insisted that these applied to the whites as well. His countrymen did engage in sharp business practices, have a habit of telling lies, and were miserly. However, "I would only say without meaning in the least to defend them, let those that are without sin cast the first stone". Finally, Gandhi rejected the rest of the criticisms altogether. The Indians did not neglect their children, nor the latter their parents. And they did not have a low sense of mutual loyalty. Indeed, in all social matters the English are far more fitted to sit at the feet of the Hindus and learn as disciples, said Gandhi quoting Frederick Pincott. Gandhi found that his White audience rarely entered into a dialogue with him and that when it did, it repeated old stereotypes, relied on anecdotal evidence, gave credence to unchecked stories and displayed utter lack of objectivity.

Gandhi noticed too that on many occasions he was confronted not so much with traditional and deeply entrencehed prejudices as crude self-interest dressed up in the disguise of a philosophical and moral theory. The Whites had for decades been in the habit of recruting indentured Indian labourers. When Indian traders began to arrive, the whites felt threatened by their competition and demanded immigration control. Rather than admit their real reasons, they argured that the presence of the Indians posed a threat to the integrity of Western civilisation. Some said that the Indians had no or an inferior civilisation. Others argued that it was wholly different and that the two suffered from close contact. Gandhi produced testimonials from such authorities on the subject as Maine, Andrew Carnegie, Munro, Charles Trevelyan, Willians Hunter and Max Muller to prove that ancient India had developed a great civilsation and chalked up remarkeble achievements in mathematics, the natural sciences, political science, philosophy, comparative religion, psychology and the science of grammar. He even assured his audience that Indians were descended not from an inferior stock but one that had produced the Greeks, the Romans and the English themselves. For Gandhi this point was particularly important, as one-half or even three-fourths' of the indignities inflicted on them were justified in terms of the alleged racial inferiority. Gandhi also reeled off the names of S.N. Banerjee, Pherozeshah Mehta, Mutuswami Aiyer and Christodas Paul to prove that modern India too had thrown up men of great eminence. Gandhi was saddened to find that his White opponents were not at all interested in the debate and only used the language of civilisation to legitimise their self-interest.

Gandhi concluded that the head and the heart, reason and morality, were inseparable. Men found it almost impossible to be objective about those they loathed or found strange and alien. If they were reflective and self-critical, they might to some extent rise above their hostility and consider others' interests with some degree of impartiality.

For Gandhi then ahimsa meant both passive and active love, refraining from causing harm and destruction to living beings as well as positively promoting their well-being. Himsa was the opposite of ahimsa. Since the ancient Indian thinkers took himsa to be a positive concept, they defined ahimsa in terms of it. Gandhi equated ahimsa with the positive and self-contained concept of love and adopted the opposite approach of defining himsa in terms of it.

In Gandhi's view, love implied identification with and service of all living beings. Its oppositers were malevolence and selfishness. Malevolence implied ill-will towards or hatred of others a wish to harm them even when they posed no threat to one's interests and simply because one enjoyed seeing them suffer. Contrary to what some of his commentators have said, Gandhi distinguished between self-interest and selfishness. Self-interest consisted in securing those conditions without which no man could live a fully human life. Since the earth provided 'enough for everybody's needs but not enough for anybody's greed', Gandhi thought that there was no conflict between the self-interests of all men. By contrast, selfishness meant putting oneself above others and pursuing one's interests at their expense. It was inherently aggressive and limitless, and necessarily led to conflict. While the pursuit of self-interest was morally legitimate, selfishness was not.

For Gandhi, then himsa meant inflicting harm or destruction upon another living being out of selfishness or ill-will. As he put it, it consisted in causing 'suffering to others out of selfishness or just for the sake of doing so'. A surgeon's use of a knife was ahimsa, and a sadist's use of it were repectively motivated by selfishness and malevolence and constituted himsa. In the Indian traditions, harm was defined widely to include not only physical but also psychological, moral and other forms of pida or klesa (pain). Gandhi accepted this broad definition of it. In his view, physical harm or destruction was the most familiar form of violence and could be caused in different ways. One might harm or kill a man by shooting him or by denying him the basic necessities of life. Whether one killed him 'at a stroke' or 'by inches', the result was the same and the individuals involved were guilty of violence.

Insulting, demeaning or humiliating others, diminishing their self-respect, speaking harsh words, passing harsh judgements, anger and mental cruelty were also forms of harm. They might, and generally did, result in physical harm, but it was not necessary that they should in order to be considered acts of violence. A lack of punctuality was also an act of harm as it caused anxiety to those involved and deprived them of their time. Not answering letters was also a form of mental cruelty and even torture, and thus an act of violence. For Gandhi violence was a property not only of conduct but also of thought. Thoughts of violence paved the ways for acts of violence, and were just as bad. Like most Indian thinkers, Gandhi refused to draw a qualitative distinction between thought and action. Thought was potential action or, rather, action in its early and embryonic stage, and action was operative or active thought. The two were integral parts of the same process and constituted a continuum. A thought was therefore never a 'mere' thought.

Ancient Indian thinkers had argued that a man could be guilty of violence by committing it himself aiding and instigating it or by watching it being committed without protest. Gandhi went further and contended that a man also committed violence by participating in or benefiting from a harmful practice. Since agriculture involved violence, the Jains avoided it. However, they could not survive without its products and depended on others to engage in it. For Gandhi, this was profoundly hypocritical. It implied encouraging others to engage in violence in order that one could practise non-violence oneself, and involved enjoying the benefits of violence while disowning all responsibility for it. He observed:

> The very idea that millions of the sons of the soil should remain steeped in himsa in order that a handful of men who live on the toil of these people might be able to practise ahimsa seems to me to be very

> unworthy of and inconsistent with the supreme duty of ahimsa. I feel that this betrays a lack of perecption of the inwardness of ahimsa.

Gandhi observed that a similar situation occurred at the political level. Many votaries of non-violence condemned the institutionalised violence of the state, but enjoyed the order and security provided by it. And though they did not themselves fight in wars, they happily paid soldiers to do so for them. For Gandhi, this too was hypocritical. The violence of the state did not disappear merely by shutting one's eyes to it, and one did not become non-violent by conveniently transfering the moral burden of inescapable violence upon the shoulders of others. Such non-violence fed off and and was made possible by the violence of others, and did not absolve the individul concerned from his responsibility for the violence involved. Indeed, insofar as his conduct added hypocrisy to violence, it was doubly reprehensible. Like salvation, non-violence was indivisible. Either all were non-violent, or none was. It simply could not be practised by running away from the world, it can be practised only by entering and changing it. Gandhi's departure from the Indian traditions could not have been more radical and decisive.

Although Gandhi vacillated on the subjects he seems to have thought that self-inflicted or self-directed harm was not violence. The Indian traditions contained scattered references to atma-himsa (violence to oneself) and atma-ahimsa (non-injury to oneself), but they generally defined violence as injury to para (another being). Gandhi shared this view and remarked on several occasions that violence meant 'causing injury to another' For Gandhi a suicide was guilty of cowardice, not violence. It would seem that Gandhi was inconsistent in taking this view. As he defined it, infliction of harm or destruction was violence when motivated by selfishness or ill-will, and it is certainly possible for a man to be guided by either in his relation to himself.

For Gandhi then, ahimsa meant active love and involved both refraining from causing harm to others in the broad sense in which he used the terms, and helping them grow and flourish. Himsa meant harming others out of ill-will or selfishness. Harm caused to others in the course of pursuing one's legitinmate or just self-interest was not himsa. Although Gandhi broke with the Indian traditions in several crucial respects, his break was not complete. His view of non-violence retained a subjectivist orientation characteristic of them, as he too defined it in terms of the motives of the agent. For them, as for him, himsa involved ill-will, a wish to harm others and hence harm did not constitute himsa if the element of malevelence is absent. Again, the Hindu had argued that harm caused in the interest of *loksangraha* and the maintenance of dharma was not himsa. Gandhi came close to sharing this dharmic view of violence, as he too argued that harm caused in the pursuit of legitimate or just self-interest did not amount to himsa. The dividing line between self-interest and selfishness is thin and not easy to draw. And, as for the concept of legitimate or just self-interest, it is normative and open to dispute. Not surprisingly, like the Hindu view, Gandhi's definition left room for considerable disagreement and even casuistry.

Insofar as Gandhi departed from the Indian traditions of ahimsa in significant respects, many of his opinions and actions surprised his countrymen. One relatively trivial incident acted as a catalyst and brought home to both the radical novelty of his docrtine. A calf in his ashram was badly maimed and in acute agony. All possible medical treatment was given to it. When a surgeon whose advice was sought declared it past hope, Gandhi asked him to administer it a lethal injection. His action provoked a storm of protest, some accusing him of senility and some even wishing him death. The Jains who, like many of his commentators, had made the predictable mistake of taking his theory of ahimsa to be substantially similar to theirs, were most bitter; the Hindus only a little less so.

Gandhi's critics raised four objections. First, according to the Indian doctrine of ahimsa life was sacred and inviolable and the deliberate killing of a living being was never justified. Second, although Gandhi talked about love, his action betrayed a lack of love for the calf, for love could never kill. Third, if we were consistent, he would have to kill a human being under similar circumsatnces, and that would be most immoral. Finally, he was under 'Western' influence in thinking that the alleviation of pain was far more important than the preservation of life.

Gandhi was deeply hurt and, judging by the tone of his reply, angered by the criticisms. Not surprisingly, he used the occasion to launch a scathing general attack on the three Indian traditions, especially the Jain. He rejected the view that killing was never justified and that all killing was violence. His critics had 'wrongly' assumed that death was always worse than life, for sometimes life was so painful and unbearable that death was preferable. When a living being was in unbearable and incurable agony, not to kill it was an act of himsa. Gandhi said he had killed the calf in its own 'interest' and for its own 'benefit'. He had tried to nurse it and soothe its pain. When it was found there was no hope and help, he was left with no choice. There is violence when the intention is to give pain, otherwise it is only an act of killing'.

Gandhi rejected the charge that his act betrayed a lack of love for the calf. Love implied care and concern for others and a desire to do all one could to relieve their suffering. He had killed the calf because he loved it and wanted it to meet its certain death without any more pain. The 'horror of killing' displayed by his critics was not ahimsa but effete sentimentality. They made a 'fetish of non-killing, and this had so'drugged' their conscience that they did not even know what 'true' ahimsa was. The equation of himsa with killing and ahimsa with non-killings 'blind' to the whole range of activities. His wealthy critics, Gandhi argues, paid their workers substandard wages and did nothing to relieve widespread poverty and degradation. Since they did not kill anyone, they assumed that they were non-violent. In fact they 'committed violence on a large scale in the name of non-violence' and were guilty of 'crass hypocrisy'. There was 'far more violence in the slow torture of men..and wanton humiliation and oppression of the weak and the killing of their self-respect than in mere benevolent taking of life'.

As to whether he would have acted in exactly the same way if the calf had been a human being, Gandhi answered in the affirmative with the important qualification that 'natural differencs' between man and animal ruled out 'a complete analogy'. Gandhi was realistic enough to recognise that weak and disorganised men and women did not always find it easy to resist the use of violence, especially when confronted with determined and ruthless opponents. Although such violence was regrettable, it was 'understandable' and 'pardonable'. In 1942, he gave several important interviews to Louis Fischer in the course of which he discussed the likely peasant movement in independent India.

The struggle for human dignity and freedom in general and political independence in particular was of special and immediate interest to Gandhi. He was convinced that the reign of violence could not be ended by adding to it and that non-violence struggle was the only answer. However, he realised that non-violence did not come easily to those not fully trained in and committed to it, and that most ordinary men and women resorted to violence when provoked 'beyond endurance'. Although morally unacceptable, such violence was 'understandable'. While all violence was 'bad and must be condemned in the abstract', it was important to distinguish between its different forms and contexts. Defensive violence was morally superior to the offensive, as it was largely reactive and provoked by the opponent. Spontaneous violence was a result of accumulated frustration and superior to premeditated violence. The violence of long-suppressed groups lacking the capacity for concerted action was more 'understandablc' than that of those with an opportunity to participate in political lifc and to develop organised strength. Though regrettable, the violence of those who had been humiliated and brutalised for centuries was not 'senseless' and served the useful purpose of helping them acquire a sense of power and dignity. Desperate violence by isolated individuals and groups in the face of an overwhelming violence by their oppressors was often the only available way to preserve their human dignity. Indeed, since it was largely symbolic and 'unequally matched', it was 'really' or 'comparatively' non-violent. The Polish resistance to German invaders during the second world war was, like the resistance of a mouse to a cat, 'almost non-violent'. Although it was 'thoughtless', the violence committed during the 'Quit India movement of 1942 was born out of 'sheer desperation' and 'provoked by the government'. When Gandhi came to know that prisoners were tortured in some of the princely states of India, he advised them that if they could not do so non-violently, they should 'resist the tortures with all the violence they can summon from within'.

Finally, Gandhi argued that although non-violence was far superior to violence, the latter was 'infinitely' better than cowardice. A coward lacked 'manlines' and was commited to nothing more elevated than sheer survival. By contrast, a man prepared to use violence had pride and self-respect and was prepared to die rather than surrender. Forgiveness was certainly better than vengeance, but the latter was 'any day superior to passive, effeminate and helpless submission. Furthermore, a violent man might one day be won over to non-violence, whereas a coward was beyond hope. We do want to drive out the beast in man, but we do not want to emasculate him. Gandhi also thought that violence had at least some deterrent effect and might reduce its future incidence whereas cowards only fed the voracios appetite of the bullies.

Gandhi carried ahimsa much further than any other theorist of it had ever done. Unlike most of them, he did not merely attack wars but also the institution of the state, including armies, the police and prisons. And unlike almost all of them, he showed a remarkable sensitivity to the non-human world and insisted on the 'absolute efficacy' of ahimsa. On the other hand he permitted or condoned violence in many more types of situation than most of them had done. He drew fine, sometimes too fine, distinctions between different forms and levels of violence and even called some of them 'almost' or 'comparatively' non-violent. He freely used the vocabulary of violence and called satyagraha 'non-violent warface' or 'war without violence', his followers non-violent 'soldiers' or an 'army for swaraj', and himself their general or dictator'. He also borrowed some of its organisational tools and modelled some of his satyagrahas after the army reuwiring oaths, pledges and unquestioning obedience. His Indian and Christian critics contended that his non-violence had an air of militancy about it and shared far more in common with violence than he realised or cared to admit.

The apparently paradoxical character of Gandhi's theory is traceable to several sources of which two are relevant to our discussion. First, for him, non-violence was not the only or even the highest value and had to be reconciled with such other values as truth, national independence, courage, human survival, self-respect and dignity. He knew that these values sometimes conflicted and that non-violence could not always be given moral priority. Second, Gandhi's theory was developed in the context of and intended to guide political action. Unlike most theorists of non-violence who were religious men primarily concerned to preserve their moral integrity in the face of evil. Gandhi led a great national movement aiming to liberate and regenerate a long-subjugated and diffident people. He had therefore little choice but to adjust his theory to the inescapable constraints of political life and mass action. He knew that a principle which took no account of the logic of its context was doomed to impotence. Having condemned all acts of violence early in his political career in India, he began to appreciate that a complete embargo on it was neither realistic nor desirable. Desperate and oppressed people unused to disciplined non-violent action and provoked beyond endurance were bound, at times, to lose patience and to resort to violence. Setting them an impossible ideal not only demoralised them but also discredited the doctrine of non-violence. A calculated use of violence as a matter of deliberate policy was one thing; a spontaneouos recourse to it under intense provocation was altogether different. Gandhi thought that no inconsistency was involved in condemning the former but reluctantly acquiescing in the latter. He knew that he stood a better chance of regulating, reducing and eventually eliminating violence by acknowledging and finding a limited and clearly defined moral space for it in his political theory than by abstractly condemning, evading or prohibiting it.

Gandhi redised that his ideal of a completely non-violent society was utopian and that violence was necessary, unavoidable or understandable when used in the pursuit of such values as individual and social life, justice, the assertion of human dignity and the development of courage or when provoked by unbearable oppression. Since the values were not internally related to non-violence, Gandhi's resolution of their conflict lacked a guiding principle and remained ad hoc and a matter of his personal preferences.

Since Gandhi's moral theory contained a mass of disparate and internally unrelated values, it remained extremely loose and openended and was unable to offer much guidance to his followers. For example, they could not decide whether they were justified in launching a satyagraha when there was a risk of violence. Gandhi's theory pointed both ways. His practice did not help much either. He disapproved of peasant satyagrahas in the thirties on the ground that they were likely to lead to violence. Yet he approved of them in his interview with Louis Fischer and launched the *Quit India* movement in 1942 in full knowledge that some violence was bound to occur. Take another rather trivial case. He said that his ahimsa ruled out a non-vegetarian diet, especially when fruits, vegetables and agricultural products were available in plenty. But he also said that if a man was used to it and likely to be hurt when denied it, he should be provided with a non-vegetarian diet as the violence involved in denying it to him was greater than that of killing an animal! Accordingly, he served meat to such visitors to his strictly vegetarian ashram as Louis Fischer and Maulana Azad. Many of his Jain and Hindu followers were puzzled and some were deeply offended by his in consistent behaviour. They thought that he could have persuaded his guests to refrain from a non-vegetarian diet while they were in the ashram.

Gandhi's theory of ahimsa could better be understed with the reference to his dialogue with the terrorists. The terrorist movement could not survive let alone flourish under the vigilant colonial eye without a significant measure of popular support, especially among the Hindus. The Hindus vastly outnumbered the rest, and most of the terrorists were drawn from their ranks. Unlike the Sikh and Islamic traditions, both classical and folk Hinduism were ambiguous on the legitimacy of violence, especially when used against the established government by those lacking the *adhikara* to do so. When Gandhi appeared on the scene and preached non-violence, most of his critics were also Hindus.

In order to secure the support of and mobilise the Hindu masses, terrorists needed to do two things. First, they had to show that not just violence per so but terrorist violence had the sanction of the Hindu tradition and that it did not involve adharma or papa. Second, in the colonial context, they needed not just acquiescence but the active moral, emotional and financial support of the Hindu masses. They had therefore to mobilise the latter, to instil in them a sense of collective responsibility for terrorist violence and to show them that it was positively their dharma to support it. In order to attain these objectives, the terrorists and their sympathisers needed to reinterpret Hinduism in active, collectivist and political terms.

In Maharashtra, Tilak and his colleagues reinterpreted and collectivised the worship of Ganesh, representing both classical and folk Hinduism and combined the former's asceticism and wisdom with the latter's hedonism and devotionalism. Ganesh had colse links with Siva, as a lord and protector of gana (community) and enjoyed the reputation of being a 'conqueror of all obstacles'. Though worshipped for several centuries, his worship had been largely a private affair, at best involving friends and neighbours. From about 1894 onwards, Tilak began to collectivise his worship and give it an unmistakable political and communitarian orientation.

In Bengal, the suitably reinterpreted Durga, the goddess of Shakti, played an important political role, especially in the form of Kali. Initially a helper of Durga and an expression of her wrath, Kali had gradually developed into an independent deity and the mistress of the universe. The public worship of her in Bengal began in the seventeenth century. Like Ganesh and Shivaji in Maharashtra, Kali was closely associated with the protection of Hinduism in general and the Brahmins in particular. Described as the 'Mother of Mother India', Kali became the guardian of her honour and the two mothers were bonded in a fascinating symbiotic relationship. Her anger, energy and vengefulness received particular emphasis and she came to be interpreted as a goddess who loved secrecy and mercilessly punished all violations of it. Secret societies sprang up all over Bengal requiring vows to be taken in her presence.

Kali was supposed to demand the blood of 'wicked intruders'. Following the influential dharmic view of violence, it was widely argued that assassinations executed in her name did not amount to violence. As one of the terrorists put it,

> The Mother is thirsting after the blood of the Feringhees who have bled her profusely. Satisfy her thirst. Killing the Feringhee, we say, is no murder. Brother, chant this verse while slaying the Feringhee white goat, for killing him is not murder.

Throughout India, the two epics and the *Puranas* were reinterpreted in activist and collectivist terms. Those *Puranas* which described violent conflicts were given prominence, their central characters and episodes were interpreted in political terms, and some of their gods and goddesses were presented as proto-terrorists. The *Ramayana*, an essentially moral treatise with a large social and only a limited political content, was read in oversimplified Manichean terms. Since the violence it sanctioned was that of a ruler to whom a grave injustice had been done, it did not serve the terrorist cause and was genherally ignored in favour of the more politicaleipic the *Mahabharata*. It too, posed considerable difficulties. The Pandavas had lost their land in a game of dice to which they had freely agreed.

War became unavoidable only because the Kauravas refused to return the land even after their enemies had completed the required period of exile. Violence occurred within the context of a war. And it caused such massive destruction of human life that even the victors felt disillusioned with their victory. Since the Indian political reality did not quite fit this pattern, advocates of violence had to resort to highly convoluted interpretations of both the epics. They described Indians as Pandavas and the colonial rulers as Kauravas. The latter had 'deceived' Indians by pretending to be interested only in trade and taking 'unscrupulous' advantage of their innocence and hospitality. Indians were only fighting for their rights and their struggle for independence was really a *dharmayuddha*. Their use of violence was not only justified but really a form of *yajna* or religious sacrifice.

The terrorists found the Gita especially useful. As it satisfied a number of disparate demands, it had begun to enjoy considerable popularity since the middle decades of the nineteenth century. It was concise and self-contained and could be presented to the supercilious missionaries as the Hindu equivalent of the Bible. Being highly philosophical, it could even be shown to be superior to the 'moralistic' and 'story-telling' Bible. Since it was eclectic and contained doctrines acceptable to different Hindu sects, it was capable of uniting them all. It was set in the context of a war and no less a personage than the Lord Himself sanctioned violence. Above all, it provided the Hindus engaged in a momentous struggle against the colonial government with a much needed theory of action. Not surprisingly, there was a hardly a national leader who did not study and write about it. Since they turned to it for differnet reasons, they naturally offered different and somethings conflicting interpretations of it.

The terrorists and their sympathisers gave the Gita unprecedented importance and thought that it summed up the essence of Hinduism. Many of them read it daily, some carried around copies of it, a few wrote extensive commentaries on it, and nearly all of them invoked it in self-justification. Khudiram was hanged with a copy of the Gita slung across his neck. During his incarceration, Tilak turned to the Gita for guidance and wrote a massive treatise on it. Several secret societies required their members to take oaths with a sword and a copy of the Gita on their heads.

Terrorist writers read the Gita in political and activist terms. Though their interpretations of its philosophy differed in serveral important respects, there was a broad consensus on its moral and political message. Moksha was the highest ideal of life and could only be attained by discharging one's dharma. Dharma held society together and adharma led to its disintegration. Social life was characterised by a constant conflict between good and evil or dharma and adharma. Since social order was the sine qua non of dharma, *loksangraha* or pre servation of organised social life was the highest ploitical value. Every individual thus had a duty to fight evil and to uphold and ensure the victory of dharma. In the imperfect world, the fight against adharma sometimes required painful choices and apparently amoral actions such as taking life, breaking promises and telling lies. Though regrettable these were all fully justified. Krishna's remark, *ye yatha mam prapadyante tam tathaiv bhajakyaham was* interpreted by Tilak to mean that 'tit for tat' or *shatham prati shathyam kuryat* was an inescapable principle of political life. The fact that krishna himself had to tell a few lies and to ask Arjuna to resort to massive violence showed that even God could not function in this world without occasionally bending rules.

It was true that a sensitive moral agent often felt anguished and depressed by the need to use violence and preferred instead to withdraw from the world or acquiesce in injustices. Indeed, the Gita itself was the story of how Arjuna, a lifelong warrior, felt paralysed by the very thought of violence. It required all the philosophical acumen of the Lord Himself, capped by Vishwaroop darshan, to get him out of his moral despair. As Krishna showed, the maintenance of dharma was the highest good and the violence used in pursuit of it, was fully justified. Indeed, such a dharmic violence was morally innocent and a matter of sacred duty. Krishna had himself announced in the Gita that whenever dharma was threatened, he incarnated himself on earth to destory the wicked. Violence could not have a greater legitimation.

The terrorists and their sympathisers thus derived not only a theory of violence but also a wider, quasi-Machiavellian theory of political morality from the Gita in particular and the *Mahabharata* in general. In order to show that their reading of the epic was not an aberration but represented the mainstream Hindu thought, they read other Hindu classics in similar light and concluded that the dominant image of a non-violent and unworldly Hindu, assiduously cultivated by colonial rulers and uncritically accepted by many national leaders, was the duplicitous and violent ways of the world. The terrorist literature claimed to give the Hindu a true image of himself, his religion, history and cultural heritage, which every successful terrorist act was used to reinforce and popularise.

Gandhi was deeply worried about the growing influence of the terrorists. He thought that their limited successes and brilliant propaganda had convinced their contrymen of the ineviatbility of violence. Gandhi had to undermine that belief if he was to persuade his countrymen to give serious consideration to his alternative method of political struggle. He was even more worried about the influential and in his view, thoroughly mistaken and extremely dangerous terrorist reinterpretation of Hinduism. He felt that the terrorists and their sympathisers were dazzled by modern civilisation and desperately anxious to mould India in its image. To say so openly or even to admit it to themselves would reinforce the painful sense of inferiority. Consciously or unconscioulsy , they therefore retrojected modern Europe into India's past and created the image of a once strong and militarily powerful country it was the duty of every patriotic Indian to recreate. Since the terrorist violence sprang from an 'infatuatuion' with modern civilisation, he thought that his best hope of undermining its moral and emotional appeallay in subjecting the latter to a searching critique. This was why his first book, *Hind Swaraj,* was both an 'answer to the Indian school of violence' and a 'severe condemnation of modern civilisation'. For Gandhi the two were insparable. Evidently, the British shared his view for they banned both the terrorist movement and Gandhi's book.

Gandhi also had another reason for taking the terrorists seriously. Though he profoundly disagreed with their interpretation of Indian civilisation, he shared their view that Indians had become passive and lifeless, that they needed to be energised and organised and that this could only be done by a cadre of committed and courageous men. And though he disagreed with their methods, he greatly admired their bravery and high spirits. As he said on many occasions, violence was morally superior to cowardice, and those willing to fight and kill or be killed were better than those content to acquiesce and survive. Gandhi seems to have thought that if he could win over the terrorists to the cause of non-violence, he would solve two problems at once, namely, eliminate his rivals and recruit energetic lieutenants. This was why he sought them out during his crowded visit to London, attended their meetings, spent long hours discussing large issues with them and cultivated their friendship. After his return to India, he continued to seek them out and kept up a long correspondence with them. Though critical of him, many of them trusted and confided in him, sought his advice in difficult situations and saluted his courage and patriotism.

Gandhi's dialogue with the terrorists was conducted at two levels. He strongly disagreed with their advocacy of violence, and he also questioned their interpretation of Hindu religious and cultural thought, especially the Gita. Gandhi rejected violence on four grounds: the ontological, the epistemological, the moral and the practical. Being a manifestation of Brahman, every living being was divine. Taking life was therefore sacrilegious and a form of deicide. Furthermore, as a spiritual being, every man was amenable to moral persuasion. Even when he was blinded by narrow self-interest and prejudices, it was always possible to awaken his spiritual nature, appeal to his sense of dignity and fellow-feeling and to activate his moral impulses. Obviously such a 'spiritual surgery' required patience, persistence, suffering and a heart free of hatred and ill-will. Qua spiritual being man owed it to himself and to his fellow men to cultivate these qualities. The use of violence in search of instant solutions reflected 'moral indolence' and 'spiritual inertia' and was unworthy of him. It also implied that some men were so degenerate that they had ceased to be spiritual beings. Gandhi considered this an impertinent assumption for which he found no evidence whatever.

Unlike many other critics of violence, Gandhi advanced a novel epistemological argument against it. It was a fundamental and inescapable fact of human life that all knowledge was partial and corrigible. Differently endowed and situated, men saw the world differnetly, each grasping only a specific aspect of it. Their knowlegde, further, grew over time and benefited from new experiences and discussions with others. In Gandhi's view, violence denied these fundamental facts. In order to be justified in taking the extreme step of harming or killing someone, one must assume that one was absolutely right, that the opponent was totally wrong and that violence would definitely achieve the desired result. The consequences of violence would irreversible in the sense that a life once terminated or damaged could never be revived or easily put together. And irreversible deeds required infallible knowledge to justify them. Since such knowledge was beyond human reach violence rested on a false epistemological foundation. Gandhi acknowledged that, taken to its logical extreme, his theory of 'relative truth' undermined the very basis of action, for no man could ever act if he constantly entertained the nagging doubt that he might be wholly mistaken. However, he thought that one must at least acknowledge one's fallibility and leave ample room for reflection and reconsideration. Violence did not allow this. It generated feelings of anger, hatred and insecurity, none of which was conducive to critical self-reflection. It also required an investment of enormous emotional energy and commitment, and made acknowledgement of mistakes and graceful retracing of steps exceedingly difficult. Violence was doubly flawed: it assumed infallibility and ruled out corrigibility.

Gandhi also rejected violence on moral grounds. Morality consisted in doing what was right because one believed it to be right and required unity of belief and behaviour. Since the use of violence did not change the opponent's perception of truth, it compelled him to behave in a manner contrary to his sincerely held beliefs. By disjoining his belief and conduct, it created an untruth at the very heart of his being, violated his integrity and diminished his status as a moral being.

Finally, Gandhi argued that violence could never achieve lasting results. An act of violence was deemed to be successful when it achieved its intended immediate objectives. However, if it were to be judged in terms of its long-term consequences and the kind of society it created, our conclusion would have to be very different. Every apparently successful act of violence encouraged the belief that it was the only effective way to achieve the desired goal and encouraged the habit of using it every time one ran into resistance. Society thus became used to it and never felt compelled to explore an alternative. Gandhi thought that violence also had the propensity to generate an inflationary spiral. Every successful use of it blunted the community's moral sensibility and raised its threshold of violence, so that over time, an increasingly larger amount of it became necessary to achieve the same results. Inititally, throwing a stone might be enough to draw the government's attention to a grievance; soon the assassination of an officer and later that of several of them became necessary. Every act of violence led to a vicious circle of mutual fears which neither party was able to extricate itself. Each armed itself to the teeth, and not truth but superior force carried the trophy.

Gandhi argued that the obvious limitations of rationality had led many to advocate violence as the only effective method of fighting untruth or injustice. They agreed that violence was evil but insisted that it was fully justified when used to eliminate a greater evil. Although Gandhi had some sympathy for this view, he was totally opposed to violence as a method of social change. Spontaneous violence under unbearable conditions or grave provocation was one thing; to use it as a matter of deliberate policy was wholly different. First, violence was based on untruth and could never be a means of attaining truth. It dented the fundamental ontological fact that all men were essentially one and that love and goodwill, not hatred and ill-will, were the only valid base of human relationships. It also assumed that some men were so degenerate that they had lost the *atman* and could not be won over by appealing to their fellow-feeling and moral impulse. Gandhi found the assumption arrogant and preposterous.

For Gandhi then rational discussion was the only truthful way to deal with untruth. However, reason was often ineffective in practice. To insist that all matters should be resolved by rational discussion alone was therefore to confront a moral being with the equally unacceptable alternatives of either acquiescing in untruth or resorting to violence. One violated his own integrity, the other that of his opponent; both alike were immoral.

Gandhi thought that his method of satyagraha offered a way out. It combined the patience and persuasive power of reason with the urgency and energy of violence. It respected and reconciled the integrity of the parties involved, tapped and mobilisd their moral and spiritual energies, and paved the way for a better mutual understanding. It also had the futher advantage that unlike violence, it did not replace but complemented reason. It saved it from becoming irrational by locating it within a wider hospitable framework and creating the three basic conditions of rational discussion mentioed earlier. Although often presented as a simple-minded moral method relying on the power of the soul, Gandhi's satyagraha involved an ingenious and complex tripartite strategy based on a fascinating blend of rational discussion, self-imposed suffering and political pressure. The first appealed to the head, the second to the heart, and the third activated both by influencing the structure of power sustaining the relationship between the parties involved.

For Gandhi satyagraha was a surgery of the soul made necessary by the opponents's refusal to talk or to do so in the spirit of humility, sincerity and good-will. Since his psyche had been distorted by hatred, narrow self-interest and such other extra-rational factors, and since his heart had become narrow and hard', he was unable to recognise the other person as a fellow human being whose interests had a moral claim on him. The purpose of satyagraha was to touch his heart, awaken his sense of humanity and activate his moral impulse. He saw the satyagrahi as an enemy or a trouble-maker to be resisted, outwitted or forcibly put down. The satyagrahi refused to reduce himself to that level and accept his misguided definition of their relationship. He saw him instead as a fellow human being, a moral being, whose sense of their common humanity was temporarily eclipsed and which could and must eventually be restored if they were to live together as members of a community. He knew that moral opacity was in no way unique to his opponent. Inhumanity was a shared human predicament, not the monopoly of a few and eliminating the opponent did not reduce but only compounded and intensified it.

4

Non-violence

Gandhi's work seems to put into a new context the perennial debate of whether non-violence is always right or whether violence might sometimes be justified, and if it is, how and when. Gandhi's concept inaugurates a new debate, the content and significance of which has not been captured by previous concepts.

Gandhi calls for a reasoned understanding of the moral ideals of non-violence and its application:

> The virtues of mercy, non-violence, and love in any man can be truly tested only when they are pitied against ruthlessness, violence, hate and untruth. It is incorrect to say that Ahimsa [Skt.-lit., non-killing, non-harming] is of no avail before a murderer. Ahimsa in the face of a murderer is to seek self-destruction. But this is the real test of Ahimsa. It is another matter that our non-violence has not reached such heights. It would be wholly, wrong for us to lower the standard of Ahimsa by reason of our own frailty or lack of experience. Without true understanding of the ideal, we can never hope to reach it. It is necessary for us, therefore, to apply our reason to understand the power of non-violence.

Gandhi's concept, metaphysics, principles of action, methods and criteria are, however, merely part of his mission to propagate non-violence as a practical rejoinder to the commonsense argument for the justified use of violence or force.

It should be noted that Gandhi's absolute practical claim does not translate consistently into the absolute proscription of violence that it logically ought to, and that most believe to be his ultimate value judgment on violence. Our critical study attempts to construct Gandhi's "best case". It represents the fullest account of the position he held as a reflective and self-critical ideologue. But, in fact, it is difficult to say he has the consistency claimed or imputed. Gandhi repeatedly and explicitly makes statements preferring violence to cowardice. He advises violence to his son, were that the only means by which he could protect his mother and sisters, in 1908 in South Africa. Again, he allowed violence to the Indian Government in 1947, in defense of Kashmir, as preferable to injustice and cowardice.

That Gandhi does not in fact give violence an absolute negative value corresponding to the absolute positive value he ascribes to non-violence, reveals an ambivalence in his thought. The positive value he sees in violence must be born in mind throughout the argument. The argument must focus on Gandhi's ideology—but Gandhi the man is often inconsistent with Gandhi the ideologue and moralist.

Non-violence denotes a spiritual force and connotes a related moral ideology. Though Gandhi's work is highly experimental and pragmatic, it is referred to as a "moral ideology". His concept of non-violence is situated in his wider philosophy and moral thought.

The exposition of Gandhi's concept must center on the fact that non-violence denotes a substantive moral and spiritual force—the soul's force. According to Gandhi, non-violence "is a force which is more positive than electricity. At the center of non-violence is a force which is self-acting."

Gandhi writes that just as the soul does not depend on the physical body for its existence, "similarly, non-violence, or soul-force, too, does not need physical aid for its propagation or effect. It acts independently of them. It transcends time and space." His concept and methods are constructed on the basis of attributes and powers he believes to be inherent in that force, and he conceives his activities to be channels for it. Activities that Gandhi describes as non-violent are those whose effectiveness consists in displacing violence by means of soul-force, thus nullifying evil.

Gandhi coined the term non-violence to translate "ahimsa". He writes that non-violence is the greatest and the activist force in the world. One cannot be passively non-violent. In fact non-violence is a term I had to coin in order to bring out the root meaning of ahimsa. In spite of the negative particle 'non', it is no negative force".

The negative construction describes a restraint of expected violence. Gandhi believes this restraint to be the chief and invariable effect of spiritual force. He contrasts this non-violence with un-violence. It should be remembered also that non-violence comes into play only when it comes in contact with violence. One who refrains from violence when there is no occasion for its exercise is simply un-violent and has no credit for his inaction.

Gandhi's reference to truth and non-violence can be described as "Gandhite' ideology and the means of propagating it by actually living these principles". "Violence/non-violence" is the principal dichotomy of Gandhi's moral ideology, and he insists that all analysis proceed in terms of this dichotomy. This is the first characteristic.

The second characteristic is Gandhi's equation of "violence" with "evil". He writes that "in the sense in which I have defended violence its good use is inconceivable." It is on the basis of this equation that Gandhi derives the normative claim that non-violence is always right and its obverse that violence is always wrong.

The third characteristic of Gandhi's ideology is the programmatic aim of demonstrating the universal applicability of non-violence. He claims that it is his "mission to demonstrate that there is no remedy for the many ills of life save that of non-violence."

The fourth characteristic of Gandhi's ideology is his definition of Truth as moral authenticity. Moral authenticity means the effort to bring inner states and outer conduct into congruence by speaking and acting on one's convictions. Gandhi believes that this effort brings into the world the moral equality denoted by Truth, and this justifies his absolute prescription for moral authenticity and forth-rightness.

The fifth characteristic of Gandhi's ideology of non-violence is the equation of truth with non-violence. He usually speaks of non-violence as the means to realize Truth. But since he believes in the convertibility of means and ends in every moral action, Gandhi equates non-violence with the truth that it serves to realize. Conversely, he believes that the truth involved in moral authenticity will surely lead to non-violence. "We have to live a life of Ahimsa in the midst of a world of himsa and that is possible only if we cling to Truth. That is how I deduce Ahimsa from Truth." "Ahimsa is my God, and Truth is my God. When I look for Ahimsa, Truth says 'Find it through me.' When I look for truth, Ahimsa says: 'Find it through me.'

Finally, Gandhi often defers to his definitions to answer arguments. This is a chief characteristic of ideological justification. However, Gandhi uses these definitions also to formulate a course of experimental moral action. He constructs his experiments in terms of the opposition of violence and non-violence (which by his ideological equation are "evil" and "good", respectively). Conversely, he uses the results of his experiments to justify his definitions. This circularity is the first critical point to note.

It is a way of moral-political action for attaining Swaraj for resolving basic social conflicts. For Gandhi, Satyagrha is something more than a method of resistance to particular legal norms; it is an instrument of struggle for positive objectives and for fundamental change. It is non-violent direct action.

Gandhi's political theory cuts across several moral, religious and philosophical traditions and rests on an unusually broad philosophical foundation, showing both the rich harvest that can be garnered from and the problems involved in a cross-cultural dialogue. Enjoying access to several cultures, he is overwhelmed by none of them and is able to carve out an autonomous space from which to evaluate them. Like a multi-lingual novelist skillfully playing with words and images drawn from different languages, Gandhi borrows ideas from different traditions, all of which he regards as part of his common human heritage, and produces ingenious combinations, some unstable, some beautifully integrated, but all fascinating.

He takes over the Hindu concept of Ahimsa, finds its passive and negative aspects. Christian concept of love helps him understand and redefine it. He realizes that love is an emotion, compromises the agent's autonomy and builds up attachments to the world, and so he redefines it in the light of Hindu concept of *anasakti* or detachment. Gandhi's double conversion, his Hinduisation of the Christianised concept, yields the fascinating concept of a non-emotive, serene and detached but positive and active love and non-activist life of action. Although the concepts contain tensions, they are highly suggestive and beyond the reach of either tradition alone. Again, he takes over the Christian concept of vicarious atonement, combines it with the Hindu practice of fasting as a panacea and arrives at the profound notion of fasting as a form of voluntary crucifixion undertaken by amoral leader to atone for, redeem and uplift his temporarily deviant followers.

By ahimsa, Gandhi did not mean merely non-injury to others. That would be a more negative or passive connotation of ahimsa which has also positive or active meaning namely, love or charity. Gandhi writes:

> In its negative form it (ahimsa) means not injuring any living being whether in body or mind. I may not, therefore, hurt the person of any wrong-doer or bear any ill-will to him and so cause him mental suffering. In its positive form, ahimsa means the largest love, the greatest charity. If I am a follower of ahimsa, I must love my enemy or a stranger to me as I would my wrong-doing father or son. This active ahimsa necessarily includes truth and fearlessness.

In the light of what has been said earlier, we may conclude that for Gandhi, action based on the refusal to do harm to others is a negative test of moral or practical truth. Its positive test is action meant to promote the welfare of others. Our desires and interests may be divided into two classes—selfish and unselfish. All selfish desires are immoral, while the desire to improve ourselves for the sake of doing good to others is truly moral. The highest moral law is that we should unremittingly work for the good mankind. We have so far considered two elements of Satyagraha, namely, Satya (truth) and Ahimsa (non-violence).

Gandhi's ultimate aim in all his activities is spiritual realization. Satyagraha is the means by which he hoped ultimately to achieve that aim. However, Gandhi's immediate aim was to establish an abiding thought current and disposition (*sraddha*-lit., "faith"; what one holds onto;) according to Gandhi, a vital faculty cleansing, whetting and informing disciplined reason from the supra-rational standpoint of the Spirit which have the power to conduct one to this ultimate realization.

By "realization" Gandhi does not mean "knowledge" in the empirical or discursive sense. His aim is to come into possession of this spiritual awareness or thought current as a vital and permanent experience, not as a piece of information. This realization and faith are specific to the individual, and so essentially incommunicable. Gandhi believes that complete realization is in fact impossible in the embodied state. But since when Truth obtains means and ends are convertible, and inner and outer states reflect each other, therefore, the accurate and intelligent modeling of oneself and one's environs as an external counterpart of the spiritual reality within is a progressive means to the individual's spiritual self-realization. This produces in physical, emotional and mental life a progressive substitution of Truth for untruth and of soul-force for brute-force. The demonstration of superior moral and practical efficacy becomes for Gandhi a visible, measurable aim expressive of, and a means to, the primary inward spiritual realization, actually its exact outer counterpart.

It is necessary first to understand the aim of spiritual realization that gives the content of Gandhi's entire work. Gandhi describes the realization he seeks as self-realization, God-realization, realization of Truth and *moksa*. He says that such realization means essentially coming into a consciousness of reality which transcends that consciousness given by the five senses and the mind. It is therefore indescribable. This reality is recognized as permanent while all that the senses experience passes away. One who has this realization is more sure and more aware of that existence than of the contents of sensory experience. In contrast, sense experience seems an ephemeral, insubstantial and impotent superimposition on the surface of a changeless substantial potent reality.

Gandhi calls faith, a faculty or sixth sense which can be progressively awakened into cognition of that reality by judicious training and purification.

Gandhi writes that this reality can be called "God" since it is self-active and all-pervading, more vital and more instinct with intelligence than the totality of sensory and mental life. It is possessed of an inborn bliss that is finer and superior to all sensory pleasure, or pleasure of the heart or intellect. It seems to be omnipresent, omniscient, omnipotent and omnibenevolent.

Gandhi ascribes to this Reality, known as God, the attributes of creator *(Brahma)*, and ruler *(Isvara)*. He describes it as a conscious law which combines in its operation intelligence, self-awareness and force, as if law, law-giver and executor were "rolled in one". He identifies this ruler with the sum of *karma* (action and consequences), creatures, or of life, immanent in all existence but also transcendent of it, and he describes it as a oneness or unity that subsists within and sustains all diversity, and that makes "kin" of all existences.

As law or supreme will, Gandhi calls this reality "Fate" that allows freedom of actions but reserves to itself power over results. Gandhi sums up his conception as follows:

> This God whom we seek to realize is Truth. Or to put it another way Truth is God. This Truth is not merely the Truth we are expected to speak. It is that which alone is, which constitutes the stuff of which all things are made, which subsists by virtue of its own power, which is not supported by anything else but supports everything that exists. Truth alone is eternal, everything else is momentary. It need not assume shape or form. It is pure intelligence as well as pure bliss. We call it *Isvara* because everything is regulated by its will. It and the Law it promulgates are one. Therefore it is not a blind Law. It governs the entire universe."

This Truth to be realized is also the God and the power that is the satyagrahi's soul-force. Soul-force originates in that power. Its attributes define points of contact and linkage needed to bring that reality into practical relation with material life.

Each of these attributes is significant for satyagraha because it inheres identically in soul-force which Gandhi asserts is the "decisive factor" in satyagraha. Further, Gandhi structures the entire conception of satyagraha, viz., doctrine, methods and application, on the notion of a living and potent link with this reality, either by direct realization or by cultivation of a vital faith that suppresses the claims of sensory experience and mental dogma.

Gandhi believes that the only means to this realization is exact conduct based on the ideals of Truth and non-violence, progressively refined and strengthened by constant self-examination, application and correction in light of those ideals. Satyagraha denotes an experimental inquiry into the form of non-violent exact conduct for solving every conceivable problem of human relations, and satyagraha thus constitutes a *sadhana* or *karma*, a means of spiritual realization through practical activity.

The non-violent conduct of satyagraha is physical activity the characteristics of which are ideally attributes of the state to be realized—qualities for which one is striving. According to Gandhi, the *sine qua non* of this realization is the establishment in consciouness of an equanimity (as is the *sthitaprajna),* peace and self-sustained joy.

Corresponding to this realization in consciousness is an accession to power and release of force that converts one's material make-up, influences the conduct of others and infects one's surroundings with the same qualities of equanimity, power and joy. This realizational and transformational capability of non-violent conduct is the potent core of satyagraha.

Satyagraha translates as "holding to Truth", to which Gandhi, as author of the term, adds, "in thought, word and deed" according to his concepts of Truth and non-violence. Exact conduct denotes the physical aspect of this "holding to Truth". As the focus of the entire concept and method, its practice changes one's attitude and outlook. The entire material existence and all practical activities become a vehicle both of the expression and the realization of God known as Truth.

Gandhi claims to see God face-to-face in the spinning wheel, service to the untouchables and the principle of Hindu-Muslim unity. Thus Gandhi believes that realization of Truth progresses in step with the widening scope of the practical application of non-violence through that exact non-violent conduct. The form of this practical expression of realization is self-dedication in reform, redress and service, and in non-retaliation when these activities are resisted. Since for Gandhi the full realization of Truth is an eschatological problem, the focus for the study of satyagraha must be on the means for its progressive approximation in material and practical life.

Because Gandhi's moral ideal of Truth requires that means and ends be convertible, the progressive effort to approximate the practical to the ideal by means of exact conduct will increasingly confer the ideal qualities of spiritual reality on the material elements and energies. Since spiritual Truth is all-inclusive, therefore its practical means should be universal and infallible. Thus an essential component of Gandhi's efforts for spiritual realization is the program to demonstrate that only the translation of non-violence to exact conduct and non-retaliation as satyagraha is capable of the universal application and perfect practical efficacy implied in the progressive realization of Truth.

This radical practical claim constitutes the differentia between Gandhi's satyagraha and all other methods of non-violent action. Non-retaliation as the chief expression and principal mechanism of soul-force applies without exception to all empirical dimensions of activity, so it provides the absolute core of exact conduct in satyagraha. Physical non-retaliation is a visible *sine qua non*, Gandhi stresses the difficulty of specifying this claim because of the number of unknown factors involved in any religious movement, the unanalyzable complexity of human action, the invisibility of the mass of spiritual effects and the lack of a defined means of measurement in spiritual matters. But Gandhi insists that satyagraha holds true without exception or qualification, independent of any conceivable conditions of application.

Gandhi asserts that inapplicability is always the result of ignorance of the actual application conditions, and that faithful inspection of them and examination of oneself in terms of the ideals of Truth and non-violence will invariably reveal the true conditions. If these ideals are in fact the law of life as Gandhi believes, then he can know *a priori* that there will never be a set of material conditions, whether physical, psychological, social or political, for which exact conduct in terms of those ideals cannot be prescribed, and which would fulfill those conditions and bring the laws of Truth and non-violence into manifest practical operation.

Gandhi claimed that these principles are not his original discovery. The most ancient and time honored texts of all religions were based on the same laws. He only made new experiments with them on as vast a scale as possible. This effort merely constituted his mission to demonstrate their universal validity and thus to propagate their use. The critical debate over their validity centers on his extensions in the scope of the practical application of non-violence.

Gandhi believes that non-violence is a law not only for highly qualified spiritual practicants, but even more so for the common man. "Treat all as one's brother," could not be a command only for the specially qualified individual.

Gandhi extends this principle to include relations among groups and nations. He reasons that if it is the law of life, then it should he applicable everywhere and in any manner, towards anyone and through everyone. Gandhi lists the fields of this extended experimentation as non-violence against abuses by constituted authority, against dacoity and criminal culture, against communal conflicts and rioting and against invading armies. Self-defense, defense of one's ward or entrusted property and national defense are test cases since they involve direct jeopardy to one's own life, and since they imply the clearest and strongest opposition by overt violence. Gandhi does not hesitate to claim that in these cases as well, non-violent resistance is more efficient than the violent methods it replaces. Gandhi's claim is that satyagraha, relying on soul-force, is a complete substitute for methods of violence relying on brute-force.

For Gandhi, this external aspect of spiritual realization, while no less important than its internal aspect, is subordinate to it as means to ends. The form of the means will change with circumstances and spiritual growth. Gandhi writes that his politics were a wage on his pilgrimage of spirit, and that his involvement in demonstrating the validity of non-violence in the political field was dictated by the fact that his work in social service and social reform involved him in politics and political reform. He states also that his politics were universal because they had to do with inner growth, and that being universal and operating at this fundamental level, they were naturally peculiarly effective.

The basic sources for Gandhi's investigations were the *Upanisads* and the *Bhagavad Gita*. According to Gandhi, the *Upanisads* provide a compendium of spiritual knowledge, and the *Gita* elaborates the means by which that knowledge may be gained through practical action and daily activity. The *Upanisads* provide the root concepts of that elaboration.

Gandhi viewed the Upanisadic texts as a record of their authors' experiments in the spiritual field. These are the oldest and most catholic such inquiries we have, and Gandhi considered their conclusions to be verified by the conforming experience of sixty years of his own research, and by the similar findings of numerous co-workers. Many by reason and experience have thought the Upanisads to report metaphysical investigations without equal, model philosophical and scientific treatises both in content and expression. Gandhi claimed that his satyagraha merely continued the researches reported in those texts. Gandhi speaks of his mission of non-violence and Truth as teaching the people to leave the ephemeral and seek the Real.

In these texts the distinction between the material and the spiritual translates as that of the ephemeral and the permanent or Real. The Upanisads teach what constitutes the Real, what constitutes the ephemeral and what is the relation between them. This is the principal distinction for understanding Gandhi's metaphysical analysis of the realization of Truth and his metaphysical interpretation of logical principles that he uses to aid that realization through mental understanding.

Satyagraha is based on the Upanisadic analysis of reality as *atmabrahma*, which Gandhi translates as *satya*, Truth. There are two aspects of Reality: *atman*, essential self-conscious reality, single but thought of as many from the point of view of the individuals who comprise its external but non-separate parts; and *brahman*, the "large" or "full" all-inclusive reality of the Absolute, also self-conscious but rather of itself as the individual Whole, the Body composed of, and the materials composing, all the externalized *atmans*- phenomenal individuals.

The key to the Upanisadic analysis of Reality is the identity of these two aspects and their total non-difference in ultimate reality, a transcendental identity undefinable except relatively through these two aspects. The key to Gandhi's satyagraha is the set of logical principles that he derives from this identity, and the categorical difference between Truth and Reality thus realized and the finite truth and reality apprehended in empirical consciousness.

The basic features of Upanisadic reality as Gandhi perceives them are as follows: The eternality of the Absolute corresponds to the immortality of the soul; their realization as such is not the result of any *karma* (action) since the infinite and eternal reality cannot be seen by means of a finite and ephemeral body. They are therefore beyond good and evil (which are attributes of action), unless those actions are being judged good or evil relatively to realization of *atmabrahma*. The content of the realization of *atmabrahma* is the consciousness of one's infinite self-existence as the Eternal, the Infinite, made of absolute power or existence, absolute intelligence or consciousness and absolute bliss, *sat-cit-ananda*.

The Upanisads also analyze reality more abstractly as Being *(sat)* and not-being (asat), and as Truth *(satyam)* beyond these both. Gandhi considers Truth, *satyam*, to be the best designation of God or Reality. He finds *sat* the designation most useful for aiding his own realization, so far as this relies on preparation of consciousness by serious thought. To Gandhi, *satyam* comprehends all aspects of reality, i.e., spiritual, metaphysical, logical, psychological, scientific and ethical.

Gandhi derives his logico-metaphysical principles as follows: *atmabrahma* can be pointed to only negatively as the complete or full Truth *(satya)* to which all contradictory predicates refer equally, but which is real beyond the grasp of any such dual notion (being and non-being), and so is essentially indescribable. Its unique logical status may be appreciated by the process of negating every possible predication by *"neti, neti."* (not this, nor this). His logical principles are derived from this inapplicability of any predicates because affirmation would exclude the predicates' opposite and inclusion of all contradictories is the logical property that is special and unique to*atmabrahma,*

Through the Upanisadic equation of *atmabrahma* the equation of the microcosm with the macrocosm becomes a fundamental principle of explanation and discovery. Gandhi takes the Upanisadic formula, *yatha pinde tatha brahmande*,- "as within, so without", "as the atom, so the universe", "as here, so there"-as the basic positive formula of Truth when Truth appears in dual or plural form, as it does to empirical observation.

From this principle the Upanisads derive the methods of scientific inference—knowing the large by examining the small, knowing the far by examining the near and knowing the unfamiliar by examining the known. They derive logical principles of analogy, negation, extrapolation and interpolation, and these become the central principles of spiritual investigation by reversing the direction of inquiry from outside to within.

Gandhi writes that all one needs to know is "as without, so within". The outer world may be known by looking within, since the same totality of Reality is comprehended in either direction. Moreover, the totality is directly accessible only to consciousness within since only there is consciousness independent of the limiting adjuncts of the subtle material instruments of empirical knowledge and discursive understanding, viz., apperception and individuating ego-sense *(ahankara)*, discriminating intelligence *(buddhi)*, conceptualizing mind *(manas)*, perceiving senses *(jnanendriya)*, and motor senses *(karmendriya)*,

Gandhi expressed his growing appreciation of the Upanisadic formula, *brahma satyam jagan mithya*, "*Brahma*, Spirit, alone is Real, True; all else, the World, is unreal, false". By affirming all value of Truth only to the Spirit and denying all value of Truth to the phenomenal reality, this formulation directly turns consciousness away from material limited reality towards the spiritual unlimited reality. Since this equation is equivalent to the identity equation "as here, so there", one can substitute any empirical expression for world, and any attribute connoting changelessness or ultimacy or uniqueness or completeness, for *brahma*.

In each application of the formula, "*brahma satyam*". "performs the function of "*neti, neti*". Through any specific predication and knowledge content this formula annuls the entire empirical reality as essentially illusion while simultaneously affirming its substantial reality as no different from *brahma* known anywhere else through any other predicate and knowledge content.

By this process of logical substitution Gandhi translates the "material/spiritual" distinction to the "ephemeral/real" and "illusory/ true" distinctions, and by the process of reversal and substitution, he constructs his concept of non-violence. These substitutions, positive and negative, are not merely abstract and logical, they are interpreted through the spiritual view of reality. In that view, the "violence" that is negated in the term "non-violence" refers to an entire category which includes all material existence, all phenomenal reality.

Thus the Upanisadic logical principles Gandhi uses are metaphysically informative and create a potent current of faith, only when the primary term is contemplated as unrealized by oneself though known by those who have realization, while the derivative term, though familiar, is contemplated as essentially unknown.

Gandhi connects his aims of spiritual realization and the demonstration of his practical claim by a similar logico-metaphysical interpretation of the pragmatic distinction between ends and means. This interprets *"yatha pinde"* from the practical standpoint. From the standpoint of the ideal, all reality is one uniform, vital substance, and from that standpoint, whatever reality is comprehended as means will be found to be identical with whatever reality is comprehended as ends. From the standpoint of Truth all predication, including ends and means, is false.

Gandhi's peculiar ideological interpretation adds to this spiritual pragmatism of the Upanisads the moral prescription of *satyagraha* that one ought always to act so as to reveal in the "means" its intrinsic identity with the "ends", and so in every action to strive to manifest the truth of *"yatha pinde"*, and *"brahmasatyam "*. This is the aim of his non-violent exact conduct.

Gandhi derives his program for the demonstration of his practical claims for non-violence from these considerations of the Upanisadic principles of Truth. By action in terms of true practical ends-means relations something of the Truth is manifested by success *(siddhi)*, and in the theory of *satyagraha*, this accumulating demonstration of practical success is inherent in the application of a pure spiritual principle. Truth is a force whose attributes include the power to unfailingly determine a true ends-means relation by action on true principles; this is the definition of Gandhi's morally exact conduct.

Thus Gandhi finds in the Upanisads a moral connection between one's orientation towards Truth and the means of spiritual realization. He writes that the materialist believes that desire makes one seek the knowledge which is necessary for its fulfillment; so the materialist believes that the multiplication of wants leads one progressively towards knowledge of the infinite. The spiritualist believes just the opposite. He believes that no accumulation of finite empirical information can give realization of the infinite. Reduction of wants, which by nature thrive on difference, is the correct preparation for realization of Truth. Truth reveals itself when there is not the empirical superimposition that desire inherently produces.

Although Gandhi derived the central means and core doctrines of satyagraha primarily from the *Gita* on the basis of logico-metaphysical analysis, he later believed that the first verse *(mantra)* of the *Iso Upanisad* contains the essence of the *Gita* and of all the Upanisads. He believed this single verse was the best means of teaching people Truth and non violence. Gandhi interprets this verse as: "God has created out of himself all that there is and is himself its Ruler (Is*vara)*. Renounce it all, since it truly is not yours, and then you should enjoy what your Father will give you for your needs and duties. Do not covet the possessions of your brothers."

This interpretation of renunciation, and the logico-metaphysical extension of the spiritual fact that existing beings constitute a conscious family, are the two key bases of Gandhi's doctrine of realization and demonstration. Renunciation is prescribed as a means to a second birth into spiritual awareness inasmuch as it is intended to lead to a detachment from the entire empirical and illusory reality. To Gandhi the verse advises "trusteeship" of what is given, and its use in service of all as the means of this renunciation. The type of the renunciation is implied in the ideas of the brotherhood of man and the fatherhood of God, and in the principle of non-covetousness. The second birth attained by such renunciation is thus a birth into the one universal spiritual family.

In sum, the verse suggests a practical means to realize the infinite. The means is renunciation based on an outlook that recognizes the facts of one's spiritual origins in Truth, or soul, and one's spiritual relation to all creation as one's family. Without knowledge that there is a favorable state to be attained and that one is in a comparatively unfavorable state, no realization of a greater reality is possible.

Gandhi believes that the Upanisadic texts give the necessary impetus and direction. He believes that the arguments presented in those texts represent experienced-realized knowledge and have the flavor of reality. They bring one to conscious recognition of one's ignorance as a "plight", and they give faith in the possibility of a way of its amelioration. The texts give the assurance that "Truth (as the only reality} shall prevail" *(satyam eva jayate).*

Gandhi believes that serious and faithful study of the texts bring one to feel the need of disillusionment and transmit the triumphant quality of the declaration *"satyam eva jayate"*; this creates the current of faith that is the basis of satyagraha. These all combine to create a real impetus and urge to reach those states and realize the Truth the Upanisads proclaim.

Besides knowledge of the state to be realized and recognition that one ought to realize it, the votary needs scientific knowledge of the condition he is in and what it is for that state to be negated.

The Upanisads describe the normal state of self-identity as the ego-complex of knowing, willing and feeling centered in the material elements of body, senses, mind and intellect. This ego state manifests as arrogation of individual existence and doership and as desire of possession.

Although the material elements of this complex successively dissolve at death, a subtle storage capability in the soul persists as the repository of experience and qualities gained through these material vehicles. Experiences are assimilated and the seed of a new personality is put forth, suitable to the soul's further evolution. This causal structure creates a new ego structure. This structure connects up with a body appropriate to its karmas and continues its illusory experience as an ultimate separate entitative consciousness.

Gandhi accepts this account of transmigration and the perpetuation of illusion. He defines *moksa,* liberation as the culmination of realization of one's true status as soul. This recognition has the power to cut through the ego-centered illusion and annul the consciousness which identifies itself with the structures whose laws of transformation constitute the process of transmigration. The state of ignorance and illusion depends on maintaining and periodically reconstituting the provisional ego structure.

Gandhi notes that this recognition is essential to satyagraha because one cannot have use of his own soul-force if he has no vital recognition of his spiritual status. He is like the "lion raised among lambs" and so cannot resort to his true lion-nature even for self-defense. The primary illusion and cause of its continuation is the belief that one is himself the doer of action, and is therefore, by the law of karma, perpetually entangled in nature's reactions to his actions.

The law of karma says that for the entire category of material or phenomenal reality, characterized by constant motion of actions and qualities, every action has its opposite and equal reaction, all forces of any transaction are conserved in the resultant; and in any transaction, quality is preserved through the chain of actions and consequences.

The soul, by means of the ego-body structure, misidentifies itself with some point in the causal nexus and believes itself to be an originator of actions. This creates innumerable relative points of view and agency in the material field. They are sustained by that illusion in consciousness which causes the misidentification. This misidentification allows the flow of the soul's force, the power of reality, to repeatedly cause to coalesce an ego-agent structure. This structure in turn propagates actions that conserve its energies in binding reactions and transferences of qualities. Thus the soul continues in the illusion.

Gandhi believes that recognition of the nature of this moving and changing reality and especially of the triviality of its isolated passing events, is "more than half the battle" in reidentifying with one's true nature and escaping the illusion of separate mortal existence. Study of this knowledge given by the Upanisads accomplishes this change in both perception and outlook and thus gives new values and feelings, and, consequently, a new orientation towards reality and a new basis to action and practical life. This disillusionment and reorientation based on the deeper facts of individuality, personality and evolving soul, is a significant second step in the process of spiritual realization.

Gandhi insists that satyagraha is a continuation of the line of researches represented in the Upanisads so far as they are guides on a path of progressive realization that is essentially experimental and experiential in nature. The texts present a mounting awareness of more comprehensive, deeper and subtler realities, and a liberating culmination. They present a map of the progressive stages leading to that realization.

Gandhi considers these texts to be uniformly testable by reason and experience, since they are based on reason and experience, and to be scientific since they lead to uniform spiritual experience when similarly applied. He asserts that this general validity of the texts is demonstrated hy the uniform transformation in the conduct of those who, with a critically reasoned faith, apply those texts to their daily lives.

Gandhi thus believes that without applying this knowledge to pursuit of Truth in activity, there is no occasion to pursue or to swerve from Truth, and so there is no occasion to test one's realization and apprehension. Though what Gandhi calls Truth is by definition eternal and its laws uniform and unchanging, its correct application is always a matter for fresh experiment. Material reality is by nature constant activity, changing quality and ephemeral structure. Application conditions and the actual operation of Truth must be a matter of judgment and discovery so long as one is embodied and identified with the ego-agent complex as the doer of actions in such a material field.

Gandhi considers the Bhagavad Gita to be a commentary on the *Isa Upanisad*, in that it shows how to give "eternal verities" active shape in practical actions that lead to spiritual realization. The problem in devising satyagraha, defined from the Upanisadic point of view, is thus the metaphysical and scientific problem of substituting the real for the ephemeral by means of practical activity. Gandhi based his satyagraha explicitly on the Gita. He studied it daily for almost sixty years, and he considered the Gita to be his "dictionary of conduct".

But Gandhi did not find in the Gita a "code of conduct" to be blindly applied. To him the Gita gives the findings of an experienced Krishna, both a king and as The Master of Yoga of the Vedic-Upanisadic tradition. These findings take the form of an analysis of the state to be realized, the realities to be spanned, the human condition of bondage and the universal principles of action, *anasakti* (non-attached action) and *yajna* (action of sacrifice).

Gandhi believes that this analysis, similarly to that of the Upanisads, is presented as universal and scientific findings based on realizable fact. They cannot be correctly interpreted aside from application and experience in the medium of action. He believes that here, as in any matter of Truth, experience is the final guide and criterion, and he claims to cite only verses the Truth of which he himself had realized in experience.

Gandhi claims that his doctrines of satyagraha, though originally derived from the *Gita* and the *Upanisads*, stand on their own, independently of the texts, as any reasoned and scientific knowledge must do. He cites the canons of trained and sober reason, of disciplined and refined moral sense when reason can be applied, and of faith in the uniform experience of trusted guides or companions where understanding involves states of awareness not accessible to mind and intellect in their present state of evolution, or to senses where facts are not deducible from phenomenal experience.

In applying the Gita analysis for his satyagraha investigations, Gandhi gives a moral interpretation of the distinction between the ephemeral and the real by equating evil with the ephemeral and material, and good with the real and spiritual. The Gita is a 700-verse text set in the 100,000-verse *Mahabharata* epic. Gandhi interprets this epic as an allegory of the ascent of the soul through its history in human evolution. To him it represents the battle between the forces of good and evil that incessantly goes on within the individual.

This inner moral battle is the context in which satyagraha must be understood since it is from this battle of good with evil that Gandhi evolved the doctrine and method of satyagraha as a means to realize the state beyond good and evil, beyond the life and state of alternating happiness and suffering. Since the battle is within and perpetual, the Gita's principles must apply to every act, and the exact conduct of satyagraha must be based on these same principles.

The Gita depicts the beginning of the great war to save justice and civilization, in which the protagonist, Arjuna, a prince and a chief warrior for the force of justice, shrinks on seeing his nearest relations, teachers and friends in the opposing army. Arjuna is required by duty, as warrior in a righteous war *(dharmayuddha)*, to kill these relatives, companions, teachers and elders.

Arjuna brings the arguments that those he would have to kill are those for whom alone he would want to win the kingdom. His victory would serve no purpose and lose all taste from his standpoint. Killing one's relatives is the worst of sins. Its consequences would be ruin of the family and destruction of custom, tradition and the total moral order that rests on the family structure and kin affinities. There could be no justification for this sin considering consequences both for himself and for the social order. Even if the enemy were guilty, it is out of ignorance. The wise, knowing better, should rather accept death without resistance as a noble course. Arjuna appeals to Krishna for guidance. But the bow slips from his hands and he says he cannot fight.

Krishna upbraids him as a coward in order to bring him back to his real character and to awaken him to his duty as a warrior for the side of right, who must fight without regard to personal ties. Krishna gives a short argument from the Upanisads to relieve Arjuna from guilt of sin that he believes would result from killing kin. The soul is immortal and untouched by any action while bodies are continually born and destroyed in the natural course of things. The knower neither slays nor is slain-only bodies kill and are killed. All embodied beings will die. Arjuna, performing his duty, fighting for justice at the threat of its annihilation from the world, will not only not sin and incur demerit in the present war, but he will have glory in heaven if he dies fighting, and victory and glory on earth if he wins.

Sin and ignominy lie rather in abandonment of duty and righteousness. The real moral order is sustained by duty and justice, not by institutions among bodies. Hence there is only the fight to be carried through. Arjuna should take pleasure and pain, loss and gain, victory and defeat as equal, and fight. These all belong to the body and have no lasting value. They only cloud the apprehension of duty and right.

Krishna promises Arjuna also that this fight with the attitude of detachment in duty is not only not sin, but it is right action in this world, and it is the means of realizing the supreme state beyond all opposites, beyond all qualities and beyond all activity and bondage.

Krishna enunciates the key principle of the *sadhana* or *yoga* of karma "Your right is to work only, but never to the fruit thereof. Let not the fruit of action be your object, nor let your attachment be to inaction". Krishna tells Arjuna that equanimity, sameness towards all material concomitants and consequences of action, frees one from bondage and brings him to the "blissful supreme state of brahma."

On the basis of his logical principle *"yatha pinde"*, Gandhi equates the outer and inner moral battles. But on the basis of his moral ideology, he gives the equation a bias and says that the "real" battle is within, and that the Gita does not teach fighting war as such. It teaches self-examination and struggle with one's ego-desire" self.

Gandhi interprets the opening scene of the Gita as depicting the origin of conflict. Arjuna does not refuse to fight on principle but from attachment to his relatives and friends. Gandhi writes in his commentary on the Gita that the root of evil is the ego-sense which puts pride of self, "I", and pride of possession and power, "mine", behind all acts.

The Gita locates the seat of evil in the mind, intellect and senses. Gandhi says that the root of sin is ignorance of one's true nature as soul beyond sin. To be beyond sin is to be rooted in that true nature and therefore to be unswayed by the activity of intellect, mind and senses that are most often merely the vehicles for realizing the claims of "I" and "mine". Gandhi finds these claims to be the cause of all conflict. The empirical "Is" contend over ephemeral objects that by nature cannot be possessed equally and simultaneously by two "Is" who each wants to enjoy them exclusively. It is the ego-sense that imposes the distinction between relatives and strangers or the enemy.

This corresponds to the tendency in the human mind to like or dislike, to be attracted or repulsed, on an arbitrary basis, due to the narrowed focus of consciousness and reason. Gandhi believes that the solution to this conflict is ridding the mind and senses of their inborn tendencies, thus removing the ego's imposition of "I" and "mine" that sustains and is sustained by those tendencies.

If the origin of conflict is this indiscriminate and arbitrary distinction and untruth, partiality and injustice, then the means of its resolution is the establishment of Truth wherein all interests are viewed and protected equally. Gandhi finds in the Gita's theory of action the science of materially accomplishing this substitution of Truth (Peace) for conflict.

Arjuna's dejection and despondency are the result of a confusion about duty. It comes from ignorance. Duty as the Truth of action and relations is clear so long as there are no personal considerations. Duty is spontaneous. But when there is an upsurge of ego and desire which is not in accordance with Truth, confrontation and conflict result—usually bolstered and augmented on both sides by untruth and self-deception, as reason aligns with ego to justify desire.

Action is demanded by circumstances and by Arjuna's previous actions and commitments, but because of attachment his energies go out of balance with Truth, inner complexity is created, he is bound to the extent of paralysis and cannot act. In such circumstances the human condition of bondage becomes evident. For Gandhi the importance of the Gita is in its demonstration that the natural condition of all human action is perpetuation of bondage in ignorance born of ego and desire.

As in his interpretation of the Upanisads, Gandhi notes that the first condition of seeking knowledge is recognition of ignorance, of one's condition of bondage and of the need for liberation. The Gita depicts this same state from the standpoint of action and of the common experience of conflict between duty and desire.

Fear and attachment predominate in this state of ignorance even when there is no overt conflict between the demands of duty and desire. The elements of the ego-desire complex are never at rest; conflict is their nature, and visible violence is incipient, maintaining a constant subliminal tension always on the verge of manifesting. The Gita teaches the method of renunciation, as does the *Isa Upanisad*, for escaping bondage and realizing Truth.

Gandhi finds that, in both the Upanisads and the Gita, knowledge completes action and only action based on Truth can accomplish its projected purposes. Likewise, the acts of renunciation of the *Isa Upanisad* and the Gita are only effective when there is knowledge of the deeper and wider factors involved in the action.

What is true of the physical aspects of action is true equally of the spiritual aspects, as indicated by "*yatha pinde* ". Renunciation can only be effective if there is knowledge of the state to be attained by the renunciation, knowledge of the relation between that state and the present one and conscious self-awareness of what constitutes the renunciate or sacrificial character of one's action.

In Gandhi's interpretation of Truth, if Truth obtains, the two are actually aspects of the same reality; when the subjective material state is not a knowledge-state, and more than an habitual response is called for by circumstances, states of dejection and paralysis are the natural result. The Gita's purpose is to inculcate the knowledge and wisdom needed to prevent this condition. This understanding functions in the process of realization itself and Gandhi notes that without practice and experience it does not become a part of the subjective make-up. A dogmatic understanding cannot make it a vital part of the subtle subjective material state and therefore an effective factor either in practical reason or in the action. Building of the knowledge-state and the true knowledge content are one and the same process.

The Gita gives a categorical analysis of the phenomenal field in which all activity has its origin and propagates its effects. Based on this characterization of the whole field as a singular unit, the Gita then gives an analysis of the state of non-doership and the detached mode of action that achieves it.

In the Gita there are five main analyses of the condition of bondage that are important from the standpoint of satyagraha. Liberation is described for each distinction as non-attachment from that point of view through the two fundamental characteristics of *sthitaprajna*—evenness of temperament and equality of treatment, with regard to all that is described under that distinction.

The fundamental mechanism of bondage is always ignorance of the true nature of the binding elements and processes and of the way they are actually operating in the individual and the situation, and of the reactive mode of action that this ignorance sustains. The final means of release is always realization of the reality beyond this condition by detachment with knowledge and faith.

One is swayed by hot and cold, pleasure and pain, success and failure, virtue and sin, merit and demerit, honor and dishonor, etc. Truth cannot be known where these dualities pull the understanding in different directions. These are characteristics of merely individual states and actions and therefore create forces contrary to those of non-individuated reality. One who is established in atman, in Truth, is *nirdvandva* (without dualities) and is called a *yogi*.

The Gita gives general and complex analyses of action, conduct and knowledge in terms of the *gunas*. It analyzes the empirical ego as a material formation sustained by a concatenation of forces which may be described in terms of the proportions of these *gunas*. The ego and passions appear to be causes, but are themselves only limited movements of the *gunas* of *prakrti*. These in turn are produced and controlled by the divine *maya* (creative power and delusion, mystery).

Satyagraha is based on the surrender and nullification of ego. This nullification, according to Gandhi, allows God's plan and power to work manifestly through the satyagrahi. Gandhi derives this doctrine directly from the Gita in analysis of action as the independent interplay of the gunas and material forces. This analysis is repeated many times in the Gita in order to make clear from many points of view, the principle of the non-doership of the soul.

This argument is summed up in the concluding chapter of the Gita. Gandhi gives the core of the analysis as follows:

> There are three things that inspire action: knowledge, the object of knowledge, and the knower. And there are three constituents of action: the organ, the deed, and the doer. The thing to be done is the object of knowledge; the method of doing it is the knowledge; and he who knows is the knower. After he has thus received an impulse to action, he performs an action in which the senses serve as instruments. Thought is thus translated into action.

The possible forms of interactions of these elements ;are described in terms of the three gunas. Thus if one is truly the soul, then he is free to separate himself from bondage in the circle of karmas by realizing that the ego really is no cause of results at all. Gandhi completes his paraphrase of the argument in terms of the analysis of the causes of action and consequences:

> He who does not abandon the fruits of action, must enjoy or put up with the natural consequences of his own acts, and is thus a bond-slave for ever. But he who gives up the fruits of action, achieves freedom. And why should a man feel attachments for action? It is idle for anybody to imagine that he himself is a doer. There are five causes for the accomplishment of all actions, namely, this body, the doer, the various instruments, efforts, and, last but by no means the least, Providence."

The last cause, Providence, is at the center of Gandhi's anasakti and satyagraha. Gandhi writes repeatedly that no action is complete aside from God's completion of it. The activity of the ego-body complex is only a reflection of the divine will. The divine will, "the Inscrutable One" here called "Fate", is the sum of incalculable other factors that conspire to produce any given resultant of action.

Gandhi concludes:

> Realizing this, a man should give up pride. He who does something without egoism, may be said to be not doing it in spite of his doing it, for he is not bound by his action, a humble man, has reduced himself to zero.

In the Gita's analysis of the attached state there is an escalation of self-tearing which leads to self-destruction. By brooding on objects of sense, attachment is born. This special contact repeats itself as there is occasion and becomes desire, an active seeking. This desire, inevitably and invariably frustrated, turns back on itself to become anger. Anger clouds the mind and leads to stupefication, which leads to loss of memory. Loss of memory disables reason, and with destruction of reason, the individual is destroyed.

The point at which to break the chain is at the level of the senses before attachment develops. Control of the senses is the recommended practice to break the chain and make reason steady. But this self-control is known to be a very difficult and dubious process. The Gita says even the wise are swept away by the sense currents. We are born with and develop sensory and mental tendencies or habits before the process of self-control can begin.

It was previously noted that desire and anger are the causes of sin, even for one who knows their nature. They are constituted of the gunas and reside in the organs of knowledge which are also constituted of gunas. The goal is to reach beyond the gunas, but the organs of knowledge and of action are constitutionally incapable of this emancipation.

The Gita solves the dilemma by pointing out the paths of knowledge and devotion. If one constantly turns the mind to remembrance of *Isvara*, it cannot get stuck in the objects of sense. By the law of *purusakara-karma*—you become what you do, believe, or yearn after—whose exercise is *abhyasa*, devoted practice, this remembrance would bring vision of that Divine Reality. That realization has the power to burn up the ego structure and the lower tendencies that it supports.

Further, the Gita ranges the subjective organs strategically in an ascending order and advises their progressive enlistment in the fight against sin. The senses *(indriyas)* are more subtle and powerful than sense objects; the mind *(manas)* more subtle and powerful than the senses; the intellect *(buddhi)* more subtle and powerful than the mind; desire, the enemy, is subtler and more powerful even than this *buddhi.* But the soul is the "subtlemost"and most powerful reality, and by confidence, or faith in oneself, the force of the soul can be drawn down and used to attack the enemy, desire and anger, in his camp, the mind, intellect and senses, and to destroy the subjective convolutions and complexes in which those tendencies and qualities inhere.

But one who is constantly called upon to act in daily life may not be able to develop this practice. Gandhi says that the Gita prescribes renunciation of the fruits of action as a universal duty, and as the means to achieve the state of detachment. He claims that this striving is man's sole obligation. It is in this state that soul-force becomes the natural instrument of action and of spiritual realization and a part of one's constant consciousness as such.

Anasaktiyoga, the gospel of selfless action, is Gandhi's interpretation of the Gita's doctrine of renunciation. The votary renounces the fruit of his actions and thus exhausts the externally binding, material interests since their continued strength requires the exercise of pursuing those fruits. The votary completes the external renunciation by dedicating the actions to *Isvara*. He renounces his internal makeup as well by the attitude of surrender of mind and soul to the *brahma (brahmasamarpana).*

In its positive form, detached action consists of *yajna*, sacrifice. This is the principal concept in the Gita's analysis of non-binding action, or action that leads to realization. The Gita states that only action for sacrifice does not bind. The ego-sense limits interest to satisfaction of material inclinations of the individual structure. This is a denial of Truth.

The Gita's analysis of the field, *kshetra*, includes the fact that with creation of material existence, sacrifice was born as the inherent tendency and urge to interdependence. The movement of *prakrti* is a reflection of the total benevolence of its creator. Every movement is geared to the benefit of all. The laws by which actions bear fruit and bring knowledge inhere in nature and consciousness. According to Gandhi, action that accords with that law and will is service to the entire creation. Action prompted by the ego-sense is necessarily in conflict with the law of sacrifice and operates to favor only the individual.

Only action devoid of ego-sense will exhaust its energies in the act since such action will address the fullest reality of its field and objective. When ego interferes, most of the energy of the action will be only incidental to the ego's intentions, and its actions will so far draw reactions, not foreseen nor prepared for, and these will necessarily bind the doer in externality. This is the self-bondage of attachment to material consequences of action for which one has to remain embodied or take up new bodies that can receive these consequences and exhaust the potentialities created by earlier actions.

Gandhi finds in the Gita the satyagraha doctrine of self-purification by which the votary seeks to reduce the ego-sense to zero and become an instrument of the divine will. This requires the intelligent renunciation and the obedience to divine law that lifts consciousness to the realized state of *anasakti yoga*, the detached soul. This state makes action the spontaneous response of the subjective organs and body to the divine will which is presiding over every force that impinges on them. Gandhi considers the process of conscious sacrifice, the balanced use of mental, physical and spiritual faculties in service of all, to be the *sine qua non* of the path of self-purification, the ascent to knowledge and the final realization. He finds here the practical means to realize the first verse of the *Iso Upanisad*.

Anasakti and yajna form the inner and outer conditions of unerringly perceiving and following duty. Action stemming from duty is action that reflects the Truth. One follows the method of renunciation of fruits by assuming the attitude of detachment and sacrifice in which there is no scope for personal consideration of consequences and concomitants. Duty or Truth become the natural mode of one's activity.

Yajna has value because in it means and ends are convertible. It is self-sustained and self-contained action. The key is renunciation of fruits. Sacrifice is both a means to realization and the reflection of that realization when it is achieved as the end. If there is desire for fruit, e.g., reward for virtue of sacrifice or duty, then the action loses the quality it was valued for—convertibly both means and end of realization, Truth—there is now an extraneous end involved. Such an action does not fulfill the definition of Gandhi and the Gita as inspired by modes of knowledge able to purify action of its binding capabilities.

It is significant for Gandhi's ideology and satyagraha that in the Gita's analysis of action as sacrifice, sacrifice is continued after realization of the end. Sacrifice is thereafter purely a means for corporate realization, while it had been only partially so on the way to the individual's realization. Realization is not the end as such. A basic principle of satyagraha is propagation of Truth, directly via the inner state of the realized actor, and indirectly via external apprehension by the unrealized votary and opponent. The Gita teaches the propriety of continuing to act on the means even when the ends seemed to have been realized. Similarly, according to Gandhi's ideology, since detachment and duty are part of the means of sacrifice and devotion, conversely they aid in establishing detachment and duty. Achievement of a perpetual dynamic state and activity of pure sacrifice is the end, not any static achievement, or objective.

Those who follow the path of action and devotion, having abolished the ego-sense, having burnt up all impelling sense and mental impressions, and feeling no lack since fulfilled by the source of bliss from within, remain active in activities of sacrifice, totally detached. They serve as an exemplar to others of the means by which their own spiritual realization may be furthered and completed. Gandhi adds that such a life exhibits also the highest beauty—the special beauty of Truth itself. We may know it, in part, as "moral beauty" of satyagraha. Satyagraha postulates that the actions of a realized being have the power to reveal that Truth into which he has merged himself.

In an age of action, eternal principles must meet the problems of action and the active modern life. Gandhi considers the purpose of religion to be the spiritualizing of the mundane; to him this is equivalent to "true happiness" and "true beauty". But with the Gita he believes that no other action than sacrificial (sacred) action can free one from bondage and painful qualities; sacrifice is the core of religion. Gandhi considers the principles of detachment and sacrifice to be eternal laws of conscious being, but the form of action through which these self-modifying attitudes may express and increase themselves is determined by the age, social customs, traditions, family and body into which the soul has been born. Gandhi takes the Gita as a timeless teacher, an allegory of the inner battle that characterizes the embodied condition, viz. whenever ksetra and ksetrajna, prakrti and purusa, matter and soul are connected.

According to Gandhi, the Gita, as a scientific treatise on spiritual realization and its means, cannot answer questions of conduct in terms of a code or casuistry. The problems of freedom and bondage are related to specific practical problems of the material life and environment. The problem of release is how to relate the facts of the soul's existence and the unity of all existence to daily action and life that seem to deny those facts. Gandhi writes that the world will eternally be an alien place for the soul; although existence in it is essentially evil, it also provides the vehicle (body and mind) and occasion (the environment differentiated as good and evil) for action by which that evolution can be self-consciously aided.

Satyagraha seeks practical means. Besides knowing the relation of consciousness or spirit to matter in general, the universal principle must meet specific problems having a definite material form and locale. Gandhi writes that though the Gita represents perfect knowledge of these eternal relations,

> This should nor mean that we can obtain from the Gita direct answers to all the questions that arise from day to day, just as we find the meaning of words by looking up in the dictionary. This would not be desirable even if it were possible, for, in that case, there would be nothing like progress or discovery for mankind. Human intelligence would then simply atrophy from disuse.

Therefore, questions that arise in each age must be solved by the people of that age through their own effort. Our difficulties at present, such as world war, must be met by applying the general principles derived from the Gita and similar books which can only be of help to a limited extent. Real help can come only from our endeavours and struggles."

> Gandhi explains by his principle of analogy: "In books on medicine, we find various virtues attributed to a number of drugs. But their descriptions can serve only as guides. So long as these drugs have not been tested in actual practice, our theoretical knowledge of them not only serves no useful purpose, but is even burdensome. The same is true of the questions in life that clamour for solution.

Gandhi believes that though there are various religions and codes of conduct, they have only a few immutable principles at their bases, and that these are common to all true religions and moralities. But the form of the code will change with the conditions of application in the given age. They may change with each generation according to the customs and needs of the times.

Anasakti, yajna, and brahmasamarpana are immutable principles invariant with respect to the problems they confront, and the ideal of sthitaprajna is a timeless ideal. Gandhi deduces satyagraha mainly from these principles as the form that the Gita and The Upanisads should take in this age.

Again, truth and non-violence are basic principles unchanging from age to age. But as Gandhi considers satyagraha to be a practical corollary of these two, as such it becomes an object of research and experiment to find specific remedies for evils of the particular age and locale.

As truth and ahimsa take on the form of anasakti, yajna and brahmasamarpana considered under the distinction between material and spiritual, so these take on the form of satyagraha when applied under the distinction between good and evil.

Gandhi's satyagraha is his attempt to define and find a type of action which effectively connects the spiritual and empirical wills in order to extirpate the seeming difference between the material and the spiritual. Gandhi believes that to suit this "democratic" age, such a means must fit the average. It must be suitable for man ignorant of self and caught in consciousness of agency. And it must itself manifest visibly that truth—a means impossible but for an extraordinary supernatural force such as Gandhi claims soul-force to be.

Gandhi often writes from the point of view of an anonymous sage in order to give his deduction a sense of historical validity and timelessness. Though his writings may not be historically accurate, they represent his deepest conviction as to the authenticity and validity of his principles and interpretations as in fact deriving from established traditions. They give insight into his concepts and methods. Gandhi is that sage and scientist.

But when Gandhi says that sages have taught the means of realization from the truth of their own realization, it is not a scholar's or scientist's study he is reporting but that of an ideologist. Behind his views can be found the ardent religious and social reformer. This caution should accompany the study of his deduction of satyagraha doctrines and methods from their classical sources.

But again, though Gandhi's analysis is simple and straightforward, it is neither naive nor simplistic. Writing about the incalculable Hindu-Muslim violence of 1946-47, Gandhi states that "India knows, the world should, that every ounce of my energy has been and is being devoted to the definite avoidance of fratricide culminating in war." He is engaged in a delicate analysis of the situation in terms of war and non-violence. Again, Gandhi stresses the "logical" connection between practical options and outcomes. Note the similarity of the situation below with that depicted in the Gita.

Gandhi said in his post-prayer speech. He had been an opponent of all warfare. But if there was no other way of securing justice from Pakistan, if Pakistan persistently refused to see its proved error and continued to minimize it, the Indian Government had to go to war against it. War was not a joke. Now one wanted war. That way lay destruction. But he could never advise anyone to put up with injustice. If all the Hindus were annihilated in a just cause he would not mind it.

He was wedded to non-violence for all time and could never advocate war. He was merely pointing out the various possibilities. India and Pakistan should settle their differences by mutual consultation and failing that fall back upon arbitration. But if one party persisted in wrong doing and would accept neither of the two ways mentioned above, the only way left open was that of war. They should know the circumstances that prompted his remark.

Time and Again Gandhi seeks to avoid misinterpretation and writes:

> Not a single mention of war in my speeches can be interpreted to mean that there was any incitement to or approval of war between Pakistan and the Union. I claim that I rendered a service to both the sister states by examining the present situation and definitely. stating when the case of war could arise between the two states. This was done not to promote war but to avoid it as far as possible. Was it wrong to draw public attention to the logical steps that inevitably "followed one after another? India knows, the world should, that every ounce of my energy has been devoted to the definite avoidance of fratricide culminating in war.

It should be noted how carefully Gandhi maintains the balance of his statements to keep the distinction between understanding the conditions of war, its causes and circumstances, and advocating, justifying or even allowing war. Yet he does allow and even advocate it with his very posture. It is also arguable that it was in his power to call for a general mutiny, or to intervene directly with the authorities and he chose not to.

For purposes of the present argument it is enough to note that (1) Gandhi considers the chain of events logical and inevitable, and that (2) he does not himself feel the non-violent power to break that logic of events, and that (3) he does not mind the war for justice. All of this is tacit abdication of his practical claim, an abdication not nullified by qualifying disclaimers. His inconsistency is patent here. Gandhi did feel justified, however, given his disclaimers, in asserting universal scope for his principle, and in taking war to be the prototype of violence.

To accomplish this universalizing, Gandhi has to make the contents of the maxim the circumstances of its practical application homogeneous at a more fundamental level than the facts and experience drawn upon by the counter-intuitions of common sense and the *prima facie* case when they define an overriding necessity that seems to cancel the moral maxim.

This is the locus of the cluster of confusions which leads Gandhi to a *prima facie* untenable position and which does not on clarification support retaining that position against the *prima facie* intuitions. Here is rooted his confused and falsifying analysis positing the moral and practical homogeneity of the spiritual and practical spheres.

Since in Gandhi's view, war is the basic form and fullest culmination of violence, the appropriate focus of this critical investigation is (1) his analysis of the genesis of war as he derives it from the Gita, and his judgments in actual instances of war that he dealt with during his sixty years as an active war-resister; and, (2) his *satyagraha* intended as a complete substitute for war (representing all violent methods in any conflict.

It is necessary to see, in concrete contexts and in detail, how Gandhi's ideological and homogenizing interpretation of the key maxim is bound by confusion and contradiction and how it fails to do justice to the real situation. According to Gandhi's principle of micro-macro-cosmic identity, *"yathd pinde"*, examining his views on war is equivalent to examining his views on violence in general.

War is only the outermost and externalized form of violence. The shape and quality of all violence are the same. The same laws are found operative and the same moral rules and methods apply. War involves the same entanglement in outer form—binding retaliations and escalation of violent reprisals that the Gita elaborates in the escalation of the violence of desire and anger. But the Gita and the Mahabharata are not only the source of Gandhi's analysis of war and violence and the justifiability problem, they are the locus classicus of these issues.

Gandhi finds in the Gita the depiction of the moral battle within, but he elaborates on this in his judgments about physical war and in his analysis of the pacifist position and methods of war resistance.

Though it may not be incorrect for Gandhi to point out an analogy and parallel here from the standpoint of principle, he is not justified in reversing the direction of his application of this logical principle to assert from the standpoint of perception that the ideal and the real are identical. That the Truth is the truth and what is true within is reflected without are valid propositions, notwithstanding.

The problems Gandhi wants to solve by this principle are the identification of violence with intention and motive and the proper characterization of violence and non-violence for moral application to practical purposes.

It is a confusion to base a theory of practical moral truth on the application of a logical principle without modifying it for application from the practical standpoint; Gandhi does this in his satyagraha and his radical practical claims. He uses these not as instruments of inquiry to guide investigation and to focus and clarify perception, but as *a priori* rules to determine moral definitions and principles of action.

From an *a priori* moral standpoint, on the basis of his assimilation of the real to the ideal, Gandhi justifies his assimilation of the spiritual, practical and moral. He seems to be incognizant of the categorical differences that enter when the assimilation is reversed and the significant difference becomes precisely that of appearance and reality. He is aware of this as a fundamental problem in explanation and judgment when he tries to convey the difficult truth that the same act can be prompted and guided by entirely different motives which determine opposing qualities and sets of results. This is a decisive recognition in terms of the present argument. Gandhi writes :

> the question raised is of very great importance and has always caused me the greatest difficulty, not so much in deciding upon the action to be taken at a given moment but in justifying my conduct in terms of ahimsa. For the same action may outwardly be taken by the believer and the unbeliever. At these times the motive alone decides its quality.
>
> But Gandhi writes also: "Non-violence of two persons occupying different positions will not outwardly take the same shape. Thus the non-violence of a child towards his father would take the shape of conscious *voluntary* submission to this violence when he loses his temper. The father would take the child to his bosom and instantaneously sterilize the child's violence. In each case it is of course assumed that the outward act is an expression of the inward intention.

Supporting the inference from appearance to reality is a large problem in any theory but Gandhi does not address it on the theoretical level. He merely assumes the unmodified reversal of the micro-macro-cosmic identity principle, and ignores the categorical truths by insisting on the primacy of absolute, ideal truth as if regard for the latter cancelled validity of the former. This disregard of difference and distinction ignores the non-commutivity conferred on the principle by the practical context of its application.

For the core and most extensive part of Gandhi's analysis, this assimilation functions as if valid since it is all within the category of phenomenal reality. The principle functions, as Gandhi wishes, to raise one's sights towards guiding ideals. But this causes confusion and leads to contradictions in the limiting cases where he shifts categorical perspective without regard for categorical realities, and for the requirement of a cross categorical perspective. Because of this assimilation and confusion of categories, the real and the ideal, the apparent and the real, Gandhi places too high a value on life, giving it an absolute value when it is only a relative category.

In spite of recognizing the spiritual principle as fundamental existence, Gandhi values transient life as if it were permanent existence. He makes its protection and quiescent state, i.e. non-violence and pacifism, his absolute values and aims.

In answer to the argument that he strained the Gita into an allegory just to support this idealizing. Gandhi writes that though "the Gita is not a treatise on non-violence nor was it written to condone war. What 1 have done is to give an extended but in no way strained meaning. I hold that the logical outcome of the teaching of the Gita is decidedly for peace at the price of life itself. It is the highest aspiration of the human species."

From this valuation, Gandhi derives the imperatives for total non-violence and for proving the unjustifiability of war by any moral value, supposed necessity or putative practical result. Gandhi repeatedly states that he finds war to be an "unmitigated evil", unjustifiable under any circumstances or for any cause, even for the defeat of insuperable evil-directly contrary to the prima facie criteria introduced above. To illustrate:

> The tyrants of old never went so mad as Hitler seems to have gone with religious zeal. He is propounding a new religion of exclusivess and militant nationalism in the name of which any inhumanity becomes an act of humanity to be rewarded here and hereafter. If there ever could be a justifiable war in the name of and for humanity, a war against Germany, to prevent the wanton persecution of a whole race, would be completely justified. But I do not believe in any war. A discussion of the pros and cons of such a war is, therefore, outside my horizon or province.

Gandhi writes more specifically :

> I do not believe in short— violent cuts to success. However much I may sympathize with and admire worthy motives, I am an uncompromising opponent of violent methods even to serve the noblest of causes. But were not "motives to decide?" It must be asked: "Why then, only not here'?"

Again Gandhi opposes to the putative moral worth of war his absolute moral value of non-violence, which he holds is universally valid and not temporally conditioned by any circumstantial provisos.

Gandhi understands this value to be true practical expedience and efficiency, since thus any supposed moral value or apparently justifying "good result" of a particular war will necessarily be cancelled in the long run, whereas non-violence, as an ultimate and comprehensive value, has the practical consequence that it alone can permanently break the circle of violence. Every violent attempt to do so, though justified on every other ground, must in fact fail to realize permanently that practical translation of ultimate value which is really the basis of any serious justifying arguments. According to Gandhi's assimilation of categories and valuations, "permanent breaking of the circle of violence" is merely the practical and physical counterpart of ultimate moral value. Thus Gandhi concludes that peace and non-violence are the same thing.

Gandhi asserts that ignoring the ultimacy of non-violence results in mere change in the form of violence and extension and deepening of the original violent motivation, "for ultimately, force, however justifiably used, will lead us into the same morass as the force of Hitler and Mussolini. There will be just a difference of degrees."

The root fact of violence is that no matter what justification and arguments are made from the standpoint of abstract valuation, divorced from the equation of the moral, practical and spiritual, what we call violence can only in fact instigate opposition and produce a. mirror reaction in the opponent. It merely deepens the violence and brutal proclivities in agent and victim both.

Note that for Gandhi, appeal to principle is identical with appeal to expedience—intrinsic evil cannot help but lead ultimately to bad results, and he writes "To every Briton" of the World War,

> I appeal for cessation of hostilities, not because you are too exhausted to fight, but because war is bad in essence. You want to kill Nazism, you will never kill it by its indifferent adoption. Your soldiers are doing the same work of destruction as the Germans. The only difference is that perhaps yours is not as thorough as the Germans. If that be so, yours will soon acquire the same thoroughness as theirs, if not much greater. On no other condition can you win the war. In other words, you will have to be more ruthless than the Nazis. No cause, however just, can warrant the indiscriminate slaughter that is going on minute. I suggest that a cause that demands the inhumanities that are being perpetuated today cannot be just.

In terms of the new debate on justifiability and the advent of the atom bomb, Gandhi reaches the same conclusions. He points to the logic of the debate as another and final proof and unavoidable vindication of his arguments in the practical sphere. He wrote in 1946,

> So far as I can see, the atomic bomb has deadened the finest feeling that has sustained mankind for ages. There used to be the so-called laws of war which made it tolerable. Now we know the naked truth. War knows no law except that of might. The atom bomb brought an 'empty victory to the allied arms but it resulted for the time being in destroying the soul of Japan.

The moral to be legitimately drawn from the supreme tragedy of the bomb is that it will not be destroyed by counter -violence. Mankind has to get out of violence only through non-violence. Hatred can be overcome only by love. Counter-hatred only increases the surface as well as the depth of hatred.

To the question: "Had it (the atomic bomb) antiquated non-violence?" Gandhi's reply was :

> On the contrary, non violence was the only thing that was left in the thing that the atom bomb cannot destroy. I did not move a muscle when first heard that the atom bomb had wiped out Hiroshima. On the contrary, I said to myself, unless now the world adopts non-violence, it will spell suicide for mankind.

For Gandhi, the ultimacy of incipient atomic violence throws into relief the ideal status, character and superior practical potency of non-violent force (a spirital force) and the ultimacy of non-violent values.

Thus, in Gandhi's view, the atom bomb had not only not "exploded" his "faith" in non-violence, but had "clearly demonstrated that the twins and truth non-violence-constitute the mightiest force in the world. Before it the atom bomb is of no effect. The two opposing forces are wholly different in kind, the one moral and spiritual, the other physical and material. The one is infinitely superior to the other which by its very nature has an end. The power of the spirit is ever progressive and endless. Its full expression makes it unconquerable in the world."

According to Gandhi, not even the pretense of justifiability of violence and war is thus possible, given the contemporary world situation of nuclear armament, immediate global impact and amplification of minor and local violence or conflict, with its probable rapid magnification and escalation to global and nuclear proportions.

Further, according to Gandhi, the possibility of justifying violence and war by success, when used against large nations by oppressed and weak nations, is logically ruled out :

> You cannot successfully fight them with their own weapons. After all you cannot go beyond the atom bomb. Unless we can have a new way of fighting imperialism of all brands in the place of the outward one of a violent rising, there is no hope for the oppressed races of the earth.

Thus for Gandhi there is no possible justification for "war on war", judged on any possible .criteria of results, spiritual, moral or practical. The thing itself is evil and there is absolutely no ancillary consideration of results possible; no justification is possib1e given the contemporary situation. Therefore, non-violence alone has the potency to solve the problems usually addressed by violence; and so non-violence ought always to be used.

This is the conclusion Gandhi has consistently sought in the practical demonstration of his radical claims. The suicide implicit in violence is unavoidably visible in its nuclear expression. Gandhi takes the analysis he has given of violence in general to be vindicated and demonstrated by the logic of the atomic debate. In one sweeping practical display is revealed the final poverty and impotence of violence and the corresponding potency, viability and necessity of non-violence.

But Gandhi caused difficulty for other absolute pacifists by his not only allowing war but actually supporting the call to training in arms and war, and himself participating in the Boer War, the Zulu rebellion and recruiting for the British in World War I.

It must be noticed that the fundamental value in Gandhi's idealism is Truth and its first form is authenticity. Gandhi writes that though he participated as stretcher-bearer and recruiter in three acts of war,

> My repugnance to war was as strong then as it is today; and I could not then have, and would not have, shouldered a rifle. But one's life is not a single straight line; it is a bundle of duties very often conflicting. And one is called upon continually to make one's choice between one duty and another. As a citizen not then, and not even now, but a reformer leading an agitation against the institution of war, I had to advise and lead men who believed in war but who from cowardice or from base motives or from anger against the British Government, refraining from enlisting. I did not hesitate to advise them that, so long as they believed in war, and professed loyalty to the British constitution, they were in duty bound to support it by enlistment. Though I did not believe in the use of arms, and though it is contrary to the religion of Ahimsa which I profess, I should not hesitate to join an agitation for a repeal of the debasing Arms Act which I have considered amongst the blackest crimes of the British Government against India. And I have not hesitated only recently to tell Hindus that if they do not believe in out and out Ahimsa and cannot practice it, they will be guilty of a crime against their religion and humanity, if they fail to defend by force of arms the honor of their women. And all this advice and my previous I hold to be not only consistent with my profession of the religion of Ahimsa out and out, but a direct result of it.

> Gandhi explains further: Life is governed by a multitude of forces. Non-violence works in a most mysterious manner. Often a man's.actions defy analysis in terms of non-violence; equally often his actions may wear the appearance of violence when he is absolutely non-violent in the highest sense of the term and is subsequently found so to be. All I can claim for my conduct is that it was, in the instances cited, actuated in the interests of non-violence.

Gandhi admits that his arguments in explanation of "choice of duties", or "necessary compromise" in the interests of the principle of non-violence that he wanted thereby ultimately to someday govern all conduct, may be self-deception.

> "I claim to have done every act described by me for the purpose of advancing the cause of peace. That does not mean that these acts really advanced the cause of peace. I am merely stating the fact that my motive was peace. What is possible, however, is that I was weak. I observe daily how capable we are of utmost self-deception. For the time being, however I am not aware' of my self-deception.

Or, his reasonings may be badly expressed. He reiterates and insists that no result in action or argument can compromise the essential unjustifiability of war and violence. He writes that "there is no defense of my conduct weighed only in the scales of *Ahitnsa.*"

> Gandhi adds: For me the matter does not admit of reasoning beyond a point. It is one of deep conviction that war is an unmixed evil. Because of the very nature of the analytical problem, reason often confuses itself in applying principle to practice; The very thing that one war resister may do in the interest of his mission may repel another war resister who may do the exact opposite, and yet both may hold the same view about war. This contradiction arises because of the be wildering complexity of human nature. I can only, therefore, plead for mutual toleration even among professors of the same creed.

> And, Gandhi concludes: I would therefore urge fellow war resisters not to mind my faulty or incomplete argument and still less to mind my participation in war which they may be unable to reconcile with my professions about war. Let them understand me to be uncompromisingly against all war. If they cannot appreciate my arguments, let them impute my participation to unconscious weakness. For I would feel extremely sorry to discover that my action was used by anyone to justify war under any circumstance.

> Gandhi's chief argument for his participation in war: Notice though as an individual I was opposed to war, I had no status for offering effective non-violent resistance. Non-violence resistance can only follow some real disinterested service, some heartfelt expression of love. I felt that by sufficient service I could attain the power and the confidence to resist the Empire's wars and its warlike preparations.

Unless he was totally non-cooperative with the government and renounced to the utmost of capacity the privileges it offered. Gandhi could not avoid direct participation and service that might shorten the war and give him status for propagating non-violence.

Gandhi believed that living in an evil, warring society was as deeply supporting that evil as direct participating in war, and since he could not without suicide non-cooperate with a society and government that he believed to be basically good for the world, he must therefore openly and directly support it in its life and death struggle.

Gandhi places war participation in the same category as his helpless killing of any life by possession of and action in the human body. He explicitly equates war with all fundamental violence.

> My opposition to and disbelief in war was as strong then as it is today. But we have to recognize that there are many things in the world which we do although we may be against them. I am as much opposed to taking of life of the lowest creature alive as I am to war. But I continually take such life, hoping some day to attain the ability to do without this fratricide.

Thus, from every possible angle Gandhi denies the equation of justifiability with any form of necessity, factual circumstances or principle, for whatever reason. Denying justifiability of war, Gandhi denies any practical, moral and spiritual efficacy to war and all violence whatsoever. Even that complicity in war which is intended to further the ideal and force of non-violence and which involves a certain necessity of unavoidability in the given circumstances, cannot justify the violence. It cannot undo the evil or avert its necessary consequences; injury once done is unmitigable and the evil cannot be annulled. Thus against all orthodoxy, Gandhi argues that "the author of the Gita never advocated violence. It is a sermon on non-violence."

Most importantly, in spite of Krishna's direct command to Arjuna to fight to protect justice and fulfill his ksatriya duty, in service of society, Gandhi writes that "I do not believe that the Gita teaches violence for doing good, and, that I have the courage of saying that Krishna never taught violence in the Gita.

Gandhi argues that the Gita would be meaningless as a sectarian treatise describing a minor historical event, and not worthy of being spoken by Lord Krishna. He argues that Krishna's advice to Arjuna has to do specially with Arjuna's particular situation and dilemma of facing a war of fratricide, though clearly in protection of justice.

Gandhi praises Krishna as a teacher for giving Arjuna exactly what he needed in the historical situation, inciting him to duty in an age where the question of participation in war was raised in terms of of caste duty or cowardice. He writes that Arjuna was not averse to killing in general, but only to killing his own relatives. Therefore, Krishna suggested that doing one's duty, one may not treat, one's relations differently from other people. In the age of the Gita, the question, whether one should or should not wage war, was not raised by any important person.

Gandhi writes that war then was no more looked upon as an abridgement of ahimsa than cereal eating is today. War posed the problem of conflicts of duty in a forceful and poignant way but there is nothing in this that is intrinsic to the problem of action in the context of war.

But the duty of a warrior is a particularly vivid case and lends itself to poetic narration. It also represents the universal struggle of common everyday experience that Gandhi takes as the archetype of conscious moral experience. Gandhi reveres Krishna for presenting the universal and eternal doctrine of ahimsa under the severe constraints of such arguments justifying participation in a small local war, one historical event.

To Gandhi the eternal battle is the inner one against passions and the ego-sense. It is the moral battle inviting universal study, and according to Gandhi the Gita teaches the battle's science and practice as the Yoga of equability – peace which comes by renunciation of fruits of action and non-attached duty. These are the means of controlling the senses and the mind, and ultimately thereby destroying the passions and rooting out the very sources of violence and war; clearly a universal teaching. But in the narrative this teaching is locally applied to the historical situation and may appear more restricted than it is.

Gandhi asserts that the purpose of the Mahabharata is to depict the struggle of man in his eternal ascent and to declare the way of right action. According to this interpretation of the Gita, the outer narrative form merely depicts Arjuna's dilemma of duty in order to instruct those caught in the consequences of past actions and commitments. This raises no question of non-violence. Gandhi considers Arjuna's arguments for pacifism to be valid if they are understood to support the universal moral doctrine of absolute non-violence and pacifism.

But Gandhi believes that Arjuna has no status to raise these deeper questions because, as Krishna rightly explains, Arjuna's aversion is not sincere and creedal, arising from urgent commitment to an eternal ideal. It is only an expression of attachment and the resultant fear of killing close realatives, friends, teachers and elders.

Generally, it is really social reality that constitutes one's moral reality. Kinship cannot determine activity in terms of objective social norms; social duty must carry an overriding obligation if the larger social unit is to survive. Arjuna is no believer in non-violence and pacifism as a universal ideal and law; he must at least be impartial in wielding violence and his battle skills not for exclusive benefit of personal relations.

Gandhi concludes that the advice of Krishna "to fight" speaks only to this moral minimum demanded of Arjuna in his particular circumstances and cannot be generalized.

Gandhi writes

> It was not in a spirit of *ahimsa* that Arjuna refused to go to battle. He had fought many a battle before. He fought shy of killing his own kith and kin. Arjuna never discussed the problem of killing as such. Krishna told him "Thou hast already done the killing. Thou canst not all at once argue thyself into non-violence. Finish what thou has already begun.". To say that the Gita teaches violence or justifies war, because advice to kill was given on a particular occasion is as wrong as to say that himsa is the law of life, because a certain amount of it is inevitable in daily life.

Gandhi writes further

> Not that the actual physical battle is out of the question. To those who are innocent of non-violence, the Gita does not teach a lesson of despair. He who fears, who saves his skin, who yields to his passions, must fight the physical battle whether he will or not; but that is not his *Dharma* law, path of conduct in the widest sense. *Dharma* is one and one only. *Ahimsa* means *Moksa* and *Moksa* is the realization of Truth. There is no room for cowardice, and despair is not the way. Better far than cowardice is killing and being killed.

According to this reading, Arjuna's arguments are only counsels of fear and they bear no relation to moral argument. They could not possibly support a universal teaching.

Krishna will go on in the rest of the Gita to establish a framework of values, and of spiritual facts demonstrating the validity of those valuations, so that action can have an objective basis outside of material or social relations and motives. Material relations, motives and institutions have no permanent basis. In the final analysis they reduce to the mere advocacy of changing perceptions, decisions, aims, affectations, affiliations and sentiments. Duty without attachment, anasakti of Gandhi, is the practical form of that teaching.

Gandhi, however, by the confused use of the *"yatha pinde..."* principle, reads from Krishna's argument the doctrine of non-killing: World is "brother" and killing brother is essential sin. Killing any is killing "kin". Any killing is necessarily "sin"!

Delusion as to the Truth of Reality, nature and self-identity, as soul and spirit, atman and brahman, and as to their empirical reflection in the oneness of all life, leads to the false view that "kin/ non-kin" determines "right/wrong".

The practical doctrine and ethics of both social-and self-realization, that both the Gita and Gandhi derive from these fundamental spiritual facts, is that Truth of conduct by right effort is effort to fulfill the duties of one's station in larger social life in accordance with one's present material and spiritual status and state, and one's stage in moral and spiritual evolution, *svadharma*.

Right effort at duty is possible only with objective perception, which implies unconcern about results, since they are not within one's control. Objective perception and pure impersonal reason are possible only with equability resulting from this inner renunciation of one's fixations on doubtable consequences and personal fruits.

Such right effort at self-duty, regarding and serving wider truth *(anasakti* and *yajna)*, by itself leads to realizing the freedom *(moksa)* inherent in soul or self. But Gandhi adds that "truth of conduct" can be non-violence and absolute pacifism, only because Truth of existence and life *entails* the brotherhood of all life without exception.

Gandhi's assertion that "two wrongs don't make a right" seems self-evident and the natural unchallengeable expression of the ideal. It thus seems to confirm the moral validity of his non-retaliation.

But the second wrong is not necessarily wrong unless there is justification for asserting the identity of static fact and moral, dynamic reality independently of Gandhi's commutative use of "yatha pinde.

However, the situation is more complex than can be understood through Gandhi's homogenizing dichotomies. In the analysis of this situation there are factors of motive and of total results, besides the immediate quality of the action. Scientific inquiry would seek to analyze and not to legislate the role and relevance of motive and total results in determining the full moral dimensions and consequences of situations of action.

Since Gandhi admits morality must manifest practically in production of good results over evil, it is necessary to understand this requirement in the uninterpreted context of the complexity of action which involves agency and use as independent factors.

Violence may be intrinsically evil as a quality of action, as the general commitment accepts. But the wider uninterpreted view does not assure that this quality is the only and final determinant of the good/ evil quotient and that other emergent factors may not be discovered that are equally or more determinate of this final quotient. There may be a real resultant quality of the transaction as a whole, qua moral. This analysis of the moral resultant as an outcome of multiple factors and possible emergent qualities allows the possibility of showing how use of violent action can produce less evil —how the second wrong may be found not to be wrong in the context of the whole transaction. This would be to suggest that ends as a whole may justify otherwise morally invalid means.

Gandhi's analysis of violence as a quality equated with evil, and thus the absolute determinant of moral validity and sole basis of moral justifiability, is the result of assuming an *a priori* dichotomization; it is not the result of looking at the situation for its component parts, contributory causes, moments and possible emergent and discoverable qualities.

But Gandhi also goes behind the immediately evident quality of action and results when he asserts that non-violence should not be equated with mere non-killing and that, though often violent and non-violent action may look alike, motives are decisive of the moral quality and final outcome at every level. Hence, only divine judgment can truly know that quality of intent and real aim. For man this is a practical judgment about the immediate quality of the outer action and likely immediate consequences. But the accumulating results progressively reveal the full moral dimensions and subtler moral qualities of the transaction.

Nevertheless, in elaborating on the violence or non-violence of his own participation in war or on the character of any act in terms of violence and non-violence, and in analyzing its justifiability, Gandhi finds motive, not outer form, decisive.

Gandhi would rather forfeit argument and stand by conviction, if argument seems to betray his purposes in justifying that conviction. He retains or cancels at will the distinction between quality of act and quality of motive. But Gandhi's equation of the moral and the practical makes it necessary that motive or qualities, as criteria, have tangible counterparts in the. form of practical results.

If life in the body is constant battle, and if practical life merely mirrors this, every act and state must be a compromise between non-violence and violence because according to Gandhi's strict interpretation material reality is violent in nature. The votary must act so as always to extend the scope of non-violence, and to push back the dividing line in justification of that particular act.

> Gandhi writes: Indeed life is made of such compromise. ahimsa simply because it is purest, unselfish love, often demands such compromise. The conditions are imperative. There should be no self in one's actions, no fear, no untruth, and it must be in furtherance of the cause of ahimsa. The compromise must be natural to oneself, not imposed from without.

Gandhi argues for a violence/non-violence distinction relative to circumstance and act. He will not let the motive of compassion redeem the existential involvement in violence or evil. Rather, he insists that the outer shape of the act necessarily compromises and qualifies the motive. This is an important point to detail:

> Ahimsa is a comprehensive principle. The saying that life lives on life has a deep meaning in it. Man cannot for a moment live without consciously or unconsciously committing outward himsa. The very fact of his living-eating, drinking and moving about necessarily involves some himsa, destruction of life, be it ever so minute. A

> votary of ahimsa therefore remains true to his faith if the spring of all his actions is compassion, if he shuns to the best of his ability the destruction of the tiniest creature, tries to save it, and thus incessantly strives to be free from the deadly coil of himsa. He will be constantly growing in self-restraint and compassion, but he can never become entirely free from outward himsa.

And, "In life, it is impossible to eschew violence" campletely. Now the question arises, where is one to draw the line? The line cannot be the same for every one. For, although, essentially the principle is the same, yet everyone applies it in his or her own way. What is one man's food can be another's poison. Evil and good are relative terms. What is good under certain conditions can become an evil or a sin, under *a* different set of conditions. At every step he has to use his discrimination as to what is ahirmsa and what is himsa.

Gandhi works out a practical solution, but his theory remains in contradiction:

> Life is an aspiration. Its mission is to strive after perfection, which is self-realization. The ideal must not be lowered because of our weaknesses and imperfections. One who hooks his fortunes to ahimsa the law of love, daily lessens the circle of destruction, and to that extent promotes life and love; he who swears by himsa, the law of hate, daily widens the circle of destruction, and to that extent promotes death and hate.

Yet again, Gandhi insists that there can be only one criterion and allows that there *is* one principle for drawing the line of justifiability of apparently violent uses of physical force, viz. that it be an act of love, and so of ahimsa, in its most basic sense, that the only active motive be the good of the recipient of the act. That line is absolute;

> Once you admit the lawfulness of the use of physical force for purposes other than the benefit of the person against whom it is used as in the case of a surgeon against his patient, you cannot draw an arbitrary line of distinction.

Is the motive determinant or only the instrument of necessary compromise and participation in evil? A modified reading would allow a type of justifiability by results, a balance of good over evil, even in terms of non-violence and violence.

This would of course violate Gandhi's strict ideology, unless he allows the motive of non-violence to have a *sui generis* quality and special material expression that is not liable to the previous categorical characterization. He makes no such provision, but this is the effect when he speaks of non-violence as a force and assigns to its idea a creative power of initiating spontaneous action. This, in practical effect, eliminates subjective, material, intermediary formations and impulsions.

In this case, motive would denote only a set of statements that are the inspired result of reflection on the action of that force in moral consciousness, and this would answer to Gandhi's description of the irresistible inner voice that, according to him, is the inseparable cognitive aspect of the activity of non-violence within oneself.

This again has the consequence that since the motive comes into play in practical application, it must still have an overt material counterpart to satisfy the strict ideological equations. This can only be expressed as a balance of such non-violently produced material components with ordinary mediately agitated ones, whose movement cannot but be tainted by empiricality, i.e. inherent violence and evil. The motive must in some way materially decide the outcome if it is to figure in the moral cum practical justification.

Gandhi gives the following very telling moral "physics":

> Passive resistance is a misnomer for non-violent resistance. It is much more active than violent resistance. It is direct, ceaseless, but three-fourths invisible and only one-fourth visible. In its visibility it seems to be ineffective, e.g. the spinning wheel which I have called the symbol of non-violence. In its visibility it appears ineffective, but it is really intensely active and most effective in ultimate result. A violent man's activity is most visible, while it lasts. But it is always transitory. But the effects of non-violent action persist and are likely to grow with age. And the more it is practiced, the more effective and inexhaustible it becomes, and ultimately the whole world stands agape and exclaims a miracle has happened. All miracles are due to the silent and effective working of invisible force. Non-violence is the most invisible and the most effective. I may say all kinds of sweet words to you without meaning them. On the other hand, I may have real love in me and yet my outward expression may be forbidding. Then

> outwardly my action in both cases may be the same and yet the effect may be different. For the effect of our action is often more potent when it is not patently known. Thus the unconscious effect you are making on me I may never know. It is, nevertheless, infinitely greater than the conscious effect. In violence there is nothing invisible. Non-violence, on the other hand, is three-fourths invisible, and so the effect is in the inverse ratio to its invisibility. Non-violence, when it becomes active, travels with extraordinary velocity, and then it becomes a miracle. So the mass mind is affected first unconsciously, then consciously. When it becomes consciously affected there is demonstrable victory. When the spirit of non-violence pervades the people and actually begins to work, its effect is visible to all.

Thus Gandhi notes that many acts of non-violence are necessary to yield one visible non-violent resultant. On our modified reading, the motive materially decides the quality and justifiability of the act because through it the resultants of many more acts than the present one alone are brought into combination. The final resultant may never be considered purely non-violent, nevertheless, it will necessarily have an identifiable distinctive action corresponding to the contributory motivations of preceding acts.

Thus even according to Gandhi's strict reading of the equation of moral and practical, non-violence can be legitimately defined as the balance of total non-harm over immediately present harm, regardless of the appearance of the forces used.

But Gandhi further mistakenly identifies violence with immediate results of force as if that were the whole phenomenon; so he continued to contradict himself even as he ceaselessly tried to answer conundrums about the apparent failure of non-violence in terms of the necessity of combining several resultants spread over time as they empirically mature to give one tangible non-violent result. The 100 or so volume corpus of his writings documents his more than sixty years' attempt to answer these "conundrums" of his critics — he himself constantly posed them in ceaseless self-examination The contradictions could not but remain since they are built into the terms of that reflection and examination.

The contradictions remain, partly because though Gandhi requires that motive decide character of similar looking actions, he gives no scientific analysis for this in consonance with the rest of his ideological analysis, and its pragmatic and experimental investigation of how this differentiation is discovered. This merely avoids the above implications for the problem of justification.

Though Gandhi's definition of non-violence and his analysis of non-retaliation are reasoned out as if on scientific lines, connecting real effects of moral qualities with forces governed by laws and predictably manipulable, he invariably falls back on abstract and moralistic reasoning in problems of justification and the application conditions of his practical doctrine.

Gandhi stressed that war is an unmitigable evil unjustifiable on any grounds. Yet he acknowledges that it evokes admirable bravery and many other noble and intrinsically good qualities and actions; "War is an unmitigated evil. But it certainly does one good thing, it drives away fear and brings bravery to the surface." And, "if war had no redeeming feature, no courage and heroism behind it, it would be a despicable thing, and would not need speeches to destroy it." This argument sounds like a Hegelian argument for the justification of war!

Thus, Gandhi acknowledges that war is a complex fact and that there is no unmixed evil in the world or in human nature. He can conclude that war is an unmitigated evil, absolutely unjustifiable only if he assumes that war can produce evil effects regardless of its non-ideal material mechanism.

If war is a material fact and does not have only ideal reality it can only be considered absolutely disallowable by the imposition of an absolute dichotomy of real and ideal which superimposes an ideal quality on phenomenal activity, as Gandhi attempts by equating violence with evil.

If in the world there is no unmixed evil and real war must have some good, then on what grounds can the justifiability of war be analyzed as if it were an ideal existence? Without justification Gandhi identifies the ideal "concept" of war with the "fact" of war. Therefore, war in the real world might be justified by a real overbalance of facts of bravery, nobility, charity, etc as its real outcomes.

Against this conclusion, Gandhi has argued that no cause could justify war's "indiscriminate slaughter" which was so fully exhibited in the prelude and beginnings of World War II. But the logical extreme has in fact never been realized, as Gandhi himself asserts in his arguments to establish that non-violence is the law of being.

Gandhi cannot dogmatize from his concept of ideological purity that all war must degenerate to an absolute barbarity. Neither is there more validity to his analysis of non-violence than to that of war, nor less to war than to his satyagraha, so far as they must be treated on a par as equally ideal concepts or equally factual states.

Gandhi has said of the Gita, as a text on "eternal verities", that its logical outcome is "peace at the price of life itself." He writes also that "the first condition of non-violence is justice all round in every department of life," and that peace is impossible without non-violence and truth.

Then the outcome of justice must be more fundamental than that of peace, and a balance of justice, a materially just war, should be justifiable in terms of non-violence. It can be argued that in fact the world has gone on after war because whatever the appalling aspect presented in terms of violent means and physical suffering and devastation, nothing short of that could have destroyed incorrigible evil and saved the modicum of justice on which the succeeding order could be based and continue to evolve.

War never does reach its logical conclusion and admittedly has many noble aspects. If the aim is truly corporate and mass application and widening the scope of non-violence in the world rather than individual propriety and salvation, than analogies are available by which to ascribe the same love, motives and surgical activities to the large scale reality of war as to states and activities of the individual. Such analogies can be derived from the criteria of the just war.

The application of the categories of good and evil through the dichotomy non-violence/violence magnifies the outer destructive aspects of war, as well as its moral destructiveness, and gives a distorted but compelling depiction of the fruits of war and violence. Gandhi disallows justification analogous to the just war model in order to retain the ideological purity embodied in his equation of violence with evil. But this equation itself only reflects his more basic assimilation of appearance to the ideal—and that again is based on an unsupported imputation of commutativity to the micro-macro identity principle in its practical application. Again, it is evident that Gandhi's arguments pro and con justifiability thus are woven throughout with categorical confusions.

Gandhi argues, finally, by idealizing the relation of means and ends as if here also a complex fact could have a morally meaningful outcome only in purely moral terms. Gandhi gives the law of *karma* a simplistic punitive interpretation and by interpreting war as a simple, single wholly evil action, a single totally bad end is assured and logically no new material order can emerge. But this ideally bad end also can have no material counterpart and Gandhi is again arguing ideal goods against ideal bads in terms of ideal realities and relations. He is again bypassing the categorical reality in terms of which the practical efficacy of non-violence must ultimately be calculated if he also wishes to sustain the equation of the moral and the practical. His moral physics and metaphysics are inadequate to sustain both his ideological presuppositions and the practical outcomes.

When Gandhi writes that not even a "noble end" could justify violence and war, he adds the practical rider that "experience convinces me that permanent good can never be the outcome of untruth and violence." But "experience" cannot teach that "permanent" evil is the definite outcome of violence. Defference to experience as if it had such a logical function indicates the "*a priori*" is merely ideological. Again, Gandhi confuses categorical realities at a fundamental level of his analysis.

Finally, Gandhi does allow, even require, moral support for the exploited victim against the exploiter and aggressor. His moral support extends naturally to non-violent assistance. He writes,

> If war is itself a wrong act, how can it be worthy of moral support or blessings? I believe all war to be wholly wrong. But if we scrutinize the motives of two warring parties, we may find one to be in the right and the other in the wrong. For instance, if A wishes to seize B's country, B is obviously the wronged one. Both fight with arms. I do not believe in violent warfare, but all the same, B, whose cause is just, deserves moral help and blessings. And, whilst all violence is bad and must be condemned in the abstract, it is permissible, for it is ever the duty of a believer in ahimsa to distinguish between the aggressor and

the defender. Having done so, he will side with the defender in a non-violent manner, i.e., give his life in saving him.

The limitation to non-violent means is of course the ideological requirement but, given the claim's acknowledgment that a right is at stake, the ideological commitment to only specially designated means stands out thereby as arbitrary in even greater contrast to the commonsense position of the general commitment to non-violence. If the end is admittedly good how can any means that actually achieve it be considered wrong? Gandhi's contradiction of this follows naturally from such a narrowed view of what constitutes the action and its effects, as his ideological and arbitrary conception betrays in such cases.

All of Arjuna's and Gandhi's arguments against war, based on identification of highest values with narrowly defined material results, fail to win confidence for absolute pacifism as a valid or viable answer to the present necessities of impending war to protect justice. Gandhi misinterprets not only the practical categorical reality but the spiritual as well by his interposition of the homogenizing moral dichotomy and principles.

Gandhi's biased use of the micro-macro identity principle and the resultant confusion of appearance and reality, and of reality and ideality in terms of violence and non-violence, lead him to a contradictory analysis of the moral standard as heteronomous and of *anasakti* as a contradictory, morally qualified state. In the one direction, Gandhi imposes his moral ideal on practical reality and in the other direction, he imposes it on spiritual reality.

Gandhi's synonymy of the spiritual, moral and practical does not represent the non-dual advaitic reality and the micro-macrocosmic logical principle, but the superimposition of an external form and standard. Thus the ideological assumption of the moralistic viewpoint results in that radical heteronomy introduced above in the explication of Gandhi's overvaluation of life. This is the origin of the heteronomy of ethical standards which was shown to extend to the roots of Gandhi's philosophy of non-violence.

According to advaitic principles, "*yatha pinde*" would be interpreted to reveal the same one reality both transcendent of and immanent in material existence and life. It would not extirpate the difference between the categories of being and becoming, ideal and real or existence and life, which do have their functions in practical and moral consciousness.

The reflection of this logico-moral identity principle and *advaitic* basis is properly the Gita's principle of *svadharma* which Gandhi accepts as the unique, simultaneous means and expression of the individual's progressive self-realization. Freedom is the result of this self-less action.

> Interpreting the Gita, Gandhi writes, If each does his duty selflessly according to his nature, he will reach perfection. A man remains free of sin when he performs the task naturally allotted to him, as he is then free from selfish desires; the very wish to do something else arises from selfishness. For the rest, all actions are clouded by defects as fire by smoke. But the natural duty is done without desire for its fruits, and thus loses its binding force.

Gandhi gives the Gita a moral interpretation of material existence, characterized there as movement, and movement characterized as necessarily violent and therefore evil. Therefore, unless he admits that there can be activity, friction, etc. without an evil quality being produced, then uniquely dutiful action of *svadharma*, even aside from his heteronomous ethics of non-violence, cannot result in free action and freedom from reaction or consequences.

To hold the duty ethics of the Gita, as a means of acting without binding results, the possibility is required that all immediate "tearing", "friction", "violence", etc. that seem inherent in activity, be completely cancelled either by an emergent counter-quality or by a neutralizing and balancing of forces observable when a larger resultant or wider perspective is assumed. Therefore Gandhi's ideological equation of violence with evil and these with activity, vitiates the attempt to establish a viable duty ethics that would produce free action as a means to spiritual realization.

According to the principle of *svadharma*, the rightness of each action is totally and uniquely determined by the entire history of the *jivatma* (evolving self). The utility of the action is determined by the degree to which it either bypasses or dismantles the ego-desire complex or strategically satisfies and strengthens it, geared in either case-to the single aim of immediate self-expression as means, and to ultimate self-realization as end.

Gandhi's spiritual position is also self-contradictory. Gandhi writes:

> Anasakti transcends Ahimsa. He who would be anasakta (selfless) has necessarily to practice non-violence in order to attain the state of selflessness. ahimsa is, therefore, a necessary preliminary, it is included in Anasakti, it does not go beyond it. whilst we are in the flesh and tread the solid earth, we have to practice ahimsa. In the life beyond, there is no himsa or ahimsa.

This state is preeminently the state of dispassion, non-attachment and equilibrium. It is of the nature of spirit not affected by modifications and movements in phenomenal reality. Hence is simultaneously for Gandhi the sine qua non of non-violence as means, and the transcendent aim of non-violence. Since anasakti is Gandhi's name for the state beyond the gunas, it is therefore beyond himsa and ahimhsa which describe qualities, actions and forces. He defines himsa morally from the standpoint of motive and intent; so that "himsa is impossible without anger, without attachment, without hatred, and the Gita strives to carry us to the state beyond sattva, rajas, and tamas to a state that excludes anger, hatred, etc." More fundamentally, behind all himsa is found "the desire to attain the cherished end."

Gandhi writes that in the "balanced state of mind, of mental equipoise, himsa, violence and killing are impossible because that state "can be achieved only after killing all your passions. It is not possible to kill your brother after having killed all your passions. And, "A man who is free from the action of the pair of opposites is incapable, like the perfect man of *the Bible*, of injuring any living thing on earth."

Gandhi thus also reads into the factual state of *gunatita* the moral heteronomy that characterizes and distinguishes his non-violence. But a correct interpretation and practical use of *anasakti* must recognize its definitive character as beyond any quality or opposition at all — moral as well as natural. Its interpretation, for moral ideological purposes, may explore its practical relation to moral action in terms of favored moral distinctions or properties as Gandhi does. But the definitive character of the state must not be assimilated to the interpretation.

The very differentia of anasakti from the material and moral states, given in the Gita and Upanisads-Katha Upanisad, Svetasvatara Upanisad and Chandogya Upanisad is its status beyond good and evil and its realization independently of these qualities.

Gandhi is at variance with his sources. His "anasakti" superimposes on the non-moral end-state the moral means and criteria that he ideologically favors for its realization.

The essence of Gandhi's argument is that the Gita teaches non-violence as an ideal and a means, and the man of equability, *sthitaprajna, anasakta, gunatita*, cannot be imagined to be violent. Gandhi's moral imagination cannot dissociate outer violent action and subjective states of anger, hate, etc. that experience seems to show him are invariably at its root.

Gandhi describes the state of anasakti as beyond the gunas and then contradicting himself, says that that "state excludes anger, hatred". Gandhi writes, "I can even now picture to my mind Arjuna's eyes red with anger every time he draws the bow to the end of his ear."

The question of moral truth is not a question of the scope of one's individual moral imagination. Artistic or moral inspiration and imagination may lead to great discoveries in these fields but they cannot substitute for scientific or logical inquiry. Whatever the vividness of Gandhi's moral imagination, the intensity and breadth of his moral experience or the dramatic appeal of his rhetorical argument based on these, they cannot of themselves validate his ideological analysis and radical practical claim.

Identifying violent appearance of activity with essential himsic violence (the inevitable expression of anger, hate, fear, etc.), and drawing the sharp contrast between inner and outer reality with the spiritual and moral on one side and the material and evil on the other, Gandhi insists on the allegorical interpretation of the Gita in order to justify his conclusion that "the author of the Gita never advocated war or violence. It is a sermon on non-violence. Fight, without anger and passion, can only be spiritual.

But again, Gandhi is saying that the "spiritual" is not a status outside of *prakrti,* beyond determination by the gunas. He is describing categorical facts but again reading in the ideological dichotomy that makes a logical necessity of equating violence with evil motives.

Gandhi goes so far as to assert that realization of this state has the subjective consequence that "where detachment governs our action, even the weapon raised in order to strike an enemy falls down out of our hand, and the objective consequence that though of "a humble man, who has reduced himself to zero it may be said that he does not kill though he kills, this does not mean that the man inspite of his humility may kill and yet be unaffected by the killing. For, no occasion can arise for such a man to indulge in violence.

Gandhi, for whom struggle and the inner moral battle are the sine qua non of spiritual and moral growth and evolution, writes that

> The *Bhagavad Gita* is a purely religious, not historical treatise. It deals with the war that is eternally waging between the forces of evil and good, Ormuzd and Ahriman, Hyde and Jekyl in the human breast. We cannot do enough violence to all the evil passions that well up on that little *Kurukshetra* (the field of battle).

> Gandhi believed: "the Gita represented the eternal duel between forces of evil and good, and inculcated the duty of eradicating evil within us without hesitation, without tenderness. The real battle is only the one. within, against the mind's submission to the prevailing distinctions and motives of "1" and "mine" and the attitude it gives rise to of attachment and repulsion. These are the roots of sin and the radical origin of all conflict, inner and outer.

> The real battle is against compulsion by sense life and desire which, when one has not the vision and the assistance of the Lord, are more powerful than any individual can with stand. The real battle is the individual effort to attain and maintain that "confidence in soul-force" by which "everything else becomes easy as a matter of course. And desire and anger and their countless hosts hold no terror for him who has mastered the senses, the mind and the intelligence, by the soul which is the greatest of all.

According to Gandhi's reading of the Gita, the inner battle is the only real battle and recourse to and reliance on soul-force is the only real means of waging it. Thus the condition of realizing the potency of and enlisting soul-force is the exact conduct of truth and non-violence and the non-cooperation strategy of satyagraha.

But it is an arbitrary conclusion of Gandhi's analysis that this is the only battle and that only this inner battle is spiritual, moral and effective. Sometimes it has been argued that Hinduism's stand on violence is ambivalence. Any scholar to investigate Hinduism's stand on the morality of violence must do so through appeal to the Vedas, the revealed scriptural foundation of orthodox Hinduism. But no sooner does he turn to the Vedas than he discovers that they fairly abound in passages which unequivocally condone, which just as unequivocally condemn, acts of violence. To illustrate the Vedas seeming ambivalence, if not sheer contradictoriness herein, consider two representative sets of texts. These we shall label, respectively, the Vedas' dharma and ahimsa views of violence.

First, the dharma view. Though multi-dimensional Hindu term, Dharma will do for present purposes to cite the Bhagavad Gita's terse remarks thereon. "All mankind," the Gita avers, "is born for perfection and each shall attain it will he but follow his own duty [dharma]." According to the Gita, then, dharma signifies a personal duty which it is incumbent on one to perform, and which is the indispensable means to reaching the common human end of perfection. But if the end of humankind is a shared one, not so the means to this end. The Gita envisions one's dharma as an inviolably personal affair, a unique quest after perfection. And so it must be, the Gita declares, for dharma is the very "law of one's nature," and as such, entails one's "natural work," a work which "no one should give up even though he does it imperfectly." Indeed, so insistent is the Gita on the unshareability of one's dharma, that not even the successful assuming of another's dharma is deemed sufficient warrant to forsake one's personal dharmic path. Such alleged success is illusory, and insidiously illusory at that, since, admonishes the Gita, "the duty of another will bring you into great spiritual danger."

If we apply the dharma view to the question of violence's ethicality, the implication is clear: for certain individuals acts of violence may well be meritorious and conducive to their perfection, a perfection which the Gita asserts is of a "spiritual" nature. But the Gita is not content merely to imply as such. Elsewhere, we find Krishna exhorting the reluctant warrior, prince Arjuna, in these commanding terms:

> To a warrior, there is nothing nobler than a righteous war. Happy arc the warriors to whom a battle such as this comes: it opens a door to heaven. But if you refuse to fight this righteous war, you will be turning aside from your duty. You will be a sinner and disgraced.

The latter paragraph presents what would appear to be the ultimate vindication of the dharma view: not only may violence be activity conducive to one's moral and spiritual evolvement, but also Krishna's express reference to "sin" serves notice that violence may be no less than God-sanctioned behavior as well — only provided, of course, that such behavior issues from one's natural dharmic propensities.

Yet, if Hinduism expressly extols, at least for a certain class of individuals, deeds of violence, difficulties arise when we notice that these same scriptures appear also to espouse a view smacking of uncompromising pacifism. This second, seemingly contradictory, position have presented the ahimsa view. Ahimsa denotes "non-violence" or "harmlessness," a term which, due largely to the influence of the great Indian practitioner of ahimsa, Mahatma Gandhi is fairly well-known in the West.

One of the frequently-mentioned repudiations of violence occurs in the great Hindu epic, the *Ramayana*. Thus, after the demon-king, Ravan, has been slain in battle, Hanuman seeks to avenge Rama's spouse, Sita, by killing the women who so cruelly held her captive. But Sita will not permit this would-be slaughter, and appeals for clemency by first confronting Hanuman with the disarmingly direct question, "Who in the world is blameless?" Immediately afterwards, as if in oblique reply to her own question, Sita adds: "It is the part of noble souls to be compassionate towards all — sinners as well as good people."

Evidently, the suppressed premise of Sita's enthymeme is the universality of human. This being so, noble souls will not delude themselves with thoughts of personal innocence, nor will they pretend to innocence so as to deceive others. Noble souls are rather who, having sincerely searched their own hearts—and precisely *because* they have searched their own hearts—cannot but own their, as well as others', moral failings. Self-knowledge born of such introspective candor thus becomes the moral goad to a global compassion, a compassion, that is, which embraces "sinners as well as good people."

But if Sita's advocacy of universal compassion goes a long way toward encouraging 'ahimsa,' it docs not appear to do so unqualifiedly, and for two primary reasons. In the first place, to maintain that noble souls are possessed of global compassion does not thereby imply that violence is never warranted. It is part of one's human, all-too human, fallenness will, doubtless much mitigate one's violent proclivities, but it does not, for all that, necessarily proscribe the use of. violent measures, say, for a just end not prompted by vengeful motives. The context of Sita's remarks, it must be remembered, is her opposition violence and the concomitant forgetfulness of one's own culpability. Supposing, then, a person who is no guilt, and who is untarnished by vindictive motives, is there anything in Sita's remarks to prohibit this person morally from resorting to violent means to bring about what he perceives to be a righteous end? In fact there any thing to prevent this individual from contending that compassion is more perfectly served when one's actions accord with justice than when they do not, since the wilful failure to work toward a just end, which,' because it is just, might benefit many, is in itself a particularly flagrant form of non-compassion. Granted, one may be hard put to produce such an unimpeachable case, but this is not really to the point. The point rather is that Sita's defense of ahimsa in the name of compassion does leave this moral loophole to the sincere proponent of violent means, and thus cannot stand as an unqualified endorsement of ahimsa.

A second drawback of Sita's vindication of 'ahimsa' is its exclusivity. As stated, the practice of non-violence does not extend beyond human reality. Conspicuous by its absence is any explicit, or even implicit, reference to animal and plant life, not to mention the so-called inanimate order. Later, we shall discuss in some detail why Hinduism considers such exclusivity incompatible with an authentic understanding *o*f ahimsa. For now we would simply point out that a rationale for ahimsa which fails to take into account the rest of the natural order defeats the purpose. Violence tacitly brooked against whims of nature does not seem conducive to the develpment of ahimsic attitude toward human nature. An ahimsic attitude would seem to presuppose an inner disposition, a habitual way of seeing and responding to reality. Essential to the formation of any habit is, of course, practice, whereby a response becomes ingrained and so, automatic. To confine one's practice of ahimsa to human beings, to the exclusion of the balance of reality, thus seems counterproductive to the very practice that is essential to build an ahimsic disposition.

In short, from Sita we learn that any appeal for ahimsa which fails of inclusiveness and which is not unequivocally opposed to violent behavior, be the end ever so just, cannot be accounted an unqualified success. For a truly unqualified expression of the ahimsic persuasion, consider the following citation from one of the oldest and most revered of Hindu scriptures, the *Chandogya Upanishad*. It reads:

> This did Brahma to Prajapati; Prajapati, to Manu; Manu, to human beings. He who according to rule has learned the Veda from the family of a teacher; he who has concentrated all his senses upon the Self; he who is harmless *(ahimsant)* toward all things elsewhere than at holy places—he, indeed, who lives thus throughout his length of life, reaches the Brahma-world and does not return hither again — yea, he does not return hither again!

In this citation, 'ahimsa' is taken to be both universal in scope and a necessary means to realizing Brahma, an aspect of the Hindu Godhead, Brahman. Now, one who realizes Brahma, we are advised, "does not return hither again," that is, escapes 'samsara,' the excruciating wheel of birth and rebirth on this plane of existence. One is condemned to 'samsara,' and so to rebirth, Hinduism teaches, because one's *karma* is unexpiated. 'Karma,' in the present context, betokens the Indian equivalent of Christianity's "As you sow, so shall you reap," only extended over multiple lifetimes.

The passage's meaning, therefore, is clear. Harmful deeds generate karmic or moral debt, which binds one to *samsaric* existence. And since, as the text further suggests, those who wilfully and habitually injure another, human or otherwise, are not fit to enter the Brahma-world. It would seem that individuals of violent disposition are ultimately locked into the *samsaric* track because their conduct is out of step with God's moral law, as revealed in the Vedas.

And with this, the opposition between the *dharmic* view and the *ahimsa* view would appear to be complete and irremediable. For the former, violent behaviour may well be virtuous behaviour; for the latter, virtue is decidedly all one with non-violent behavior. Again, for the former, violent behaviour is virtuous precisely and insofar as it receives divine approbation; for the latter, non-violence exclusively warrants divine sanction, whence virtue perforce entails non-violent behaviour. Such are the polar moral views on violence authoritatively expounded in, and founded upon, the one and the same Vedas!

5

Suffering

Self-suffering is the third element of Gandhi's theory of Satyagraha. Action based on love towards others, is a positive test of truth. From this Gandhi goes on to say that tapas or self-suffering is the test of such love. Suffering injury in one's own person, writes Gandhi, "is the essence of non-violence and is the chosen substitute for violence to other". Self-suffering by satyagrahis, it must be understood, is not out of their cowardice or weakness; it is based on higher form of courage than that of those who resort to violence and it is meant to aid in the moral persuasion of one's opponents or oppressors.

Suffering of non-violence may make its deep appeal to the human moral consciousness, its nobility and dignity; but joy of existence, of fullness of being and activity even in the form of war and fight for noble causes, makes its effective appeal also. Gandhi fully acknowledges his failure to realize the true method of non-violence, and the full practical program to which he aspired. His own failure, as its originator and most accurate and intense practitioner and investigator, is the best argument against the radical viability and practicability that he claimed for his ideology and praxis.

Gandhi is unlikely to have an equal in his experiments, and "1,000 years hence" he will scarcely be believed to have walked this earth, as Einstein is often quoted about him. It is almost impossible to imagine an equal, much less a more thorough effort.

The last two years of his life Gandhi tried to face massive inter-religious and fraternal violence with his techniques of non-violence in Noakhali, Calcutta and Delhi. Without a study of historical records and first hand accounts, it is hard to grasp the magnitudes of the violence and to gauge the dimensions of his efforts and comparative success. Gandhi's own assessment of these campaigns was failure of his technique and insufficiency of his own spiritual evolution and purity measured in terms of ahimsa. Applied to the problem of criteria and mass application, he writes :

> That art of true self-defence by means of which man gained his life by losing it, had been mastered and exemplified in the history of individuals. The method had not been perfected for application by large masses of mankind and India's satyagraha was a very imperfect experiment in that direction. Hence, during the Hindu-Muslim quarrel it proved a failure on the whole.

In the satyagraha mode of conflict resolution, self-suffering plays a complementary role to that of reasoning. Persuading the other through reasoning is indeed the essence of satyagraha. But satyagrahi recognizes the limits of reason in resolving fundamental social, religious, political or ideological conflict in which a rational consensus may not be easily or quickly forthcoming. Here Gandhi offers an anticipated critique of Habermas's theory of communicative ethics. In fact, Gandhi insisted that the direct action techniques of Satyagraha are to be resorted to only after employing the usual process of reasoning with the opponents or oppressors and only for securing their rational consent or conversion. He writes:

> Since Satyagraha is one of the most powerful methods of direct action, a satyagrahi exhausts all other means before he resorts to Satyagraha. He will, therefore, constantly and continually approach the constituted authority, he will appeal to public opinion, educated public opinion, state his case calmly and coolly before every body who wants to listen to him; and only after he has exhausted all these avenues will he resort to Satyagraha.

In a Satyagraha campaign, the contested truth of a social system or norm is sought to be validated through three steps: (1) persuading the opponents through reasoning and being open to, and inviting the counter-persuasive efforts of the opponents : (2) appealing to the opponents through the self-suffering of the satyagrahis; and (3) non-cooperation and civil disobedience.

The various method of Satyagraha are: (1) purificatory or penitential actions by the satyagrahis, such as pledges, prayers, and fasts; (2 acts of non-cooperation, such as boycott, strikes, hartal, and the like; (3) act of civil disobedience, such as picketing, non-payment of taxes, and defiance of specific laws; and (4) works or constructive programme, such as the promotion of inter-communal unity, the removal of untouchability, adult education, and the removal of economic and social inequalities. At each stage of the programme, the satyagrahis, while holding on to the truth as they see it, assume their own fallibility and give the opponents every chance to prove that the satyagrahi's position is erroneous. Satyagraha excludes the use of violence because man is not capable of knowing the absolute truth and therefore, not competent to punish. The idea to be kept in mind is that of a self-regulated society of communitarian truth in which every one "rules himself in such a manner that he is never a hindrance to his neighbours". "The claim for Satyagraha", writes Joan Bondurant, "is that through the operation of non-violent action the truth as judged by the fulfillment of human needs, will emerge in the form of a mutually satisfactory and agreed-upon solution." Hence the important operative principles to be observed by the satyagrahis are the admission of truth as relative, non-violence and toleration, and the self-suffering of the Satyagrahis. Gandhi justified these operative principles in the following passages:

> In the application of Satyagraha. I discovered that in the earliest stages that pursuit of truth did not admit of violence being inflicted on ones' opponent, but that he must be weaned from error by patience and sympathy. For what appears to be Truth to one may appear false to the other.

The golden rule of conduct, therefore, is mutual toleration, seeing that will never all think alike and we see truth in fragment and from different angles of vision. Conscience is not the same thing for all. While, therefore, it is a good guide for individual conduct, imposition of that conduct upon all will be an insufferable interference with everybody's freedom of conscience. People's conceptions of true interests and just laws differ. That is the main reason why violence is eliminated and a satyagrahi gives his opponent the same right of independence and feeling of liberty that he reserves to himself and he will fight by inflicting injuries on his person.

Gandhi links the principles of Satyagraha to the spirit and ethos of democracy. In his opinion, evolution of democracy is not possible if we are not prepared to hear the other side. We shut the doors of reason when we refuse to listen to our opponents, or having listened, make fun of them. If intolerance becomes a habit, we run the risk of missing the truth. While, with the limits the nature has put on our understanding, we must act fearlessly according to the light vouchsafed to us, we must always keep an open mind and be ever ready to find that what we believed to be truth was, after all, untruth. This openness of mind strengthens the truth in us.

Gandhi was opposed to armed struggle because it would take many, many years for the Indians to arm themselves in a matching or effective manner more than this practical difficulty. Gandhi disapproved of the moral consequences of Indian freedom movement's adopting the method of violence. He pointed out that "to arm India on a large scale is to Europeanise it" or, in other words, to continue to be reduced by the morally flawed modern European civilization.

Indian metaphysical and religious thinking sees not so much evil, as suffering, as the chief problem. The theist of the Judaeo-Semitic tradition with his insight to God as the embodiment of goodness in His Divine Person grapples with the undoubted presence of evil in the world. The forces within and without involve him in this cosmic drama, and that suffering is part of his lot is accepted as a fact of his existence. It is no less a fact that he is capable of reaching peaks of joy, in human relationships and in the creative work of art and craft, and these give a foretaste of a bliss which is beyond imagining and yet which is mirrored in the mood of celebration which dominates most forms of Indian art. A cyclical view of time reconciles man to the repetitive phases of his destiny. The cycle of births and deaths strikes a man in a fearsome way if he sees it as the prospect of further chains of suffering. Suffering then, in the Indian mind, has always posed itself, to the philosophers and sages, as something to be got rid of, that is, as a practical problem.

Bondage, however, is not the last word. The different systems along with their analysis of the causes of bondage, or to change the idiom, in their probing of the depths of human finitude, also set out of the maze. Divine grace may, or may not, feature in the system, depending on whether the theistic hypothesis is present or not, and, as in theologies of other traditions, on the extent to which man is conceived to be imperfect. It is striking that all Indian systems, barring the Carvaka, take it for granted that the central target of ethico-religious endeavour is the removal of suffering. In working out how this was to be done, Indian thinkers were in a bit of a quandary. The activist alternative, presented interalia quite unmistakably in the Gita, carried along with it a danger. To act is to accumulate further karmas and thus to add to one's bondage. Even though the possibility of evening up the account through further births might be consolatory, very opposite effect might be brought about.

Reformist Hindu thought from the nineteenth century onwards was bold enough to attempt to cut through this problem. But it was not until Gandhi that we find the innovatory idea of suffering the richest treasure of life itself beings regarded as a way of dealings with suffering. This paradox will have to be elucidated. Gandhi is traditional in seeing the central human task as that of getting rid of suffering and in seeing this as a practical matter. But he sees the sufferings of men in a particularistic way, rather than, as the philosophers had seen it, as a general cosmic condition. Secondly, he centres on the sufferings of others as the focus of our meliorist efforts, not the shuffling off of the chains of bondage for our own personal liberation. The sufferings to be got rid of stem from the injustices that beset the poor; they derive from wickedness in high places as well as from wickedness within the human heart. Gandhi is not concerned with finding a metaphysical justification for suffering or with speculating about its cause. His scientific eye diagnoses the diseases of society, his heart responds to those in distress, and he works out a new tapasya, a new marga for tackling human miseries.

In a manner which is strikingly contemporary, Gandhi pinpoints violence as the chief malady of our times. If anyone asks Gandhi what is wrong with violence he has his answers ready. Once violent. action leads to another for example, violent speech provokes angry retorts from the other side. Secondly, violence concentrates power in the hands of a few. He is thinking here of the violence typified in colonialism and the economic system which deprive the poor by concentrating wealth in feudal and capitalist structures. Thirdly, violence leads to suffering and degradation. His Ambulance Corps work in the Boer and Zulu wars brought him face to face with the misery caused by war. Warfare is the externalisation of violence in the human heart. Violence is evil. This is why the words 'ahimsa paramo dharma' posses for Gandhi seeing man as a reservoir of powers for good and evil. The task set us is to channelise man's energies in such a way that good predominates. It was not enough to search among metaphysical systems for a remedy for suffering. We need to revolutionise our social environment, and this can come about only through a revolution in the human heart. A method is needed which not only the spiritually strong can use, which those who have adopted sannyasa, or those who are pursuing closistered virtues can employ. A method is needed for every man, a moral equivalent of warfare which will release the constructive energies that all men possess and which will enable man to build up a good life for all. Gandhi believed this method to be the method of non-violence, the voluntary assumption of suffering by an individual and by a group as a self-purificatiory act, an example to other, and as a way of converting the-heart of the oppressor.

The difference between voluntary suffering and involuntary suffering was a very basic one for Gandhi. The sufferings of the poor were not of their own choosing. Gandhi strongly rejects classic excuse that one's condition in this life is the result of bad deeds in previous lives. Social injustice is a challenge to be faced here and now. Reality has to be changed. The world, and that in so doing we chime in with reality at a deeper level since we are thereby operating according to the law of love. Voluntary suffering or self-sacrifice is what Gandhi puts in place of the ancient yagna or sacrifice. The reign of love is to be brought about not through the sacrificial love of God's son on the Cross but through every man's acts of self-sacrifice. Gandhi often uses the images of the Cross to drive his message home. In 1927 he wrote :

> God did not bear the Cross only 1900 years ago, but He bears it today, and He dies and is resurrected from day to day. It would be poor comfort to the world if it had to depend upon a historical God who died 2000 years ago. Do not then preach the God of history, but show Him as He lives today through you.

These words were addressd to a Christian audience. Gandhi very evidently believed in the power of suffering, for some years later he wrote: 'I saw that nations like individuals could only be made through the Cross and in no other way.' But if the power of suffering is not to be seen paradigmatically in a redemptive act, how then is it to be seen? To answer this we need to return to his South African experience out of which the whole gospel of non-violence was born.

It was a gospel in the sense that it amounted to the good news that the poorest of the poor were shown a way of using their non-violent strength; that out of man's very weakness he could accomplish mightily. For Gandhi himself this was by no means as Pelagian a strategy as it sounds. His own life was conducted, in the presence of God and it was his own experience the God came to the help of the helpless. Gandhi himself recalled how he came to forge the weapon of satyagraha in South Africa when mere talk, petitions, negotiations had failed:

> It came to me that we should refuse to obey legislation that was degrading and let them put us in jail if they liked. Thus came into beings the moral equivalent of war. Since then the conviction has been growing upon me, that things of fundamental importance to the people are not secured by reason alone but have to be purchased with their suffering. Suffering is the law of human beings; war is the law of the jungle. But suffering is infinitely more powerful than the law of the jungle. for convering the opponent and opening his ears, which are otherwise shut, to the voice of reason. The appeal of reason is more to the head but the penetration of the heart comes from suffering. It opens up the inner understanding in man. Suffering is the badge of the human race, not the sword.

It is a long quotation but richly creative in content. It may seem paradoxical that the man who speaks of satyagraha as a science in the making should confess the limits of reason. It can be looked upon in this way. How can one persuade the fanatic, the man who through stubbornness, vested interest, ingrained orthodoxy or whatever, is not be be persuaded in favour of what we believe to be right and just. The method of reason comes up against 'stoppers', and perhaps everyone who has argued about the role of reasoning in ethics has granted that this is so. To think of man as a rational animal scarcely cuts ice, and the Greeks were perhaps in the best position of all to appreciate that man's psyche cannot be confined within the straightjacket of reason, those who thougtht in terms of rule and those who thought in terms of telos might have wished it were otherwise. But the nature of man has its shallow pools and swamps, its depths and heights, and what is religious life but a coming to terms with all these many territories.

Gandhi's was not the method of injunction of preaching, because he believed that the ears of those who are determined not be hear are unlikely to be unstopped through mere talk. One can of course, through reason, established theories, found systems and so forth. But what was at stake was not systems but 'things of fundamental importance to the people'. This includes the securing of civic rights, the gaining of national independence, the ending of the exploitation of the of poor by the rich. Discussion and negotiation may take us to the part of the way but they will not take us to the end of the road. Self-suffering is more than a tool of conflict resolution, it is a way of 'changing reality'. That suffering is the badge of the human race had been the belief of generations of people living in India reflected in the philosophers' obsession with 'dukha'. Christianity made the Cross and the Resurrection the central events in the redemption of man by God in the form of the one who was both Son of Man and Son of God. The fact remains that the revolutionary potential both of the Mahavakyam of the Upanishads and the message of 'Love God and thy neighbour as thyself' had some how got lost along the way.

Gandhi found that what is most inescapable about human life, the fact that man must suffer, can be turned to good account. Gone was the traditional belief that suffering was at all costs to be got rid of. Gone too was the idea of individual suffering of an isolationist kind, undertaken through austerities, in quest of self-perfection. In place of the Jain concept of the spiritual hero who recovers the pristine purity of a soul which has become tainted through karmic difilement, Gandhi puts the heroism of the group of satyagrahis who undertake a movement to redress economic, civic, social or political grievances. The 'conversion' aimed at is not a conversion of belief externalised in a formal changing of religious labels. Gandhi does use the word conversion, and he is very well aware of its religious overtones. The opponent is to be converted, to undergo a change of heart, when he sees that the satyagrahis are willing to stake their all for what they believe to be true.

Why should anyone voluntarily add to his sufferings when, as it is, suffering is the common lot of men? Many elements enter into Gandhi's thinking at this point. As a Vaishnava, he has faith that man is a being who is capable of being touched by another' woe. The reverse is also the case. Man can harden his heart and refuse to regard another's suffering as any business of his own. But Gandhi believed that since men share a common humanity, sooner or later the opponent will be won over. This apparent conquest by the satyagrahis was, however, not a defeat for the other side, but a conquest for them too, in that they had been able to rise above the factors which had previously stood in the way of understanding. But there are several conditions which had to be fulfilled first on the part of the satyagrahis. We have seen that Gandhi was a great believer in the importance of discipline for spiritual-growth, and with the wisdom of a spiritual master he had his finger on the pulse of those he led, sensing their readiness or otherwise for embarking on a particular campaign. Here again there are overtones from the past. In both the Hindu and Jain modes of ascesis, a distinction is drawn between the discipline proper to a house-holder and what is proper for the sannyasi or the monk. Gandhi's reaction to this traditional distinction is complex. While on the one hand he stresses the importance of stages-a major example is found in the stages of the national movement which he led over a period of decades-he is no less insistent that the techniques of self-suffering, sacrifice for a cause, is something which the humblest man, including the householder, can use, provided of couse, he under goes the necessary preliminary training. This discipline included what Gandhi called non-violence in thought. But ideas have a natural outcome in action and non-violent actions have a persuasive power greater than that of words.

It may be useful to mention an example of non-violent action in a context which involved an apparently reiligious matter, to get the feel of how the principle worked. Vykom in Kerala enters modern Indian history as the place where in 1925 an important satyagraha movement took place to vindicate civic rights of the untouchables to pass down a particular road, and eventually opened up the whole discourse of the right of any Hindu, whether caste Hindu or otherwise, to enter a temple. There are interesting features about this particular campaign. First of all it illustrates Gandhi's insistence that each religious community must put its own house in order. Untouchability was a blot on the name of Hinduism, a cancer, a disease. Since it is a matter which concerns the Hindu community it is no solution if the untouchables run away and became Buddhists as Ambedkar advised. Each must find his salvation within his own community. But this required non-violent definance of the brahmins' edict not to use a certain road, a willingness of the untouchables to undergo hardship in so doing, and a parallel constructive effort on their part to improve their own life by observing cleanliness, improving their crops through the use of compost, spinning, and a host of other things involved in Gandhi's conception of rural reconstruction. It is those who bear the brunt of a particular injustice who must learn to mobilise their non-violent strength in order to improve their condition. This was why he did not allow the Sikhs to open charitable kitchens in Vykom, commented discouragingly on Christian efforts to eradicate untouchability, and spoke against the dole system.

What then becomes of the principle of bearings one another's burdens? Straight off it must be said in answering this question that Gandhi is not at all hamstrung by any philosophical allegiance to separate karmic lines. It is a principle that must be carried out first, and foremost with those with whom we are immediately associated. Here Gandhi has something very signifincant to say in the light of the caste allegiances of Hindu society. When he went to Noakhali on his historic peace-making tour in 1946, he urged the riot-stricken people to organise themselves as fisherfolk, as weavers, as peasants; let the unit of collective action be the immediate goal in daily work. Here was a new teaching regarding identification of one's neighbour. Later, when Gandhian workers tried to organise peace brigades in other parts of the country, it was on a neighbourhood basis. So it happened that even in the midst of terrible communal conflagration the import of 'who is my neighbour' was not totally lost and there were heroic cases, both in Bengal and Punjab, of Muslims sheltering Hindus and Hindus sheltering Muslims, often at the cost of their own lives.

The independent observer may have some difficulties over Gandhi's embracing of suffering as an operative principle. In pre-Independence days the satyagraha weapon, seemed to be nothing less than a form of political blackmail. But a generation familiar with Martin Luther King and Danilo Dolci, with French worker-priests, and the politically involved clergy of many countries in Latin America, and familiar moreover with the catastrophic effects of violence (including assassinations, the taking of hostages, urban guerilla strategies, and isloated acts of terorism which wipe out innocent civilians) is in a better position to appreciate what Gandhi was about. The mighty weaponry of powerful states has not proved itself able to control violence, still less to neutralise it. In so many parts of the globe today there are stalemate situations where the man in the street suffers, entire governments are held to ransom and futher spells not hope but panic as to where terror will strike next. That we are in dire need of a method of defusing the loci of violence in our society would be readily conceded today.

But will the method of self-suffering work in dealing with every kind of situation? The method presuppose a certain gallantry in the adversary. It is easy to think of cases in the past and present where that gallantry was, and is, comspicuously absent. Here Gandhi would say that such considerations did not show up the method as ineffective. It rather showed that our preparation had been wanting. The supporting constructive work which was an indispensable parallel activity to the voluntary assumption of suffering in order to right injustices, had been absent or inadequate, or our timing had been wrong. If a situation were allowed to deteriorate beyond a certain point, it is this deterioration, rather than failure of the method of self-suffering, which was to blame. Gandhi did provide a criterion which is sometimes forgotten. In conditions where cowardice and violence are the only alternatives, then violence is the lesser evil. In spite of giving the impression at times of seeing things in black and white, Gandhi had in fact his own way of assessing the pros and cons of a situation, and no decision was taken without thorough inquiry into the factors concerned, especially the human element, as was possible in the circumstancs. That self-suffering will eventually move the heart of the opponent was an article of faith with him. But even if it did not, he belived it was better to be killed than to kill, apparently to fail, than to give in to tyranny. Gandhi was pragmatist as well as an idealist. He used the weapon of self-suffering over a period of many decades, beginning with the South African period of his life. He showed it could be used to alter economic, social and political situations, and the very movements he led brought out the extent to which they were inextricably related. But towards the end of his life he confessed that the weapon was a new one, yet to be perfected, a technique which was still in an experimental form. Without the preliminary self-purification on which he laid such stress, the method, *'Gandhigiri'* could degenerate into a form of blackmail or sheer coercion 'dadagiri'. Whatever methods we use, they are, after all, carried out by men, and men are fallible beings.

It is worth marking the difference between this approach and two others. The Jain reverence for life which is taken to an extreme point in customs like covering the mouth and nose, feeding ants with sugar, and which led to the avoidance of agriculture for it cannot be carried out without the destruction of life, resulted in directing the Jain community into business. The Islamic belief in theocracy has amounted to a refusal to distinguish religion from politics and an attempt to shape every aspect of life strictly according to theological tenets derived from the Koran. Gandhi's attitude appears in a very different light from both of these. He had no partience with the ant-feeding type of Jain, who, following the insect theme, strained at an ant but swallowed a camel for example who adulterated ghee. Gandhi's approach to scriptures was always very liberal. If there was anything in scripture which offended against reason or conscience, so much the worse for scripture. In any case man's God-given powers of scrutiny and criticism should be turned on the written word no less than on institutions- all were man-made.

We have already seen that Gandhi did not believe that the human mind or human society could be divided into watertight compartments, social, political and religious. One has only to observe any big rally today in India to see how all three are inter-connected. Since the spiritual law does not work in a field of its own but through the ordinary activities of life, it works in the political sphere also, even though at times, and these are the words Gandhi himself uses, politics may encircle us like the coils of a snake. The symbol is significant. The snake is a symbol of power in Indian mythology and no one appreciated better than Gandhi that politics is to do with power. How can this power be humanised? This was the crux for Gandhi. And the answer is only through the counter- power of soul-force. In spite of Gandhi's passionate adoption of a life-style of self-purification for himself, he was not one with Tolstoy in relying on this alone. Time was running out and the people perish. New institutions must be built up in a progressive manner; social structures must be transformed, and political instruments forged which could be responsive to the will of an enlightened people. We have yet to elucidate two very important facets of Gandhi's teaching on self-suffering, that ahimsa is the farthest limit of humility, and that there is such a thing as the law of love. There is no room for being puffed up about our own particular view when other views are possible and are actually held by our fellow human beings. This is why Gandhi says: Out of truth emanate love, tenderness, humility increaes with his observance of truth.' Humility is the very reverse of self-assertivencess which springs from ego and makes for discord within man and within society. To wish to reduce onself to zero reveals the utmost humility. The question was for Gandhi by no means a theoretical one. Constructive workers in the villages were advised to move among the villagers with humility. It could not be assumed that the townsman's ways were the best. A life of service must be one of humility. But this involves 'most strenuous and constant endeavour'. Humility is the condition of growth.

We turn next to the theme of love. Gandhi says of satyagraha: 'Its root meaning is holding on to truth, hence truth-force. I have also called it love-force or soul-force.' The bhakti (devotion) tradition, as distinct from the dhyana (meditation) tradition in India, speaks of love between man and God. The Vaishnava hymn which Gandhi was fond of, celebrate this relationship. But Gandhi's lauguage and idioms are peculiarly his own when he comes to eludidating what he means by love. The Radha/Krishna symbolism appeals to him far less than does the analogy of Rama and Sita, the idea of faithful consortship. But all the thelogies are left behind when he identifies truth-force with love-force which are both to be understood as totally differnet from brute-force. In 1925 he once addressed an audience in Kutch as follow:

> What is worth learning from me is my love and not my strength to give a fight. My fighting strength is only small fraction of my real life. And even that strength is the outcome of my truth, my sympathy, my love. All my fights, and fighting spirit are worth nothing without that love.

C.F. Andrew spoke with deep understanding of his friend. Gandhi when he wrote to Romain Rolland that in his inner life 'it is the passion for others which is supreme'. Those close to him who saw how Gandhi allotted his time during the day have testified to the hours he devoted to listening to the woes of streams of visitors who consulted him on a vast range of personal problems even medical ones. No letter was too insignificant to get a personal reply from Bapu, sometimes a brief message on a postcard. With the eye of love he was able instinctively to intuit the other's need. To women in East Bengal who had lost their husbands, sons and brothers he came with a message not of consloation, but of courage. In touring from village to village in East Bengal, he went all the way back to give an ailing child the anema he needed. Such selfless giving attracted in full measure the rich friendship of men like Charlie Andrews, Rabindranath Tagore, Romain Rolland, Jawaharlal Nehru, Maulana Azad, and not only the giants of those days but the humble villagers with whom he identified himself in diet, dress, and style of life. So it came about that he drew so many to himself. Madeleine Slade (Mirabehn) was right when she wrote to Romain Rolland that: 'with Bapu it is his life and acts that speak more than words.'

What he is talking about is far more like agape than it is like eros or philia or even caritas. Ahimsa is 'the largesst love' because it is self-sacrificial love. We can compare it, then both with yagna ritualistic relationship between man and God celebrated so appealingly in India's devotional music. Ahimsa casts out cowardice; perfect love casts out fear. Gandhi never lost his faith in human nature in spite of having experienced man's inhumanity to man first hand, both in South Africa and in India. The Hindu tradition spoke of the divine spark in man, the Gita of the Lord as friend, and as Gandhi put it, 'Buddha taught us to defy appearances and trust in the final triumph of Truth and Love. The Sermon on The Mount had also made a deep impact on young Gandhi, an impression fortified by Tostoy's message of 'inward perfection, truth and love'. What Gandhi was looking for was a manly conception of love which he did not always find in the literature of his own Gujarat, much as he was devoted to it. He once wrote to Maganlal Gandhi, his nephew and close associate, that the love taught by Swaminarayan and Vallabhacharya was 'effeminate sentimentality', and that there was more of purusartha (manly endeavour) in the couplets of Ramdas. As for the grihasta ties with their inevitable tinge of possessiveness, they appeared in the garb of bondage to one who had donned the mantle of a national mission or perhaps had it thrust on him by the course of events. Human love as seen in the ties of comradeship which bind workers in a common cause was perhaps the form of love most intelligible to Gandhi, a self-sacrificial love which was seen in a specially intense form in ashrem life. But it was an outgoing love which reached the village child, the riot-ridden citizen, the British constable, not excluding the 'tallest in the land'.

The Sanskrit words beginning with the prefix 'a' conceal a positive meaning behind their apparently negative grammatical form. Gandhi thought it was necessary to bring this positive meaning out. This is why he says that in its positive form, Ahimsa means the largest love, the greatest charity. "If I am a follower of Ahimsa, I must love my enemy or a stranger to me as I would my wrong-doing father and son.' He is humble enough to include at the end of this statement what he at the time was finding a source of stress, his relationship with one of his sons Harital. Gandhi's frankness about his personal relationships has often puzzled others. But this was all part of the pursuit of truth, of authenticity in so far as one was capable of it.

There is a further dimension to this. The crying need for peace was never very far from Gandhi's mind. How can one 'live at peace with both friends and foe' if it not be through making a friend of the foe? The central anguish that contemporary man has to surmount is the anguish of war. Archbishop Cosmo Lang once spoke of Gandhi in unsympathetic terms as a mystic, fanatic and anarchist. We do not believe that the first two charges are just. But there is an element of anarchism in Gandhi, an enlightened anarchism in which he fancied and gloried. He really belived that the efforts of ordinary people to multiply the bonds of love and fellowship around them operated as peace-making forces in the world.

The concept of dharma involves a chain of duties rather than a chain of love. The Jain concept of the unity of all living things provides a sanction for non-injury to all beings, great and small. The Mahayana Buddhist concept of compassion, of return to the world out of concern for those still in bondage, examplified in the lives of bodhisattvas, brought more strongly into the tradition of India the sense of the positive transforming power of the gentler virturs.The purificatory role of both fire and water are familiar in the tradition of many peoples. Likewise also the purificatory role of austerities. At what point then does Gandhi bring in somethings new? It would be easy to say that Gandhi's encounter with Christian communities had introduced him to the idea of the power of love. The answer is unfortunately not so simple. In this history of the Crusades and in the rapacious economic structures he observed in South Africa, the influence of the Sermon on the Mount was conspicuous by its absence. For Gandhi it is not the Holy Family which provides the paradigm but a capacity for a long-suffering bearing with others which he found in the human family and perhaps even more in the village of his dreams. His first encounter with the New Testament and, in particular the Sermon on the Mount made him 'simply overjoyed', for it confirmed in with what he already believed to be true. The language of I Corinthians, Ch.13 is strangely echoed in the following: 'Satyagraha is gentle, it never wounds. It must not be the result of anger or malice. It is never fussy, never impatient, never vociferous. It is the direct opposite of compulsion.' Gandhi is full of surprises. He assimilates the idioms of other and they come out in his writing as if they were his own, even for example an echo of Spinoza when in speaking of 'this grand law of love' he asks wonderingly 'are not all good and great things difficult to do?'

Gandhi believed that the 'law of love', as he called it, was actually at work. That life goes on in spite of death and destruction, he took to be evidence of this. But, as in the case of dharma, we encounter here a principle which at once sustains all things and yet which requires man to guard and tend it. The cohesive force which already exists among men needs to be utilised. In other words Gandhi believes we have at our disposal a power whose full potential has yet to be realised. There is an interesting Jain echo of the notion of subtlety in his opinion: 'The more efficient a force is, the more silent and the more subtle it is. Love is the subtlest force in the world.' But although Gandhi so often spoke of soul-force on the analogy of other forces, his intention was really to point out how different it was from other forces. The ultimate test of the satyagrahi is his willingness to die, the choice of death, the adoption of self-suffering to the extremest limit. Can such a spirit of self-sacrifice be possible for one without faith in God? Gandhi believed that non-violence in the positive sense, that is, love, can only 'permeate' the man who has 'a living faith in God'. It was for this reason that Romain Rolland had many misgivings about the prospects of non-violence as an active principle in a desacralised world.

Gandhi sincerly affirmed that a satyagrahi relied on the power to suffering. Confronted with untruth he sought a dialogue with his opponent. When this was denied or reduced to an insincere exercise in public relations, he took a stand and accepted whatever punishment was meted out to him. Since his sole concern was to evoke a moral response in his opponent, he did everything to put him at ease and nothing to harass, embarrass, anger or frighten him.

In the meantime he suffered the punishment without hatred or ill-will in the hope of igniting in him a slow, intensely personal and highly complex process of self-examination. The moment his opponent showed the slightest willingness to talk in a spirit of genuine goodwill, he suspended his struggle and gave reason a chance to work in a more hospitable climate.

In all his satyagrahas Gandhi observed several basic principles. Before it was launched almost every one of them passed through three stages: a clear and reasoned defense of its objectives, a popular agitation to convince the government the intensity of popular feeling, and an ultimatum to give it the last chance for negotiation. Throughout the satyagraha, the channels of communication with the government were kept open, the attitudes on either side were not allowed to harden, and intermediaries were encouraged. Gandhi insisted that since a satyagraha was a deeply moral act, only those with the highest moral character and generally in the habit of obeying the law had the adhikar or moral right to participate in it. Violence was never encouraged and every satyagrahi was required to take a pledge to eschew it. He was also required never to complain about his punishment or to hit back, or resist arrest or the confiscation of his property, to impede, harass or spread gossips and innuendos against government officials or to insult the Union Jack. Similar rules were laid down for the satyagrahi prisoner who was expected to be courteous, ask for no special privileges, do as ordered and never to agitate for conveniences 'whose deprivation does not involve any injury to his self-respect.

Gandhi seems to offer three related but different explanations. First, he sometimes referred to the psychoylogiical impact of suffering. In his view it was most difficult for a human being to continue to inflict suffering on another. Sooner or later he became emotionally exhausted and morally worn out, especially when the victim offered no resistance. Richard Gregg, of whom Gandhi thought well, compared to the Japanese Jiu-jitsu style of wrestling in which a wrestler used the weight of his opponent to throw him off balance and subdue him. Violence confirmed the opponent's expectations and paradoxically sustained his morale and self-confidence. Since the satyagrahi played the game by wholly different rules, he confused and unhinged him, undermined his moral self-confidence and created in him a psychological space for critical self-reflection. The greater his opponent's anger and violence, the greater was the psychological energy available to him to create a sense of guilt and subtly transform him.

Second, sometimes Gandhi stressed the spiritual power of love. Like the natural world, the spiritual realm had its laws and a unique mode of operation. Even as electricity and gravitation worked in ways only a scientist could comprehend, one spirit acted on another in mysterious and hitherto unexplored ways, of which the continuing influence of Christ on the Cross was an obvious example. The satyagrahi's love, sustained even in the midst of most brutal treatment, released a silent and unseen force that touched the innermost spiritual being of his opponent, activated his sense of their shared identity and broke through the barriers of ill-will.

Third, and this seems to be Gandhi's well-considered view, he stressed the complex interaction between the spiritual impact of love and the psychological impact of suffering. The satyagrahi's love and moral nobility weakened his opponent's feelings of anger and hatred, awakened his sense of decency and humanity and morally transformed him; his uncomplaining suffering generated a sense of shame in him, denied him the pleasure of victory, mobilised public opinion and created a mood conducive to calm introspection. The two together triggered off the complex process of critical self-examination on which a satyagrahi relied for its success. Love by itself was not enough as otherwise the satyagrahi could quietly expostulate with his opponent without launching a campaign. Self-imposed suffering by itself was not enough either, for it had little value and was even counter-productive if accompanied by hatred and anger. Self-imposed suffering was effective and indeed acceptable only when born out of and sustained by love, and love was effective only when expressed and articulated through such suffering. Love spiritualised suffering, which in itself had only a psychological value; suffering gave love a worldly and visible manifestation as well as psychological energy and power.

Gandhi realised early in his political career that suffering love had its limits. His satyagraha against the 1907 Registration Act of the Transvaal Legislative Assembly went on for months and produced no targible result. The one against the Natal immigration bills was even more painful and protracted. The provisional settlement he reached with the government included no major concession, and even then the government tried to wriggle out of it by putting dubious glosses on its important clauses. As the satyagraha dragged on, the government resorted to the familiar tactic of harassing, dividing and tiring out its opponents, misrepresenting their case and misguiding public opinion. Predictably they became demoralised, and their numbers began to decline drastically. If suffering love was all-powerful, numbers would not have mattered. Gandhi realised that they did, for he could not exert any pressure on the government without mass support. After a few months he decided to draw in the indentured labourers whom he had hitherto ignored by including their demand for a repeal of the three pound tax in his programme. He called them out on strike in 1913 and travelled around the mining districts bringing out the workers and discouraging those showing signs of returning to work. This put pressure on the coal owners and eventually on the government. The strike also spread to the coastal sugar districts and had a considerable economic impact. Gandhi now acquired the bargaining power he desperately needed to negotiate with the government on more or less equal terms.

Although Gandhi continued to maintain that suffering love was omnipotent and, when pure, was capable of 'melting even the stoniest hearts', he knew that the reality was very different. Most satyagrahis were ordinary human beings whose tolerance, love, determination and ability to suffer had obvious "limits and who could not 'act beyond their capacity'. When confronted with a deeply prejudiced and obstinate government that paid no heed to and totally insensitive to its subjects their suffering, they had little chance of success. As Gandhi put it in the course of his South African struggle:

> I do not believe in making appeals when there is no force behind them, whether moral or material. Moral force comes from the determination of the appellants to do something, to sacrifice something for the sake of making their appeals effective. Even children instinctively know this principle.

Gandhi saw this even more clearly on his return to India where he was fighting not a weak provincial government but a powerful empire determined at all costs to protect and defend its vital interests. The Jallianwala Bagh massacre convinced him how ruthless the government was prepared to be and how little it was influenced by the 'innocent suffering' of hundreds of women and children. Not surprisingly he felt it necessary to redefine satyagraha and to add to its 'armoury' the novel and highly effective weapons of social, economic and political boycott, civil disobedience, non-payment of taxes, non-violent raids, strikes and other forms of non-cooperation, none of which relied on suffering love alone and which were all designed to compel and force the government to listen and negotiate. Even his description of satyagraha underwent a radical change, and he began to call it non-violent 'warfare', 'peaceful rebellion', a civilised form of warfare' and a 'war bereft of every trace of violence'. With all these changes in his manner of action and language of discourse, the very concept of satyagraha came under strain, and it is doubtful if the social and economic boycott, strike and non-payment of taxes could be called satyagraha in the moral sense in which he had used the term so far. As usual Gandhi's praxis outpaced his theory.

As Gandhi realised that the satyagraha against the government was very different from that against a private individual, and as he saw the need to put economic and political pressure on the government, he began to analyse the nature and basis of political power and the way it sustained oppressive and unjust systems. His reflections on his South African experiences led him to several interrelated discoveries. First, all power was ultimately derived from the victims. It was because they thought and behaved as if they were powerless that their masters acquired power over them. Second, all systems of oppression ultimately depended on and were maintained by the co-operation of their victims. Third, the oppressed were a party to and responsible for their oppression and never wholly innocent. Fourth, no system of oppression could come into being let alone last unless it was rooted in the minds and hearts of its victims. The victims accept the willing bondage.

When the Natal government passed discriminatory laws against the Asians, the latter either accepted or resorted to devious ways of circumventing them. When Gandhi urged them to protest none was ready and they expected him to do their fighting for them. Not surprisingly the government became bolder and passed increasingly vicious anti-demenatic laws. Again, when it passed the Asian Licensing Act, making it extremely difficult for the Asians to obtain trading licenses, rather than unite and fight they went about bribing the officials and procuring the licenses. In sheer frustration Gandhi remarked, 'Shall we blame the Whites alone for these things? We at any rate cannot. If we behave like worms, we are bound to be trampled upon.' The white South Africans were not angels and were naturally tempted to pursue their interests at the expense of the Asians. However, they would not have dared put their intentions into practice if they had feared fierce resistance. Since the Indians behaved like worms, they encouraged, even invited the Whites to trample on them with impunity. Whenever there was a coward, argued Gandhi, there was bound to be a bully. Indeed it was the coward's fault that he had allowed someone to become a bully. He was thus doubly guilty for his own dehumanisation as well as that of the bully. By freeing himself from his cowardice, he also liberated the bully from his bullying tendencies. Sometimes Gandhi got carried away and advanced the untenable thesis that the oppressed were themselves to be blamed for their condition. For the most part, however, he was content to argue that while the oppressors were not blameless, their victims were not innocent either, and that the latter should devote their energies to organising themselves and fighting against the oppressive system rather than blame and hate their masters.

As Gandhi vividly realised in the course of the Natal satyagraha of 1910, the entire economic system of South Africa was sustained by the labour of its workers. If they were to stop working, it would not last a day. They were thus not its helpless victims, and had the power to overthrow it. It continued because and as long as they co-operated with it; they were therefore accomplices in their own exploitation. Similarly British rule in India owed its existence to the fact that the Indians co-operated with it, supplied the necessary manpower, and above all accepted its legitimising ideology. If they stopped co-operating with it in all areas of life including the ideological, it would not last a day. The government had no power of its own; it derived it from their co-operation. Gandhi's continued emphasis on non-cooperation from the time he assumed leadership of the Indian National Congress was based on this theory of power. Since co-operation was the source of the government's power and its people's powerlessness, non-cooperation was the only way to reverse the situation.

The belief that the oppressor had all the power was, of course, a myth. However, insofar as it was taken to be true by both the parties and formed the basis of their expectations and mutual responses, it became self-fulfilling. This was broadly the Hindu doctrine of *maya*, on which Gandhi drew heavily. Every system of oppression rested on *maya* which veiled the underlying *satya* that the oppressor had no power save what his victims chose to give him. It was simply a false consciouness. The Raj was able to exercise an ideological hegemony over the Indians.

For Gandhi a system of oppression derived its strength and durability from two interrelated sources: first, the victim's illusion that his oppressor was all-powerful and he himself powerless; and second, his incapacity for action. Since the victim believed himself to be powerless, he fell into the habit of looking after himself at the expense of others and lacked the courage or capacity to organise himself. The oppressor took advantage of the resulting vacuum and built up a formidable apparatus of coercion that further strengthened the power of the illusion. Those wishing to change the system must therefore act at two levels; they should help the victim see through the illusion of powerlessness and build up his self-confidence and capacity for concerted action. Political education and political praxis were inseparable and neither had a chance of success in the absence of the other. They were also dialectically related in the sense that each was both a precondition and a consequence of the other.

This was precisely what Gandhi's satyagraha aimed to accomplish. It educated the people and demystified the system. It also organised them, built up their political power and threatened the system. It sought popular 'awakening', an evocative term with a strong religious resonance, by means of and as a prelude to political action. Each of his satyagrahas was a well-calculated step towards a necessary moment in the dialectic of national regeneration. Remedying a specific injustice was its immediate goal through which it aimed to realise its far more important long-term objectives. Each satyagraha carefully selected a target that met the three crucial criteria of dramatically exposing the evil character of the system, mobilising popular attention and energy and standing a good chance of success. Its success partially lifted the veil of maya, gave people both a better insight into the nature of the system and a sense of power, weakened the government's self-confidence and morale and slightly shifted the overall balance of power in favour of the people. More satyagrahas followed, each progressively giving a further nudge to the shifting balance of power, until a point was reached when the awakened masses had seen through the ingenious mechanism of colonial rule and were no longer prepared to put up with it.

Gandhi's satyagraha then as an ingenious combination of reason, morality and politics, relied on the powers of argument, suffering love and organised pressure, and appealed to the opponent's head, heart and interests. Although each satyagraha brought in all three elements which it combined differently to suit different conditions, they were not all equally important. Reason or rational discussion remained its ultimate goal. It was because reason had failed that the satyagraha had become necessary. The constant aim of the satyagrahi, of which he was never to lose sight, was to get the dialogue going in the spirit of goodwill. Self-imposed suffering was not important in itself, but accepted only in order to facilitate and unblock the exercise of reason. As for organised political pressure it contained the element of coercion and did not appeal to the opponent's moral nature. Strictly speaking it was therefore not moral and was only intended to activate the head and the heart.

The satyagraha as Gandhi understood it, then, had both moral and political dimensions, and relied on the moral power of self-imposed suffering as well as the political pressure exerted by social, economic and other kinds of action. Since political pressure was only designed to facilitate and intensify the moral, Gandhi underplayed its role and saw the satyagraha as essentially a moral method. His opponents viewed it very differently. They felt and responded to the impact of political pressure and regarded it as basically a political method like any other, whose moral component was incidental, marginal or even a mere smoke-screen. While he interpreted its political dimension in moral terms, they saw its moral dimension in political terms. The results were often fascinating even puzzling.

When Gandhi called a *hartal,* he said that it was not so much a strike as an expression of collective sorrow and grief at the untruth committed by the government. That it also involved cessation of work was only its incidental consequence. When he launched social and economic boycott, he said that it was meant not so much to put pressure on the government as to express his countrymen's moral determination to withdraw co-operation from an unjust government which they had every right and duty to do. When a satyagraha led to a settlement, he claimed that it had 'touched' the government 'heart' and 'converted' it. The British saw the whole thing in opposite terms. A *hartal* involved a strike, and the fact that the strikers subjectively saw it as a *hartal* did not alter the objective fact that it was and had all the consequences of a strike. This was equally true of the economic boycott which was not merely an assertion of the moral right to non-cooperate but also and primarily a refusal to buy British goods and cause considerable hardship to the workers in British textile mills and put pressure on the government.

Their conflicting understanding of satyagraha also led to differences in the way each approached the other. Gandhi was always anxious to establish some kind of moral relationship with the government and lift their discussions to a new level. He often addressed the Viceroy as a 'friend', articulated his demands in moral terms, appealed to his 'conscience' and 'sense of justice' and wondered how a man of his moral sensitivity could wish to live with untruth. For his part the Viceroy studiously stuck to the conventional language of politics where he had an advantage over his spiritual opponent. He addressed him as 'Mr Gandhi', used the formal language of official communication, asked him for a 'clear statement' of his demands and warned him of the 'illegality' of his contemplated course of action. Each skilfully resisted entering an unfamiliar territory and talking in a language of which he had an insecure grasp. During a series of such encounters involving fascinating manoeuvres, each scored limited victories. Gandhi did on occasions manage to evoke a moral response from and establish a friendly and at times even warm and trustful relationship with his antagonist. For their part the British government from time to time forced Gandhi to speak in conventional political idioms, descend from his high moral pedestal and negotiate as an ordinary politician.

Gandhi's satyagraha also led to an innovative style of negotiation. He was primarily concerned to evoke in his opponent a spirit of goodwill and deepen their mutual understanding. During the course of the satyagraha he therefore probed him in his characteristic ways to reassure himself that his opponent was better disposed than before, meant well and could be trusted. Once he was satisfied, he treated the detailed negotiations as a relatively minor matter. Establishing a basis of goodwill, one of the essential conditions of a meaningful rational discussion, and paving the way for a better future relationship represented a vital long-term gain and mattered most to him. As for the specific issue in question Gandhi felt sure that since his opponent was well-disposed and knew the strength of popular feeling, he was bound to concede at least some of his demands. Since, however, he could not wholly transcend his point of view and the considerations of self-interest, he obviously could not concede them all. The practical outcome of the negotiations was therefore more or less certain, the only question being whether he should hold out for more than he was likely to get. He knew that he could increase the pressure and insist on more. However, if that was likely to vitiate the atmosphere of good will, Gandhi did not consider the price worth paying and preferred to wait for a more opportune moment. It would seem that almost as a matter of policy he left some ambiguity in the final settlement. This was his way of testing, even tempting his opponent.

In addition to such methods as economic and social boycott, non-cooperation, refusal to subscribe to government loans, strike, civil disobedience and non-payment of taxes which he tried out on different occasions with varying degrees of success, Gandhi also introduced the highly controversial method of fasting. It is not entirely clear whether he classified it as satyagraha. He rarely referred to it as one, although it probably satisfied all the relevant criteria. He fasted on 17 different occasions, none of his fasts lasting more than a week unless he had set himself a longer duration. Of these, three were against untouchability, three for Hindi-Muslim unity, four against violence, one to encourage the Ahmedabad striking textile will workers to stick to their pledge, three for self-purification and only three against a government. Of these last, one was against the Thakore of Rajkot, one against the colonial government's refusal to allow him to continue Harijan work in the prison, and one as a protest against the Viceroy holding him responsible for the violence of his followers. He never fasted against the colonial government to extract political concessions or to exert political pressure. There is only one recorded occasion when a group of people fasted against him, but he was able to dissuade them from it within a couple of days.

Gandhi knew that his fasts caused considerable unease among his critics and followers, and went to great lengths to defend them. He argued that over the years he had thoroughly identified himself with his countrymen and devoted his entire adult life to their service. They had reciprocated his love for them, trusted him and given him their unstinting support and loyalty. He had thus become a vehicle of their longings and a universally accepted custodian of their conscience. As a truly representative being who had become one with his people, he thought that he had both acquired the *adhikara* to rebuke and reproach them and incurred a *dharma* to accept responsibility and atone for their misdeeds. He was not fasting against strangers, for that would be coercion, nor for personal gain and glory, for that would be moral and emotional blackmail, but on behalf of those to whom he was bound by the mutually acknowledged bonds of love in order to wean them away from what they themselves accepted as grave moral lapses. His fast was really a 'voluntary crucifixion' of his flesh for their moral uplift, which he had both a right and a duty to undertake. It is worth noting how Gandhi took over the Christian concept of vicarious atonement and Hinduised it. Like Jesus on the Cross he sought to atone for his countrymen, but thought that he could only do so because and after he had earned the *adhikar* by virtue of his *karma*.

Gandhi argued that his fast had three objectives, First, it was his way of expressing his sense of sorrow and hurt. He could not bear to see those he loved degrade themselves and wanted them to know how much they had hurt and disappointed him. Second, as their leader he felt responsible for them, and his fast was his way of atoning and accepting responsibility for their misdeeds. And third, it was his last desperate attempt to stir their 'sluggish conscience', 'sting them into action' and awaken and mobilise their 'moral energies'. It was an 'intense spiritual effort', a penance, intended to 'burn up' the dross of their ill-will and hatred. For a variety of reasons his countrymen had temporarily lost their senses as in the case of communal violence, or become insensitive to injustice and suffering as in the case of untouchability, or shown utter lack to self-discipline as when a satyagraha became violent. By suffering himself and inducing sympathetic suffering in them, he intended to activate the process of moral self-examination in them. Gandhi conceded that a fast could easily become a form of moral blackmail, and imposed four limiting conditions. It should only be undertaken against those to whom one was bound by the mutually acknowledged bonds of love, only when their conduct was outrageous and admitted by them to be such; it should aim at their reform, and should be undertaken only after all other methods had failed.

Gandhi agreed that his fast exerted pressure, even perhaps coercion, on his intended targets, but insisted that the coercion was purely moral, 'the same kind of coercion which Jesus exercises upon you from the Cross'. Human life was necessarily interdependent and men could not avoid exerting pressure on one another. Furthermore, every man had a right to preserve his integrity and stop co-operating with those he considered misguided or evil. And when the evil was contagious and widespread, a votary of non-violence had no other remedy available to him save that of a fast. Gandhi asked what he was to do when his countrymen were busy murdering one another or treating some of them as worse than animals. Either he remained a helpless spectator, in which case he was a party to the evil, or he acted, and the only effective form of action open to him was the fast. Since it was only intended to get them to reflect on their behaviour and observe the values they themselves claimed to hold, Gandhi contended that the coercion it exerted was really the coercion of conscience and inherent in all moral conduct.

Although this could not be said of all of them, some of his fasts exercised a profound and essentially moral influence. Take for his Calcutta fast at the age of 78 in poor health against one of the most horrendous waves of communal carnage India bears testimony to his failure.

It has been suggested that we can understand Gandhi's concept of truth if we substitute the word 'Reality' for it, but this evidently does not fit his sense of the term in many passages. His slogan 'God is Truth' or 'Truth is God', if interpreted in this way, a suggest a Spinozan or Hegelian nature monism, with no great ethical content. But Truth, for Gandhi was the focal point of all his moral ideas. Often he describes himself as 'a humble searcher after Truth' or something similar. Self-claimed 'seekers after truth' are legion, both in the East and the West, and the term here can be taken in its literal English sense. The same is the case when Gandhi says:

> 'I have no policy save the policy of truth and ahimsa. For me truth is the sovereign principle. This Truth is not only truthfulness in word, but truthfulness in thought also, and not only the relative truth of our

> conception, but the Absolute Truth, the Eternal Principle, that is God. I worship God as Truth only. I have not yet found Him, but I am seeking after Him. Often in my progress I have had faint glimpses of the Absolute Truth, God and daily the conviction is growing upon me that He alone is real and all else is *unreal*.

We can perhaps find passages in Western literature in various languages where the word is given so many meanings, but in fact Gandhi's concept of truth, implying not only factual truth, truthful speech, honesty, and the resolute carrying out of vows, promises and plans, but also ultimate reality, can scarcely be paralleled outside India.

We have no evidence that the Upanishad had made any impression on the young Gandhi when he left for London, and it is probably that at that time he had never heard or read them, for the Upanishads were not the usual religious literature of the Indian Vaisya classes of those days. But his concept of Truth did not need the Upanishads to inspire it. Gnadhi's nurse, Rambha taught him to call on the name of God, in the form of Rama. One of the commonest ejaculations of popular north Indian Vaisnavism is Ram-nam sach hai, 'The Name of Ram is true'.

Unlike the English 'truth', which is related to such words as 'trust' and 'troth', satya is semantically akin to the word sat, 'existence', 'beings', the first property of the Absolute Essence or Brahman according to Vedanta philosophy. Its overtones are therefore more metaphysical than those of the corresponding English word, and in both Sanskrit and modern Indian languages its range of meaning is wider.

Thus the fundamental concept of Gandhi's philosophy owes nothing to Western sources. It was developed from the Hindu tradition in which he was brought up. Truth for Gandhi seems to incorporate some of the content of the pregnant Indin word *dharma*, especially in its Buddhist usage, as the eternal moral law by following which a man may achieve bliss. His knowledge of Buddhism does not appear to have been very profound, and he acquired whatever knowledge he had from his London days onwards. The coincidence is striking, however, for Buddhism tends to exalt dharma to the status of divinity. Another possible parallel to Gandhi's 'Truth' is the Vedic concept of Rta, the divinely ordained course of nature, which was associated in the minds of the Aryans with truth, honesty, regularity and carrying out one's resolutions.

Gandhi's frequent use of the slogan 'Truth is God' and certain passages from his speeches and writings taken out of their context might be used to suggest that he at heart a rationalist or at least an *advaitin*, believing only in an impersonal Absolute. In one well-known passage he declares: 'I am a part and parcel of the whole and cannot find Him apart from the rest of humanity'. He read something of Hindu and Buddhist philosophy, and of Western humanist and rationalist literature no doubt, and with typically Indian catholicity he tried to make room for the attitudes of other schools of thought. In a remarkable passage he admitted the influence of the typically Jain doctrine of *anekantavada*, which in its orignal form, implied that a proposition might at the same time be true and false from two relative points of view:

> I am advaitist and yet I can support dvaitism [dualism]. The world is changing every moment, and is therefore unreal, it has not permanent existence. But though it is constantly changing, it has a something about it which persists and it is therefore to that extent real. I have therefore no objection to calling it real and unreal, and thus being called an *anekantavadi* or *syadvadi*. But my syadvada is not the syadvada of the learned, it is peculiarly my own.

This aspect of Gandhi's thought is typical of Indian philosophy, which admits relative truth and degrees of truth, without references to Aristotelian logic, according to which truth is an absolute quality and a proposition must be either true or false. Whatever intellectual theories he may have had, he was emotionally a simple theistic Hindu, with absolute faith in God. His faith never wavered and was evidently strengthened by mystical experience.

Gandhi's willingness to compromise on matters which he considered inessential, and his admitted inconsistencies, hardly invalidate his sincerity. He believed firmly in the doctrine of rebirth, which is the hallmark of the religions which originated in India, and sharply distinguishes them from those of the West; and he even justified such difficult aspects of Hinduism as cow worship: 'It is for me a poem of pity. I worship it and I shall defend its worship against the whole world.'

Ahimsa

Non-violence for Gandhi was a principle second only to 'Truth' in importance. Indeed, sometimes it even appears to transcend Truth. 'Non-violence', he wrote in 1922, 'is the first article of my faith. It is also the last article of my creed'. Ahimsa is a common enough word in ancient Indian literature and Gandhi claimed to be following in up-to-date form an ancient Indian ideal, which he had also read in 'the teachings of all the greatest teachers of the World—Zoroaster, Mahavir, Daniel, Jessu, Muhammad, Nanak, and a host of others'.

The classical doctrine of ahimsa was interpreted differently in the light of *varna* and *ashrama*, class and stage of life. It involved not only such considerations as participation in warfare and meat-eating, but also the forcible apprehension and punishment of criminals and self-defence.

Warfare was rarely condemned in ancient India. The Bhagavad Gita, which was one of Gandhi's chief sources of inspiration, was composed partly with a view to justifying participation in righteous war, even when the war was waged against one's own kith and kin. The ksatriya, or member of the warrior class, had the positive duty to fight, loyally serving his king in all circumstances. Similarly the policeman or other officer of the king was justified in using force in apprehending a suspected criminal, the judge in sentencing him to mutilation or death, and the executioner in putting the sentence into effect. Only in a few Buddhist texts and in the edicts of Asoka we find explicit condemnation of war.

Ideally, however, war was an affair of the ksatriya class—the fighters and rulers par excellence. Though the members of other castes often took part in fighting or served as non-combatant, it was not their caste duty to do so. The priesthood in particular should ideally remain 'above the battle', though there are many examples of martial Brahmans. The right of self-defence was generally conceded to the layman. If a learned Brahman of the highest sanctity made a violent attack on a man of lower class and the latter could only save his life by killing the Brahman, he incurred no sin and was not liable to punishment. In the realm of politics was generally conceded that the subjects had the moral right to rise in revolt and put a tyrannical king to death.

In classical Hiduism the most significant aspect of ahimsa was in respect of killing animals for food and meat-eating. Many injunctions in the *Smriti* and other literature led to the spread of vegetarianism among the higher castes. It was by no means universal, however. The low castes were never averse to eating meat. At the other end of the scale, the warriors traditionally hunted, and ate the game they killed. In Bengal and some other regions, fish was by convention looked on as an aquatic vegetable. The Tantrists ate meat as part of their ritual. However, the general sentiments of classical Hinduism were much in favor of vegetarianism and the preservation of animal life. The Jains were particularly emphatic in this respect.

It must be remembered that the ahimsa described in the foregoing paragraph refers to the ordinary layman, the grhastha. The ascetic was bound by much more stringent rules. There were many castes of hypocrisy and laxity, but the ideals set before the forest hermits and wandering ascetics, for instance in the Law Book of Manu, were rigid in their insistence on absolute ahimsa. The hermit must be a complete vegetarian and, moreover, should eat only food which he had collected from wild plants and trees, avoiding all cultivate food, presumably because this involved injury to life in the process of ploughing, reaping and so on. The wandering ascetic might only eat what was given to him, and it is not expressly stated that he should always be a vegetarian, though this seems to have been the usual case. He should be absolutely non-violent, even carefully scanning the ground on which he walks to avoid treading on insects. And in the face of threatening violence he should always remain calm, unruffled, and benevolent.

The ascetic ideal was even more strongly emphasized in Jainism, which so deeply influenced the life of Gujarat. The hylozoistic philosophy of Jainism resulted in regulations verging on the fantastic, calculated to avoid injury to the minute and humble forms of life in air, water, metal, and fire. Even the eating of vegetable food was looked on as an unfortunate necessity. And unconscious injury to life, such as accidentally treading on an ant, was almost as dangerous to the soul as an act of violence consciously committed. The discipline of strict ahimsa applied in its full force to the Jain monk, and even the layman was encouraged to follow the monks' example as far as possible, and to undertake retreates, accepting monastic discipline for limited periods. In any case no Jain layman could legitimately eat meat or kill a flea, even thought the Jains in earlier times made exceptions in the case of rulers and their servants, who were permitted in this degenerate age to take part in war and to punish criminals.

Thus in nineteenth-century Gujarat, so strongly influenced both by later devotional Hinduism and by Jainism, ideas of strict non-violence and devotional Hinduism and by Jainism, ideas of strict non-violence and vegetarianism dominated the ethical systems of the middle classes. The boy Mohandas Gandhi rebelled against them. He ate meat secretly and only gave up his vice through his devotion to 'Truth' and his shame at having to tell lies. When he arrived in England he did not really believe in ahimsa, but he remained a vegetarian because he had given his word to his mother to do so. It was only after reading a now-forgotten English book on the subject that he become 'a vegetarian by choice'. Later, the Sermon on the Mount strengthened his belief in non-violence, which was confirmed in South Africa by his study of Tolstoy. Yet the foundations of Gandhi's non-violence were obviously laid in his childhood. He tells us that his first reading of certain verses of the sermon on the Mount. These lines are echoed in the bhakti poetry of all the languages of India, and their more positive interpretation of ahimsa, as returning good for evil rather than refraining from definite physical violence, is to be found in much Hindu devotional literature. Thus the Sermon in St Matthew's Gospel seems to have acted as a potent stimulus in reviving and developing in his mind ideas which had been implanted in early childhood, and which were based on the religious ideology of nineteenth-century Gujarat.

Gandhi's non-violence differs from the orthodox Indian concept of ahimsa in that it is conceived in positive terms, and can serve as a very effective political weapon. 'The self-sacrifice of one innocent man is a million times more potent than the sacrifice of a million men who die in the act of killing others. Non-violence does not involve running away from a violent situation, or turning a blind eye to cruelty and oppression. Where there is a choice between cowardice and violence, violence is to be preferred. But far better than either is non-violence, which is the very antithesis of cowardice, 'the summit of bravery'.

In many respect Gandhi's non-violence admits exceptions which the orthodox Hindu would not agree to. 'In fear and trembling, in humility and penance' he was willing to do injury to monkeys which damaged and destroyed the crops of Sabarmati ashram, 'hoping some day to find a way out'. On one occasion a calf which was incurably sick and in great pain was put to death on his instructions, and he vigorously defended his action. He did much to help the British in the Boer War and the First World War. And he declared that those who sincerely believe that violence is right are morally justified in using force.

Thus Gandhi's non-violence is an extension of the classical Hindu principle of ahimsa, which involves merely doing as little injury to living beings as possible, in the direction firstly of 'loving one's enemy' and secondly of positively inviting injury in a non-violent spirit, as a form of resisting evil. For the first, there are many Indian precedents in Hindu, Jain, and Buddhist sources. For the second these are less easy to find, though they are not wholly absent. Buddhism contains several stories of pious monks who suffered persecution and torture without resentment and with complete calm. The legends of Asoka tell that he was a converted by this means. A story certainly known to Gandhi in his childhood was that of Prahalad, the son of the demon Hiranyakasipu. Prahlada's devotion to Vishnu so enraged his father that he ordered his son's destruction. They boy endured torture and suffering of all kinds without complaint, and his spiritual power was such that steel, poison, and flames had no effect on him. He did not, however, bring about the conversion of his father, who continued in his evil courses until he was destroyed by the Narasimha, incarnation of Vishu. On at least one occasion Gandhi referred to Prahlada in this connection, in the rules and regulations of the satyagraha ashram at Sabarmati. But in a passage repeated in more than one anthology of Gandhi's writings he mentions only Jesus Christ, Daniel, and Socrates as 'the purest form of passive resistance or soul force', and Tolstoy as 'the best and brightest modern exponent of the doctrine'. In India, he goes on, 'the doctrine was understood and commonly practiced long before it came into vogue in Europe', but he gives no concrete examples. Probably he was thinking in terms of the general ethical doctrine of ahimsa, as it was applied in classical Hinduism to the ascetic and in Jainism and medieval Hindu bhakti to the layman also.

Satyagraha

Gandhi's boyhood experiences can have provided few precedents for his techniques of passive resistance, deliberate infringement of the law, and open invitation of arrest and imprisonment in order to bring about political or social change. Nevertheless, some practices did exist which may have inspired him in his later career. One such, which has been often noted, was *dharna*, or in Sanskrit prayopavesa, the custom of recovering a debt through the creditor sitting doggedly, perhaps for days, at the debtor's door. This custom is very ancient, being referred to in the legal texts of Apastamba, Manu, and several others. Dharna was generally accompanied by fasting on the part of the creditor, and it had a very potent effect upon the debtor. Not only was the publicly put to shame, but also, if he held the beliefs current in his time and place, he felt himself endangered by the spiritual power produced by the creditor's persistence. The performance of dharna by a creditor might be counteracted by a similar performance on the part of the debtor. Thus there would ensure a sort of contest in the display of will power, which might result in a friendly compromise.

The practice of dharna might be put to other uses, for it was even thought possible to influence to the gods by this means. A supplicant, despairing of less drastic means of obtaining a boon, might sit and fast for days at the door of a temple or shrine, and thus virtually compel the divinity to favour him. The whoel diea of dharna is closely linked with the widely held and very ancient Indian belief, not unknown elsewhere, the metal or physical concentration has a positive effect upon material things, and that self-inflicted suffering in the form of tapas or asceticism generates an immense power that may even shake the gods on their heavenly thrones.

Dharna-like picketing was sometimes carried out by groups. A man performing dharna might be accompanied by his family members. The Kashmir Chronicle contains several cases of dharna against the rulers on the part of aggrieved subjects. Thus the wife of a dead Brahman performed a fast in order to compel King Candrapida to find her husband's murderer. The king then himself fasted for three days and nights in a temple of Vishu and was rewarded by a dream which showed him the means of detecting the criminal.

We know of no record of similar mass protests in other parts of medieval Hindu India, but this may be merely due to the fact that no detailed chronicles exist for any region but Kashmir. One remarkable incident shows that the practice of mass dharna was known to the Brahmans of north India at a somewhat later period. Sultan Firouz Shah decided to impose jizya or poll-tax on his Brahman subjects, who hitherto had not been expected to pay it. The Brahmans of Delhi appeared before the sultan and declared that rather than pay the tax they would colleted dry wood and burn themselves to death. The sultan refused to make any concession, telling them that they could burn themselves rather than expect him to let them off. They fasted outside his hunting lodge for several days, until they were near death. When the Hindu citizens of Delhi heared of their plight they offered to pay the jizya on the Brahmans' behalf. Ultimately the sultan agreed to a compromise, and accepted jizya from the Brahmans at the lowest of the three rates fixed, ten tankas par head per annum. It is to be noted that this case of mass dharna was partially successful, even though it was directed against a ruler antagonistic to Hinduism.

In later periods, cases of mass dharna are not known to us, though they may have taken place. Peaceful demonstrations against the re-imposition of the jizya certainly occurred in the reign of Aurangzeb. In one of these, in 1679, the whole road between the Red Fort at Delhi and the Jama Mosque was blocked by an unarmed crowd of Hindus. They refused to disperse in order to allow the emperor to go to prayer at the mosque, and were trampled down by elephants. There is thus enough evidence to show that the seeds of satyagraha were already present in the Indian soil before Gandhi nursed them into growth.

We have found no account of anything resembling prayopavesa of this type of Tulsi Das's *Ramayana*, and it is not likely that Gandhi knew of the Kashmiri prototype of satyagraha before his return form England. The *Rajatarangini* was first fully translated into English only in 1901, five years before his passive resistance movement in South Africa. At that time it is unlikely that it would have come to his notice.

However, certain events in the port of Surat, not very far from Gandhi's birthplace, may have had some influence in the formation of his policy of satyagraha. The merchants of Surat had always formed a compact and wealthy community, and the well-do-do Gujarati merchant had a tradition of participation in politics going back to Hindu times. We have several records of protests of a more or less non-violent type, mounted chiefly by the mercantile population, but with considerable support from the masses.

It is hardly likely that Gandhi was unaware of these demonstrations, and it is very probably that they, and others like them in other parts of India, had a considerable effect on his later policy. Indeed, it may be said that civil disobedience, in the form of the more or less non-violent protesting crowd which refuses to disperse when ordered to do so, is traditional in Indian life.

Belief in the power of the concentrated will, especially when accompanied by fasting and penance, was common to Hindu and Jain alike, and such ideas must have been known to the young Gandhi from his early boyhood, long before he began to read in the Gospels of mountains being moved by the power of faith. We need seek for no Western prototypes for his doctrine of 'soul force', which is derived from the Indian conceptions of punya or spiritual merit, and tejas, the supernatural power accumulated from asceticism and meditation.

It must be recognized that satyagraha is ethically a great refinement of dharna or prayopavesa. The creditors performing dharna and the Kashmiri Brahmans performing mass prayopavesa evidently had no sentiments of love or compassion towards the objects of their fasts and vigils. They pinned their hope of success rather on their wills than on their moral fervour, though no doubt they were usually convinced of the justice of their cause. On at least one occasion, in 1921, Gandhi wrote against the practice, and sharply distinguished it from his own methods, calling dharna 'barbarity' and a crude way of using coercion', since the practitioner of dharna knows that he will not be injured by the object of his fast. But, in fact, the relationship of dharna and prayopavesa to the techniques of civil disobedience seems closer than he was willing to admit. Gandhi gave those old Indian practices a more moral content by insisting that civil disobedience volunteers should, as far as it lay in their power, cherish thoughts of love and benevolence towards their persecutors. This high ethical tone is certainly in keeping with the Sermon on the Mount but it is equally consistent with Hindu bhakti, as exemplified in the Gujarati verses quoted by Gandhi himself in his *Autobiography*. Gandhi's techniques may have been learnt in part from the West, but the practice of satyagraha, dependent as it was on belief in the 'soul force', was in no way un-Indian. Gandhi's very puritanical attitude to sex no doubt also derives from his youth. The incident on the night of his father's death would be sufficient in itself to encourage any sensitive young Hindu, on reaching maturer years and producing a family, to resolve on a life of celibacy. Celibacy is prescribed for both the Christian monk and the Hindu sannyasi, but in the two religions the motives behind the taboo on sex differ somewhat. Christina ascetic thought looks on sex with suspicion as one of the most potent sources of infatuatioin, and a very serious distraction of a man from his true aim, which is the worship of God; hence the Catholic priest or monk may not marry. Hinduism, Jainism, and Buddhism agree with Christianity on this point, but the two former emphasize another improant reason for celibacy, which is also not unknown in Christian circles—sex is believed to sap both vital and spiritual power. India has many legends of saintly hermits who, as a result of a carnal lapse, lost all their supernatural power and were no longer able to perform miracles. Gandhi's vow of brahmacarya, significantly taken just before his first South African civil disobedience campaign in 1906, was largely inspired by this motive, interpreted in modern terms.

Assessment

We suggest that several of Gandhi's concepts are fully in keeping with Indian tradition, and were probably developed from ideas which he absorbed in his childhood and youth, fertilized and brought to fruition by his contact with the West. Only two major planks in his platform—the dignity of manual labour and the emancipation of women—seem to have had no prototypes in India's past. He was no doubt a great innovator, but he built firmly on the foundation of his own tradition. It is possible that if he had never read the Gospels, Tolstoy, Ruskin, and much Western literature, Gandhi would not have entered politics at all, or, if he had done so, would have devised techniques and policies different from those which he actually did devise. But if he had not been brought up in middle class Hindu-Jain environment of the type that was to be found in nineteenth-century Porbandar and Rajkot, his techniques and policies would have been very different indeed. His genius was even more successful than that of, earlier reformers in harmonizing non-Indian ideas with the Hindus dharma, and giving them a thoroughly Indian character; and he did this only by relating them to earlier doctrines and concepts.

Concerning Gandhi's theory and praxis of satyagraha, several critics maintain that non-violence and self-suffering are impractical methods against violent oppression. The Gandhian way, they say, is "other worldly" and "anti-humanist". For instance, Lokmanya Tilak argued that Gandhi's project of integrating politics and morality are unsuited to this worldly concerns. In his famous letter to Gandhi, he wrote that politics is "a game of worldly people and not of sadhus" and that approach of Sri Krishna is more suited to this world than the Buddhist approach.

In his reply to Lokmanya Tilak, Gandhi insisted that non-violence and self-suffering were "not for the unworldly but essentially for the worldly." He did admit that those principles were very difficult to practice but insisted that we need to, and can keep on moving along those lines. "Perfect non-violence whilest you are inhabiting the body, he wrote, "is only a theory like Euclid's point or straight line, but we have to endeavour every moment of our lives." Gandhi rightly maintained that it is desirable to bring about a predominantly non-violent society.

It may still be objected that Satyagraha demands the satyagrahis self-suffering even unto death. It is true that self-suffering is a major element of satyagraha. However, self-sacrifice is also involved in the case of violent resistance. Sacrifice even unto death is thus the common element in both the violent and non-violent resistance against oppression. That is why Gandhi approved of the use of satyagraha only in case of conflict over fundamental issues and only after all milder methods of non-violence have failed. "I should be deeply distressed," he wrote in 1921, "if on every conceivable occasion every one of us were to be a law unto oneself and to scrutinize in golden scales every action of our future National Assembly. I would surrender my judgment in most matters to national representatives." But when a situation of violent oppression persists even after all milder methods of non-violent resistance have been tried, Gandhi maintained that the self-suffering even unto death of the non-violent fighter for communitarian truth is a truer assertion of individual freedom than is the death-in-defeat of the violent resister.

In conclusion, we may ponder over two assessments of Gandhi's Satyagraha by western writers. In his book *Philosophies of India*, H. Zimmer writes: Gandhi's programme of Satyagrah is a serious, very potentially vastly powerful experiment in the ancient Hindu science of transcending the sphere of lower powers by entering that of the higher. Gandhi is confronting Great Britain's untruth (asatya) with India's truth (satya); British compromise with Hindu holy dharma. This is wizard priest-battle, waged on the colossal, modern scale, and according to principles derived from the textbooks, not of the Royal Military College, but of Brahman.

Similarly, in his book, Science, Liberty and Peace, Aldous Huxley writes: In the year ahead it seems possible that Satyagraha may take root in the West, not primarily as the result of the "change of heart", but simply because it provides the masses, especially in the conquered countries, with their only practicable form of political action. The Germans of the Ruhr and Platinate resorted to Satyagraha against the French in 1923. The movement was spontaneous; philosophically, ethically and organizationally, it had not been prepared for. It was for this reason that it finally broke down. But it lasted long enough to prove that Western people—and a people more thoroughly indoctrinated with militarism than any other-were perfectly capable of non-violent direct action, involving the cheerful acceptance of sacrificial suffering.

Non-violent Power Coercive?

Power in the Gandhian sense is persuasive and not coercive. Coercive and persuasive aspects of power constitute its two significant dimensions. A further categorization on the basis of legitimacy is possible. Richard Schermerhorn has indicated four such dimensions of power, namely: (1) Legitimate and coercive. (2) Legitimate and non-coercive, (3) Illegitimate and coercive. (4) Illegitimate and non-coercive. According to his classification boycotts, non-violent resistance etc. would be marginal cases depending upon the social context. Boycotts and non-violent resistances can have a coercive dimension that not under all circumstances. And surely the Gandhian non-violent resistance was not coercive but persuasive. However, there are scholars who take a different point of view. As for example, Joan Bondurant says that, "despites the protestations of a few followers of Gandhi and that satyagraha is always persuasive and never coercive," she believes "that the method does contain a positive element of coercion," Coercion, she defines, as "the use of either physical or intangible force to compel action contrary to the will or reasoned judgement of the individual or group subjected to such force" and "non-violence (used in connection with satyagraha) as the exercise of power or influence to effect change without injury-which includes psychological as well as physical harm—to the opponent." While making these conceptual clarifications she maintains that there is a "difference between violent coercion in which deliberately injury is inflicted upon the opponent and non-violent coercion in which injury indirectly results." It is sheer distortion and misunderstanding of the Gandhian principle of non-violence to suggest that in a true satyagraha of Gandhian stipulation injury results indirectly to the opponent. On the contrary, in such a situation not only that injury does not result but the opponent is uplifted, liberated from the bonds of his own violence and there results a relationship based on positive love and altruism. To dismiss those who take the position that non-violent power can only be persuasive and no coercive as 'followers of Gandhi thereby implying subjective bias for their opinion is not the same as producing a sound argument to sustain her own position. Both Joan Bondurant and Clarence March Case, who contend that satyagraha involves non-violent coercion, stand on shaky positions. Bondurant says:

> In the case of non-violent coercion there is willingness on the part of the one who would coerce to submit himself to suffering in contrast to one who uses violence to coerce intentionally causes suffering to his opponent.

Case says:

> The non-violent coercion causes inconvenience and suffering to those who wield it, as well as to those against whom it is involved, in this it is exactly contrary to non-violent methods.

Willingness and coercion do not go together; agreeing to do

certain things under coercion is not a voluntary decisions-making or willing cooperation. Similarly inflicting self-suffering by the satyagrahi is not to bring suffering on the opponent, it is for the contrary. Inflicting self-suffering, a satyagrahi offers panacea and tapasya and offers opportunities for the opponent to ponder over issues and arrive at a just decision. A satyagrahi does not offer satyagraha except for a just cause and after undergoing a purificatory course and observing other conditions stipulated by Gandhi.

Satyagraha itself is directed against violence and coercion of all kinds, 'Truth is non-violence. That force that is born out of an intense desire to follow the path of truth cannot be coercive in any respect. All coercion involves and implies elements and varying degrees of violence. Therefore, to consider the power of non-violence as coercive, even if it is maintained that non-violent coercion is different or qualitatively superior to violent coercion, tantamount to a distortion of the Gandhian thesis. Non-violence and coercion are violent power and can only be different levels and degrees of persuasion depending upon the satyagraha's situation and social compulsions. But never would a satyagrahi desire forcing a decision on his opponent. What ever decision the opponent takes must be completely voluntary. If such a decision is not completely voluntary, then to that extent the satyagraha is not successful. A successful satyagraha should generate a non-violent power which should persuade the opponent to arrive at the just decision.

Non-violence would be the ordering principle in Gandhi's democracy. Majority rule based on the Western model would be inappropriate, however, because Gandhi believed it ignored the great mass of the people. And majority rule based on violence was 'terrorism' and 'worse and really more godless' than minority British rule. Decision-making would be highly diffused and there would be few 'political' issues, as such. He believed some of the problems which confronted the village could be solved through decision and agreement rather than through the edicts of political authorities or specialists who buttressed their solutions with the threats of violence. But the best way for the political system to practice non-violence was to be relatively inactive. Following Jefferson and Thoreau, Gandhi held, 'that state is perfect and non-violent where the people are governed the least.'

In one of his last self-evaluations, Gandhi writes:

> Whatever I have said does not refer in any way to the failure of Ahimsa, but it refers to my failure to recognize, until it was too late, that what I have mistaken for Ahimsa was not Ahimsa but passive resistance of the weak, which can never be called Ahimsa even in the remotest sense. The proper way to view present outburst of violence throughout the world is to recognize that the technique of unconquerable non-violence of the strong has not been at all finally discovered as yet.

If Gandhi's own austerity, ahimsa and asceticism of his satyagraha way of life and social action could not succeed as projected, there seems little reason to think that the mass application of his methods is a tenable practical position.

Paradoxically, Gandhi acknowledges that violence and evil have equal place in God's plan and that God kept him blinded to the violence in his own mass application of satyagraha. He confessed that he had "all along laboured under an illusion. But he was never sorry for it. He realized that if his vision were not covered by that illusion, India would never have reached the point which it had today."

This is tantamount to admitting that in fact moral progress proceeds by means of violence as well as non-violence as a practical rule. This directly contradicts the absolute prescription and force of Gandhi's ideological claims and injunction.

It is concluded that as a general analysis of the working of moral consciousness and of the general commitment to non-violence in practical action, Gandhi's ahimsa and satyagraha are a valid and important contribution to the philosophy and practice of non-violence for their clarity, thoroughness and range of real application. However, the same clarity, intensity and vigor in its absolute and universal application, respecting no limitations, render it invalid so far as these radical aspects are allowed to distort the theory and application as a whole. Gandhi's work fails on both logical and practical grounds to prove its practical claim and to make good its absolute case against the justifiability of violence. Gandhi's basically sound and generally applicable analysis should be rendered a powerful, practical aid once its limitations are recognized. The practitioner may assume that not ideal purity, but the need and aim in the total situation and the total projected outcome, must determine the correct action.

The new debate on the justifiability and use of violence and practical uses of non-violence is set by both the advent of nuclear arms and the advent of Gandhi's satyagraha. The atom bomb and the new generations of other mass-destruction weaponry make direct engagement with evil and old methods of direct revolution on a popular scale obsolete. Local insurgency may go on, but anything on a larger scale, or in strategic positions, has direct implications for the nuclear powers. But for the balance and deterrent fear among them, their nuclear self-annihilation, from even minor misreading of intent and resolve—or of a faulty surveillance system, is a strong possibility—some say inevitability.

All conflict must be seen in the light of escalation to nuclear conflagration, mostly an unthinkable event. However, the magnitude and sui generis moral dimension of these powers and scenarios of such an escalation, raises the issues of peace and conflict with a new vividness, force and urgency. This debate is further sharpened by the contrast with Gandhi's non-violence, his own example against the British Raj and his work in South Africa, and by efforts of proponents in various parts of the world—notably Nehru in his non-alignment movement, Martin Luther King's civil rights movements in the United States and various South African congresses in coalition campaigns against apartheid.

Gandhi's satyagraha has been the chief resource in studies of non-violent change and conflict resolution. It may be found by future historians that Gandhi's faith in his practical non-violence have forestalled nuclear confrontation by the stark contrast they give to atomic warfare and the hope they offer to emerging peoples and nations who might otherwise have precipitously or more concertedly engaged oppressive powers with violent means where the net effect might have been rapid nuclear escalation—weak peoples or sectors of larger nations also have then a means of engagement.

But it seems that violence cannot be ruled out in today's world where the current is so manifestly towards decolonization, self-determination, freedom and self-development, and where rife injustice is no longer tolerable. The aim and moral thrust of historical and social forces seem to be justice and freedom. There has been in this century a swelling refusal on the part of smaller nations to accept the oppressive debilitating peace of the status quo. The proclaimed aim is also evolution of a "family of nations" as an "organic unit", where only non-violent methods are naturally and reasonably chosen to adjust claims, as between states within a nation.

But though the aim is an ideal community of nations, the starting place is a complex plurality of peoples, histories, and aspirations, and a conflicting array of claims rising out of the unchastened plurality that has not yet found its equilibrium. What will work to gain justice and freedom? There are many perceptions and claims, none wholly true and none purely justified, yet all largely valid also. There are great bulwarks of historical inertia to overcome.

What will work in a factually fractured, plural worrld where this organic sense of cooperation and solidarity is the exception, and exists only within nation-states not between them; when materialism is the ruling outlook, and its natural concomitants of greed and competition the ruling international motives—for both have and have-nots? What means can be used where the established oppressive and exploiting states have the monopoly on police technology and non nuclear military power?

The question must be what, in such a world, will move humanity, and each nation's humanity, towards the goals of justice and freedom? If there is no automatic universal non-violent method always available and a priori guaranteed to succeed in realizing justice and freedom regardless of material circumstances as Gandhi claimed, and if the fight must progress somehow, then there must be some other way than the restricted choice of either purely violent weaponry or Gandhian non-violence—plural methods, not chosen through any monolithic value system and adapted to specific situations and occasion.

Violent methods must be equally acceptable when, to their sincere practitioners, intelligent use seems justified. Tolerance of all methods to advance the historical current is a natural corollary to the new debate. This intelligent use of force implies the same careful regard for Truth in both violence and in non-violence as Gandhi required for ahimsa and satyagraha. By the previous analysis, the truth would seem to be that non-violence is not the weapon of the strong in Gandhi's sense; that was the weapon of a Gandhi. As a technique it must be regarded as a weapon of the materially weak. Gandhi may have wielded that weapon with rare extraordinary strength derived from his own spiritual resources, but generally, as a socio-political technique, it is a strategic instrument whose effective operation varies with the degree of soul-force or moral strength brought to bear by the individual presiding over its use. Soul-force has its necessary place in the fight for justice. But it is not the universal, spiritual weapon Gandhi conceived it to be.

It is common knowledge that at the Calcutta and Delhi riots of 1947-48, Gandhi's mere presence had the electric and stilling effect that he had claimed was the final criterion of the active working of the force of ahimsa—"Enmity vanished in his neighborhood," and shooting stopped wherever he passed by. His presence stilled large crowds.

It need not be denied that superior force can be drawn upon and brought to bear on material reality in manifestly moral and practical terms. But the ultimate limiting factor is always there in the nature of the medium through which the force must act to express the ideal of the agent of that force.

Analysis of Gandhi's methods and practice meant to follow his lead, both fail to achieve his results because of inappropriate or inadequate empirical analysis. Empirical or scientific analysis generally fails to take into account the factor of personality and hagiography. The spiritual and moral facts cannot be discounted from the total problem any more than the empirical ones. Gandhi's work has given ample justification for study in these directions.

But violence also does not always work either. Gandhi did awaken India with non-violent means. That India did not retain the impetus and momentum only verifies the importance of the presiding personality in such methods. That the methods do work under given person and oriented conditions is a practical fact of life.

On the other hand, it is a question whether even Gandhi's non violence could have removed British colonial rule except for Hitler's violence and the momentum of historical trends. It is difficult to imagine non-violence, even with such as Gandhi leading, working today in South Africa, just as it was repeatedly questioned how a Gandhi could do anything to overcome the evil of a Hitler. In a plural world such as ours all these forces seem to work only in combination—not necessarily a rationally analyzable combination.

Localized conflict, however approached, exists against the background of the large nuclear dilemma, the pervasive materialistic value system and surging technological advance. Can unilateral disarmament solve that dilemma? No, because if the will is there; the arms will be rebuilt or surreptitiously built all along—cyclically dismantled in show of trust, and cyclically reassembled in feigned pique. Error is bound to occur in a world so technologically sophisticated, so morally cavalier and so politically irresponsible and unreflective. The cycles could not be perpetual and the breakthrough could come only by sincere change of heart, accident, or miscalculation inevitable to perception governed by ill will, mistrust and fear.

Non-violent methods especially require patience, detachment, non-possession and willingness to suffer, not merely to convert the opponent as a spiritual principle, as Gandhi believed, but simply as a practical matter to outlast the evil. Sacrifice and renunciation are the operative factors in all struggle, material as well as moral and spiritual, because what one wants determines the dimensions and particulars of what will be given up and what suffering sustained to achieve one's objective.

The efficacy of Gandhi's non-violent non-cooperation and civil disobedience needn't be underestimated. In principle there is no reason why such large and complex state mechanisms as the USSR and the US should not succumb if adequately paralyzed from within. But this is not a problem of soul-force. It is a problem of material reality and strategy.

Renunciation as mass non-consumerism would be a contemporary translation of Gandhi's non-cooperation and economic boycott. Choice of a consistent life-routine based on values not susceptible to market pressures and marketing manipulations, adopted and sustained against consumer indoctrination, is itself a matter of spiritual or moral battle, translating the principles of self-sacrifice, purification and renunciation. But the renunciation as a consequence of adopting some healthier, saner, stronger, clearer, more life-giving modes and values of life rather than the recognition of material dependence, subservience and hatred.

Gandhi's sadhana of non-violence is one such preparation and cleansing of moral and practical consciousness. Its application in daily life and domestic relation is the moral prerequisite for developing that non-retaliatory, non-hating moral consciousness and spiritual poise that is capable of sustaining love and truth in either method.

It must be noted that Gandhi's final value is not non-violence. Whatever his disclaimer and arguments, he in fact always preferred violence to cowardice—without exception. Gandhi writes, "I would rather risk violence a thousand times than the emasculation of a whole race".

We have no better indicator of real values than where one feels compelled to draw the line in practical fact, and Gandhi writes that "My non-violence does not admit of running away from danger and leaving dear ones unprotected. Between violence and cowardly flight, I can only prefer violence to cowardice. I can no more preach non-violence to a coward than I can tempt a blind man to enjoy healthy senses. Non-violence is the summit of bravery," and , "Non-violence cannot be taught to a person who fears to die and has no power of resistance." He concludes that "I do believe that, where there is only a choice between cowardice and violence, I would advise violence".

Finally, it should be reiterated that though the position argued for in the present study is admittedly a reassertion of a widely-held, commonsense one of a general commitment to non-violence which nevertheless can and ought to be set aside when overriding moral considerations require it, still it must again be recognized that Gandhi, by his absolute views and application, has shown the political importance and power of non-violence and its practical validity as no one else has shown it before.

It must be reiterated that Gandhi is therefore a resource that should be a constant reference in self-reflection and in debate on these fundamental issues; he should be studied in a way that most illumines the practical; commonsense position as it is relevant to both the daily life and the present world political situation of nuclear threat, emergent national pluralism and the need of complex adjustment where justice has had no powerful international advocate and little local constituency. It is thus important to see how Gandhi's methods and practical success depend upon his metaphysical position, the limits of those views and methods, when and how they need to be modified for a wider practical outcome and more realistic, commonsense political view and relevance.

In the key chapter of *Moral Man and Immoral Society*, 'The Preservation of Moral Values in Politics,' Niebuhr elaborates and refines his interpretations of Gandhi in 'What Chance Has Gandhi?', the article he wrote soon after his return from London. The 1931 article and the 1932 chapter constitute Niebuhr's considered estimate of Gandhi. It was of a world historical, even transcendent figure. In the decaying and desperate world of failed capitalism and failing democracy, Gandhi's ideas and practices as, Niebuhr interpreted them, provided a religiously meaningful and politically effective way to pursue 'equal justice, the most rational ultimate objective of society'. He wondered 'whether there has even been a more historic movement in the centuries than this visit of Gandhi to London'.

After this almost hagiographic estimate of December 1931, Niebuhr became more ambivalent about Gandhi. As he proceeded to write *Moral Man and Immoral Society*, he made 'a conscious declaration of independence from the pacifistic circle—liberal and socialist—in which he had worked in the previous decade. In his December 1931 article, Gandhi, the unique 'prophet' and 'statesman', combined 'translucent honesty' and 'spiritual self-discipline' with 'necessary opportunism' and 'patient application of general principles to detailed situations'.

Niebuhr arrived at the view that the responsible Christian should accept the use of force and that the use of force implied the use of violence in certain situations. He came to this position in part through a at best superficial and at worst perverse interpretation of Gandhi's use of satyagraha [truth-force], militant non-violent collective action or resistance. Gandhi, according to Niebuhr, used non-violence as a pragmatist; he was not committed to non-violence absolutely. 'Beginning with the idea that social justice could be resisted by truth force and soul force, Gandhi came finally to realize the necessity of some type of physical coercion upon the foes of his people's freedom, as every political leader must'. For weak collectives such as Indian nationalists or weak minorities such as American Negroes, non-violence was the best tactic. Having made Gandhi intelligible in realist terms, Niebuhr held that he, not Gandhi's self-appointed champion in the United States, John Haynes Holmes, was 'a true Gandhian'.

Niebuhr broke with his liberal Protestant and political reformist past by arguing that coercion, even violent coercion that liberates 'oppressed nationalities' or the 'working classes' in the name of equal justice is 'placed in a different moral category from the use of power for the perpetuation of imperial rule or class dominance'. Conflicts involving oppressed nationalities and class could not, as Gandhi though they could, be resolved through non-violence collective action that made mutual understanding and accommodation possible.

Koestler has made a scatting attack on Gandhi. He found that most Asians are either 'frauds' or deeply troubled 'neurotics'. For him Gandhi was no exception. Here is Koestler's summing up of Gandhi:

> Gandhi was an extremist in every respect. The secret of his genius, of his power over the nation's imagination, lies perhaps in his unique gift to exaggerate [sometimes to grotesque proportions] and to dramatize [sometimes to the degree of showmanship] precisely those elements in Hindu tradition, which had the deepest emotional appeal. This is true for the whole range of his activities: his vegetarian and fruitarian apostolate; his [sometimes fatal] activities as a nature healer; the Stakhanovite cult of khandi; the principles of tolerance and non-violence carried to Jacobin extremes; the martyrdom of the fasts; the prayer meetings in the patriarchal ashram; the rejection of sex, even among married couples, as a source of spiritual debility; the inhuman 'detachment' from his family in the interest of public service; and the belief in the life-long absolute right of the father to rule over his sons.

We have here an amalgam of 'queerness' and 'wackiness' with extremism and obsessiveness that, in popular parlance, translate into 'sick' and 'sickening', and in social scientific language into psychologically disturbed and culturally deviant. At the same time Gandhi's exaggeration and showmanship suggest that he is a trickster or magician, that is, a fraud. 'Naked fakir' becomes an irresistible double entendre. Once the great issue of British rule over India was removed and psychological language captured discourse, Gandhi the saint or mahatma could be treated as a celebrity and at the same time unmasked as a neurotic and a fraud whom only the gullible could reserve.

Gandhi claimed to be a saint, Geertz argues, if not in so many words, certainly in almost every action he took because a saint 'demands a moral response'. It is the triumph of Erikson's book', Geertz tells us, to uncover Gandhi's inherent moral ambiguity', the 'admiration and outrage, awe and disgust, trust and suspicion', that accompany the career of 'a man who recommends his character to the world as a saving revelation'.

After taking from Erikson's account of Gandhi that he is 'an obsessive tease', a person 'with an extraordinary capacity to make others feel furious and foolish at the same time', Geertz proceeds to explain satyagraha as a form of teasing. 'He is always taunting, testing limits, playing with other's emotions. Forged into a political instrument this becomes the famous satyagraha.' Geertz renders satyagraha as 'mass taunting' or 'collective needling'. What in the end Gandhi did to colonial India was to 'drive it to distraction'. In his conduct during 'the event', the Ahmebaded textile strike of 1917, which is the centerpiece of Erikson's book, Gandhi's teasing 'was openly exposed, and with it the fact that shaming men into virtue was a complex and treacherous business, both less selfish and less pacific than it looked'.

Geertz pictures Gandhi's thinking about non-violence as 'moral double talk' and 'hypocrisy'. Non-violence, as Geertz understands Gandhi, derives its 'moral grandeur' from the violence it contains. In a remarkable transvaluation of values, Geertz argues that the practitioner of non-violence must be powerful in the sense that he must be 'competent to strike back, even to kill. The road to true non-violence passes then through the attainment of power, that is, the means of violence. 'Because Gandhi the thinker was 'stymied by the paradox that non-violence is the reciprocal of strength,' his philosophy 'dissolved into a collection of colliding homilies and Indian eccentricities'. Geertz has trouble making sense of Gandhi because he doesn't find Gandhi's representations credible; his peasant dress, like his saintliness, were unconvincing affection. For Greetz, Gandhi isn't for real. Lacking credibility, Gandhi lacks intelligibility.

Many of those who were Gandhi's followers in the nationalist movement accepted his political leadership even while rejecting or not hearing his message of religious commitment and social reform. With each passing generation his image and ideas have declined in public understanding and acceptance. One era's inspiration has become the next era's cliché. Post-Independence Indians have little regard for Gandhi's vision of India as a nation with a special 'spiritual' vocation and with the will and means to live simply in self-sufficient villages. One hears less and less in political discourse of the Vedas, Upanishads, and Gita or of the public relevance of the quest for union with the eternal. The conception of India as a spiritual nation formulated in the nineteenth and early twentieth century by Dayanand, Vivekananda, Tagore, Aurobindo, and Gandhi himself played a significant part in shaping India's national identity and helping her to make a name and place for herself in the world. With the coming of independence and democratic self-government, new age groups have emerged for whom the nationalist struggle, in which Gandhi played so central a part, has become a history book happening or the memory of old men's youth. Castes and classes have come to power whose cultural backgrounds, political experiences, and moral concerns are less rooted in the Sanskriti tradition and its ideological norms. They pursue goals that are increasingly instrumental. Self-sufficient villages stand in the way of their quest for a release from poverty and dependence. The other worldly concerns of Gandhian followers detract from the moral and material tasks of economic development and social mobility.

The men of power in India today also have little patience with Gandhi's post-industrial critique of industrial civilization and the alternatives he advocated. Living in an era when industrialized civilization was already well-established in the West, Gandhi was of a nation that was just beginning to industrialize. He could still hear and sympathize with the critics of early industrialism, Ruskin, Thoreau, and the European and American utopian socialists, who found that it brutalized men, alienating them from self and society and depriving them of the capacity to govern themselves.

Several of India's most influential intellectuals—Rajni Kothari, Ramashray Roy, perhaps Partha Chatterjee and, in the disaspora, Bhikhu Parekh, joined Ashis Nandy in reading a postmodern Gandhi into the record of India's nationalist movement and postcolonial consciousness. He was shown as crafting an authentic Indian voice by disentangling his ideas and vocabulary from those of the Raj's colonial modernity and by reforming and revitalizing tradition. Nandy said that Gandhi spoke from 'outside the emporium ' and had freed himself from an 'intimate enemy'; Chatterjee that more than any others of his time and since, Gandhi's discourse came closest to being non-'derivative'. He was acknowledged as a key author of India's civil society and many of its associated movements. The secular-rationalist left, disposed to be suspicious of Gandhi's spiritual aspect, softened its critique. The Hindu right, disposed to suspect his religious inclusive, began to stress his commitment to Hinduism. Indeed, as Gandhi the icon and monument faded from view and a revitalized Gandhi emerged to occupy considerable political space, he became an increasingly contested multivalent signifier. Nandy's four Gandhis were no longer enough to accommodate his multiplying meanings.

Gandhi's recuperation in India had been helped by his growing significance abroad. Not least among those he influenced was Martin Luther King. King adopted Gandhi's methods of non-violent civil disobedience in his leadership of the civil rights movement in the United States. The Montagomery, Albama, bus Boycott that launched the civil rights movement in the United States began on 1 December 1955 when Rosa parks refused to yield her seat on a crowded bus to a white man. He refusal defined the city segregation ordinance. Her act of civil disobedience had a Gandhian inspiration; six months earlier she had attended a workshop in Monteagle, Tennessee where she had learned about Gandhi and was trained in Gandhian techniques.

Four days later, on 5 December, the young untested King gave 'the most decisive speech of my life, a speech that helped to launch the Montgomery Bus Boycott'. As leader of the Southern Christian Leadership Conference, King made Gandhi a household name in the US by embracing his ideas and methods. In his by now well-known passage about his commitment to Gandhi, he said: 'Gandhi was probably the first person in history to lift the love ethic of Jesus above mere interaction between individuals to a powerful and effective social force on a large scale. The whole concept of "Satyagraha" was profoundly significant to me.'

In the 1980s Gandhi began to influence Europe public life. He was acknowledge by non-violent revolutionaries in Eastern Europe—Lech Walesa in Poland and Vaclav Havel in Czechoslovakia. In the 1990s the Dalai Lama began to invoke Gandhi in his non-violent effort to gain autonomy for Tibet. In the 1990s Nelson Mandela was in position publicly to acknowledge that 'the Gandhian influence dominated freedom struggles on the African continent right up to the 1960s'. At the close of the 20th century, The *Time* chose Gandhi along with Albert Einstein and Franklin Roosevelt as the three most influential persons of the century.

6

Satyagraha in India

Gandhi had arrived in London from South Africa in August, 1914, just after the outbreak of the First World War. Radical Indian friends of his in London wanted India to take advantage of the war to wrest political concessions from England, but Gandhi still considered himself a loyal subject of the Empire; besides, he believed that a satyagrahi who had not tried to prevent a war, could not avoid taking part in it without being cowardly. He was constantly introducing and developing new variations on the theme of satyagraha. While he was in London, he again organized—with the reluctant consent of the British government—a small ambulance corps of Indian volunteers, but he never got to the front, and merely did some token nursing in England. It disintegrated within a few months, partly because Gandhi had fallen out with the military authorities by refusing to let his corps function as part of the army, and partly because he succumbed to the damp, inhospitable English climate and contracted pleurisy. A friend advised him to seek a warmer climate, and he sailed for India, reaching Bombay in January, 1915, and his health considerably restored by the voyage. He was now forty-five.

Accepting an offer of financial help from some textile merchants in his native region of Gujarat, Gandhi in 1915 established his first permanent community in India, near Ahmedabad, on the west bank of the Sabarmati river. Ahmedabad was one of the most ancient and beautiful cities of India, dotted with old mosques and medieval ruins, but it was also the center of India's textile industry—a place of belching smokestacks surrounded by filthy lanes and squalid shanties. Gandhi called his community Sabarmati Ashram. In the ancient Hindu tradition, an ashram was a retreat where a group of devout people lived, meditated, and mortified the flesh, waiting to free themselves from the body, the bondage of worldly existence. But the Sabarmati Ashram was a religious community only in a very loose sense. Gandhi carried over to Sabarmati Ashram the daily regimen perfected at *Phoenix* and *Tolstoy Farms* in South Africa and added to it spinning and weaving. He did, however, ask its members—many of whom had followed him there from *Phoenix Farm* —to live by a number of simple vows that had both political and religious aims: to practice brahmacharya, satyagraha, and ahimsa; to discipline their palates; to possess nothing; to cultivate fearlessness; to boycott imported English cloth; and to accept untouchables as equals. Some fifty or sixty million people—one-fifth of India's population— were untouchables, but the vow regarding them immediately threatened the survival of the ashram.

Gandhi had begun to fulfill his vow by accepting a family of untouchables—a father, mother, and baby daughter, whose names were Duda, Dani, and Lakshmi—into the ashram community. The other ashramites, however much they sought to follow Gandhi's precepts, found the family's presence humiliating and defiling, and avoided their company. The man in charge of the communal well protested at allowing the family to draw water from it, and cursed them and Gandhi. The Ahmedabad community as a whole threatened to stop all dealings with the ashram and drive the residents out. The textile merchants on whose charity the ashram depended for its very existence withdrew their financial support. Gandhi prepared to move his ashram to another place of the city where only untouchables lived, and have its members earn their livelihood doing the work of untouchables. But the ashram was saved when a man drove up in a big car and handed Gandhi thirteen thousand rupees. The donor, who wished his identity kept secret, was revealed later to have been the leading textile merchant of Ahmedabad, Ambalal Sarabhai.

Gokhale had strongly criticized Gandhi's manifesto "Indian Home Rule" as crude, ill-conceived, and indicative of how Gandhi had lost touch with Indian politics. He had extracted from Gandhi a promise to refrain from direct political activities and judgements until he had spent at least a year reacquainting himself with the country. Gokhale died shortly after Gandhi's return to India. Gandhi resolved to go barefoot for a time to mourn his mentor, and to reacquaint himself with the country, he began travelling through

India by train, always going in the third class, with the poor. Third-class compartments had almost unrestricted ticket sales and no reserved seats—only uncushioned benches and the compartments were crowded not only with people but with their bedrolls, bundles, trunks, baskets, and rubbish. Sometimes Gandhi had barely enough room to stand, and occasionally he was forced to sleep standing up. Everywhere he went, he saw poverty, filth, and disease. He stopped at Hardwar on the Ganges, among the holiest of the holy places of pilgrimage for Hindus, and was horrified to find it as badly dirty as the rest of the country. As an act of atonement, he resolved that thereafter he would restrict his diet in any given twenty-four hours to only five articles of food.

In December, 1916, when Gandhi had been back in India for almost two years, he attended a session of the Indian National Congress in Lucknow, which had on its agenda, among other subjects, agrarian discontent in Champaran. Gandhi knew nothing about Champaran and took no part in the debate, but afterward he was approached by a poor farmer who pleaded with him to go there and see for himself how the tenant farmers were being exploited by their English landlords. Champaran was such a remote district in the foothills of the Himalayas, in the province of Bihar that Gandhi had never heard of it, and he put the farmer off. But the farmer persisted, and followed him wherever he went—to Kanpur, to Ahmedabad, to Calcutta—and at last Gandhi agreed to make the journey. In April,1917, Gandhi and the farmer left Calcutta for Champaran.

They stopped in Muzaffarpur, which was the town nearest to Champaran, and there Gandhi learned from the local lawyers that most of the arable land in the area were owned by Englishmen and cultivated by Indian tenant farmers. Under the tenancy system, each farmer had been obliged to set aside fifteen per cent of his land for growing indigo— once Bihar's most profitable crop—and turn over all the indigo to the landlord as rent. The English landlords had the crop processed in local factories into the deep-blue dye, which they then shipped to Europe for sale. At the beginning of the century, however, the Germans had discovered a method of making a synthetic blue dye, which eventually became so inexpensive that no one wanted to buy natural indigo any more. The landlords, taking advantage of the farmers' ignorance of the German discovery, had thereupon demanded that they pay their rent in cash. When the farmers finally realized that they were growing an unmarketable crop, they felt that they had been cheated and robbed. They joined together and engaged lawyers to sue for a full refund of the cash they had paid as rent. Gandhi concluded that litigation would only impoverish the poor farmers further, and he said that what the lawyers should do instead was to go into the villages and, as the first step in reforming the whole tenancy system, collect testimony from the farmers about all their grievances. Gandhi was so persuasive that many lawyers took his advice, even though by doing so they risked imprisonment as political agitators. When Gandhi tried to talk to the landlords in Champaran, they would have nothing to do with him. As far as they knew, he was nothing but an interloper and a trouble maker.

In Champaran, Gandhi himself began collecting testimony from the farmers. Local English officials soon served him with an order to leave the district, but he bluntly refused to obey the order and was summoned to appear before a magistrate. Gandhi telegraphed these developments to the Viceroy and to various prominent friends. Moreover, word spread locally that a champion of the helpless was going on trial in Motihari, the district headquarters, and poor, emaciated farmers flocked there on .foot or by bullock cart from surrounding villages, as if Gandhi's mere presence had liberated them from their old fear of landlords and officials. Gandhi told the magistrate that he had not disturbed the peace in any way but that since he could not obey the order he was guilty as charged. "I have disregarded the order served upon me," he said, "not for want of respect for lawful authority, but in obedience to the higher law of our being, the voice of conscience." Before Gandhi came up for punishment, however, the authorities in Delhi, realizing that the local officials had bungled by making him into a hero ordered that the charge against him be dropped and that he be allowed to proceed with his work undisturbed.

With the help of lawyers and other recruits, Gandhi succeeded in collecting testimony from some eight thousand farmers throughout Champaran. "We may look on Mr. Gandhi as an idealist, a fanatic, or a revolutionary according to our particular opinions," a young British civil servant in Champaran reported at the time. "But to the *raiyats* [farmers] he is their liberator, and they credit him with extraordinary powers. He moves about in the villages asking them to bring forth their grievances before him, and he is transfiguring the imaginations of masses of ignorant men with visions of an early millennium." Gandhi was hailed as a "liberator" because he had imparted to the farmers, for the first time in their long history of exploitation by landlords, some hope of relief and courage. Eventually, at the insistence of the Viceroy, Lord Chelmsford, a Champaran Agrarian Enquiry Committee was set up to investigate the local tenancy system, and Gandhi was given a seat on it. The farmers expected him to hold out for a full refund of their cash payments, but the committee unanimously recommended that the landlords refund only twenty-five per cent of the cash. On this particular issue, Gandhi had compromised because he felt that any repayment was an acknowledgment that the landlords had wronged the farmers and because he was more interested in the triumph of principle than in the defeat of an adversary. He writes, "The superstition that the stain of indigo could never be washed out was exploded."

Gandhi stayed in Champaran for several more months and, with the help of volunteers recruited from as far away as Bombay, set about trying to teach the villagers rudimentary methods of hygiene and sanitation. Most of them suffered from chronic dysentery and chronic malaria, and from boils and scabies. They were introduced to simple medicaments—quinine and sulphur ointment along with nature cures. They were taught how to keep their huts tidy and well swept, and their lanes clear of filth. Schools were improvised in huts, and soup kitchens set up in many villages to feed the poor and teach them the virtues of eating nutritious meals at regular hours. But at the end of 1917 Gandhi was called to Ahmedabad to help settle a labor dispute. Without his inspiring presence, the volunteer workers left, and the villagers reverted to their old ways.

In July, 1917, plague had broken out in Ahmedabad, and people had begun fleeing the city, abandoning their homes and shops. The mill-owners, afraid of losing business to their competitors in Bombay, started paying the miserably poor unskilled mill hands "plague bonuses," amounting to as much as eighty per cent of their wages, to keep them in the city. No such bonuses were paid to the skilled mill hands, who were expected to stay in any case because they enjoyed certain small privileges at the mills. They began negotiating for a "dearness allowance," pleading that the war had doubled the prices of most necessities. When the plague epidemic abated, a few months later, the mill-owners stopped the bonuses and cut short al! discussion of the "dearness allowance." Together, the skilled and unskilled mill-workers numbered some ten thousand, and now—even though they all lived virtually from hand to mouth, belonged to no unions, and had no bargaining power to speak of, since they could easily be replaced—they started talking, for the first time, of striking against the mill-owners.

Gandhi received a call for help in the labor dispute from Anasuyabehn Sarabhai, who was a sister of the mill-owner Ambalal Sarabhai but was championing the mill-workers' cause. Gandhi had many friends among the mill-owners and was well known to the mill-workers as the 'sadhu' who lived in the local ashram. He agreed to help, and quickly became the spokesman for the mill-workers, who were asking for a fifty-per-cent increase in the wages they had been earning when the plague broke out; the mill-owners, acting together, were offering twenty-per cent. Gandhi recommended as a compromise a thirty-five-percent increase, but the mill-owners turned it down.

On February 21, a small group of mill-workers actually went on strike, and the mill-owners, who were experiencing shortages of materials because of the war, used the occasion to close down all the mills, declaring that the mill-workers could go back to work only when they accepted the twenty-per-cent increase. Gandhi now started meeting every day with the mill-workers under a babul tree on the east bank of the Sabarmati river, just outside the city, to pray with them and to exhort them to remain united and firm in their demand. The mill workers, after four days of no work and little to eat, began to think of settling on the mill-owners' terms, but at the meeting on the fifth day of the lockout, Gandhi persuaded them to make a pledge that regardless of the consequences, they would not return to their jobs without the thirty-five-per-cent increase, and that they would not beg or steal, loot or damage property, or resort to violence of any kind. The daily meetings continued, and the babul tree was soon dubbed the *Keep the Pledge Tree*.

Gandhi, Anasuyabehn, and other volunteers visited the huts of the mill-worker's daily and tried to provide them with a little food and keep them occupied in constructive work—repairing huts, cleaning roads, and constructing buildings across the river in the Sabarmati Ashram. But as the days passed, the mill-workers grew more and more desperate, attendance at the meetings became smaller and smaller, and it began to look as if the starving mill-workers would go back on their pledge— especially since, after the lockout had been going on for three weeks, the mill-workers again announced that the men could return to their jobs if they accepted the twenty-per-cent wage increase.

At the *Keep the Pledge Tree* meeting on March 15, Gandhi, in an effort to inspire and ignite the strikers' spirits, declared tat he would not touch food until either the mill-owners accepted binding arbitration or the mill-workers quit their jobs for good. "While I was still groping and unable to see my way clearly, the light came to me," Gandhi writes. Gandhi had never before undertaken a fast for a public cause, but, he says, he now saw that it could be an important weapon for a satyagrahi, provided that the motive for using it was disinterested and pure, and the issue involved so critical that death was preferable to capitulation. Yet, he says and he was instantly filled with self-doubt. The mill-workers and owners might capitulate not because of the justice of the cause but because of their affection for him, their concern for his well-being, or even their fear of the consequences if he should die. He tried to convince himself that his fast was true to his principle of satyagraha, but he could not overcome the feeling that it might actually turn out to be a betrayal of it. Still, having committed himself to a fast, he felt he had no choice but to go through with it. Three days later, on March 18, the mill-workers and owners agreed to arbitration. Gandhi called off his fast, the mill-workers returned to work, and eventually, through arbitration, they received the thirty-five-per-cent increase. The Ahmedabad strike was the first such organized effort by any workers in India. Two years later, Gandhi inaugurated the Ahmedabad Textile Labor Association and so helped launch India's trade-union movement. Gandhi's fast was in the Hindu tradition, for Hindus often used fasts to exert pressure on their opponents, but in justifying his own fast in Ahmedabad he later drew a distinction between a fast in the service of what he considered a "creative idea"—in this case, binding arbitration—and a fast for private gain or for the intimidation of an adversary. "I can fast against my father to cure him of a vice, but I may not in order to get from him an inheritance," he explained. In the course of the next thirty years, he used the weapon of public fasting seventeen times.

At about the time of the Ahmedabad strike-cum-lockout, the peasants in the Kheda district, near Ahmedabad, were claiming that the damage to their crops from adverse weather in 1917 was so great that it called for remission of their annual revenue assessment, which they were not required to pay if the harvest fell twenty-five per cent below the yield for a normal year. The local officials were disputing the extent of the damage and insisting that the assessment be paid. In late March of 1918, Gandhi agreed to go to the Kheda district, and there he addressed a meeting of some five thousand peasants. He urged them not to pay the assessment, and "to fight it out." Inspired by Gandhi's call, many educated men and women in the area gave up the practice of their professions and went with him from village to village encouraging the peasants to overcome their fear of authority and refuse to pay the assessment. They were eagerly received, and were helped along the way with offers of bullock carts and food and shelter. The local officials retaliated by attaching the peasants' land and cattle, but then they realized that they had gone too far—that their retaliatory measures had boomeranged. A compromise was arranged: the richer peasants had to pay the assessment; the poorer were let off. The effort in the Kheda district was Gandhi's first large-scale satyagraha movement in India. It brought him into contact with influential people in the area, who became stalwarts of his future campaigns, and it established him as a leader in a populous countryside, from which his fame quickly spread. The foundations of his national leadership and national satyagraha campaign were thus laid in his native Gujarat.

In April of 1918, Gandhi received an invitation from the Viceroy to attend a conference in New Delhi on recruiting Indians for service in the war. About eight hundred thousand Indians were already fighting in the British Army. Nationalist leaders like Lokamanya Tilak and Annie Besant objected to any recruitment in India without firm guarantees from the British that India would be granted home rule, or dominion status, when the war was over. Gandhi, in contrast, still felt that Indians, as loyal subjects of the Empire, were duty-bound to help Britain in the war. But since he was also committed to satyagraha and ahimsa, he went to the conference reluctantly. Nevertheless, once there, he allowed himself to be persuaded by the Viceroy to become an active recruiting agent. He wrote at the time to a Christian missionary friend, Esther Faering, "Indians have a double duty to perform. If they are to preach the mission of peace, they must first prove their ability in war. A nation that is unfit to fight can not from experience prove the virtue of not fighting." All the same, his decision was condemned both by his co-workers and by most of the nationalist leaders.

Gandhi started recruiting in familiar territory, in Kheda. The district contained six hundred villages and he hoped to recruit at least twenty able-bodied men from each, but he found that the peasants who had so recently cheered him, shunned him now as a turncoat. Some days, he would walk as much as twenty miles without getting anyone even to listen to him, let alone enlist. He became weak and dispirited--at the time he was living mostly on groundnut butter and lemon juice—and in August, while he was stopping over at Sabarmati Ashram, he contracted dysentery. He tried to cure himself by fasting, but, he became so hungry that when Kasturbai gave him porridge and lentils he overate, and made his dysentery worse. Nevertheless, he set off by train with a co-worker, Sardar Vallabhbhai Patel, for Nadiad, a town in Kheda twenty-nine miles from Ahmedabad, to carry on the recruiting campaign. They reached Nadiad around ten o'clock in the evening and had to walk about half a mile from the station to the ashram where they were to spend the night. "It was as good as ten [miles] for me," Gandhi writes. "I somehow managed to reach the quarters, but the griping pain was steadily increasing." He developed a fever, became delirious, and, he says, lost his will to live. He was taken back to Ahmedabad, where Ambalal and Anasuyabehn Sarabhai nursed him in their home. He was convinced that he was going to die, and he wanted to die in his own ashram, so he was moved there. The doctors pressed meat broth, eggs, and milk upon him, but he spurned them. Kasturbai, however, persuaded him to drink goat's milk by arguing that his vow against milk applied only to cow's milk. He says that the goat's milk, together with the news that Germany had been defeated and the war was over, helped him to start getting better.

In March, 1919, the British government passed the Rowlatt Act, which kept in force in India such stringent emergency wartime measures as press censorship and summary trials for political agitators, and extinguished any lingering hopes for dominion status. Gandhi, who had put his trust in the good intentions of the British, felt betrayed. He says he had a waking dream that he should call for a twenty-four-hour hartal, or general strike, as a satyagraha protest against the Rowlatt Act. During the hartal, all work would stop and the entire country would pray and fast for self-purification. He called for a day of hartal to be observed, and eventually fixed April 6 as the date. The idea of a hartal against the widely unpopular Rowlatt Act was eagerly taken up by the nationalists, and on April 6 work in a number of towns and cities came to a standstill. People pledged that, regardless of the consequences, they would not submit to the Rowlatt Act. Some prayed and fasted, but others took to violence: officials were attacked, government buildings burned, shops and houses plundered, trains stopped and looted, telephone and telegraph wires cut. Many people died in the rioting. Gandhi, horrified, called for an end to the hartal, but the violence continued.

On April 10, in the city of Amritsar in the Punjab—the scene of the worst violence—an English school teacher was assaulted by a mob. Although she escaped being killed, General Dyer, a veteran of the First World War who had also fought in Burma and on India's northwest frontier, arrived in Amritsar on April 11, and the next day he proclaimed a ban on public meetings and processions. On April 13, some five thousand of the city's residents, in defiance of the ban, held a meeting at Jallianwalla Bagh, a tract of land mostly walled by buildings. General Dyer blocked the main entrance with troops and ordered them to open fire. The panic-stricken crowd, trapped and unarmed, surged in all directions. Within ten minutes, at least four hundred people were dead and twelve hundred maimed or wounded. The following day, General Dyer decreed that all Indians passing along the street on which the English school teacher had been assaulted must crawl on all fours as penance for the crime. He further decreed that any Indian who failed to show proper respect for the British—by getting down from his bullock cart to salute a passing Englishman, for instance—would be publicly flogged. Some time later, when word of the massacre and Dyer's other excesses finally reached Gandhi (any violence against Europeans or Anglo-

Indians was widely publicized, but news of the massacre was censored), he concluded that the British would stop at nothing to keep India subjugated, but he blamed himself for the outbreak of violence, because it was he who had called the hartal in the first place. He felt his mistake to be of such proportions that he referred to it as his "Himalayan blunder." He had miscalculated the forces of evil in Indian society, he said, and had hastily summoned his people to satyagraha before they were ready for it.

In any event, the government swiftly countermanded the crawling order and appointed Lord Hunter, a distinguished jurist, to head a committee of investigation. His report was thorough and fair, but the Jallianwalla Bagh massacre, though it was exceptional in the history of the British Raj, became a byword for British brutality.

Late in 1919, the British proposed to grant Indians, among other things, more places in the Indian Civil Service and greater participation in the provincial legislative assemblies and ministries. Gandhi dismissed the proposals, known as the Montagu-Chelmsford Reforms, as a "subtle method of emasculation," and said that Indians should have nothing more to do with the British or the government. In fact, he said, they should observe a whole program of "non-cooperation"—not only stay out of the Civil Service and legislative assemblies but also boycott English the official language, the courts, British-run schools and colleges, and British goods, including textiles. And they should volunteer their services for nationalist causes, speak their mother tongues, set up Indian arbitration boards to settle their court cases, enter Indian-run schools and colleges, and, above all, wear khadi as an expression of their nationalism. Gandhi believed that he had found in non-cooperation yet another powerful weapon for satyagrahis—one that could achieve Swaraj (literally, "self-rule") for India in a year, at most. He was vague about what form Swaraj would take, speaking of it, variously, as a people's democracy, spiritual and political freedom, and the millennium.

Non-cooperation was at once attacked by other nationalists as a creed of "negation, exclusiveness, and despair;" as an anarchist scheme to undermine respect for law and authority, for persons and property; as a doomed attempt to build a "Chinese wall" between India and the West. Nevertheless, in 1920 non-cooperation was narrowly adopted by the Indian National Congress, India's chief political party as its national program. The Congress, from its founding in 1885, had been the preserve of the upper and middle classes—of anglicized lawyers educated in British-run schools and universities, who wore Western-style suits, spoke English among themselves, and were more interested in becoming partners of the British than in overthrowing them. Party meetings were likely to be devoted to rhetorical debate rather than to serious discussion. But since 1918, in view of Britain's failure to grant India any kind of home rule, the Congress had become more nationalistic and more radical. Now, in 1920, it adopted a new Constitution, drafted by Gandhi, which was designed to refashion it into a militant grass-roots movement with village, district, provincial and national committees, all democratically elected. Anyone who could afford the subscription of four annas, or one-fourth of a rupee a year, could become a member. Gandhi's success in the Congress was due in part to his ability to influence its Muslim minority, an ability he possessed because at around that time he had lent this support to the most important Muslim political and religious issue of the day. This was the Caliphate—or, as it was called in India, the Khilafat Movement, an attempt by the Indian Muslims to save the defeated Sultan of Turkey as the caliph of Islam. It was a hopeless undertaking, because the caliphate had long been as moribund an institution as the Turkish Empire. Gandhi espoused this exclusively Muslim cause for the sake of Hindu-Muslim unity; and thereby won widespread Muslim backing for the first and also the last time in his life. But it was another thing that the Khilafat Movement fizzled out in 1924, when the Turks themselves—having previously banished the Sultan and declared Turkey a republic—abolished the caliphate. In 1921, Gandhi began a dizzying tour of the country, travelling to the most remote villages to meet, direct, and advise Congress workers and recruit new ones. He now always wore a white khadi dhoti—the mendicant's or fakir's garb. Villagers who got word that he was coming mobbed his train in country station after country station simply to catch sight of him—to receive his darshana. He would often say a few words about satyagraha and ahimsa, or about his experiences in South Africa. He became renowned for his voluntary poverty, his humility, his simple, saintly life, and began to be called Mahatma.

The British at first did not take non-cooperation seriously, dismissing it as foolish, hysterical scheme, which would soon destroy itself. But as non-cooperation gathered momentum, they came to realize that it posed a threat to their entire system of law and administration. The government began to watch Gandhi's movements closely. In November, 1921, when the Prince of Wales arrived in Bombay on a visit to India, his arrival was boycotted by the local residents and there were also outbreaks of rioting and arson. Thereafter, in Indian cities, meetings and processions were forcibly dispersed, midnight searches were made of Congress offices for seditious material, and by January, 1922, as many as thirty thousand Congress workers had been put in jail.

In February, Gandhi came under pressure from his Congress colleagues to lead the country in mass civil disobedience. He resisted at first, because he could not think of one basic issue capable of mobilizing the whole country and he feared that the people would again resort to violence, as they had during the agitation against the Rowlatt Act. Then he decided to experiment briefly with civil disobedience in the county of Bardoli in Gujarat, by directing peasants to refuse payrnent of the land-revenue tax. If it worked there, he intended to raise the same issue and fight it in the same way in district after district, until the whole country was striking against the payment of the tax. But, as he had feared, shortly after he launched his Bardoli campaign on February 5, rioting broke out in Chauri Chaura, a little, out-of-the-way village in the nearby United Provinces. He called off the experiment and abandoned all thought of a national campaign, thus confounding his colleagues and followers.

Nevertheless, on March 10, at ten-thirty in the evening, a police officer arrived at Sabarmati Ashram and arrested Gandhi. A week later, Gandhi was tried in Ahmedabad on a charge of writing three seditious articles in his weekly *Young India*. "I am satisfied that many English and Indian officials honestly believe that they are administering one of the best systems devised in the world and that India is making steady though slow progress," Gandhi said in his statement to the court.

> They do not know that a subtle but effective system of terrorism and an organized display of force on the one hand, and the deprivation of

> all powers of retaliation or self-defense on the other, have emasculated the people and induced in them the habit of stimulation. I believe that I have rendered a service to India and England by showing in non-cooperation the way out of the unnatural state in which both are living. In my humble opinion, non-cooperation with evil is as much a duty as is cooperation with good.. I am here, therefore, to invite and submit cheerfully to the highest penalty that can be inflicted upon me for what in law is a deliberate crime and what appears to me to be the highest duty of a citizen. The only course open to you, the judge, is either to resign your post and thus dissociate yourself from evil, if you feel that the law you are called upon to administer is an evil and that in reality I am innocent; or to inflict on me the severest penalty if you believe that the system and the law you are assisting to administer are good for the people of this country and that my activity is, therefore, injurious to the public weal.

The judge sentenced Gandhi to six years in jail, adding that "no one would be better pleased than I if the government later saw fit to reduce the sentence." Two days later, Gandhi was taken by special train to Yeravda Central Jail in Poona, a hill station about three hundred and fifty miles south of Ahmedabad. He served only twenty-two months of his sentence partly because in 1924 he had to undergo an operation for appendicitis. Not only did this leave him weak and exhausted but the non-cooperation movement was now in complete disarray, so the government decided to release him. For the next three or four years, he mostly stayed out of politics.

Then, in 1928, the government increased the land-revenue tax by twenty-two per cent in Bardoli. Gandhi was persuaded to help organize a second civil disobedience campaign there. The peasants refused to pay the tax, and the government retaliated by arresting many of them and attaching their property. This time, there was no rioting; the peasants stoically bore the indignities heaped upon them, and, as a consequence, the government was obliged to yield. It rescinded the tax increase, released the prisoners, and restored the property. But two more years passed before Gandhi, disillusioned by British attempts at constitutional reform, finally launched a national civil disobedience campaign.

Early in 1928, the Conservative Government of Stanley Baldwin had sent a commission, under the chairmanship of Sir John Simon, to India to review its constitutional status — a move called for in the Montagu Chelmsford Reforms of 1919. Gandhi and other Congress leaders boycotted the Simon Commission, on the grounds that no Indians had been appointed to it and that, in any case the appointment of a commission was a charade, given the imperialist attitude of the Conservative Government. Both the Government and the Commission were denounced at protest meetings across the country. The meetings were often forcibly dispersed by laihi charges. During a lathi charge in Lahore, Lala Lajpat Rai, the best-known Punjabi nationalist — he was popularly called the Lion of the Punjab — was fatally in jured. In revenge a Punjabi named Bhagat Singh assassinated the assistant superintendent of police in Lahore and later bombed the Legislative Assembly in New Delhi. Once again, to Gandhi's horror, a peaceful protest had turned violent

In December of 1928, Gandhi was prevailed upon to come out of his relative political seclusion to attend the annual session of the Congress in Calcutta. The Congress leaders were bitterly divided over the question of whether India should demand dominion status or press for all-out independence, and they looked to Gandhi for an answer. Gandhi, who still preferred accommodation with the British to a complete break, and so favored dominion status, came up with a compromise: if at the end of one year the government still refused to grant India dominion status, then he himself would lead a national civil disobedience campaign for all-out independence.

Meanwhile, in June, 1929, the Labour Government of Ramsay MacDonald had succeeded Baldwin's Conservative Government and after due deliberation it proposed a Round Table Conference in London between the British and Indian representatives to debate whether India could be granted dominion status and if so, when and how. The members of the Congress decided to boycott the conference, ostensibly on the ground that they had demanded immediate dominion status, not more talk on the whether, when, and how, but actually because they knew they would have a poor negotiating position. All over India, people were divided not only on the question of dominion status versus independence but also on the questions of the disposition of some six hundred practically autonomous princely states and of the protection of the Muslim minority. Some Indians even wished India to continue under British rule or to receive dominion status in stages. Therefore, neither the Congress nor Gandhi could claim to speak for all Indians, and so neither was in a position to make a national demand at the conference. Instead, on January 1, 1930, Congress defiantly unfurled a flag for independent India and so opened its campaign for all-out independence.

Everyone in the Congress now looked to Gandhi to find an issue around which the whole country could be rallied non-violently, and within two months he did find one. His "inner voice" told him to lead a civil disobedience campaign against the salt-tax laws, on the model of his Satyagrah in South Africa. First, he wrote to Lord Irwin, the Viceroy:

> The iniquities of the tax laws in general and the salt laws in particular are maintained in order to carry on a foreign administration, demonstrably the most expensive in the world. Take your own salary. You are getting over 700 rupees per day against India's average income of less than two annas per day. Thus you are getting much over five thousand times India's average income. On bended knee, I ask you to ponder over this phenomenon. I have taken a personal illustration to drive home a painful truth. I have too great a regard for you as a man to wish to hurt your feelings. But a system that provides for such an arrangement deserves to be summarily scrapped; nothing but unadulterated non-violence can check the organized violence of the British government. But if you cannot see your way to deal with these evils and my letter makes no appeal to your heart, on the eleventh day of this month, I shall proceed with such co-workers of the ashram as I can take, to disregard the provisions of the salt laws.

The Viceroy, rather than enter into a discussion with Gandhi or arrest him, contented himself with having his secretary write a formal acknowledgment of Gandhi's letter.

Under the salt laws, the government enjoyed a monopoly on salt mining, levied a sales tax on salt, and forbade Indians to make their own salt or to use contraband salt. A large number of Indians lived on plains not far from the sea and could easily have made their own salt by drying out seawater in the sun. For the Indians, salt was as essential as air and water: most of them labored long hours in the fields in blistering heat and ate only lentils, bread, and salt. Gandhi came to look upon the salt tax as a tax on Indian sweat and blood.

On March 12, 1930, Gandhi-accompanied by scores of ashram residents and press correspondents—set out for Dandi, a coastal town two hundred miles south of the ashram, where he planned to publicly flout the salt laws, vowing that he would not return to the Sabarmati Ashram until they had been repealed. Every day, he marched about twelve miles, then stopped for the night in a village, where he held a prayer meeting and gave a talk about the salt laws and the Constructive Programme, on occasion mentioning the second Bardoli campaign as an inspiring example of both the potency of non-violence and his countrymen's capacity for it. Every evening, too, he found time to do an hour's spinning and to keep his diary and correspondence up to date. Some villagers joined the march; others sprinkled water along Gandhi's path to settle the dust, and strewed leaves and flower petals before him.

Gandhi's journey to Dandi was compared by his disciples and followers to Jesus's journey to Jerusalem ; many Hindus who could read, bought copies of the Bible and read it. Gandhi himself apparently thought that he might have to die in Dandi, as Jesus died in Jerusalem.

He and his followers arrived there on April 5 and spent the night praying on the beach. In the morning, he walked into the sea to bathe and purify himself. Then he and his followers went through the process of making salt from seawater and so became criminals in the eyes of the law. He and followers camped near Dandi for the next month making and selling small quantities of salt, and waiting to see what the government would do. At first the government did nothing, in the expectation that Gandhi's bizarre campaign would end itself. But the story of the salt march and Gandhi's illicit activities were reported around the world, and in India more and more people began going on symbolic salt marches of their own. Up and down the coasts, on the beaches, and on the banks of brackish streams—wherever there was salt to be found—people became satyagrahis and broke the law. Scarcely any violence was reported. The satyagrahis waded into the sea, collected salt water in pans, watched it evaporate in the sun, and shared the precious salt left behind. The authorities, completely underestimated the Pact, in which Gandhi agreed to go to the Second Round Table Conference, without any prior commitment concerning independence, and to call off all protest against the salt laws and every other form of civil disobedience, while Irwin agreed to release most civil disobedience prisoners and to grant Indians living on the coast permission to manufacture salt. Both Gandhi and Irwin had yielded much more than they wanted to, but each was looking to the second conference for further political gains. The salt laws were never completely repealed, so Gandhi never returned to Sabarmati Ashram to live. When he was not travelling or in jail, he lived at Sevagram Ashram, which he had established in 1936 near the village of Segaon, in central India, dedicating it to the carrying out of the ideals of the Constructive Programme.

The Congress elected Gandhi as its sole representative to the Second Round Table Conference, and he sailed for England late in August of 1931, accompanied by, among others, Mahadev Desai, Mirabehn, Pyarelal, Devadas Gandhi, and Sarojini Naidu, who together had made up for many years what was a kind of informal secretariat. Gandhi and his entourage stayed in a settlement house called Kingsley Hall, in the East End of London, about five miles from St. James's Palace, where the Second Round Table Conference was held, but Gandhi was prevailed upon to maintain an office in Knightsbridge for the convenience of his English friends and admirers and also of many well-to-do Indians living in England who were eager to talk with him.

Gandhi's visit created a great stir in England, and he made the most of it. He went to Oxford colleges and Lancashire cotton mills. He met Charlie Chaplin and George Bernard Shaw, and gave interviews to journalists from all around the world. In his encounters, he often returned to the simplistic, romantic themes he had introduced in *Hind Swaraj:* that through much of history the West had been governed by the laws of force and violence, imperialism and aggression, while the East, in contrast, had been governed by love and spirituality, by ahimsa and satyagraha, and that he was the evangelist from the East to the West.

The Second Round Table Conference met under less propitious circumstances than the first. Although the Muslim League and the princely states were once again represented, the Labour Government had been replaced by the National Government, which, though still led by Ramsay MacDonald, was dominated by the Conservatives. At the conference table, Gandhi argued passionately for independence, or, at the least, a partnership of equals between India and England, but the National Government, for all its interest in setting up a responsible federal government in India, was far from ready to give up the Empire. Moreover, the conference further exposed the underlying differences between the Congress, on the one hand, and the Muslim League and the princes, on the other. Both the Muslim league and the princes feared more than ever that if the British departed without first guaranteeing their interests, they would be overwhelmed by the Congress. Gandhi returned to India in December, 1931, a disappointed man, recognizing that he would now have to contend for independence not only with the British but also with his own countrymen; indeed, he now despaired of ever achieving independence through negotiation. He and his followers in the Congress tried to launch another civil disobedience movement for independence, but this time they were arrested at once, and were again sent to jail. They were released about a year and a half later. Gandhi called off the movement, which had lost much of its momentum, and gave up his membership in the Congress, and for the rest of the thirties he had little to do formally with politics.

In 1937, the British finally put into effect a new Constitution for India—the product of many years of debate and agitation, dating back to the Simon Commission. India was to be granted its long-awaited self-rule in stages, beginning with the transfer of most powers to the popularly elected provincial governments. The Congress was divided in its reception of the Constitution. One faction regarded it as, among other things, a means of realizing the goals of Gandhi's Constructive Programme, and urged cooperation; the other faction, one of whose leaders was Jawaharlal Nehru, regarded it as "a charter of slavery" and urged non-cooperation. Nehru, who had first met Gandhi in 1916, was an aristocrat of modern Western outlook, while Gandhi, in some respects, pictured himself as a peasant of medieval outlook. They became very close but continued to espouse opposing political principles. In part because the Congress didn't want to leave the field open to the Muslim League, and in part because it was seduced by the prospect of power, those who urged cooperation eventually prevailed, and the Congress participated in provincial elections held under the Constitution in 1937.

Gandhi was drawn back into politics by the spectacle of Indians being forced to fight in the Second World War as subjects of the

British Empire. Though he had tried to follow the political events in Europe leading to the war, he seems never to have quite grasped the phenomena of Nazism and Fascism or to have seen the war, when it came, as much more than a clash of imperialistic interests. Some of the leaders in the Congress, asserting that Indians should fight only as free people in defense of their homeland—which, as part of the British Empire, was then threatened by the possibility of a Japanese invasion— and only in support of the cause of freedom, instead of as subjugated people, now urged Gandhi to lead a mass civil disobedience campaign for independence. But Gandhi, although he was opposed to war in any form, did not want to stab the British in the back. He therefore came up with a strategy that at once satisfied the Congress and avoided undermining the British war effort: a succession of individual acts of civil disobedience in place of mass civil disobedience. In line with this strategy, he designated one satyagrahi at a time to court arrest by breaking the law—for instance, by spreading anti-war propaganda. His first choice was Vinoba Bhave, a brahmachari resident of his ashrams, whom he considered the most saintly of his followers and therefore the purest of sacrifices. Bhave was arrested in October, 1940, tried, and sentenced to three months in jail. Gandhi's second choice was Nehru, who was also arrested, tried, and sentenced—to four years in jail—and so it went, over a period of about a year, until there were some twenty-three thousand Congress workers in jail. Gandhi himself stayed out of jail to manage the campaign.

Late in 1941 few days before the surprise attack on Pearl Harbor, Winston Churchill, faced with the prospect of an imminent Japanese invasion of India and pressured by anti-colonial sentiment not only in the Labour Party but also in the United States, released all the important Congress prisoners. Then, in March, 1942, he sent Sir Stafford Cripps—a left-wing Labour member of Parliament, a nephew of Beatrice Webb, and, as it happened, a vegetarian—to India to make another attempt to work out a constitutional arrangement acceptable to Gandhi and the Congress. Cripps proposed immediate Indian participation in the government including matters of defense, but under the Viceroy's direction, and full self-government after the war—even the right to secede from the Commonwealth—but with the provison that any Indian province, princely state, or religious minority could, if it chose, negotiate a separate relationship with

Britain. Though Congress took the offer very seriously, Gandhi saw in it not the promise of a free, united India but the sinister threat of several separate Indian states. In any event, negotiations eventually broke down over the nature of Indian participation in the government and in the war effort. The British blamed Gandhi for the breakdown. At the Lord Mayor's banquet in London that November, Churchill made his famous quip "I have not become the King's first minister in order to preside over the liquidation of the British Empire." B. R. Nanda, in his *Mahatma Gandhi* suggests, that each British proposal for reform and self-government "tended to become out-of-date by the time it was actually granted." He explains, "The Reforms of 1919 might well have appeased political India in 1909; the Reforms of '1935 would have evoked enthusiasm in 1919; and an equivalent of the Cripps offer in 1940 could [in 1935] have opened a new chapter in Indo-British relations, halted the process of estrangement between the Congress and the Government and between Hindus and Muslims."

In August, 1942, Gandhi at last felt impelled to launch the mass civil disobedience campaign, demanding that the British "Quit India," which he had been trying to avoid for the past two years. He told Congress workers to consider themselves henceforth free of British rule. The government promptly arrested all the Congress leaders. Gandhi and his closest followers were imprisoned in the abandoned palace of the Aga Khan in the vicinity of Poona—quarters improvised as a jail expressly for them. Outside the jail, Gandhi's mass civil disobedience campaign quickly degenerated into mass violence, this time abetted by Marxist revolutionaries in the left-wing of the Congress.

Lord Linlithgow, who was now the Viceroy, said that Gandhi was responsible for the violence. Gandhi, shocked by the accusation, wrote a stream of letters to him from jail, maintaining that it was the government's precipitate arrest of him and other Congress leaders which had excited popular passions and provoked the violence. But Lord Linlithgow, in his replies, persisted in blaming Gandhi. And so in February, 1943, when Gandhi was seventy-three years old, he undertook a twenty-one-day fast as an appeal to God to help him settle what he called his "misunderstanding" with Lord Linlithgow. Lord Linlithgow, for his part, allowed Gandhi to be attended by teams of doctors but continued to refuse to admit that he himself had been in any way responsible for the violence. He condemned Gandhi's fast as political blackmail, as a form of personal violence, and as a denial of Gandhi's own pronouncements over twenty-five years that fasts should be used only for self-purification and for disinterested ends. Gandhi survived the fast, but his health was seriously impaired. In subsequent months, he came down with a succession of diseases—malaria, amoebic dysentery, hookworm, and acute anemia. All across the country, there was considerable agitation for his release, and it intensified after Kasturbai died in jail, on February 22, 1944. On May 6, 1944, Gandhi was finally released. By then, he had spent some five and a half years in British jails in India, much of that time as a result of his three major civil-disobedience movements—the non-cooperation movement of 1920-22, the salt movement of 1930-32, and the individual and mass satyagraha movement of 1940-42. He was never to go to jail again.

7

Satyagraha after Independence

India's political leaders paid much lip service to Gandhi and his ideals in the years after Indian independence. There was a stated desire to forge more equitable social and economic relationships in rural areas, with land reform, the regulation of rural usury and minor irrigation projects. There was considerable state investment in small-scale agriculture and support for the khadi and village industries programme, Gandhian education and ashrams, and for the sarvodaya campaign of Vinoba Bhave. Jawaharlal Nehru sought to build on Gandhi's world reputation by claiming that India's foreign policy was motivated by morality, truth and non-violence rather than power politics.

Many scholars have pointed at that time and time again, however, the policies pursued in some of the most crucial areas of concern for modern India ignored all that Gandhi stood for. India had inherited an autocratic system of government from the British, and very little of the repressive apparatus was dismantled. Power was concentrated in the hands of a centralised state that was able to take unilateral action against any form of dissidence that was seen to undermine its control. Far from there being any Gandhian-style devolution of power, the state assumed increasingly authoritarian powers. Little tolerance was shown towards Gandhian-style civil resistance.

For the first time Gandhian method was deployed by the Balmiki Dalit sweepers who went on strike for improved working conditions. They had a high regard for Gandhi, who had stayed in their slum-quarter in Delhi in 1946 in an act ot solidarity. They used Gandhian techniques such as strikes, dharnas and protest-fasts to press their demands with the Delhi Municipal Corporation. The state was caught in a cleft over this, but ultimately resorted to aggressive strike-breaking by the police. In July 1957, demonstrating Balmikis were fired on, with one Balmiki protester, Bhoop Singh being killed. Ministers of Nehru's Congress government expressed regret, but argued that for the sake of public health they could not tolerate strikes by essential workers such as public cleaners. The Home Minister G.B. Pant went so far as to say that the Balmikis had a duty to work 'because they are citizens of the councry and they have the privilege to serve the people by rendering essential services.' The Minister for Law, A.K. Sen, asserted that 'the right to strike is not a fundamental right'. On 6 August 1957 the Essential Services Maintenance Ordinance was passed in Parliament, which allowed civil liberties to be suspended in an emergency. Jayprakash Narayan roundly condemned this as an example of a 'growing Indian fascism'.

Many Balmikis regarded the police firing as their 'Jallianwallah Bagh'. In post-colonial India, it was acceptable for leading politicians to invoke Gandhi in symbolic ways, with *padayatras* and the like, but not for poor people to apply his methods of assertive non-violent protest. Their rewards were beatings and police atrocities. As Rattan Lal Balmiki stated: "The days of Gandhi are over and true Gandhians are now morose.' Today, the Balmikis maintain the room in which Gandhi stayed in their colony as a shrine, and among the relics is a photograph of Bhoop Singh, the martyr of July 1957.

The Bhoodan and Gramdan Movements

Bhoodan and Gramdan were Gandhi-inspired initiatives associated most closely with the two figures of Vinoba Bhave and Jayaprakash Narayan. Their work formed a part of the overall Sarvodaya Movement. Sarvodaya entailed dedicated work for public welfare, carried out by cadres—known as *lok sevaks*—who were trained in Gandhian institutions and Gandhian principle and philosophy.

Vinoba Bhave (1895-1982) was a Maharashtrian Brahmin brought up in Gujarat, who joined Gandhi in 1916 and was active thereafter in constructive rather than political work. A relatively unknown figure within the movement until 1948, he took the initiative in that year in founding the Sarvodaya Samaj. The day before his assassination on January 30 of that year, Gandhi had proposed that the Congress be disbanded and a Lok Sevak Sangh be established in its place. This was rejected by the Congress leadership, which believed that given the severe problems of the day, it was essential to maintain a cohesive political party to run the country. In response, Bhave set up the Sarvodaya Samaj in March as an alternative.

This was a time when communists had won strong support in rural areas, with powerful peasant movements in areas such as Telangana, Bengal, and Thana district of Maharashtra. After the movement was crushed in Telangana by the Indian army, with the landlords being in many cases given back the land which had been seized from them by the communists, Bhave — who was strongly anti-communist — toured the region, seeking a Gandhian means for mitigating the problems of the rural poor. In April 1950, a landlord donated one hundred acres of land to him to distribute to landless Dalits. Bhave saw this as a sign from God, and set about trying to persuade other landlords to make gifts of land. Thus was initiated the Bhoodan movement. He had considerable success in Telangana, and then in Uttar Pradesh. Nehru gave his moral support to the work, hoping it would provide a better climate for the government's land reform legislation. Bhave received widespread international coverage for this work, but surprisingly his anti-communist credential even helping him to make the cover of *Time* magazine, with his portrait over the caption: 'I have come to loot you with love.'

Jayaprakash Narayan (1902—1979), who was from Bihar, soon joined Bhave in this work. Like Bhave, JP had had a long and close relationship with Gandhi, but in JP's case it had been a probleanatic one, as he had moved away from an early Gandhism to Marxism, and then back, slowly and painfully, towards a synthesis between the two. JP had first joined the Gandhian movement during Non-Cooperation in 1921. His wife Prabhavati had gone to live and work with Gandhi in his Swaraj ashram in Ahmedabad, and remained there during the 1920s when JP went to the USA for higher study. There he came into contact with Marxian writings that convinced him that Gandhi was a counter-revolutionary who was working in the interests of the bourgeoisie. Back in India in 1929 he went to see Prabhavati at the ashram with mixed feelings, but Gandhi quickly won him over emotionally, if not ideologically, in part by pampering him as his 'son-in-law'.

JP participated in the civil disobedience movements of 1930-1 and 1932-4. Disgusted with the communist refusal to join the struggle at that time, he and other young socialists decided in 1934 to form the Congress Socialist Party to work within the Congress. He continued his dialogue with Gandhi during these years. He argued that spinning, and even anti-untouchability work, was irrelevant to the wider political and ideological struggle, which had to be along class lines. He also held that state power had to be seized before there could be real change. Gandhi replied that people had to be convinced intellectually before legislation could succeed. During these years, JP moved further away from the Communist Party, which he saw as apologising for Stalin's tyranny. He was committed to a strongly democratic socialism. He also followed Gandhi in believing in the need for decentralisation and a moral base to praxis. However, he refused to accept the principle of ahimsa and in the early 1940s worked actively to prepare for an armed revolt against the British. He was a leading figure in the underground movement during the Quit India movement of 1942. At the time, Gandhi publicly praised JP, but after his release from jail in 1944, he condemned the violence of the movement. He said that while he admired JP's courage, Prabhavati was the true hero, as she had remained non-violent throughout. J P, then in jail where he had been tortured, felt very bitter about Gandhi's remarks in this respect. However, the terrible carnage of the Partition period, which JP witnessed at first hand in rural Bihar, made him far more sympathetic to Gandhi's principled abhorrence of violence.

JP joined Vinoba Bhave in the Bhoodan movement in 1953. He marched through his home state of Bihar encouraging land owners to give land to the poor. Many made promises to do so. Bhave and JP then extended the movement into *gramdan*, which aimed to bring all land in a village under the control of the village community, with individual land owners agreeing to gift their land to the community. This was a radical departure from the principle of bhoodan, which was rooted in the individual ownership of land. Gramdan also involved activities such as the settlement of disputes by voluntarily established village councils without recourse to the police or courts, and the encouragement of village self-sufficiency. By the end of 1956, 1935 villages had elected for gramdan. By 1958, the movement was flagging. One major problem was that village money lenders refused to grant loans to villagers who no longer possessed individual land deeds as a security. Also, there was growing unease amongst sarvodaya workers about Vinoba Bhave's disinclination to resort to satyagraha against those who had promised to hand over land, but refused in practice to do so. Bhave believed that in a democratic country such as India, satyagraha should only be used in very exceptional circumstances. He rejected the demand made by the socialist leader Rammanohar Lohia for mass civil disobedience to force the pace of change. In 1973 Bhave went so far as to state:

> In Gandhi's days, there was no freedom of thought and expression. But in India today we enjoy the highest measure of freedom in the world. Every day the newspaper brings to us the highest indictment of the government. Satyagraha as practised by Gandhi has therefore become quite irrelevant in India.

Bhave appears to have been blind to the fact that abuses of power by the landed elites, politicians, bureaucrats and the police continued apace in independent India, in most cases being entirely unreported in the press.

The growing unease in regard to Bhave increasingly led to dissent within the ranks of the sarvodaya movement. Ramachandra Rao, who had won Gandhi's respect in the 1940s for his activism went so far as to form a separate Satyagraha Sangh that Bhave refused to support. Rao, who was from Andhra Pradesh, staged a Satyagraha in front of the legislative assembly in Hyderabad in 1960 in protest at the corruption of politics through the party system.

The Naxalite Movement

By the late 1960s an alternative surge of rural revolution was under way in which Gandhi-inspired methods were firmly rejected in favour of violent appropriation of landed property and the physical elimination of tyrannical landlords. The Naxalite movement began in North Bengal in 1967, with an uprising by peasants led by communist revolutionaries. Sharecroppers seized the land of the landlords and occupied it. Although the police crushed the rising within a few months, the ideas behind it remained alive, inspiring similar revolts in other parts of India in the following years, notably in Andhra Pradesh and Bihar.

The Naxalites had no time for Gandhi and his theories, for, in the words of the Naxalite theorist Saroj Dutta, 'Gandhi was the leader and representative of the bourgeois group which was the agent of the British imperialists." There was an emphatic rejection of the Gandhian methols, which were depicted as a bad-faithed attempts to reconcile irreconcilable class antagonisms. Gandhi's desire to create a culture of non-violent struggle was subjected to scorn and ridicule. Saroj Dutta called on naxalites to destroy statues of Gandhi and erect in their place statues of the heroes of the 1857 revolt, such as Mangal Pande and the Rani of Jhansi, thus validating and glorifying a history of violent revolt. The killing of landlords by naxalites was seen as a wholly progressive and positive step: 'The masses never make mistakes. Revolution is bound to signify excess.'

The chief ideologue and leader of the movement in the early years was Charu Mazumdar, who advocated a campaign of terror against the propertied classes, to be carried out primarily by naxalite militants operating in underground guerrilla bands in great secrecy. The Gandhian and existing communist emphasis on mass mobilisation and struggle to obtain land was rejected in favour of building a 'red army' which would eventually be able to take on the Indian state. As it was, the naxalite guerrillas were eliminated in a series of ruthless police operations, in which many villagers were killed alongside the naxalites. Within the movement, Kanu Sanyal expressed his disquiet at Charu Mazumdar's line, arguing that: 'As a result of denying any importance to politics and rejection of the path of mass struggles and mass organisations, the combat groups obsessed with actions only, were soon reduced to roving bands." He felt that a more dialogic approach in relationship to the government of West Bengal could have gained far more for the people in 1967. Instead, they had been crushed. The naxalite outbreak in Bengal proved, however, to be a defining moment in modern Indian history. The Gandhian alternative was certainly eclipsed in the late 1960s by a movement that sought to replace dialogue with terror. There were a series of naxalite-style revolts in various parts of India at that time.

Against this backdrop, Vinoba Bhave abandoned his efforts for peaceful land reform and retired to his ashram near Wardha. He refused to designate any clear successor, which left the movement in a state of drift at a crucial juncture. There were demands from within the Sarvodaya movement for sustained satyagraha against landlords as a counter to naxalite violence. This chance was lost.

In JP's home state of Bihar, naxalites established strong bases in a number of areas in the early 1970s. On the whole, their approach was more that of Kanu Sanyal than Charu Mazumdar. A firm base was established amongst low-caste and Dalit landless labourers, providing an environment in which the armed militants could find shelter between actions. The emphasis was on building a strong movement through solid work over an extended period, rather than through adventuristic acts of dramatic violence. With such a base, naxalites were able to resist the counter-attacks of the police and the rural rich, and through their presence force the latter to improve the conditions of work of their labourers.

When some naxalites issued death threats against two prominent sarvodaya workers of Muzaffarpur district of North Bihar in 1970, JP decided to go there and work to counter their influence through bhoodan and gramdan. He decided to emphasise civil resistance over and above moral appeals. He continued to insist on strict non-violence, as naxalite-style violence would only provoke fierce state repression. By adopting this approach in his subsequent campaign against the corruption of Indira Gandhi's Congress Party, JP then managed to regain much of the ground that had been lost to the naxalites. This culminated in a massive upsurge in 1974-5, known often as 'the JP Movement'.

The JP Movement

This movement, which became a particularly notable example of Gandhian-style activism in post-independence India, was inaugurated by JP in 1973 against the corruption of Indira Gandhi's government. Students were mobilised to campaign against corrupt politicians, black-marketeering, profiteering and hoarding by capitalists that led to price rises, the evasion of land reform laws, and unemployment. The movement took off in Gujarat in 1974, with the Nav Nirman Movement, which brought the corrupt Congress administration of Chimanlal Patel to its knees. Chimanlal was forced to resign offioce. The movement then spread to Bihar. JP led the protest actively there, trying to prevent it degenerating into violence by maintaining the momentum with strikes, demonstrations and marches. He called on the students to leave their studies for a year and work for 'total revolution'. Despite his efforts, there were many incidents of violence. Several Sarvodaya workers condemned the movement in this respect, even though the violence of the police was far greater. For them, state coercion did not rank as violence. VinobaBhave merely commented to JP's great disgust—'I leave it to God for his verdict'.

JP publicly condemned Bhave for this statement—the first time he had ever criticised his fellow-Gandhian in public. This allowed Indira Gandhi to set about exploiting the difference between the two men. She turned on JP calling him a 'believer in violence' and a traitor to the Gandhian movement. She gave the green signal for the formation of a paramilitary group called the Indira Brigade, which went so far as to fire on a demonstration in Patna, injuring twenty-one people. In November, while attacking a rally in Patna, the police launched a murderous assault on JP himself, aimed to maim or kill. He was defended bravely by his followers, some of whom were badly injured. JP was rescued after two of his ribs and a toe were broken. Coming round, he addressed the crowd, stating that he had not witnessed such state terror in all of his years of public life, including during British times.

At this juncture, JP made a controversial strategic decision. Seeking for allies in his struggle with the Indira Congress, he linked up with the Jana Sangh and its sinister parent body the RSS, who were eager to use this as a means to attack the 'communists' within the Congress. Although JP had severe reservations about the RSS, which he regarded as a clique which refused to open itself to internal debate, he was now linking his Gandhian-inspired movement with a group that despised Gandhi and his legacy and which stood for the most "authoritarian, intolerant and non-dialogic forms of politics." In JP's defence, it can be argued that he was hoping to bring about a change of heart in the Jana Sangh and RSS, and that he succeeded to the extent that a more moderate group emerged within this tendency under Atal Bihari Vajpayee. The mass of the Hindu right was not however won over ideologically in any significant way.

In the short term, this move greatly strengthened the protest in northern India, where the RSS had an impressive organisation. With RSS support, a huge demonstration of over half a million protesters was staged in Delhi in March 1975. Indira Gandhi was now able to state in March 1975, with some credibility, that the movement had become a front for 'fascists'. However, rather than try to woo and befriend JP away from his dubious new allies, which might have been possible with some concessions, she chose instead to crush all of her opponents together, imposing a state of Emergency on 26 June 1975 and arresting and jailing the leaders of the protest. The RSS was driven underground to continue the fight. This boosted the morale of its cadres on the one hand, and on the other helped it gain legitimacy through its participation in what was widely seen as a righteous war - *dharmyudha*.

Vinoba Bhave came out openly in support of Indira Gandhi at this juncture, praising the Emergency as an *anushasan parva* (an era of discipline) that would be good for the health of the nation. Bhave's stance split the Gandhian movement in two, with many sarvodaya workers refusing to follow his lead. They organised satyagrahas in nearly three thousand places on over five hundred occasions. The police beat up large numbers, and nearly nine thousand were arrested. Despite great provocation, they remained non-violent. Though these protests were ignored in the heavily censored press, in scale this satyagraha was comparable to many of Gandhi's own anti-British campaigns.

JP's protest against the government of Indira Gandhi, was one strand of what he called his campaign for 'total revolution' in India. This followed the old Gandhian path of deploying political discontent to drive forward a wider movement for all-round social, economic and cultural change.

After the dramatic elections of March 1977 that brought an end to the Emergency, JP appeared to be vindicated, with the way now being open for more active state support for the Gandhian programme at every level. He demanded that people's committees be established as a step towards a genuine devolution of power at village level. The response from the politicians who had now won power was less than enthusiastic and the scheme was soon forgotten. JP himself was in very poor health, and was unable to take much personal initiative in the matter. He died a sad man in October 1979.

Women and Anti-Liquor Movements in India

In recognition of the strong movement against liquor which had been inspired by Gandhi and which brought about an empowering mobilisation of many women within the struggle, prohibition was implemented in certain provinces of India after independence in 1947. Enforcement was however lax, and in most cases the policy was abandoned after a few yeats. Anti-liquor work was left on the whole to Sarvodaya activists. In Uttar Pradesh, Sohanlal Bhubhisuk, a follower of Vinoba Bhave, launched a dharna outside certain liquor shops in 1962, himself staging a fast on the steps of the Legislative Assembly in Lucknow. This movement never really took off, however. In the following year Vimla and Sunderlal Bahuguna, a couple who were active in the Sarvodaya movement, started a far more powerful movement in the Uttarancha! region of the state. After they launched a satyagraha against the awarding of a contract to sell liquor in a village close to their ashram, the government agreed to cancel the arrangement. The movement spread in 1966, with women picketing liquor shops and forcing them to close. Protests continued in the following years, with many women being jailed. In one demonstration in 1971 over ten thousand women took part; with fifty-six being arrested and jailed for picketing a liquor shop. Eventually, in 1972, the government agreed to impose prohibition in Uttaranchal. In the process, many women were politically empowered, feeding into their remarkable participation in the Chipko movement in the same area in the following years.

There were similar anti-liquor campaigns elsewhere in India at that time. In Dhule district of Maharashtra, for example, activists with Gandhian leanings started one such movement amongst Adivasi women. After a women's camp was held in 1973, many women in the area went in groups to smash up illicit village liquor distilleries.

In most cases, initial successes were not consolidated. In Uttaranchal, for instance, the subsequent emphasis on forest protest saw a marginalisation of the liquor issue. Soon, many illicit distilleries sprang up, so that within a few years it became one of Uttaranchal's major cottage industries. In 1980 the government decided that the policy had been a failure, and allowed the sale of liquor once more in three districts of Uttaranchal. This led to a resumption of the anti-liquor movement in the region in the early 1980s by a youth group called the Uttarakhand Sangharsh Vahini. There were strong protests in 1984, with demonstrations at the time of liquor-shop auctions and picketing of liquor shops. Women were to the fore in this activity. The Sarvodaya-led anti-liquor movement continued in Uttaranchal, feeding in recent years into the movement for what is now the separate Uttaranchal state.

In the early 1990s, there was a powerful anti-liquor movement in Andhra Pradesh, launched after the state government had set up a new machinery to market arrack in a more efficient and, for the government, more lucrative way. Village women saw that their husbands and brothers were squandering their meagre family earnings on this high-priced arrack. The last straw proved to be the subsequent withdrawal of the state subsidy on rice for poor families. In Andhra, numerous poor women had become more assertive of their rights as a result of literacy programmes run in part by the Communist Party (Marxist-Leninist) and the Naxalite Peoples War Group, in part by the state. Women launched a series of raids on arrack-shops on their own initiative. Besides smashing liquor containers, they also attacked excise jeeps bringing the arrack to their villages. They put pressure on the men of their families to renounce liquor, fining some of those who continued to drink. Their main grievance was against the high price of the government arrack, which was causing great poverty in families, rather than against liquor as such. They had no strong objection to the consumption of home-made liquor.

A wide range of politicians and NGO workers of various political ideologies supported the movement, hoping thereby to further their own agendas. This included Gandhians, who introduced a call for temperance as a moral principle. The leader of the Telegu Desam Party, N.T. Rama Rao—then in opposition to the Congress government— took up the issue in 1992, invoking the memory of Gandhi's opposition to drunkenness and his encouragement of women to lead the fight against this evil. Under this pressure, the state government announced in October 1993 that there would be a ban on arrack throughout Andhra. When the Telegu Desam Party won power in the following year, Rao—now chief minister—announced that liquor would be prohibited throughout the state from immediate effect. A Gandhian temperance agenda had been imposed, although the women in the movement itself had not put forward any demand for complete prohibition.

The Chipko Andolan

The Chipko Andolan, which was started and led by Gandhian activists, was a protest against the forest policy of the government in the Uttaranchal division of Uttar Pradesh.T his was a mountainous region that until the 1960s was thickJy forested. There was a long history of protest m Uttaranchal against government forest policy, stretching back to 1906. From 1921, this protest had been linked to that of the Gandhian Congress.

With the extensive construction of roads in the region in the 1960s, trucks were able to enter the hills and remove timber on an unprecedented scale. Politicians took bribes to ensure that timber-felling contracts were awarded to industrialists and timber dealers at concessional rates. Local sarvodaya workers tried to resist this initially by establishing locally-controlled forest co-operatives, so that the benefits would come to the people of the region rather than outsiders. However, they lacked both political clout and money-power, and could not obtain the contracts for the co-operatives. In late 1972 a series of demonstrations were held, demanding an end to the contract system of forest exploitation and the supply of forest produce to local people at cheap rates.

At the same time, a more critical attitude was developing amongst the local Sarvodaya workers towards forestry in general. They had been active in mobilising women in the strong anti-liquor campaign of the late 1960s and during the course of this struggle had learnt from the women that the destruction of the forest was causing them severe hardship. Fuel-wood for daily cooking needs was becoming hard to obtain, and even springs were drying up as rainwater was running off the hills unchecked, and thus not replenishing underground springs. The fast run-off. also caused floods and landslides.

The movement entered a new phase in 1973, with protest against a case of gross discrimination against local people in favour of a rich industrial concern from the plains. In late 1972, the government awarded a contract to a large sports manufacturer of Allahabad to cut hundreds of trees from a forest in the hills. Earlier, it had refused permission for a small local firm run along Gandhian lines which specialised in processing of forest produce to take a few trees from the same forest. The man in charge of this organisation was Chandi

Prasad Bhatt, a sarvodaya worker who had been involved already in work against untouchability and liquor consumption. He decided to launch a campaign of civil disobedience that involved physical prevention of the tree-felling. The local-people themselves devised the idea of'hanging on' *(chipko)* to the trees, thus giving rise to the name of the movement. They managed to get the cutting stopped. When the company tried to move its operations to a neighbouring forest, they organised a similarly successful protest there. Soon, villagers all over the region were preventing forest clearance through this form of protest. Village women were in the forefort, though men were also strongly involved.

Although the Chipko moverment became known as a woman-centred movement in which village women fought to preserve the forest around their villages, this represented only one element of the stuggle. In Uttar Pradesh as a whole, the particular needs of Uttaranchal were often ignored, for even though it was an extensive area, its people made up only four percent of the total population of the state. Politicians, traders and industrialists of the plains exploited Uttaranchal as a resource, but little was invested in return to improve the condition of the people. Hill agriculture was hard and with low returns, forest resources were largely monopolised by the forest department and there was little industrial employment. As a result, most people of the region lived in poverty. Many were being forced to migrate out in search of work. To a large extent, the protest was against this general state of affairs,

The movement continued throughout the 1970s, with sarvodaya workers such as Sunderlal Bahuguna and Chandi Prasad Bhatt in the forefront of the leadership. They insisted that there be complete non-violence, despite much provocation by the authorities and others. In a few cases, the women found themselves fighting alone, as when Gaura Devi—a fifty-one-year-old widow—led some women of her village in a protest against tree-felling that the men of the village were keen to allow, as they earned money from renting their houses to contractors and their workers, and were also themselves employed by the contractors to cut trees. The village men launched a social boycott against Gaura Devi, making her position very difficult. Her son was beaten up, and she received death threats. It was only with the strong moral support of Chandi Prasad Bhatt that she was able to keep up her struggle. In Dongri Paitoh village also a few courageous village women stood against the men, being subjected as a result to threats and insults.

Bahuguna believed that the movement had the potential to bring a wider transformation in India, stating that 'I am waiting for the day when the non-violent movement of the hill woman will help turn upside down the centres of power in this country." In 1979 he launched a fast to force the government to stop cutting of trees by contractors. He was arrested on the thirteenth day, but continued his fast in jail. On the twenty-fourth day the authorities agreed to discuss the issue, and he withdrew his fast. In 1980, Indira Gandhi invited the Chipko Andolan leaders to Delhi for talks, and as a result banned commercial forestry at a height above a thousand metres in the Himalayas for the next fifteen years. Food, fodder and fuel-bearing trees were to be planted close to villages, and people were to have the right to take dry twigs and leaves from the government forests. This represented a major victory.

The movement succeeded for a number of reasons. It provided a striking example of a Gandhian-style protest driven by a sense of moral outrage against a corrupt and rapacious regime that was impoverishing the people and their environment. It was led by respected Sarvodaya workers who insisted on a rigid adherence to non-violence and who had good relations with many leading Gandhian politicians as well as top government officials. The state had to tread carefully against a movement so clearly informed by the Gandhian ideals. Because of this, the movement escaped the sort of vicious repression experienced by many other protest movements of the day. In the end, they also drew the attention of the prime minister, Indira Gandhi. She had come out in favour of environmental protection at the First International Environmental Conference in Stockholm in 1972, and the appeal was addressed to her on that basis, with considerable success.

Chipko became well known throughout the world as an example of Gandhian green movement with the image of women embracing trees becoming an icon of the green movement as a whole. Chipko gave rise to a series of protests since that time in which activists have embraced trees or established tree houses, so as to prevent commercial felling operations.

Narmada Bachao Andolan

One of the most powerful campaigns of civil disobedience since 1980 has been against the construction of a huge dam on the Narmada river, just below the point at which it flows into Gujarat state. The resulting lake—called the Sardar Sarovar in honour of Sardar Vallabhbhai Patel— will displace from between 100,000 and 250,000 people—the figures are disputed—in about 450 villages. Of these about two-thirds are in the Nimar plain of Madhya Pradesh. These are mainly relatively prosperous high-caste farmers who have benefited from the Green Revolution. They will lose their fertile lands to submergence. About one-third of those affected are Adivasis living in the hills directly behind the dam. The bulk of the finance for the construction was to come from loans from the World Bank and from the Japanese government.

The organisation that was formed to fight this project—the Narmada Bachao Andolan is often described as 'environmental'. It has in consequence received support from many environmentalist groups around the world. However, the chief stated goal of the movement itself is that of creating an alternative political culture based on the Gandhian principles. It has been driven by a very Gandhian belief that modern developmental projects supported by the state run roughshod over the economic needs as well as civil rights of the mass of the rural poor, and that the only way to counter such tyranny is through non-violent mass resistance. The merits of satyagraha as against participation in electoral politics, or even violent resistance, have been debated at length in the movement, and it is generally accepted that non-violent methods are most appropriate. The two main leaders, Medha Patkar and Baba Amte, have also used fasting as a weapon, often with some success. The Narmada Bachao Andolan is best seen, therefore, as a campaign for economic and civil rights that employs Gandhian-style satyagraha to powerful effect.

Protests against the proposed dam began as early as 1978 in Nimar, but the movement flagged in the early 1980s. It was then taken up by local NGO workers active in the Adivasi areas which were due to be submerged, with a series of rallies and protests in the mid-1980s. Medha Patkar came to the area first in 1985 as a member of a research team that was investigating the resettlement of peasants affected by the project. She was deeply disturbed to find that the people were being evicted from their land and livelihood with no proper compensation. She also felt that the adverse environmental effects of the dam had not been fully appreciated, as no proper environmental studies had been carried out. In 1987 she decided to settle in the valley and fight against the big dam.

Their first success came in 1990, when the NBA managed to persuade the Japanese government to withdraw all further funding for the project on environmental and human rights grounds. In the same year, the much-respected Gandhian social worker Baba Amte became actively involved in the struggle. He was known for his dedicated work amongst lepers in Maharashtra. In 1985 he had led a mass protest against the construction of two dams in Bastar that threatened to displace the Adivasis of the area. The two dams were never built. In 1989, he turned his attention to the Narmada dam, publishing a booklet called *Cry of Beloved Narmada.*, in which he argued that the desire for large dams was a form of modern superstition and that the future lay with small-scale watershed projects. In 1990 he decided to take up residence on the banks of the Narmada at Kasravad, where he established an ashram at a spot that was scheduled for submergence. He vowed to stay there and fight the dam to his last breath. In May 1990 he staged a dharna in Delhi before the residence of the then prime minister, V.P. Singh, demanding that construction work be stopped. The prime minister, under pressure from the Gujarat government, rejected the demand.

In December 1990 three thousand people who were threatened with displacement started out on a march from Nimar to the site of the dam. After eight days, the state police stopped them at the border of Gujarat. Rather than go back, they sat down in protest. Volunteers tried to break through the cordon, their hands tied in front of them to show their non-violent intentions. They were beaten back by the police and some were arrested. Medha Patkar and five others launched an indefinite fast. The Gujarat government then orchestrated a counter-demonstration at the border by supporters of the dam, which included some noted Gandhian workers such as Harivallabh Parikh. Baba Amte tried to reason with them, but they rejected his appeals, something he found both sad and disconcerting. The Gujarat government likewise refused to enter into any dialogue; every suggestion from the NBA was turned down flat. The stalemate continued until a group of independent citizens agreed to review the matter, after which the fast was called off having lasted twenty-two days. The NBA leaders decided to abandon their sit-in. Despite the failure, the protest had received huge publicity, and Medha Patkar had become an all-India, and indeed international figure. The World Bank decided to investigate the matter by setting up a commission of enquiry.

The report that this commission submitted in 1992 thoroughly vindicated the NBA. It was highly critical of the whole project, both in terms of its impact on the environment and for the way in which the displaced people were being treated. As a result of this report, the World Bank withdrew its financial support for the project in 1993. Angered by this setback to their ambitions, the political leaders of Gujarat launched a yet more vicious campaign of repression. The police thrashed demonstrators, an Adivasi boy was shot dead, and the NBA office in Baroda was ransacked. They continued to build the dam and dig the canals that it was to feed, financing these works from state resources. Soon, eighty percent of the entire irrigation budget of Gujarat was being poured into the work, starving other irrigation projects of funds.

The NBA had meanwhile challenged the legality of the project in the Supreme Court of India in New Delhi in 1994. It was argued that the way rehabilitation was being carried through, violated the terms under which the project had been passed by the government. The court accepted that there had been various irregularities in the implementation of the project. It ruled that construction work should cease for the time being at a height of 88 metres pending a review. As the projected height of the dam was to be 138 metres, this was considered a major victory for the NBA.

The NBA continued its campaign to prevent the waters of the Narmada being dammed at all. However, many people who were sympathetic towards the protest began to feel that the dam was now a *fait accompli.* The majority of Adivasis affected by the existing submergence had by then been resettled, albeit in very inadequate and often squalid camps, and it was argued that rather than go on opposing it in an outright fashion it would be better to work to obtain a better deal for those who were being displaced.

Medha Patkar refused to accept this, arguing that the whole project continued to violate her deepest feelings. She advanced the

Gandhian argument that the struggle was for decentralisation of power, with local people having the right to decide how their resources should be utilised. She now focused the campaign on annual protests in villages that were being submerged by the reservoir each monsoon. Activists stayed with the peasants in their villages as the waters rose, refusing to move, even at the risk of drowning. This was called *jal samarpan*—which means 'give one's life to the water'. The first such protest was in 1993 at Manibelli, a village very close to the site of the dam. In 1994, Baba Amte and his wife refused to move from their house by the river and were only saved from drowning by being forcibly removed by the district collector. There was a highly publicised protest along such lines during the monsoon of 1999, when Medha Patkar went to stay in Domkhedi—one of the villages which was being rapidly submerged by the rising waters. She and sixty other protesters were arrested by the police, dragged away and kept in detention until the water receded after the monsoon.

Patkar was joined in the late 1990s by the celebrity author Arundhati Roy, who threw her weight behind this uncompromising stand with a powerful polemic in favour of the movement which gained a lot of media attention both in India and abroad. In January 2000, Roy was arrested while leading a protest march against the dam. Roy's intervention gave a major fillip to the protest after a period of demoralisation.

In October 2000 there was a grave setback to the movement when the Supreme Court ruled by a 2-1 majority that construction work on the dam could be resumed to bring it up to 90 metres, and thereafter in stages to an eventual height of 138 metres. The Gujarat government, now controlled by the BJP, celebrated this news with fireworks, and then organised a big function at the site of the dam to inaugurate the restart of construction. It was held on 31 October 2000, the 125th universary of the birth of Sardar Vallabhbhai Patel, and the man after whom the reservoir is named. The celebrations cut across party lines in Gujarat, with the leader of the Congress opposition in the state, Amarsinh Chaudhary, also attending. However, the chief ministers of the three other states affected by the project, Madhya Pradesh, Maharashtra and Rajasthan, did not come. The function was presided over by L.K. Advani, the then home minister of India, who had a conceit of being the true heir to Sardar Patel. In his speech he spoke darkly of the 'anti-national forces' that were opposing both the dam and India's nuclear weapons: 'I sometimes wonder whether these people are working at the behest of our own people or outsiders. I want to be proved wrong, but it surprises me. Why is there so much opposition to developmental projects? This attitude clearly suits those who do not wish to see India becoming strong in security and socio-economic development."Patkars response to this was: 'At least they have understood us well when he said that we were against Kargil and Pokhran. They have understood that we are against violence."

Patkar and Roy refused to compromise at all, launching an immediate campaign to have the Supreme Court verdict reversed. The Gujarat government is now pushing ahead with the building work, hoping that they will eventually be allowed to take the dam to the full height of 138 metres. As the Supreme Court is only allowing the height to be raised in stages, depending on whether or not there has been compliance with the terms of the agreement, permission for each stage is likely to be fought out bitterly. In January 2001, the government of Maharashtra— which is generally more prepared to listen to Medha Patkar than the government of Gujarat—let it be known that it is unlikely to agree to a height greater than 110 metres unless very good reasons are given. The struggle thus continues.

To what extent has this been a Gandhia*n* movement? Although Baba Amte is very clearly a Gandhian, Medha Patkar makes no such claim. Yet, in the words of Shripad Dharmadikari, who has been with the NBA since 1988; "Gandhi was never a "mantra' within the Andolan. Yet all its activists saw themselves as fighting the battle against Nehru's version of "development" and for something closer to "Gandhi's" version which, fifty years ago, had been pushed aside by the forces of history." And, as Sanjay Sangvai—another leading figure in the NBA—has pointed out, the tactics that have been adopted exemplify the Gandhian method of struggle.

As in Gandhi's own campaigns and JP's movement, the protest has depended on the leadership and drive of charismatic figures, most notably Medha Packar and Baba Amte. Initially, the people of Nimar were suspicious of Patkar, who they suspected was motivated by personal political ambitions. But when they saw that this was not the case—that she was driven by a rage against the injustice of such development projects—they became ardent followers, regarding her as almost a goddess-like figure in whom they could repose their faith. She and Baba Amte were widely seen to be above narrow party politics and to be true champions of the people—as were Gandhi and JP. Through their inspired leadership, Patkar and Amte managed to bring together rich farmers and Adivasis within one movement, even though the two groups of this region have very little in common in most respects and in the past have generally viewed each other with considerable distrust.

Just as Gandhi managed to win international attention through his adept use of symbols, so the Narmada Bachao Andolan has proved a master of publicity. Adivasis staged their protests wielding bows and arrows. They held meetings in which—in front of the cameras of the world press—they scooped up water from the Narmada and held it in their hands while vowing never to leave their ancestral lands. When portions of their villages were submerged, they were photographed standing in the rising water declaring that they would let themselves be drowned rather than accept rehabilitation.

They learnt to use language that went down well with environmentalists, such as that they were children of the earth who were being torn from their mother's breasts. The image of the movement that was thus projected was that of simple Adivasis who had lived in the area since time immemorial in harmony with their environment being brutally displaced by a callous and unfeeling developmental state. The fact that the majority of the people due to be displaced were prosperous farmers of Nimar rather than poor Adivasis tended to be overlooked in all this.

Although the appeal to environmental sensibilities has in many respects been extremely successful, it has also opened up the movement to an attack that seeks to trivialise it. The leaders are thus described as 'youngsters' from urban areas who are driven by romantic concerns about 'trees and tigers'. Also, as Michael Dove has argued, environmentalism is easily turned round by states to justify repressive developmental policies, by refusing local people access to forests on the grounds that they are destroying the forest ecology.

Similar problems are encountered in the attempt to project this as a religious struggle. The Narmada is considered one of the seven great sacred rivers of India, revered by many as 'Narmada Mai', or the goddess Mother Narmada. There are a string of temples along the banks from its source to its mouth, and it is considered particularly religious for Hindus to trek on foot from one to the other along the entire length of the river, travelling east on the north bank and back west on the south. This is known as the *Narmada parikrama* and it takes many months to complete. The construction of the Sardar Sarovar and other dams along the river will destroy this ancient pilgrimage trail and submerge many old and historic temples. There are no plans to save them in any way. The feeling that religious sensibilities are being trampled underfoot by the state provides an added moral defence for the movement. This has been reinforced by a free use of religious symbols in demonstrations and protests.

The uncompromising attitude of a succession of Gujarat governments—whether of Congress or the BJP—towards the NBA has made this a particularly difficult test of the Gandhian method of resistance. Medha Patkar and Baba Arnte have been able to carry on fruitful dialogues with the governments of Madhya Pradcsh and Maharashtra. The government of Gujarat, on the other hand, has resisted all dialogue, preferring to react with calumny against the leaders and police action against the protesters. Despite all the provocation, the resistance has remained non-violent.

Realising that they had lost the moral high ground in the affair, the supporters of the dam in Gujarat have deployed a counter-tactic, namely the mobilisation of their religious spokesmen to advance a claim that the dam is *dharmik*. They argue that it will bring the holy water of 'Narmada Mata' to the homes of people throughout Gujarat. A rally to this effect was held in Bombay in 1990, addressed by high-profile Hindu religious figures, such as Morari Bapu and Pramukh Swami of the Swaminarayan sect. The building of the dam was described as a 'yagna'.

The strongest grounds for this struggle are neither environmental nor religious but those of the rights of citizens to a livelihood, a decent standard of living and freedom from arbitrary acts of state coercion. All of these basic rights are violated most blatantly by the Narmada project. The stuggle began as a local demand for social justice, but in the process it expanded to providing a fulcrum for a critique of a whole system of rule which was prepared to ride roughshod over the basic needs of one section of the population for the sake of development projects which enrich those who are already well off. While the state claims that this furthers national interests, it in fact strengthens class divisions and is thus socially divisive. This can hardly be said to represent a healthy participatory form of national development.

Gandhi and the Pacifist Movement

Gandhi and his movement were of central importance in the development of modern pacifism, which stands for a principled rejection of the use of violence at all levels of politics in any form. This emerged in the West as a full-fledged doctrine only in the 1930s. It originated in protests against the military-industrial complex during the First World War.

After the war, anti-war protesters came to see Gandhi as a shining symbol of pacifism in action. Frederick Fisher has noted how in this respect, Gandhi appeared on the world stage at just the right psychological moment. Earlier, his message would have been almost certainly ignored. As it was, he struck an instant chord with a generation that longed for peace and demanded that future international conflicts be resolved non-violently.

A central figure within the newly emerging pacifist movement was the Dutch anarcho-syndicalist Bart DeLigt (1883-1938). A Christian pastor, he was imprisoned by his government during the First World War for making anti-war speeches. His church did not support him in this, and he subsequently became disillusioned with Christianity as it was practised in his day. He studied Greek paganism and Eastern religions, moving towards a belief in more cosmic and universal truths. In the 1920s he became active in the Dutch labour movement, giving it a strong anti-militarist thrust. He came to see pacifism as something rooted in such long-standing traditions, but providing at the same time a revolutionary means towards a transformation of popular consciousness in an age of mass politics.

During these years DeLigt corresponded with Gandhi and met him in Switzerland in 1931. In his book *The Conquest of Violence*

(1937) he argued that the non-cooperation of syndicalist strikes should be joined with Gandhi's principled non-violence. He was however critical of Gandhi in several important respects. He felt that he was often inconsistent in his non-violence, as during the First World War, when he supported the British war efforts. Also, he criticised Gandhi's demand that the Indian people should control their defence forces, when in fact he should have been seeking to disband. them. He felt that in these respects Gandhi's nationalism came into conflict with his non-violence. He also disliked the tendency for Gandhi to be idolised as a new and infallible messiah, for there needed to be a continuing critical scrutiny of his practice.

De Ligt was not altogether fair in his criticism. Although Gandhi had supported the British during the First World War, going so far as to lead a recruiting campaign, he admitted his error soon after the war had ended. An Indian who had visited the battlefield at just after the slaughter, made a point of seeking him out and telling him that he had been wrong to support a conflict that represented the very antithesis of civilized values. After listening to the description of the carnage, Gandhi commented: 'I am sorry I had anything to do with this war. 1 believed Woodrow Wilson's dream; that it was a.war to .end war. But I now see that force can never banish force."

In America, pacifist theory was developed by Ricard Gregg a lawyer who was active in the labour movement in the 1920s. Impressed by Gandhi's campaigns against the British, he went to India to study the Gandhian movement at first hand, and became converted to the principle of non-violence. He published various books on the subject in the 1920s and 1930s. Gregg helped to popularise Gandhian theory in the USA. Following from this, a committee for non-violent revolution was founded there in 1946, which opposed the armaments industry and encouraged people to refuse to serve in the armed forces or work in arms factories, deploying mass civil disobedience if necessary. This fled into the movement against nuclear weapons that emerged in the 1950s in both America and Europe. Gandhi had been an outspoken critic of nuclear weapons after the American atomic bombing of Japan in 1945. He condemned 'the supreme tragedy of the bomb', stating that it revealed most starkly that: 'War knows **no law** except that of might.' Also that: 'I regard the employment of the atom bomb for the wholesale destruction of men, women and children as the most diabolical use of science." He refused to accept the argument that possession of nuclear weapons acts as a deterrent against war, on the grounds that there can be no lasting, durable or moral peace through such means.

Another important international initiative that has flowed from the peace movement has been that of the *Peace Brigades International* which was founded in 1931. It was inspired in part by the work of the Gandhian *Shanti Sena* in post-independence India. The Peace Brigade has three main strands, first, to send unarmed volunteers to protect people who are threatened with repression and provide publicity for violations of human rights, second, to train people in techniques of non-violent resistance and conflict resolution, and third, to document successful non-violent initiatives as an example for others. It has carried out such work in trouble spots in central America, the Caribbean, the Balkans, Palestine, Sri Lanka and South Africa. Volunteers have put their lives on the line in very dangerous areas to protect local peace. In India, JP was the leading spokesperson for peace in the period before 1980. He consistently opposed Indian military action in wars against Pakistan, China, the Nagas, and in the conquest of Goa in 1960. He saw war as a crime against humanity and demanded international disarmament. During the armed occupation of Goa, and during the Indo-China war of 1962, JP had wanted to take an active role in stopping the conflict. He was dissuaded from this by Vinoba Bhave, who supported the use of military force by the Indian state and who insisted that Gandhian workers should engage only in social work within India. Although JP felt that Bhave's position was very un-Gandhian, he agreed to keep quiet in deference to his position as elder statesman of the movement. As it was, some people branded JP as 'unpatriotic'. There was a similar divide between the two leaders over the issue of nuclear weapons. When Indira Gandhi exploded an atomic bomb in May 1974, ostensibly for 'peaceful purposes', Bhave took her at her word and stated that nuclear bombs could help to irrigate land and thus wipe out poverty.

Few prominent opponents like Praful Bidwai and Achin Vanaik and Arundhati Roy campaigned long and hard against India's endorsement of the nuclear option. Although not Gandhians, in their writings, they cite Gandhi's principled stand against nuclear weapons as an inspiration.

Since then, doubts and cynicism have emerged, as Pakistan quickly went nuclear in response, and then a year later launched an invasion of Indian territory at Kargil in Kashmir. Nuclear weapons were of no avail in what turned out to be a very conventional form of warfare. From then on, the anti-nuclear movement took off, with protest groups springing up all over India. In 1999, coinciding with the first anniversary of the tests, there was a march from Pokhran to Sarnath, the place near Banaras where the Buddha lived and preached. Some 30,000 to 40,000 people participated, including some old Gandhians who had participated in the nationalist movement. A month later, a large National Convention for Nuclear Disarmament and Peace was held in Delhi, attended by over 600 delegates, including representatives from Pakistan.

The convention led to the formation of the Coalition for Nuclear Disarmament and Peace, a network of over 200 groups. Many of these came from groups with a substantial Gandhian influence, like the Narmada Bachao Andolan, although to be inclusive it did not endorse non-violence as an absolute principle.

Gandhigiri on World Stage

Gandhi's theoy and pradice was not limted only to India, its impact was felt all over the world. For large numbers of people in countries which had been colonised by Europeans, or who were tyrannised by authoritarian or racist rulers, Gandhi became an icon who symbolised and stood for the assertion of the oppressed. His position in this respect was secured by the salt march of 1930, the progress of which was reported by the world media on a daily basis. Coming at the dawn of the age of the rapid transmission of sound, photography and film around the globe, this was one of the first such media event in history. The march was mounted as a visual spectacle that focused on the figure of the thin, scantily clad old man surrounded by his khadi-wearing comrades, together defying the might of the empire with strict non-violence. Gandhi employed the language of what is now known as the sound-bite: e.g. 'I want world sympathy in this battle of Right against Might or 'We are entering upon a life and death struggle, a holy war; we are performing an all-embracing sacrifice in which we wish to offer ourselves as an oblation." Americans in particular lapped it up, jubilant at what they saw as a further vindication of their own historic rejection of

British imperialism. A few months later, *Time* magazine paid tribute to Gandhi by declaring him its 'Man of the Year."

India's winning of independence in 1947 was widely believed to vindicate Gandhi's method of non-violent resistance. In most parts of the world it was recognised that armed struggle against authoritarian states was hardly an option, due to the massive discrepancy between the military might of the rulers and people. Violent revolts could succeed only in a few exceptional circumstances, as in China. It came to be seen that modern governments, with their strong and often secretive and authoritarian bureaucracies, but with a nominal commitment to a rule of law, were particularly susceptible to principled non-violent protest. A resistance which revealed the moral failings of those who exercised power while remaining strictly non-violent had the advantage of appealing to many of those in the ranks of the police, bureaucracy and army who propped up the regime. The government, it was argued, would prefer to compromise rather than find itself crumbling from within. This would appear to have been borne out in the case of Iran in 1979, where an autocratic government found its authority eroded so rapidly through mass protest and demoralisation within the police and military that it was forced to surrender power.

The chief opposition to such a strategy came from those who were encouraged by the armed victories of the people in countries such as China, Cuba, Algeria and Vietnam to embrace a romantic notion of the power of revolutionary violence. This was epitomised in the cult of Che Guevara and Franz Fanon. It was argued that in the last instance all states would defend themselves with a ruthless display of violence. Therefore, however much the state may be put on the defensive by mass strikes and other forms of civil resistance, the movement would at some stage have to escalate to the stage of armed struggle. Some who followed this line formed underground revolutionary terrorist groups such as the Angry Brigade, the Red Army Faction and, in India, the Naxalites.

It has been argued, following from this, that Gandhian-style non-violent civil resistance has had a greater global impact since 1945 than armed struggles and violent resistance. Such a formulation begs many questions, such as the role that US armed aggression played in shaping struggles during the second half of the twentieth century. Also, there has been often a complex interaction between civil resistance and more violent forms of struggle. It also leaves out of account the question of leadership, for the Gandhian method depends very strongly on the presence of an inspired and charismatic moral leader.

The African-American Struggle in the USA

Gandhi was admired among African-Americans in the USA from the 1920s onwards. His work was publicised by Marcus Garvey and W.E.B. Du Bois among others. In 1936, Howard Thurman (1900-1981)—a distinguished Baptist minister, theologian and academic who was from the American South—led a delegation of prominent African-American Christians to India to meet Gandhi. Gandhi quizzed him and the others about racial discrimination in the USA, and then expounded on his principles of non-violent resistance to injustice. Mrs. Thurman pleaded with Gandhi to come to the USA: 'We want you not for white America, but for the Negroes; we have many a problem that cries for solution, and we need you badly.' Gandhi said that he still had much to do in India, but when he felt the call, he would not hesitate to travel there. Thurman said that what Gandhi had told them resonated strongly with their Christianity. Mrs Thurman then sang two well-known spirituals, and Gandhi obviously moved—observed that 'it may be through the Negroes that the unadulterated message of non-violence will be delivered to the world."

Gandhi also inspired Bayard Rustin (1910-1987), who was from an African-American Quaker family of Pennsylvania. He joined the Communist Party in the 1930s, but refused to accept their dogmatic line that racial discrimination would disappear once socialism was established in the USA. He broke with the party in 1941 when it ordered its members to stop fighting for Negro rights, as the USA and Russia were now allies and such internal dissent would, it claimed, detract from the struggle against Hitler. Rustin linked up with A. Philip Randolph, the African-American leader of the Brotherhood of Sleeping Car Porters, a trade union. Together they established the Congress of Racial Equality (CORE) in Chicago in 1942.

Rustin had already been in contact with Krishnalal Shridharani, who after studying at the Gujarat Vidyapith—Gandhi's university in Ahmedabad—had taken part in the salt march of 1930 and had been subsequently jailed. In 1934 Shridharani emigrated to the USA, where he became a prominent advocate of Gandhian non-violence. In 1939 he published an influential book on Gandhian techniques called *War Without Violence*.

Rustin himself refused to serve in the army during the Second World War, and was jailed for three years as a conscientious objector. After his release, he took up the cause of Indian independence, picketing the British embassy in Washington, and being arrested on a number of occasions. In 1947, he and his fellow activists travelled on buses through the South to test a Supreme Court ruling that Negro passengers could sit wherever they wanted to in buses. Rustin was beaten up and jailed for six months under local segregation laws, a sentence which he accepted in a true Gandhian style and spirit. After his release, he took up an invitation to visit India as a guest of the Congress party. There were further protests, beatings and imprisonments for Rustin in the early 1950s — an experience he described, humorously, as 'going Gandhi'.

While Rustin was carrying on his protests, Martin Luther King was studying at Morchouse College, Connecticut, Crozer Seminary, Pennsylvania, and the School of Theology of Boston University. King, who was born in 1929 in Atlanta, Georgia, was the son of a Baptist minister who was active in fighting for the rights of the African—Americans of that city. While studying at Crozer Seminary, Martin Luther King Jr. attended a lecture on Gandhi by Mordecai Johnson, who had just returned from a visit to India. Johnson argued that Gandhian non-violent protest could be used in the battle for African-American rights. King stated later that the 'message was so profound and electrifying that I left the meeting and bought a half-dozen books on Gandhi's life and works.'

King was particularly impressed by the way in which Gandhi had directed his anger at injustice into a constructive and creative non-violent engagement. He realised that such a resistance provided a deeply Christian weapon that could provide a strong base for the mass mobilisation of African-Americans. King stated: 'He was probably the first person in history to lift the love ethic of Jesus above mere interaction between individuals to a powerful effective social force on a large scale."

King was also influenced strongly by Howard Thurman, who had led the delegation to meet Gandhi in 1936. Thurman was a professor at the School of Theology of Boston University when King was studying there for his doctorate between 1951 and 1954. In 1949 he had published his most important book *Jesus and the Disinherited*, which was inspired in part by Gandhi — sought for a Christian means for combating oppression. Thurman argued that Jesus, who was from a poor Jewish family, had devoted his life to fight for his people. He stood for the self-pride and assertion of the colonized under the tyranny of Rome. Jesus understood, however, that the Roman Empire could not be fought by force and that the battle had to be of the spirit. Christianity was thus forged 'as a technique of survival of the oppressed. Wherever his spirit appears, the oppressed gather fresh courage; for he has announced the good news that fear, hypocrisy, and hatred, the three hounds of hell that track the trail of the disinherited, need have no dominion over them." Thurman argued that the anger generated by injustice must be transformed into a constructive force. Later, King used to carry this book with him for inspiration during his campaigns.

In 1954, at the age of twenty-five, King was appointed as pastor of the Dexter Avenue Baptist Church in Montgomery, the capital of Alabama. He could have stayed and worked in the less-segregated North, but he chose deliberately to fight segregation at its core. His chance came soon enough, when in December 1955 an African-American teacher called Rosa Parks refused to give up her seat on a crowded bus to a white man. She was arrested and charged with breaking the local segregation laws. It is perhaps no coincidence that it was a similar experience of racial discrimination on public transport that had first politicised Gandhi in South Africa. It was an experience that King himself had been through. At the age of fifteen, King won an oratorial prize by celebrating the ideals of the United States Constitution. Riding in a bus on his way home from the speech, King was ordered out of his seat. Reflecting behind the veil that was between him and the white passengers, King recalled, "I was the angriest I have ever been in my life.'" When the court punished Parks with a fine of $14, King and other civil rights activists decided to protest the law by organising a boycott of the city's buses. Bayard Rustin, who had long experience of such Gandhi-inspired protests, came to Montgomery to work as an adviser in the campaign. This was the start of a long and fruitful comradeship between two great proponents of non-violence. Rustin prevailed on King to dispense with armed guards and to embrace non-violence as a key element of the struggle. King asserted that they were putting democracy into practice in a truly Christian way and insisted that they should bear no enemity towards their opponents and that they should observe complete non-violence. Rustin also helped forge strong links with African-American radicals of the northern cities who raised funds to support the Montgomery campaign.

After a year of resistance, the Supreme Court gave erdict in favour of the protesters, with bus segregation being ruled illegal. King declared that 'Christ furnished the spirit and motivation, while Gandhi furnished the method." In this way, the protesters had occupied the moral high ground in a way that proved irresistible. Although King was always modest about himself, declaring that he had no Messiah complex, he believed strongly in the need for powerful and charismatic leadership. As he stated in 1960: "people cannot devote themselves to a great cause without finding someone who becomes the personification of the cause." In this, King was influenced by Hegel, whose work he had studied at Boston University. Hegel had argued that throughout history certain 'world historical individuals' who had the vision and intellect to understand the spirit of their age had been able to provide inspiring moral leadership at critical historical junctures. King understood Plato, Aristotle, Lincoln and Gandhi to be such persons. For all his modesty, he saw himself in such a mould.

Like Gandhi, King was nevertheless all too aware of his fallibilities as a leader. Not all of his Southern campaigns were successful. For example, in 1962, he agreed to take personal charge of the campaign in Albany, Georgia, and was soon arrested. There were however various rival groups amongst the local African-Americans, and one paid King's fine, so that he found himself ejected from jail against his will. The local police chief had studied Gandhian methods and was careful to keep his men in order and to treat the protesters with decorum, so that the newspapers were deprived of the usual photographs of police brutalities. King also made tactical mistakes in Albany, as when he agreed to obey a federal court injunction that ruled against the protest, as he did not want to alienate the federal authorities. This angered the radicals in the movement, who saw it as a betrayal. Soon after, there was a riot, in which two thousand African-Americans attacked the police with bottles and stones. King was inevitably accused of encouraging this violence. The protest lost its momentum and petered out without any substantial gains.

King's methods were nonetheless redeemed by some remarkable successes, as in the campaign in Birmingham, Alabama, in 1963. The target here was the segregation of eating-places in a city that was notorious for the hardline racism of its white population. Only recently, the local Ku Klux Klan had castrated an African-American and dumped his mutilated body in the road. Unlike in Albany, King and his colleagues planned their campaign meticulously. They decided to focus on some prominent retail outlets, such as Woolworths, harassing them with sit-ins and boycotts that would hit business where it hurt most—in the pocket. They were also careful to ensure that there were plenty of protesters willing to go to jail, so that the jails would be filled in a way that would embarrass the authorities. King anticipated that the local police would not react in a disciplined manner, as they had in Albany. This was crucial, for he wanted to expose the true nature of Southern racism to the outside world, so that the federal government would be forced to intervene. As King stated, he intended to provoke the 'oppressor to commit his brutality openly—in the light of day with the rest of the world looking on.'

The police commissioner of Birmingham declared that he was not going to tolerate any 'nigger trouble makers' in his city. Many of the local African—Americans feared what might happen, and King had to use all of his powers of oratory and persuasion to instil the necessary solidarity and enthusiasm for the stuggle. He ran workshops on non-violent resistance, in which the volunteers were trained to resist police provocation without rancour. The jails were soon filling with protesters. When the Alabama state court served an injunction forbidding the protest, King defied it by leading a march. The day was Good Friday, and he talked of 'the redemptive power of suffering', and said that he was heading for jail as 'a good servant of my Lord and master, who was crucified on Good Friday."

His supporters compared him to Jesus, as he marched at the head of a procession, dressed in the faded denim of the African-American worker, and was arrested and jailed.

In prison, he wrote a manifesto that became famous as the 'Letter from Birmingham City Jail'. This was addressed to some prominent white clergymen of Alabama who in January 1963 had published an open letter condemning King for his confrontational tactics at a time when, they alleged, desegregation was being achieved through court rulings. They feared that King's activities would provoke disturbances. King told them that the whites of Alabama had consistently refused to obey court orders in the past and had ruthlessly enforced their own local segregation laws. They had learnt that an oppressor never handed out freedom willingly — it had to be demanded and fought for by the oppressed. They had therefore decided to bring matters to a head: 'Non-violent direct action seeks to create such a crisis and establish such creative tension that a community that has consistently refused to negotiate is forced to confront the issue."

King went on to justify his breaking of selected laws, and made a very Gandhian distinction between just laws which accorded with morality and the will of God which were to be obeyed and unjust laws, which they had an obligation to disobey. He argued that any law that degraded a human being could be considered unjust; and also any law imposed by a majority on a minority that was not binding on the moinority. When he was released from jail after eight days, King found that the campaign was flagging. He then took the risky step of mobilising children to court arrest. He knew that he could be criticised for using children, and that some of them might get hurt. But, he reasoned, they were being hurt everyday by whites. He also saw the photo-opportunity provided by the symbol of young children marching against a pernicious segregation. They proved to be exemplary protesters, courting arrest with youthful and fearless enthusiasm in a manner that caused immense logistical problems for the police.

The protests continued with ever-increasing vigour, as the campaigners sensed that they had forced the white racists of the city on the defensive. Then, confronted by a massive demonstration on 5 May, 'Bull' Connor's men refused to obey him when he ordered them to disperse the crowd by force. As the protesters marched through their ranks, some of the firemen stood holding their unused hoses and wept. Five days later, it was agreed that eating-places throughout the city would be desegregated. King announced that this was a demonstration of the power of non-violence in its purest form; 'I saw there, I felt there, for the first time, the pride and the power of non-violence.'

In his application of non-violent resistance, King was far more confrontational than Gandhi. He actively sought out situations in which he could deploy his techniques of protest, so that his life consisted of a series of engagements in rapid succession, with some being carried on simultaneously. He was always on the front-line himself, heading marches, giving inspirational speeches, courting jail and negotiating with the authorities. Gandhi himself rarely led mass campaigns, and later in life preferred to fight alone rather than risk mass protest that could go awry. King, by contrast, constantly exposed himself to the huge risks involved in such experiments in mass non-violent resistance.

King learnt to carry out careful research on a situation before he evolved a strategy suited for that particular place and historic moment. If the conditions were not right, he was hesitant about launching a struggle. What he required above all was a local African-American community with strong internal solidarity and willingness to fight non-violenty, and a white population that would react in a ham-fisted and self-defeating way.

Like Bayard Rustin, King adhered to Gandhian non-violence without trying to follow the Maharma's ascetic and disciplined way of life. King enjoyed good food and fine wines. He stayed in costly hotels on his tours, relishing the luxury. He dressed impeccably in smart and expensively tailored suits. After visiting India in 1959 to tour places associated with Gandhi, King vowed to set aside a day each week for fasting and meditation. The vow was soon forgotten. King had neither the time nor will-power to carry it out. He was also very bad at keeping time, but shrugged off his frequent late arrivals at meetings as being an inevitable case of what he jokingly called CPT, or 'Coloured People's Time'. He had extra-marital sexual relationships with some of his women-followers and admirers. One such intimacy was recorded on tape by FBI agents in 1964, and it was to do him considerable political damage over the next four years, as it allowed the sinister FBI howevr to mount a smear campaign that undermined his moral reputation and authority. King was guilt-stricken by his failure in this respect, and he resolved constantly not to allow it to happen again.

The period 1964-5 was a turning point for the civil rights movement. The year 1963 had been a year of triumph, with the victory in Birmingham, followed by the great march on Washington, where King delivered his powerful 'I have a dream' speech. In 1964, President Johnson backed civil rights legislation that made it illegal to practise segregation in any public place in the USA. But in the same year, New-york, Harlem, Chicago, Philadelphia and Jersey City exploded in race riots. King was jeered at when he went to Harlem at the invitation of the mayor of New York to try to cool tensions. Harlem was the stronghold of Malcolm X, who in that year denounced what he characterised as the 'Christian-Gandhian groups':

> Christian-Gandhian I don't go for anything that's non-violent and turn the other cheek. I don't see how any revolution—I've never heard of a non-violent revolution or a revolution than was brought about by turning the other cheek, and so I believe that it is a crime for anyone to teach a person who is being brutalized to continue to accept that brutality without doing something to defend himself. If this is what the-Christian-Gandhian philosophy teaches, then it is criminal— a criminal philosophy.

Although Malcolm X revealed here a profound misunderstanding of both Gandhi and King's non-violence, for both believed in confronting an oppressor most actively, his words struck a chord with his own followers.

Malcolm X was what was known at the time as a 'Black Nationalist'. He demanded that African-Americans should fight for a separate nation-state in which they would hold power for themselves. He himself rejected Christianity and had converted to Islalm. In a debate with Bayard Rustin in 1960, he had criticised the civil rights position that African-Americans should struggle to assert themselves within the American polity, arguing that in a racist society they could never become fullfledged citizens. He said.:

> People come here from Hungary and are integrated into the American way of life overnight, they are not put into any fourth or third class or any other kind of class. The only one who is put in this category is the so-called Negro.

He condemned what he called 'the passive approach' which he saw as a mere palliative preached strategically by liberals. Arguments such as these began to exert a dramatic hold over the imagination of young African-Americans of the northern **cities.** Their problems were different from those of the South, for they already had the vote and there was no segregation by law. The vast majority, however, lived in poverty in squalid ghettoes where they were rack-rented by slum lords. Many were unemployed and they were victimised on a daily basis by policemen who 'treated every Negro as a criminal merely because he was a Negro. Their anger exploded periodically in so-called 'race riois', in which they lashed out at their oppressors and were shot down in the streets.

King decided that he had to extend his movement to the North. In early 1966 he set up home in a cramped and soul-destroying apartment in a Chicago ghetto and launched a movement for integrated housing in the city. He contacted a number of youth gangs, met their leaders and spent long hours in persuading them to embrace non-violence and act as marshalls in demonstrations. He held workshops in non-violence, persuading them that the southern protests had gained far more than the northern riots. Some two hundred gang members—enthused by the attention given to them by such a famous and charismatic leader— agreed to give non-violence a chance. It was at this juncture that King was faced with a rebellion in his ranks. Several young Northerners had been inspired by the civil rights movement and had gone south to participate in the protests. By 1966, however, some of them were becoming disillusioned with King's methods. Matters came to an impasse in June 1966, during a protest march in Mississippi. After a white man had shot one of the marchers, King overheard some of his fellow-protesters saying that the days of non-violence were passing. Some began to arm themselves with guns so that they could fight back. Others accused white sympathisers of trying to appropriate the movement and told King that they didn't want any whites marching with them: 'This should be an all-black march. We don't need any more white phonies and liberals invading our movement". This was a direct rejection of King's stress on inclusion.

During the next three years, King devoted his energies to countering what he saw as the profound errors of Black Power. He understood the anger which had produced this new militancy, and he was always more sympathetic to it than the white liberals, most of whom felt not only threatened by the slogan, but bitter that a movement with which they had sympathised had spawned—so they believed—such rabid hatred. King felt, however, that the Black Power celebration of violence was completely misguided. They could never hope to defeat white America in a show of force, and their relatively feeble violence would provide an excuse for white racists to unleash a wave of genocidal killings of blacks, no doubt under the slogan of'White Power. King went on to argue that in advocating violence, Black Power was not adopting a revolutionary line.

One of the great paradoxes of the Black Power movement is that it talks unceasingly about not imitating the values of white society, but in advocating violence it is imitating the worst, the most brutal and the most uncivilized value of American life. King also condemned Black Power for its repudiation of all whites as racists:

> I reminded them of the dedicated Whites who had suffered, bled and died in the cause of racial justice, and suggested that to reject white participation now would be a shameful repudiation of all for which they had been sacrificed.

For all the rationality of his arguments, King was well aware that what mattered most were results. He had to prove to the African-Americans of the northern cities that they would gain more through non-violent protest than rioting in the streets. In this respect, Chicago became of crucial importance to his movement. He decided to launch mass civil disobedience in the city. He was heckled by supporters of Black Power at one of the first meetings in July 1966. Although bitterly upset, he took it as a challenge and pressed ahead with protests. He was not, however, able to generate any 'creative tension'. There were street riots that July, and although not connected in any way with the campaign, they underlined the extent to which King's movement was a mere sideshow in the violent life of that city. King rushed from riot-spot to riot-spot, calming the people and persuading the authorities to act in a constructive manner. He met with the gang leaders and took from them renewed promises to remain non-violent. The rioting stopped before it gained any further momentum, and several commentators felt that King had been instrumental in this.

King then pressed ahead, announcing a series of marches to all-white neighbourhoods. They were met with racist taunts by working-class white men and women, who waved American Nazi Party insignias and Confederate flags and taunted them with cries of'you monkeys' and 'Nigger go home!' The white suburbanites even taunted the police who protected the marchers with being 'nigger-lovers' and 'white trash'. Rocks, bricks and bottles were hurled at the marchers. On one occasion a brick hit King, bringing him to the ground. A knife was also thrown at him, but missed its target. King was astonished at the sheer venom of the reaction—he stated that he had seen nothing like it in the South. He rejoiced, however, that the young gang leaders who had marched with them had remained non-violent.

There were further riots in the northern cities in 1967. In the last years of King's life, non-violence was losing its moral authonity on the American imagination. Radicals everywhere were celebrating the cathartic power of revolutionary violence and terror. Black Power was only one example of this tendency. To counter this, King wrote his last book *Where Do We Go From Here: Chaos or Community?*. Published in 1967, it represented a heart-felt plea for the continuing relevance of non-violence. He argued:

> Returning violence for violence multiplies violence, adding deeper darkness to a night already devoid of stars. Darkness cannot drive out darkness: only light can do that. Hate cannot drive out hate: only love can do that.

He demanded a politics that was driven by love and not hate, 'What is needed is a realization that power without love is reckless and abusive and that love without power is sentimental and anaemic." Black Power, he asserted, divorced power from love and based itself on hatred. He refuesed to accept that love was associated with resignation of power. "Power at its best is love implementing the demands of justice. Justice at its best is love correcting everything."

King's point of view, the error of separating power from love has been tragically compounded by Christian thinkers who, in divorcing their ethereal Platonic version of love from their temporal struggles for power, left themselves open to Nietzsche's withering attacks. As Nietzsche rejects the 'Christian' concept of love, Christians reject the 'Nietzschean' will to power. All this mutual rejection is unfortunate in King's view, because the two concepts are not really 'polar opposttes' but necessary co-conceptions of ethical. King himself claimed that Gandhi had been the first to grasp this great truth: 'What was new about Mahatma Gandhi's movement in India was that he mounted a revolution on hope and love, hope and non-violence.

King always knew that his life was in danger; death-threats were an almost everyday feature of his life. When he heard the news of John F. Kennedy's assassination in November 1963, his first reaction was 'I don't think I'm going to live to reach forty." Although he proved to be prescient in this respect (he was thirty-nine years of age when shot and killed in Memphis by a white racist on 4 April 1968), his faith in God gave him the strength to carry on with undiminished militancy despite the threats. What mattered, he said, was the quality and not the quantity of one s life. In a speech during a demonstration in Alabama in 1965 he stated:

> I do not know what lies ahead of us. There may be beatings, jailings, and tear gas. But 1 would rather die on the highways of Alabama than make a butchery of my conscience. There is nothing more tragic in all this world than to know right and not do it. I cannot stand in the midst of all these glaring evils and not take a stand.

King's assassination had been preceded by that of Malcolm X three years before. During the last year of his life, Malcolm X had been moving towards King in spirit, and had begun to try to patch up their differences in the weeks before his death. Although in certain respects the antithesis of King, he was also a man of strong moral principles and a brilliant and charismatic leader in his own right. Despite his harsh comments on King's non-violence, his courageous struggle for the moral self-assertion of the poor African-Americans of the northern cities was in practice also waged without the use of violence. He just refused to accept non-violence as a principle. As he stated at a mass meeting in 1965 'I don't advocate violence, but if a man steps on my toes, I'll step on his. Whites better be glad Martin

Luther King is rallying the people because other forces are waiting to takeover if he fails." The Nation of Islam, in which Malcolm X was a leading figure until his acrimonious break with the organisation in the final year of his life, sought to inculcate an upright, puritanical, moralistic, disciplined and deeply religious approach to life. Followers were expected to give up liquor, drugs and tobacco. Breaking such lifelong habits helped inculcate what Malcolm X saw as 'black self-pride'. The founder of the Nation of Islam, Elijah Muhammad taught that 'idleness and laziness were among the black's greatest sins against himself, and Malcolm X himself was punctilious in keeping to time. In these particular respects he was closer in spirit to Gandhi than Martin Luther King ever was.

Although Malcolm X refused to be associated with Gandhian non-violence, there were certain parallels between the two men. Malcolm X may have attacked Gandhian non-violence, but he was a great admirer of the man who had fought the British imperialism in India. He regarded Gandhi as a great 'leader of the people' who had been politicised by his experience of white racism in South Africa. Both were fighters against injustice and were charismatic figures who based their message on a strongly moral appeal that was rooted in a firm faith in God. Malcolm X's strong anti-white message was intended to shock people out of their amnesia in a way that paralleled Gandhi's sweeping rejection of Western civilisation in *Hind Swaraj.* In the last year of his life, Malcolm was moving towards new forms of dialogue—with white sympathisers, pan-African nationalists, the radical regimes in Algeria, Tanzania, Cuba, and with Martin Luther King and the civil rights movement. It was almost certainly this attempt to build a powerful new alliance of those opposed to American racism and imperialism which proved the last straw for certain forces within the American state system. Like Gandhi, Malcolm X died fighting intolerance and hatred. Martin Luther King was to die three years later while struggling to build a similar solidarity of the oppressed.

Although King's death in 1968 brought an end to the period of the great campaigns for African-American civil rights, the movement had changed the political scene in the USA in a radical new direction. Gandhian techniques of resistance had been shown to work in an American context, in a way that legitimised them for a generation of

Americans. It had forged a whole vocabulary of protest, with songs such as 'Freedom Now!' and 'We Shall Overcome' becoming the new anthems of dissent. In his last two years, King himself became a leading figure in one such protest, that against the war in Vietnam. Besides massive marches and street demonstrations, there were public burnings of draft cards. Such protest was then extended into campaigns for women, gay and lesbian rights, and the environmental movement.

The Revolt Against Apartheid in South Africa

After Gandhi left South Africa in 1915, he placed his third son Manilal in charge of his work there. Manilal ran the Phoenix Ashram, published *Indian Opinion*, and kept up the struggle for the rights of Indians. In 1946 he played a leading role in a major campaign of protest against new legislation that discriminated against those of Indian origin that built directly on the legacy of Gandhi's own resistance to the White regime three to four decades earlier. The satyagraha continued for two years, with mass rallies and the picketing of and squatting on of land reserved for Whites only occupation. Indians of all classes were involved—men and women alike and around two thousand were jailed, including the two main leaders, Yusuf Dadoo and G.M. Naicker. Although confined to the Indian community, many blacks were deeply impressed by the power of the protest. As Nelson Mandela later wrote:

> It instilled a spirit of defiance and radicalism among the people, broke the fear of prison, and boosted the popularity and influence of the NIC [Natal Indian Congress] and TIC [Transvaal Indian Congress], They reminded us that the freedom struggle was not merely a question of making speeches, holding meetings, passing resolutions and sending deputations, but of meticulous organisation, militant mass action and, above all, the willingness to suffer and sacrifice. The Indians' campaign harkened back to the 1913 passive resistance in which Mahatma Gandhi led a tumultuous procession of Indians crossing illegally from Natal to the Transvaal. That was history; this campaign was taking place before my own eyes.

Blacks felt a novel sense of solidarity with a community hitherto regarded by them as being little better than lackeys of the Whites. The 5th Pan-African Congress, which had met in Manchester in

1945, had already endorsed the Gandhian passive resistance as the preferred method for resistance to colonialism in Africa. In 1949 the African National Congress (ANC) in South Africa committed itself to non-violence in its struggle against apartheid. Manilal Gandhi wanted them to state that non-violence was a moral principle to be observed at all costs, but the majority of the ANC leaders saw it as a tactical matter, arguing that in a situation of an overwhelming control of force by the white regime, violent resistance would have been futile. This became the official ANC line, despite Manilal's vigorous objections.

In 1952 the ANC launched a campaign against the pass laws in which blacks violated the law by entering White areas. There was however some violence, which gave the rulers an excuse to crush the movement ruthlessly. Non-violent protest continued in the 1950s and 1960s under the leadership of Albert Luthali (1899-1967), who was strongly committed to non-violence as a principle. This courageous Zulu chief was awarded the Nobel Prize for Peace in 1960.

Long before this, however, many of the ANC leaders had begun to question the strategy of non-violence. New laws were being passed which criminalized even the mildest displays of dissldence. Protesters could now be detained indefinitely without trial. As Mandela stated:

> I began to suspect that both legal and extra-constitutional protests could soon be impossible. In India, Gandhi had been dealing with a foreign power that ultimately was more realistic and far-sighted. That was not the case with the Afrikaners in South Africa. Non-violent passive resistance is effective as long as your opposition adheres to the same rules as you do. But If peaceful protest is met with violence, its efficacy is at an end. For me, non-violence was not a moral principle but strategy; there is no moral goodness in using an ineffective weapon.

The matter came to a head after the Sharpeville massacre of 1960, in which sixty-nine non-violent protesters were shot and killed by the police in cold blood. The ANC leaders retaliated by burning their passes in public, which led to a declaration of martial law and their being thrown in jail. Many of these leaders felt that non-violence had had its day. After their release, there was a heated debate within the ANC, with Luthali standing up for non-violence. He was supported by J.N. Singh, an Indian ANC leader, who advanced the Gandhian argument that: 'Non-violence has not failed us, we have failed non-violence'. Eventually, the Gandhians were forced to bow to the majority line— that there should be underground violent resistance. The military wing of the ANC was however to be separate, and be under the leadership of Mandela, Walter Sisulu and Joe Slovo.

Mandela did not however turn his back on Gandhi entirely. He could never forget J.N. Singh's words—they continued to reverberate in his head even thirty years later. He continued to be a passionate admirer of Gandhi, whom he saw as a champion of the rights of the colonised and racially oppressed. He never forgot that Gandhi's fierce anti-colonialism was born in South Africa from bitter experiences of racial discrimination and from seeing the brutal repression of the Bambata rebellion by white British troops. Mandela argued that Gandhi did accept violence in extreme circumstances, in particular when non-violence was a cover for cowardice, or when honour was at stake. Mandela believed that what mattered was not so much whether a movement was strictly non-violent so much as the balance maintained between non-violence and violence. 'Violence and non-violence are not mutually exclusive; it is the predominance of the one or the other that labels a struggle." He therefore advocated a limited form of violence, involving acts of sabotage against government installations and property, taking care to avoid injuring people. Mandela felt that it was vital that they did not set off a blood feud between black and white: Animosity between Afrikaner and Englishman was still sharp fifty years after the Anglo-Boer war. Non-violent civil resistance continued with strikes, demonstrations, boycotts and moral pressure from church leaders such as Desmond Tutu and Alan Boesak. The work of these latter figures greatly enhanced the moral power of the struggle.

Although he had turned his back on strict non-violence, Mandela understood that a struggle that created bitterness between opponents made it harder in the long term to reach a lasting solution to a problem. He himself had an almost saintly ability to refuse to think badly of his enemies, believing very strongly that: 'Man's goodness is a flame that can be hidden but never extinguished." He felt himself vindicated in this when he saw certain Whites rise above their prejudices—men such as Justice Rumpff who in a celebrated judgement of 1961 refused on the basis of the evidence before him to convict the ANC leaders for acts of violence or being communists, even though the government demanded it. Even during the long and terrible years in jail, Mandela continued to appeal to the humanity of his jailors, and a small number of these hardest of people responded with sympathy. After his release, he sought to bring these qualities to his negotiations with President W.E de Klerk: 'To make peace with an enemy, one must work with that enemy, and that enemy becomes your partner."

By the late 1960s, it was clear that the ANC strategy of violent underground struggle was going nowhere. Many of its best leaders were in jail and silenced, while those in exile found that they could do little to pursue their strategy to any effect, and began to quarrel amongst themselves against this background that a new leader emerged who reasserted the principle of struggle through open and non-violent resistance in a most powerful way. This was Steve Biko, who was born in the Eastern Cape Province in 1946. While a medical student in the late 1960s, he had taken the leading role in formulating a new creed ot 'Black Consciousness.' There were strong parallels between Biko's position and that of Malcolm X. Like Malcolm X, Biko criticised the blacks for their complicity in their own subjugation: 'The type of black man we have today has lost his manhood. Reduced to an obliging shell, he looks with awe at the White power structure and accepts what he regards as the "inevitable position". He argued that there could be no genuine liberation until the blacks learnt to be proud of themselves and consider themselves to be the equal of the Whites. He rejected the ANC strategy of building a multi-racial political alliance, as this tended to reinforce a mentality of dependency on Whites. Biko was the most articulate and charismatic of this new generation of young black activists, and was soon the acknowledged leader of the new Black People's Convention. Discussion groups were set up, and local community self-help projects inaugurated, involving educational, health, welfare and cultural activities.

8

Gandhi and Rawls on Civil Disobedience

There are interesting similarities and dissimilarities between John Rawls and Gandhi on civil disobedience. Gandhi believed that civil disobedience 'to be civil has to be open and non-violent[1]Rawls defines civil disobedience as a public, non-violent, conscientious yet political act contrary to law usually done with the aim of bringing about a change in the law or policies of the government. They both agree that the civil disobedient should voluntarily submit himself to punishment. They both take the view that civil disobedience should not be coercive, though Gandhi and Rawls understand this requirement somewhat differently. They.both think that for civil disobedience to be justified, it is necessary that there should be fundamental violations of rights. Thus Gandhi maintains that in less serious cases there should be compromise rather than resort to civil disobedience; and even when more serious issues are at stake, Gandhi would agree with Rawls that there is a presumption that they should first attempt to achieve an honourable settlement through normal legal channels. Gandhi thinks that civil disobedience should not be resorted to lightly, and that if the practice of civil disobedience is not to be abused, it must only be resorted to by those individuals who are qualified to embark on it; the major personal qualification being that the person who embarks on it must have already acquired 'the habit of willing obedience to laws without fear of their sanctions' and those who have not learnt to obey laws for the right reasons do not have the right to disobey the law. Moreover, people undertaking civil disobedience must have, according to Gandhi, considerable powers of suffering and patience, and be devoted to truth, non-violence, service to the community, etc. For Gandhi, 'disobedience without civility, discipline, discrimination and non-violence is certain destruction'.

Rawls admits that some stringent conditions must be satisfied before civil disobedience is justified. For instance, it must be limited to 'instances of substantial and clear injustice' (*TJ*, p. 372). But unlike Gandhi, Rawls is almost totally unconcerned with the personal qualifications that the individual must possess before he can acquire the right to undertake civil disobedience. This diffference may be explained in part by the fact that Rawls is dealing with a state of near justice where individuals are not so morally deficient as they may in a corrupt society; but a more important explanation is that Rawlsian civil disobedience is a much more cosy, less demanding practice than Gandhian civil disobedience, and consequently it does not require, to the same extent, such high moral qualities among civil disobedients.

Rawls and Gandhi both assume that there is an objective answer to the question: Has an injustice occured? Thus Gandhi talks of the pursuit of *Satya*, i.e. Truth, and though he believes that men are fallible (which incidentally is one reason why he recommends non-violence rather than violence), he thinks that there is a truth in moral matters that men should aspire to; Satyagraha, the movement he championed, 'is literally holding on to Truth, and it means therefore. Truth-force'. And civil disobedience is for him 'a form of Satyagraha. Rawls not only believes that justice has an objective basis, but goes further and applies his model of civil disobedience only to just or near-just regimes where these objective principles of justice 'regulate the constitution and social institutions generally' (*TJ.*, p. 365). Gandhi had much greater faith in the value and efficacy of civil disobedience, even for societies that are unjust and corrupt: 'civil disobedience is based upon an absolute efficiency of innocent suffering'. True, Gandhi was concerned about the violence that may accompany civil disobedience; but this risk would, he thought, be minimized if those who undertook civil disobedience possessed the relevant moral qualities. Gandhi did not despair, for he thought that the relevant moral qualities could be striven for even by 'the lowliest among us'

So Gandhi, unlike Rawls, was willing, in principle, to extend civil disobedience against unjust regimes as well. For Gandhi, unlike Rawls, civil disobedience not only appeals to the principles of justice already accepted by the authorities; it can also help to reform the evil rulers and persuade them to give up their old ways. Satyagraha constitutes an open and dialectical search for the truth, the resister inviting the opponents to join him in this search for the true principles of justice; while from Rawls's model the impression one gets is that the true principles have already been discovered and are in operation in near-just societies. Rawls is reluctant to commend civil disobedience against basically unjust regimes because he fears that such regimes may, unlike near-just regimes which would act more humanely be aroused to 'more repressfive measures if the calculation of advantages points in this direction' (*TJ p*. 387). This fear of Rawls's may also partly explain another feature that distinguishes his theory from Gandhi's, namely that for Rawls civil disobedience is a form of address to the sense of justice of the community and he does not permit civil disobedients to exert pressure on the state by non-cooperation of the kind that Gandhi commended. Gandhi was not so afraid of reprisals by the authorities. Indeed he thought that if people's grievances were not channelled into non-violent forms, violent protests would take over and lead to even more severe reprisals. He was convinced that in the long run non-violence leads to the least amount of total suffering. Of course there is another possibility, namely that protesters in basically unjust regimes should use non-violent methods of protest, including breaking the law, but not voluntarily submit themselves to punishment. But Gandhi would criticize resisters on the grounds that it would destroy the civil, open, and non-violent nature of the protest movement; moreover, since Gandhi had great faith in the efficacy of innocent suffering he would not advocate that non-violent registers evade the penalties.

Rawls advises the resister in basically unjust regimes not to submit voluntarily to the legal penalty, for to so submit would 'not only be to play into the hands of forces that he believes cannot be trusted, but also to express a recognition of the legitimacy of the constitution to which he is opposed' (*TJ p*. 367). It may be plausible to maintain that, other things being equal, a law-breaker has a greater duty to submit to the legal penalty of a regime that is near-just than of one that is basically unjust. One may even take the line that the unjust regime is acting in an unconstitutional and immoral manner and that a law-breaker has no duty to submit to the legal penalties of such a regime. But it would be wrong to infer that if the law-breaker in an unjust regime volunttarily submits to the legal penalty, he would in any important sense be expressing a recognition of the legitimacy of the regime or of any constitution to which he is opposed. If the constitution is a good one and the wicked regime is constantly flouting it, then the resister would not be opposed to the constitution but only to the regime; if however the constitution itself is also basically corrupt, even then the resister would not, by submitting to the penalties be expressing his approval of the constitution. To acknowledge that the law-breaker has no duty to submit voluntarily to the legal penalties of an unjust regime does not imply that he has a duty not to so submit. Or again, even if you take the line that you, as the law-breaker, have a duty to submit voluntarily to such penalties, it does not commit you to the view that the regime that inflicts such penalties is legitimate; for it may be that you regard it as a duty to submit to the penalties because you acknowledge that you have a duty to help the victims of the unjust regime, and that you can do so most effectively by suffering in prison. Admittedly, when a law-breaker voluntarily submits to the legal penalties inflicted by the unjust regime, he does in a sense acknowledge that this regime exists; it does not follow that he acknowledges that this regimes ought to exist.

Of course, if a person's reasons for voluntarily submitting to such penalties are reasons of the kind that Socrates advanced in *Crito* then his voluntary submission to the penalties of such a regime will be an expression of his allegiance to that regime. But no such conclusion follows if civil disobedients voluntarily submit to the legal penalties because they believe (rightly or wrongly) as Gandhi did, that their sufferings in jail will help to put an end to the injustice being committed by the regime. Of course, voluntary co-operation with the institutions and policies of a really unjust regime is an important way of showing one's support for that regime. But even here the presumption can be rebutted. For instance, a person may possess good evidence to show that though he voluntarily joined, say, the civil service or the cabinet, he did this in order to assassinate the tyrant, or to subvert the regime, to exert a moderating influence on that regime. The charge that civil disobedients supported the regime is so far as they voluntarily submitted to the legal penalties inflicted by that regime is not so difficult to rebut. For if the civil disobedients wanted to support the wicked regime, why should they have bothered to go in for civil disobedience at all? Co-operating with the wicked regime by voluntarily suffering in the regime's jails is surely not on a par with co-operating with that regime by joining its civil service. There is the argument that the civil disobedient who voluntarily submits to the legal penalties would in fact unintentionally be playing into the hands of the wicked regime, by allowing the wicked regime to eliminate or put away the opposition to it. The force of this argument will depend upon certain empirical truths. For instance, this argument will become weaker if and when the legal trials and sufferings in prison and the consequent publicity and sympathy of the civil disobedients are likely to result in substantial eradication of the injustices.

To appreciate why Rawls, unlike Gandhi, rules out civil disobedience against unjust regimes, we must stress the fact that for Rawls civil disobledience is a less-demanding practice than it is for Gandhi; the Rawlsian form of civil disobedience will certainly not work effectively against a basically unjust regime, but it does not follow that the Gandhian form will not work agains such a regime. Rawls expresses the hope that when justifiable civil disobedience occurs, the penalties inflicted by the authorities will be reduced and in some cases suspended. Of course, he regards civil disobedience as a public; open, and civil act, and he is committed to the view that the civil disobedient must voluntarily submit to whatever punishment the authorities decide to impose. But he reassures the civil disobedients by saying that in fact the authorities are likely to soften and not impose the heavy penalties that the law allows. He makes it clear that he expects the civil disobedience movement when justified to succeed without involving great self-sacrifice on the part of those who take part in it; the success would come in a less demanding, more cosy manner:

> One may think that this sentiment [viz., the sense of justice] expresses itself in sincere professions of principle and in actions requiring a considerable degree of self-sacrifice. But this supposition asks too much. A community's sense of justice is more likely to be revealed in the fact that the majority cannot bring itself to take the steps necessary to suppress the minority and to punish acts of civil disobedience as the law allows its desire to give justice, weakens capacity to defend its unjust advantages.

The contrast here with Gandhi is striking. For Gandhi believed that it is through suffering voluntarily undergone that the satyagrahi melts the heart of his opponent and opens 'the eyes of his understanding'. For according to the science of *Satyagrah*, the greater the repression and lawlessness on the part of the authority, the greater should be the suffering courted by the victims. Success is the certain result of suffering of the extremist character, voluntarily undergone.

Gandhi further says:

> We expect to bear down the opposition of the Government by courting and not by avoiding imprisonment, even though it may be by showing our supposed readiness to be arrested and imprisoned, *en masse*. Civil disobedience then emphatically means our desire to surrender to a single unarmed policeman. Our triumph consists in thousands being led to the prisons like lambs to the slaughter house. If the lambs of the world had been willingly led, they would have long ago saved themselves from the butcher's knife. Our triumph consists in being imprisoned for no wrong whatever. The greater our innocence, the greater our strength and the swifter our victory.

It can be seen that while Gandhi expects great sacrifices from the civil disobedients, Rawls expects justified civil disobedient movements that do not involve great sacrifices for its participants to be followed by a noble, high-minded response from the regime. One may attempt to modify and reconcile the two theories by maintaining that the cosy form of civil disobedience is more appropriate for near-just conditions but that one is living under a basically unjust regime the civil disobedient must be prepared to make great sacrifices. However, there are other difficulties that the Rawlsian theory may have to face.

On the persuasive model of civil disobedience as advocated by Rawls and others, the protesters attempt to persuade the authorities, and they suffer patiently until the authorities are converted. They avoid measures that hurt the authorities, for they do not want to put any pressure except perhaps moral pressure on the authorities; they want the authorities to accede to their demands of their own free will. According to Rawls, civil disobedience 'while it may warn and admonish, is in ot a threat. Brian Barry finds this persuasive model an absurd one. In his important and very acute commentary on Rawls, Barry argues that the have-nots may need to resort to non-persuasive civil disobedience in order to safeguard and promote their legitimate interests; they may need to threaten the authorities with sanctions, such as the burning of property. Barry thinks that the persuasive, non-threateing protest cannot explain why we should break the law at all:

> ... any form of self-injury would do as well to make it known that one believed strongly in the injustice of a certain law; public self-immolation or, if that seemed too extreme, making a bonfire of one's best clothes would be as good as law-breaking.

Vinit Haksar has rightly argued that Rawls's version of the persuasive model of civil disobedience has grave internal inconsistencies and cannot be defended in its present form. But Barry's general criticism against all forms of persuasive civil disobedience is not, Haksar thinks, valid. He has criticized Barry's argument that the persuasive model cannot explain why the protesters should break the law at all. It seems quite rational, under certain circumstances, to go to prison in order to make one's grievances publicly known and in order to address the sense of justice of the community. True, there are other methods of demonstrating one's sincerity. But for Rawls and for Gandhi, civil disobedients are not just concerned with demonstrating their sincerity. They are also concerned with addressing the sense of justice of the public and of the regime.

We need to distinguish two different senses of addressing the sense of justice of the people, the weaker and the stronger sense. In the weaker sense one can address a person's sense of justice by, writing him a letter informing him of the injustices inflicted upon himself. When he reads his letter he is in a sense informed of his case, though he .may not necessarily appreciate it. But in the stronger sense of addressing a person's sense of justice, one addresses him by opening his eyes to the relevant grievances:

> But experience has shown that mere appeal to reason has no effect upon those who have settled convictions. The eyes of their understanding are opened not by argument but by the suffering of the satyagrahi. The satyagrahi strives to reach the reason through the heart.

The distinction between the two senses is not between merely informing a person of one's case and converting him to it. It is a distinction between merely informing him of one's case and making him appreciate it. Even after the person appreciates your case he may still, of course, fail to agree with you, for there are other considerations that he has to weigh along with the kind of considerations that are involved in your grievances. So his appreciating your point of view is a step towards converting him, but it does not necessarily guaraentee converting him.

Now, even in the weaker sense of addressing the sense of justice, one can make a case for the view that breaking the law by causing more publicity helps the protester to address the community. For alternative methods of giving the relevant information to the public, such as writing a letter to everyone, advertising one's grievances in the newspapers, etc., may be too expensive for a poor minority group. But if the oppressed attempt to address the sense of justice of the community and the regime in the stronger sense, then their case for resorting to civil disobedience can under certain circumstances become even more rational. Admittedly there are other ways of addressing the public's sense of justice—e.g. by going on a fast, burning one's clothes, self-immolation, etc. But it seems quite rational to opt for civil disobedience under certain circumstances. For civil disobedience at least does help to bring the problem of the aggrieved nearer the door of the authorities and even of the public. The trial is conducted by the state authorities and the sentences are served in the state's jails. So the civil disobedient may be able to get his message through and reach the authorities in a way in which he could not if he just fasted or burnt his property. The trial provides an opportunity for the disobedients to state their case directly to the authorities, and often, especially in liberal democracies, the trials are widely reported. Moreover, the trial often involves the state in a dialogue with the disobedients regarding the pros and cons of their movement. An excellent case in point is Gandhi's trial. Again, when the civil disobedient suffers in the state's jails, the state is in a sense inflicting that suffering upon him, and particularly if those in jail show exemplary behaviour they can make the authorities ponder about the morality and justice of their position.

No doubt if the protesters fast without going to jail, this too may make the authorities reflect about the justice of their position. But there is this difference, that the suffering that such a protester undergoes is not directly imposed by the authorities, though it may be self-imposed by the protester as a consequence of, or protest against the regime's policies. In the case of civil disobedients who suffer while being arrested (e.g. if the police use brute force against non-violent demonstrators), since the regime is directly imposing the hardships it is more likely to do some soul-searching about the justice of its position with regard to the dispute. Admittedly, a regime often becomes concerned about the fasts that its opponents undertake. The regime has to take into account the repercussions such fasts have on the population at large; and if, for instance, the faster were to die, this could create civil unrest. The British in India were at least as scared by Gandhi's fast as when they put him in jail. When fasting is used to scare the authorities it involves coercing them, and so would not be permissible under the Rawlsian model as this does not allow the protesters in near-just societies to resort to coercion. But fasting can also be used as a non-coercive device, in order to address the sense of justice of the opponents. So is it not then similar to civil disobedience in that, like civil disobedience, it can be used either as a coercive device or as a non-coercive method of addressing the sense of justice of the community. Why go in for civil disobedience if fasting and other legal methods can do the trick?

Part of the answer may be that at least under some circumstances civil disobedience may be more effective and ethicaL We must remember that when comparing the effectiveness of civil disobedience with that of fasting, etc., we must do so fairly. Often, perhaps always, a sincere fast unto death is more effective as an appeal to the public's and the regime's sense of justice than civil disobedience involving a very minor sentence or fine. But one should take into account how economical in terms of the sufferings involved the two methods are. Civil disobedience is at least sometimes more effective as a form of address than comparable methods that do not involve law-breaking but do involve the same amount of suffering. Take, for instance, the trial and imprisonment of Bertrand Russell, which achieved a lot of publicity without Russell's undergoing too much suffering. If Russell had not broken the law but just imposed upon himself an equivalent amount of suffering the results would hardly have been so impressive. Of course, if instead of breaking the law he had gone on a 'fast unto death' and then died, that would have been different. But compare that to what would have happened if he had died in Her Majesty's jail! We have seen that the state feels more intimately involved with the trial and punishment of civil disobedients, but the same is true of the public. The public feels that the state is acting as its representative and agent, and so the public too feels more involved when the state inflicts punishment than when the protesters inflict an equivalent amount of hardships upon themselves without breaking the law. And so the public, too, is more likely to go in for soul-searching about its dispute with the protesters.

Moreover, the ethics of different forms of protest must be taken into account—it is not enough to show that a method of protest, such as fasting, is effective. Fasting, destroying one's property and self-immolation are all delicate methods of protest in that they can be abused and require careful handling. One of Gandhi's anxieties was that the Satyagraha movement should not degenerate in to *duragraha* which involves coercion. Of course this anxiety extends to civil disobedience as well. It does not follow, however, that civil disobedience should never be used. For it may be quite rational to use it as a form of appeal, after a careful and judicious study of the situation, of the calibre of the individuals, and of the alternatives available.

Gandhi thought that for fasting and other kinds of penance to be ethical they must be resorted to against someone with whom one shares a bond such as love or common ideals. If you fast or resort to other kinds of penance against an enemy with whom you do not share common ideals, then fasting is likely to involve a species of violence towards him. But if someone sharing your ideas has strayed from them due to weakness, then you can fast in order to help to strengthen his resolve to live up to his own ideals. Again, if you have some other close bond with a person, such as love, you can seriously intend and expect to convert him by your suffering, without coercing him. But if you fast, or resort to other kinds of penance, such as burning your property, against an enemy with whom you do not share common ideals or bonds, then your fasting will either be ineffective, or if it is effective, will involve a species of violence towards him. For you cannot seriously intend and expect to convert him without coercing him, and your fast, if effective at all, is likely to be effective by coercing him to do what you think, rather than what he thinks, is the ideal thing to do: e.g. the opponent may give in to your suggestions not because he sees the correctness of your view but for fear of public upheaval. Though Gandhi does not allow fasting against tyrant since one does not share a common bond with the tyrant, he is willing to commend civil disobedience against a tyrant such as Hitler. And it may be asked, would not civil disobedience against a tyrant be equally coercive? Is it not arbitrary to rule out fasting against tyrants, while permitting civil disobedience?

We think one could construct the following reply on behalf of Gandhi: civil disobedience brings the protester into a closer relationship with the authorities by involving a dialogue with the authorities at the trial and the infliction of punishment by the authorities on the protesters, and so forth. Such considerations, along with others, may explain why Gandhi had greater hope in the power of civil disobedience to dissolve the tyranny of the tyrant. So he thought it more plausible to take the view that the civil disobedient can seriously intend and expect to convert the enemy to the point of view of the civil disobedient. For Gandhi it was such serious intentions and expectations that were important; he believed that even our ordinary actions often turn out to have coercive effects but that this does not necessarily make them immoral actions.

It may be asked, does not civil disobedience involve direct coercion of the authorities, in that it forces the authorities to come into a special relationship with the disobedients? Gandhi would reply that civil disobedience when conducted properly should avoid such coercion. Civil disobedients invite the authorities to try, convict, and punish them, but they should never force them to do so. The punishment is not something that civil disobedients should extract from the authorities:

> You cannot fast against a tyrant. You invite penalty from him for disobedience of his orders, but you cannot inflict on yourself penalties when he refuses to punish.

On this view, if the authorities agree to convict and punish the protesters they accept the protesters' invitation to enter into a special relationship with the protesters, since being their jailor does create a kind of relationship.

Gandhian ideas of the ethics of fasting cannot be used to defend the Rawlsian model, at any rate in its high-minded version against Barry's challenge. For on the Gandhian view fasting is not coercive when used against a person who shares the faster's ideals but has strayed from them, i.e. when it is merely used to help the other party to live up to his own ideals or principles. Now in the Rawlsian state people are living in a state of near-justice, sharing common principles of justice; civil disobedience is used when the regime has a lapse and violates those commonly held principles of justice. But if this is so, why resort to civil disobedience? Fasting can be both effective and economical, and so should suffice to remind them and bring them back to the ideals they have temporarily strayed from. In the Rawlsian model, since the people share common principles of justice, they share 'hot lines' through which they can communicate, non-coercively, with each other and send signals or appeals to each other's sense of justice.

Perhaps what one can say is that if two methods of eradicating injustice are equally effective and equally economical in terms of suffering, and if the main relevant difference is that one involves breaking the law while the other does not, then we should opt for the latter. For law-breaking involves dangers of anarchy, as well as inconvenience to others; though even here it is worth recalling that Gandhi thinks that under certain circumstances fasting can be more coercive than civil disobedience. At any rate, it seems quite wrong that penances like fasting should always displace civil disobedience as a form of address. This claim can be reinforced by another consideration. Even if we assume that, say, fasting or burning one's property is as effective and economical a form of address as civil disobedience, it does not follow that it is as effective as civil disobedience when the latter is supplemented by such penances. Sometimes, especially in unjust regimes but also in liberal democracies, when a minority is so deprived of access to the media that its case is not heard properly, what may be required is an attack on several fronts. Some could fast, others could burn their property, while still others could go to jail, and perhaps some could combine these penances with going to jail, e.g. fast in jail. Even Gandhi, who was very cautious in advocating fasts against one's opponents, thought that sometimes we are justified in fasting in jail as a last resort.

The Rawlsian model contains assumptions which render civil disobedience redundant. Rawls confines civil disobedience to instances of 'substantial and clear injustice' and assumes a state of near-justice where all share common principles of justice and respond to appeals to their sense of fair play. But if so, why should the protesters break the law at all, .why should they even go in for any form of self-sacrifice such as fasting or burning their own property? Why not just point out to the authorities that certain 'clear and substantial' injustices are being inflicted by the authorities. Rawls assumes that before civil disobedience is resorted to there is a presumption that the normal appeals to the political majority have been made in good faith and they they have failed. The legal means of redress have proved to no avail, the existing political parties have shown themselves indifferent to the claims of the minority or have proved unwilling to accommodate them. Attempts to have the laws repealed have been ignored and legal protests and demonstrations have had no success.

But if the majority is so insensitive to such appeals from people who are suffering from 'substantial and clear' injustice, how can they be said to be living in a state of near-justice? And if the majority and the regime is so insensitive to such appeals through the conventional channels, what makes it suddenly so sensitive to appeals from civil disobedients? The Gandhian model can perhaps answer this last question by appealing to the power of sincerity and suffering to convert the opponent. But the Rawlsian model is, as we have seen, a cosy one that does not involve substantial sufferings, and there is no reason to see how Rawls could answer this question adequately. Or again, if we assume that we are living in a basically unjust society where certain minorities are denied fair access to the media and are unable to appeal to the majority through the normal channels, they may be compelled to make their case known through extra-constitutional channels such as civil disobedience. But in the Rawlsian model it is not that the minority does not have recourse to appeal to the majority through the normal channels; they have that recourse and make the appeal, and yet fail to move the majority. There is no reason to think that in such circumstances the cosy kind of civil disobedience will always achieve what conventional forms of protest failed to achieve. So the victims of injustice may sometimes be compelled to resort to less cosy forms of civil disobedience.

Rawls points out that in his near-just society 'ruthless tactics that might be contemplated in other societies are not entertained as real alternatives'. Now it would seem quite consistent to take the view that in a liberal democracy such as the USA the majority may on certain occasions be insensitive to the justified protests that a minority makes through the normal channels, yet when the same minority makes its protests through civil disobedience the majority cannot tolerate the use of ruthless measures to suppress the protesters. It is one thing to reject their claims when made through normal channels, but quite another to employ ruthless measures against them when they indulge in civil disobedience. Liberal-democratic regimes either because out of weakness and softness or out of principle are much less ruthless than authoritarian regimes.

But even if we admit that the majority and the regime in liberal-democratic society will not resort to ruthless measures against civil disobedients, this does not entail that they will give in to the demands of civil disobedients. There are other alternatives; for instance, the authorities can decide to punish civil disobedients for short periods or not punish them at all. Neither these nor other alternatives would necessarily imply that the authorities would agree to the demands of the civil disobedients. Suppose a minority is deprived of the liberty to vote and eventually goes in for non-coercive civil disobedience. The authorities may decide to punish them less severely, or to let them off altogether, but this would not necessarily involve giving the minority their liberty to vote. Of course, in practice things may not be so simple. If the authorities refuse to punish severely, the minority could continue being a nuisance and by continuing to break several laws eventually compel the authorities either to ruthlessly suppress the civil disobedients, or to give to their just demands. So if the authorities here will not resort to ruthless suppression, it follows that in these circumstances they will eventually submit to the demand. But does this really help the Rawlsian model? The Rawlsian model is a non-coercive one where the protesters appeal to the authorities' and public's sense of fair play; the gentlemanly and considerate protesters are not allowed to put pressure on the authorities by becoming, or threatening to become a perpetual nuisance to them.

Rawls says that his near-just society implies that 'there exists a constitutional regime and publicly recognized conception of justice'. Sometimes he seems to use 'near-just society' in a fairly wide sense, to include societies where there may be considerable injustices. Barry has taken Rawls to include at least some existing countries like the USA among near-just societies. However, some of Rawls's arguments will only make sense if he uses 'near-just society' in a fairly strict sense where people including the authorities act in a much more high-minded way than they do in any existing liberal democracy.

Rawls seems to be on the horns of a dilemma. Either he uses the term 'near-just society in a fairly generous way, so that some existing liberal democracies like the USA are near-just societies, in which case the cosy model of civil disobedience will not necessarily be effective on all the relevant occasions. For as we have seen, if the majority is insensitive to appeals through the normal channels from an oppressed minority, why should it necessarily get converted when the protesters resort to the cosy form of civil disobedience? For remember the Rawlsian protesters are neither allowed to coerce anyone nor are they expected to suffer much, yet it is expected that they will somehow always bring about a change of heart among the oppressors. It is not even dear how they convince the public and the authorities of their sincerity. The Gandhian civil disobedient shows his sincerity by his willingness to submit to substantial punishment. Of course the actual infliction of such punishment is not necessary, it is sufficient if the civil disobedient is willing to face the threat of substantial punishment. But if we adopt the cosy form of civil disobedience there is not even a real threat of substantial punishment facing those contemplating civil disobedience. True, under the Rawlsian model the law may permit the authorities to impose substantial penalties on the civil disobedients, but under this model the civil disobedients can rely on the authorities being too civilized to impose such penalties.

Alternatively, Rawls could use 'near-just society' in a narrower sense, confining it to societies where people act in a high-minded way or where, when they depart from the right course, they can be brought back to it by an appeal to their sense of fair play and justice. But now he will be confronted with the other horn of the dilemma. For, in this ideal society, although the cosy form of civil disobedience will be sufficient to convert the authorities, it is not at all clear that it will ever be necessary for that purpose. In this ideal society civil disobedience should be redundant for the legal forms of protest should be able to achieve the same result.

In view of this, it would perhaps be best to interpret the Rawlsian model of civil disobedience in such a way that it is applicable to at least some of the existing liberal democracies such as the USA. One way out of some of the difficulties would be to modify the model so that it permits forms of civil disobedience that require a considerable degree of self-sacrifice on the part of the protesters. Rawls would have to abandon his view that this requirement is too severe, that it asks too much. This modification of the Rawlsian model would make it less vulnerable to atleast some of the objections and also bring it closer to the Gandhian model. But can even the Gandhian non-coercive civil disobedience model, which involves considerable suffering tor the protesters, be certain of success in liberal democracies, even if we assume the great power of suffering to melt the opponent? For if the authorities simply refuse to punish the civil disobedients, how can the latter, without coercion, continue their efforts to convert the authorities through civil disobedience? Even if the protesters were to resort to fasting and other forms of self-inflicted suffering, that would not be civil disobedience.

Another difficulty for the Rawlsian model arises from the fact that Rawls confines civil disobedience only to obvious and clear cases of substantial injustice. We shall now try to examine some of the conclusions he attempts to derive from this requirement, and also the difficulties that arise as a result of his requirement. He thinks that his requirement would imply that civil disobedience should not be used against violations of the 'difference principle' (according to which inequalities should be arranged so as to maximize the expectations of the worst off) on the grounds that infractions of this principle are not easy to ascertain:

> There is usually a wide range of conflicting yet rational opinion as to whether this principle is satisfied. The reason for this is that it applies primarily to economic and social institutions and policies. A choice among them depends upon theoretical and speculative belief as well as upon a wealth of statistical and other information, all of this seasoned with shrewd judgment and plain hunch. (*TJ. p*.372)

He wants to confine civil disobedience to serious infringements of: the principle of equal liberty and to blatant violations of the principle of fair opportunity. Thus when certain minorities are denied the right to vote or to hold office, or to own property and to move from place to place, or when certain religious groups are repressed and thus denied various opportunities, these injustices may be obvious to all. The establishment of these wrongs does not presuppose an informed examination of institutional effects.

Now it seems that Rawls is quite wrong here. The examination of these wrongs, at any rate of such wrongs that one encounters in near-just societies, will involve an informed examination of institutional effects. It is not at all clear that liberty should get the high priority that Rawls gives it. Sometimes the claims of a particular liberty will have to be balanced against claims of another liberty, and sometimes they may have to be balanced against other values such as security. Such balancing will involve 'shrewd judgment and plain hunch'. We can think of clear, substantial, and unjustified violations of principles of equal liberty, for instance the treatment of the Jews in Nazi Germany; but the examples that come to mind in societies that are near-just are not so clear-cut and obvious. We do not deny that in countries like the USA serious and clear-cut infringements of the principle of equal liberty may take place from time to time, e.g. the denial of the vote to blacks. But then can a society which allows such clear-cut violations to take place be regarded as a near-just society? And what guarantee is there that a society that allows such clear-cut cases of substantial injustice will reform itself when confronted with the cosy form of civil disobedience? Rawls could get out of this difficulty by modifying his model so as to allow non-cosy forms of non-coercive civil disobedience. But then there is another problem here. If we do allow that in near-just societies such clear and substantial violations of the principle of liberty can take place, why cannot constitutional entrenchments and independent tribunals such as a Supreme Court be adequate to correct such injustices? Why should there be any need for civil disobedience? Brian Barry argues unfairly that on Rawls's premises there are just two alternatives:

> If people pursue justice single-mindedly it sacrcely matters how the rules for decision making are drawn up, since the results can hardly fail to be good; if they don't do this then all is lost.

Barry rightly points out that Rawls has no place for the kind of Benthamite constitutional engineering which assumes that individuals are motivated primarily by self-interest and which attempts to channel these motives by a system of incentives, so as to produce good collective decisions. But Barry wrongly concludes:

> It is difficult to see why on Rawls's premises, there is any reason for the constitutional entrenchments of the personal liberties dealt with by the first principle of justice, since if we behave justly, they will vote to preserve them anyway.

Barry fails to notice that Rawls's premises do allow another possibility, namely that individuals are fairly high-minded and normally pursue justice single-mindedly, but not always; occasional lapses do occur, but even if we dispense with Benthamite constitutional engineering, all is not lost for since the individuals and the authorities are basically just they can be brought back to the just path by an eloquent appeal to their sense of fairness.

We do not agree with Barry that constitutional entrenchments are redundant on Rawls's premises; for once we allow for the possibility that even high-minded people can suffer occasional lapses due to fits of weakness, we can make a case for such safeguards as constitutional entrenchments backed up by independent courts. There is the argument that constitutional entrenchments should be redundant, because whatever injustices occurred could be corrected by, for instance, civil disobedience or by protesters who appeal to the authorities and the public by fasts and other penances. But this argument is not a good one. It is surely better to prevent an injustice from occurring rather than give up the preventive techniques because you know how to correct substantial injustices after they have been allowed to occur.

The problem facing Rawls here is this: though constitutional entrenchments are not redundant, do they not, along with independent courts to back them up, render civil disobedience redundant in Rawls's system? It might be suggested that it is quite consistent and desirable to have both safeguards against injustice, constitutional entrenchments as well as civil disobedience. The role of constitutional entrenchments is to prevent departures from justice, but this safeguard is not perfect, occasional departures may still take place, because the courts are fallible; so civil disobedience may still be needed to restore justice. But if we also insist, as Rawls seems to, on confining civil disobedience to clear and obvious violations of the principles of justice in a near-just society, then civil disobedience becomes redundant. For if and when the violations are clear and obvious, why can they not be prevented by the courts or by some independent tribunal? When we are dealing with infractions that are not clear and obvious, honest mistake is possible, and the fact that the courts do not strike down such injustices does not show that they are being corrupt. But if the courts allow clear and obvious infractions of principles of justice to survive, then they are conniving with injustice prepetrated by another branch of the state, and can this happen in a near-just society?

In some countries, like India, certain basic liberties get violated in spite of their being guaranteed by the constitution, and through no fault of the courts. There may be so much social prejudice over things like dowry, untouchability and caste that in spite of what the courts and the constitution say, these evils flourish. In such situations there may indeed be a case for civil disobedience to change the majority prejudices and to appeal to the government to take more positive measures to eradicate such practices—though, of course, such a case may be rebutted when such disobedience is likely to lead to anarchy. Similar occasions for civil disobedience may arise in advanced liberal democracies as well. Think, for instance, of a minority which finds that its security which Rawls regards as part of liberty or its economic interests are threatened by certain racists, and where the state is not taking sufficient positive action to fight such threats to the interests and security of the minority.

Again, we can divide rights, as the Irish constitution does, into 'justiciable' and 'non-justiciable' rights. There are some injustices, for instance in the field of economic policy, removal of slums, crime prevention, and foreign policy, that may not be enforceable through the courts. The Indian constitution makes a distinction similar to the one made by the Irish constitution; instead of the term 'non-justiciable rights', it uses the term 'directive principles', so the division in the Indian constitution is between justiciable rights and directive principles. The Indian constitution, like the Irish, provides for directive principles which it is the duty of the state to try to follow, but which are not enforceable through the courts. When the state does not fulfil such duties the people may even attempt to sack their government at election time. But if the minority is being unjustly treated in an area that is not justiciable, it may lack the power to elect a more just government or to influence the existing one in any substantial way. In such circumstances the minority may feel compelled to resort to such less conventional forms of protest as civil disobedience or fasting. Considerations of this kind show why it may be necessary to resort to measures like civil disobedience in spite of constitutional safeguards backed by the courts. But no such considerations will help Rawls against the charge that civil dsobedience is redundant in his system. For civil disobedience in the sort of areas that we have just been considering would be against the spirit of Rawls's advice. The reason why directive principles are made non-justiciable in these cases is that it is not thought that the courts will have the competence to judge whether the state is doing all that it reasonably can be expected to do to promote the directive principles.

Rawls thinks that as long as our civil and political liberties are secure, the normal political processes can be relied upon to correct injustices automatically in fields like social justice. But he is being too optimistic here. For a minority, even though it has the liberty to vote, freedom of speech, etc., may be outvoted and economically and socially exploited by a majority for long periods over issues such as income, housing, and education. It may be argued that in a near-just society a majority would not do this for long, but we must remember that we are assuming that the Rawlsian majority is capable of lapses from justice. Indeed we have seen that unless we make this and other assumptions there will be no place for civil disobedience at all. The majority, the authorities, and the courts are assumed to be capable of conniving against the interests of the minority. But if the authorities and the majority are capable of such deeds, how can they be trusted in matters of economic and social justice, where things are much less clear-cut and consequently where there is much greater scope for self-deception, prejudice, false consciousness, etc.? Rawls points out rightly that in such areas the opinions one normally forms depend upon theoretical and speculative beliefs, upon a wealth of information, and upon shrewd judgement and plain hunch. In view of the complexities involved 'it is difficult to check the influence of self-interest'. He also rightly infers from such considerations that over such issues there is considerable scope for the biases and the prejudices of the civil disobedients to creep in. But he wrongly thinks that it follows from this that the resolution of these issues should be left to the political processes. What he forgets is that in such areas there is so much scope for self-deception, self-interest, and prejudice to blur the judgement not only of the protesters, but also of the public and the authorities. If we give the public and the authorities the final say in such matters, there is in a sense even greater danger than in the cases of injustices that are clear and obvious that they may continue perpetrating the injustices for long periods. For in the latter cases the majority and the authorities, since they are basically just, will feel guilt and shame at perpetrating such injustices and before too long they will return to the right path. They are not rogues on the Rawlsian account. But in the case of equally substantial but less obvious cases of injustices, even high-minded people can perpetrate such injustices for long periods of time, believing that they are doing what is right and just.

So civil disobedience may be needed as a safeguard even when the injustices are not clear and obvious. This point is reinforced by the following. One might argue a case for having independent tribunals, such as a supreme court, to deal with cases of clear and obvious injustices, and not with less clear-cut cases, for with the latter there is more danger of bias and prejudice and more need of expert knowledge of the kind that the courts do not possess, e.g. knowledge of economics. It is such considerations that have led some to advocate the doctrine of preferred freedoms, according to which the court should take an active line as guardian of the civil and political liberties, but not with regard to primarily economic and social legislation, except in so far as the latter is necessary for the exercise of civil and political liberties. Now if clear and obvious violations of civil liberties can be quite well protected by a supreme court while economic and social legislation tends to go unchallenged by the supreme court, one could contend that if we use civil disobedience as an additional safeguard in addition to the courts there is even greater need for it to safeguard injustices that tend to go unscrutinized by the courts, e.g. injustices in social and economic matters.

Of course not every one accepts the doctrine of preferred freedoms. But a Rawlsian can not reject such a doctrine. For the sort of considerations advanced by Rawls in favour of civil disobedience functioning as a guardian of civil liberties rather than of economic interests can be, and indeed have been, advanced in favour of the doctrine of preferred freedoms. Though Rawls does not refer to this doctrine, it is interesting to see that its proponents have used arguments to support it which run parallel to those used by Rawls in favour of the view that civil disobedience should safeguard people's liberties rather than their economic interests. For instance, supporters of this doctrine have pointed out that it is essential for the supreme court to protect the civil and political liberties, because the normal political process cannot be relied upon to correct violations of such basic liberties. So we have a sort *of reduction ad absurdum* of the Rawlsian position. For if the Rawlsian arguments are valid, then so too is the doctrine of preferred freedoms. But if the doctrine of preferred freedoms is implemented, then, for reasons given earlier, there is less to be said for the Rawlsian view that we should confine civil disobedience only to the violations of clear and obvious injustices.

It may be argued that the great advantage of confining civil disobedience to cases of clear and obvious violations of principles of justice is that if we do not so confine it there would be a much greater danger of anarchy and chaos. Just imagine what would happen if everyone could break the law whenever they felt they were being treated most unjustly in economic and social fields. But one must not overstate this point. There are other more important safeguards against anarchy. The alternative is not anarchy, at any rate not on Rawls's premises. Remember we are dealing with a near-just society where there may be substantial injustices, but where people, including the protesters, are fairly high-minded, responsible and considerate. And no one is suggesting that people should break the law whenever they feel unjustly treated. Instead of advising the protesters, as Rawls does, not to break the law if the injustice is not substantial and obvious, we could advise them not to break the law if it is not their considered opinion that a substantial but not necessarily obvious injustice is being perpetrated. Moreover, we could endorse a good deal of the caution with which Rawls accompanies his advice to those contemplating civil disobedience, e.g. that they should exhaust the normal political channels, that their decision should be a considered and informed one, and that they should ponder what would happen if minority groups with similar grievances began civil disobedience. We could also agree with Rawls's preference for limiting civil disobedience to those injustices which block the way to removing other injustices. Only Rawls wrongly assumes that violations of the difference principle that causes injustices in the distribution of wealth and income do not block the way to removing other injustices. This assumption reflects his naive belief that as long as a minority has political and civil liberties the normal political processes can be relied upon to correct, before long the injustices inflicted upon it. In fact, however, the extent to which a minority can, even in the long run, protect and promote its legitimate interests depends not just upon its possessing the civil and political liberties but also upon such factors as the amount of wealth at its disposal and the size of the minority. Other things being equal, if a minority is very wealthy it would have less need to resort to civil disobedience as a method of publicizing its cause; for it could get its adequate share of publicity without breaking the law. It is the relatively poor who may be in greater need to resort to stunts like breaking the law and fasting in order to publicize their cause. Sometimes Rawls seems to be talking about near-just societies where even the worst off are well off economically. But if we are to apply his model, as he is sometimes driven to apply it, to some existing liberal democracies such as the USA, then the worst off are at a considerable disadvantage compared to the well off in protecting and promoting their legitimate interests by advertising, hiring lawyers, etc.

There is one most important safeguard against the danger of anarchy that scholans like Vinit Haksar would like to insert but which Rawls does not, namely the threat of substantial punishment of those civil disobedients who transgress the limits of justified protest. Rawls admits that civil disobedience is potentially dangerous and has to be kept within bounds: 'there is a limit on the extent to which it can be engaged in without leading to a breakdown in the respect for law and the constitution'. But he stops at merely advising the civil disobedient not to transgress such limits; he is willing to rely upon their good sense. But why does he not advise the authorities to constrain protesters, where necessary, by threatening substantial penalties against protesters who transgress such limits? We have seen that the Rawlsian model has to assume that the majority and the authorities are capable of lapses from justice. And he does constrain their unjust behaviour, e.g. by constitutional entrenchments of civil and political liberties, by a system of checks and balances. He does not rely merely on the good sense of the authorities and of the majority to choose the just path; why then is he willing to rely solely on the good sense of the civil disobedient not to transgress the limits of justified protest? If the majority and the authorities are capable of behaving unjustly, so too are the civil disobedients. And just as he is willing to impose effective external constraints on the unjust behaviour of the majority and the authorities by a system of constitutional entrenchments etc., so too should he be willing to impose some effective external constraints when the behaviour of civil disobedients transgresses the limits set by the principle of fairness and justice. The authorities may not be brutal or to use more force than is necessary. When the danger of anarchy can be averted, as it often can, by more humane means, one may follow Rawls in recommending a reduction or suspension of sentences. But the threat of substantial penalties is something that must be there in the background, available for use as a last resort. So now we have seen another reason for rejecting the cosy model of civil disobedience, i.e. that it would not be able to prevent anarchy.

So one would criticize Rawls for being too liberal in one direction, but also too restrictive in another. He is too liberal in advising the authorities never to impose substantial penalties against the civil disobedients. He is too restrictive in advising the civil disobedients never to embark on civil disobedience unless the injustice is clear and obvious, and never, or almost never, to use it for protesting against violations of the "difference principle." He, in effect, forbids the protesters to resort to civil disobedience whenever the opponents have a rational case. Since his protesters can only go in for civil disobedience when they are convinced that their opponents have no rational case, this may lead in practice to an attitude of self-righteousness and arrogance on the part of the civil disobedients. They will find it difficult not to patronise the authorities, for their job is simply to enlighten the authorities who are either fools or cowards. On the Gandhian model the protesters are encouraged to believe that their opponents may turn out to be right or partly right, and that even if they are wrong they may have a rational case; consequently the protesters ask their opponents to join them in a search for the truth.

Of course, it would be immoral to break the law just in order to join with the authorities in a humble search for the truth. The protesters must, after considered reflection, believe that a substantial injustice has been perpetrated by the authorities; when the protesters break the law they are trying to convince the authorities that this injustice has occurred. But on the Gandhian view the protesters are advised not to take up a dogmatic and inflexible stand; they search for the truth in the sense that their original objective of getting an alleged injustice corrected is itself subject to revision, should a discussion with the authorities show that the original objection was not wholly reasonable and correct.

On the Rawlsian view it is difficult to see how the civil disobedients enter into a dialogue and debate with the authorities, for if their case is clear and obvious to everyone, all they can do is to point this out; they cannot enter into a dialogue with the authorities since the authorities have no rational case to answer! For if the issues are rationally debatable, then the Rawlsian criteria imply that there should be no civil disobedience; civil disobedience is not advised over an issue when there is 'a wide range of conflicting yet rational opinion'. Rawls says that for civil disobedience to be justified there must be substantial, clear and obvious injustice. But he also offers another test, namely that when contemplating civil disobedience preference should be given to those injustices which block the way to the removal of other injustices. Now let us imagine a situation, which Rawls never considers, where the two tests conflict, where there is an injustice that is not clear and obvious, but is believed by the protesters to be very substantial and which could block the way to removing injustices in the future.

Suppose the state during an emergency decides to suspend certain liberties for the sake of security. And the state claims that once the emergency is over, it will restore the liberties. Should we always obey the state's decision whenever it is not clear and obvious that the state has made a wrong decision? Suppose it is our considered belief that the state has made a wrong and fatal decision, that the sacrifice of our liberties is too drastic and that there is, in our opinion, a real danger that the liberties may be lost for ever. We agree with Vinit Haksar that is plausible to argue that sometimes we should engage in civil disobedience in such cases, even though the state's case is not an obviously irrational one. For when so much is at stake we may be justified in engaging in civil disobedience even though it is not obvious that we are right.

Religion and Politics

Criticism has often been made of Gandhi's use of religious and spritual idiom for communication himself and his basic thinking of a wide variety of issues. It has been said that by its nature this tended to be vioced in the language and symbols of Hindu religion and that much as he tried, he was not able to overcome this limitation. In order to be able to deal with this matter we would like to strees something that comes prior to that namely that Gandhi was, both during his lifetime and in terms of the legacy left behind by him, a "profoundly organic and self-contained being, always retaining his roots yet reaching out to the beyonds." Following a model of life that was at one and at the same time based on a union with diverse traditions, concepts, myths, belief systems, and normative inheritances and liberation from them all, he made them all deliver to him freedom for independent action suited to his social purpose and the demands of the time in which he was working out both his personal salvation and his strategy for social and political change. He often imparted new meaning s and new content to both eternal verities and shifting situations for working out his strategy at a given point of time, wrung from the various alternatives that he faced wholly new possibilities, thus kept himself a "free agent," though no doubt rooted in a set of circumstances and maneuvered his way through a jungle of both inherited norms and ideas and the need for fresh interventions as demanded by the needs of his time. Though Gandhi was not either a universalist or a relativist in his philosophical make-up, he was constantly searching for ever new ways of handling reality. Perhaps one could say that in the ultimate analysis his was a search for an alternative universal of his own creation, a universal that has both secular and religious meanings. For, Gandhi was in fact both: a profoundly religious being who was seeking his way through a praxis that was at bottom political and hence secular. Moved himself by moral and spiritual motives he was all the time aware that he was leading a major political movement in which large masses of the people had to be involved.

This brings us to the criticism mentioned above in respect of his employment of a spritual and religious idiom. There are two aspects to this issue. For Gandhi, religion provided both sanctity and inner strength to his pursuit of politics. Hence his dictum that those who said that religion had nothing to do with politics knew nothing of either relgion or politics. But, at the same time, he was constantly reinterpreting and recasting the meaning of religion, its very definition and various key concepts that had the sanctity of religion like dharma, karma, and moksha with a view to giving to the pursuit of politics a wide currency and making it meaningful for an otherwise a political society. The concept of dharma, which had traditionally been used to legitimise social hierarchy, was utilised by him to mobilise the people against alien rule (it became their obligation to fight this common curse), while the concept of karma, which had hitherto been used for personal salvation through individual deed, was utilised to further nation-related deeds and, finally, the concept of moksha was utilised to encourage identification of personal salvation to the salvation of society as a whole.

Gandhi was and continues to be the greatest politicizer that India has produced. For him, mobilising the vast masses of people belonging to diverse faiths and social systems in the freedom movement was the primary challenge. Hence his use of religious symbols for political ends. The main challenge as he saw it was political but there was need to provide roots to that effort.

In the religious field itself, he said again and again that all religions were true and had a common message (of non-violence and truth) and that each was a search for a unified approach by no means underrating the distinctiveness of each but constantly emphasising the unity underlying them all. Hence it happened that in India far from being a negation of religion, secularism and the process of secularisation was itself to be thought of as at bottom a religious and cultural process, of drawing upon a diverse pursuits after truth and in search of the sacred and integrating them into one single homogenous stream which was then made the basis of a unified nation-state which in turn was endowed with a spiritual meaning and by virtue of that wide legitimacy among all sections of the people. Such a conception of secularism could well have been dictated by the immediate exigency of the growing antagonism between Hindus and Muslims (as well as pressing social problems, above all the Harijans) and more generally with respect to apprehensions about the great plurality and heterogeneity of the country at large, all of religion in the cause of Indian nationalism and a nation-state grounded in a nationalist ideology. But of course equally basic was Gandhi's own holistic conception of self and society, continuously seeking to unify every being and all seeming opposites.

This was his basic position. Today, faced as we are by anything but a truly composite religiosity on the basis of which the foundations of an equally composite political structure could be sustained, and facing as we do a highly vitiated communal atmostphere and also facing a major authoritarian drive in the name of the "unity of the country," many are likely to feel uncomfortable with Gandhi's conception of secularism. Given this overriding desire to mobilise the mass of the people in the national movement, Gandhi also chose to employ traditional symboles that could reach out to them. Many of these happened to be of Hindu origin, though Gandhi's own conception of Hinduism was highly multi-dimensional in which all other faiths found a place and in his own life he often tried to identify with other faiths and belief systems. This often led to skepticism among leaders of other religious group despite Gandhi's effort to involve them at each stage of thinking about India's political future. This could be one reason for our failure to forge the kind of composite unity across diverse faiths that Gandhi had in mind.

We should like to make a distinction between the religion proper and the various social system that obtain at given points of time. While the propagation of Hindutva has distorted and vitiated the whole debate over the role of religion in society and politics, it is still possible to stress the catholicity and inclusiveness of Hinduism. Hinduism accepts as part of its distinctively pluralist domain a variety of other religious traditions too and has a place for them as part of its worldview apart from its being non-proselytising and being free of a centralised clergy, dogma, and scripture and to that extent more openended and hence "tolerant"than most other religious tradition. But when it comes to the social system of the Hindus, there seems to be continuing intolerance, discrimination, and humiliation meted out to the lower rungs of the system and, by extension of this in recent times, to the social segments represented by "converted" Muslims and Christians and that is where the "rot" really lies.

Having dealt with the religious cum secular import of Gandhi's thinking and message, the question arises: how does Gandhi himself stand up to scrutiny in this context? Rajni Kothari has offered an explauation reservations about Gandhi quite apart from his own sense of failure as spelt out by him towards the end of his life which had to do with Hindu-Muslim unity, with respect to his inability to restructure the Hindu social order. Perhaps it is too much to ask of any one individual, however great he may have been, to restructure a whole social order. But one can and, when it comes to a man like

Gandhi who never shied away from taking on major historical tasks, one ought to at least raise questions in respect of somethings as basic as this. There is no question in our mind that Gandhi thought this to be a major task facing India and in fact put in a big effort in raising consciousness on the most shameful aspect of it, namely the practice of untouchability, preventing continued state of degradation of a whole social segment, and trying his best to endow it with a sense of honour and dignity including giving it spiritual significance (by calling its members "Harijans" or Children of God) which in Gandhi's scheme of things meant giving it prime importance. To a considerable extent, he did succeed in raising consciousness on this issue. But the matter remained there and no more than that just as in our various efforts as Indians to raise the status and position of various segments of our society we seems to have done little more than raising consciousness, influencing public opinion and passing "progressive" legislation or provisions in the Constitution.

It may be considered by some as an act of blasphemy to say that Gandhi failed. But in matters like this it is better to state things a little more bluntly than to take refuge in verbal or intellectual sophistication. As we look at the matter carefully, we find that in Gandhi's effort to take a holistic view of creating a non-violent and decentralised social and economic order given to the pursuit of truth- his paramount value - he may have quite often given short shift to contentious social issues of which the Harijans in Hindu society turned out to be one. While he himself gave a lot of importance to the abject condition of the Harijans, he seems to have failed in two respects. He failed to carry the wide Hindu society and its subjective sense of the grave injustice that it had indulged in over the centuries and the need to consciously and collectively reverse the status quo. Given his unique model of communication, he did cast a spell for a while, but, given his own strong conviction that the necessary change could be brough about within the prevailing order, he failed to mount the necessary offensive that was needed for bringing about that reversal. It is owing to his second failure that the so-called "change of heart" remaind a pious hope, namely his disinclination to give due weightage to the "Harijan's" own subjective sense of the way history has dealt with him, played truant with him, continuosusly exploited, depraved, raped and marauded him and his kins, subjected them to all manner of atrocities or, at the other end of the spectrum, created illusions in their own subjective perception of their standing in the whole scheme of things. It is on this that the more fundamental of the exchanges between Gandhi and Ambgedkar took place, apart of course from Ambedkar's very poor opinion of rural India which, according to him, was a cesspool of both terror and superstition whereas Gandhi laid the whole emphasis of his alternative paradigm on India's villages. This state of affairs continues to this day which is why there is taking place a renewed emphasis on the Gandhi-Ambedkar debate.

Gandhi seems to have been far more successful in combating external "enemies"- including the civilizational and cultural imperial thrust rather than with the internal one in respect of the decomposition and inequity of India's civil society. Gandhi's refusal to let his Harijans find their own way and carve out their own destiny was part of his basic position of thinking of them as integral to the larger unity called India and not accepting the British view of treating diverse cultural and social entities as distinct from each other, merely deserving "representation" but not being conceived as being parts of a larger unity. But in actual practice this may well have amounted to accept their subordinate and servile state by permanently peripheralising them against which they seem to be now themselves rising after more than 40 years of struggle. That to no small extent this struggle could have benefited from both separate electorates and reservations for the "Scheduled Castes" may continue to be matter of debate. But there seems little doubt that in the mobilisation of the Harijans or Dalits, as they prefer to call themselves, in giving them a sense of potency and self-regard and in enabling them to wage struggle within the system is going to be of central importance.

In an increasingly multicultural world, political theory is presented with perhaps its most vigorous challenge yet. As radically different moral projects confront one another, the problem of competing claims of truth arising from particular views of the human good remains crucial for political philosophy and political action. Recent events have demonstrated that the problem is far from being solved and that its implications are more far-reaching than the domestic politics of industrialized nations. As the problem of violence has also become coterminous with issues of pluralism, many have advocated the banishing of truth claims from politics altogether.

Political theorists have struggled to confront this problem through a variety of conceptual lenses. Debates pertaining to the politics of multiculturalism, toleration, or recognition have all been concerned with the question of pluralism as one of the most urgent facts of political life, in need of both theorectical and practical illumination.

This chapter argues that a possible method for arbitrating among competing claims to truth, without altogether jettisoning the activity of truth-seeking from politics, is provided by Mahatma Gandhi. While various Western thinkers have offered solutions to this problem, fresh insight can be gained by turning to thinkers from the non-Western world. Gandhigiri presents fertile ground for this project, for it offers a vision of political action that includes the search for truth as integral to political life. Implicit in this vision is also the possibility that non-violence, understood in a certain way, provides a means to adjudicate among competing truth claims. We begin by articulating the ontological and epistemological premises that underlie the Gandhian vision. While these premises raise the possibility of conflict among competing moral truths, Gandhi's concept of non-violence functions as an arbiter among these competing claims. Such arbitration can be performed by the Gandhian civic virtue of non-violence which may be useful in contemporary instances of moral conflict because it presents a richer and more complex understanding of political life and a more productive approach to such conflict than other contemporary pluralists.

A new model of politics emerges from the Gandhian view. Gandhi takes pains to clarify that the commonsensical definition of politics understood solely as the quest for power, pursued through the structure of the state and through legislative and electoral processes, was to be avoided. In contrast to many modern or Western views, politics for Gandhi is not to be seen as an autonomous sphere of life, guided by its own set of assumptions and principles. Rather, Gandhi wants to broaden the political realm to include most aspects of daliy action that relate to the improvement of society at large. Gandhi repeatedly makes the distinction between what he calls "power" politics and "real" or "true" politics, which for him "must be looked upon in terms of social and moral progress. In turn, this view of politics stems from Gandhi's general objection to the compartmentalization of human life into separable, distinct realms of action. "I do not divide different activities—political, social, religious, economical—into watertight compartments. I look upon them all as one indivisible whole each running into the rest and affected by the rest." This view of the interconnectedness of different realms of activity leads to the idea that each of them must be informed by and reflect the same central purpose or concern. For Gandhi, the spiritual and the ethical quest for truth serves as the driving purpose for the other realms of life, especially for the political. In this sense, the political is no different than any other realms of human action: it is to be guded by the quest for truth. Unlike more ascetic branches of Hindu thought, which marginalize the political realm by treating it as a negative externality to be subjugated by the spiritual, Gandhi revives the political sphere by linking it to the quest for truth: politics is, for Gandhi, intrinsically a realm of truth-seeking. The challenge of politics, as with any other realm of life is constant vigilance to ensure that even as one is epistemologically limited, one's worldly actions accord with the seeking of truth.

It is important to note, however, that epistemological limitation should not give rise to political paralysis: a partial grasp of the truth is an adequate and necessary way of navigating the political world. One need only follow the truth as one sees or knows it. The task of human life for Gandhi is to contemplate and work toward the best set of truths for oneself in this life. Within the realm of worldly action, relative truth or what we might call "practical" truth- is the more accessible way of steering ourselves, rather than trying to find the Absolute or theoretical truth. This is not to say that Gandhi disavows the search for Absolute Truth through politics, he repeatedly emphasizes that the final goal or ideal should always be Absolute Truth. Certainly, Absloute Truth has a comprehensive doctrinal quality to it, akin to a theoretical truth system, covering all aspects of the good life, including questions of what is of value in human life, fundamental beliefs, virtues, and ideas of right conduct, both political and non-political. Yet, because this Truth is unavailable to humans in their embodied state, the challenge of politics—as for most other realms of human life-is about participating in and getting right a series of less ambitious, relative truths. Politics, then is a realm where it is possible to arrive, through practice, at a series of relative truths—truths about the right action to be taken in a specific situation, for a specific reason.

The framework we have just articulated now raises the following important challenges for Gandhi's vision. First, we have the epistemological issue of how we know whether our own grasp of the relative truth—truth as we see it—is an accurater one. If the truth is so multifaceted, is it not possible that our grasp of it is erroneous and not among the various relative truths that participate in the Absolute Truth? Furthermore, what happens when these partial truths conflict with one another? Finally, we have the moral or ethical issue, which, for Gandhi, rides on the epistemological one: unless we know we have arrived at some portion of the truth, how do we justify any social or political action based on these beliefs? The potential challenges to Gandhi's vision, then are twofold: the first dimension is epistemological, while the second, which rides on the first, is moral/political..

We offer a comparison between the Gandhian position with that of a contemporary pluralist such as Rawls. We focus on a Rawlsian approach since it represents a prevalent viewe about pluralism in polities and also offers a fruitful dialogue with the Gandhian model. For Rawls, the "fact of reasonalble pluralism" is a permanent feature of modern societies. Disagreement about fundamental moral and religious questions—"comprehensive doctrines," which "include conceptions of what is of value in human life, ideals of personal virtue and character, that are to inform non-political conduct"—is not a temporary condition but "the normal result of the exercise of human reason" under free institutions. The problem, therefore, is to find principle of political justice that all can affirm despite their moral, philosophical, and religious differneces. Preserving stability in the face of such pluralism calls for theories of justice to be free of controversial moral assumptions and metaphyusical foundations: "By avoiding comprehensive doctrines we try to bypass religion and philosophy's profoundest controversies." As a practical matter, no general moral conception can provide a publicly recognized basis for a coneption of justice in a modern democratic state. Rawls's solution is the famous "overlapping consensus" on the implicitly recognized basic ideas and principles within a democratic society.

Rawls repeatedly affirms that the task of ploitical philosophy is not only to provide justification and arbirtation in matters of political justice "ordering the many conflicts of justice that arise in public life" but also to preserve stability, fair cooperation, and social cohesion. The appropriate way to achieve this is a method of "avoidance" in which one avoids argument on the basis of any contested moral or metaphysical premise, any controversial claim about what is true. Instead, in justifying any principle to a pluralist community, political philosophers must make reference to the history and the shared experiences of a community to forge an "overlapping consensus" on a conception of justice. This consensus is formulated in terms of intuitive ideas viewed as latent in the public culture of a democratic society and that people with opposing religous, poilosphical and moral doctrines, are able to agree on from within their respective positions. The aim of political philosophy in pluralistic democracies can no longer be the pursuit of truth. Instead, the aim is the pursuit of" informed and willing political agreement between citizens."

The Rawlsian model is not competely indifferent to truth or to morality. Rawls emphasizes that his conception of justice is moral in that it "has conceptions of person and society, and concepts of right and fairness, as well as principles of justice with their complement of the virtues." What distingusihes his conception is that the morality it espouses is ostensibly deatached from any one particular moral and/or comprehensive view. It involves "no prior commitment to any wider doctrine," and it is constructed from a public consensus on shared principle implicit in the political life of the society. For the Gandhian model, in contrast no such restriction applies to any moral view, regardless of attachment to a particular truth system or comprehensive doctine, would be admissible in matters of public justification, so long as it is accompanied by the preceding criteria of the non-violence.

Like Rawls's political conception of justice, the Gandhian model is concerned with matters of justification on political life. Unlike Rawls, Gandhi offers an alternative account for public justification. Instead of focusing simply on the kinds of reasons, his model shifts the focus of justification for the action that go along with reason. Reason-giving continues to be important as it is in the Rawlsian model—after all, we come to the truth of a matter by weighing the reasons given on each side of an argument. However, the Gandhian model adds an additional component to the evaluative process, by subjecting the public actions accompanying the reasons to scrutiny. The Gandhian model holds us to a different ideal of the sorts of reasons that are acceptable—namely, those that are accompanied or supported by certain kinds of speech and action in the political arena (humility, discourse, and nonviolent suffering). This account arises in part from the rather different and more pragmatic way of thinking about politics that Gandhi offers. Rawls tries to separate political activity from the rest of human life. He wants to find a model of agreement that is carved out of the larger commitments of human beings with specifically political belief and action seen as being separable from other kinds of theoretical commitments. Gandhi, meanwhile, presents a vision in which thought, action, and politics are contiguous with one another, not neatly separable into distinctly theoretical or practical aspects of one's being. In such an organic view of human life, theory and praxis are equally important and come under scrutiny equally.

Using the Gandhian model as a standard of arbitration one avoids some of the considerable costs associated with the Rawlsian model in pluralist society. Moreover, contrary to popular characterizations of the Mahatma, which porttay him as a half-naked mystic, immersed in a world of bizarre living experiments and somewhat removed from reality, Gandhi offers us a model of thinking about politics that may, in many ways, be more real than the one offered by Rawls. Perhaps the main cost of the Rawlsian model is the impoverised understanding of political life and of the activity of political philosophy that emerge from it. The banishment of truth to the realm of the private, with stability and consensus as overriding conerns, leaves Rawls's enterprise looking more "political" than "philosophical." Because it is focused on establishing agreement on the acceoptaance of certain ideas rather than the proof of their truth, the Rawlsian model turns the activity of political philosophy into a political rather than a philosophical undertaking. Isn't political philosophy, we might argue, precisely the search for truth, involving argumentation about controversial metaphysical premises. Furthermore, in banishing such argumentation and subordinating the pursuit of truth to that of agreement, the members of society lose the opportunity to engage one another in a mutually enriching (if contentious) dialogical enterprise in which each substantive commitment is subject to questioning, articulation and, perhaps, renegotiation-a process that some might argue lies at the very core of democratic political life. It seems unlikely for the Gandhian (as for many others) that one's view on a matter of political justice will not already have been influenced by his commitment to a moral, philosophical, or religious view. Bracketing for political purposes our most fundamental religious or moral conviction does no good, for it is likely that we will be similarly divided on questions of political justice. Asserting the truth of the matter may be a necessary course of justification for certain kinds of political action, for political change is often driven by engaging rather than avoiding the comprehensive moral and religious doctrines at stake. For instance, it is difficult to see how one might have argued for the injustice of slavery without recourse to some comprehensive moral or metaphysical form of argumentation.

For all these reasons, the Rawlsian model imposes considerable costs on the activity of political philosophy and on political life itself, costs that can be avoided by the Gandhian model. Because Gandhi saw politics as inseparable from morality or spirituality, his model views the task of political action as precisely the rough-and-tumble engagement between comprehensive doctrines, to be rigorously engaged rather than avoided. In contrast to Rawls, the Gandhian model explicitly allows—indeed calls for the parties to a conflict to draw upon their understanding of truth in taking actions of a political nature. At the same time, it provides a way that such truth claims can confront one another in the public realm, without leading to the sorts of dire consequences that Rawls fears. In providing political actors with a way for moving beyond dialogue and by subjecting such actions to certain requirements, the Gandhian model is able to provide a standard for judging the relative merits of each actor's truth claim. The criteria of episemological humility and self-scrutiny facilitate constructive public dialogue on controversial matters and issues, while non-violent suffering allows people to base their political judgments on moral convictions, yet present them for justification in the public realm without disrespecting or harming others.

Although arbitration on the Gandhian view pertains only to specific actions rather than belief systems, the convictions or belief systems underlying these actions are always brought to the fore in the course of political action. Furthermore, because only the advocates themselves suffer for their convicitons, this use of Absolute Truth in the public arena is not harmful. The civic virtue of non-violence allows strong believers to assert the power of their conviction in some ultimate reality, yet to dramatize the strength of this conviction if necessary, in a way that is peaceful and not threatening to others. Essentially, an act of self-suffering sends the message: "This is how strongly I feel about this matter. I am willing to suffer for it, not only to show you the strength of my conviction but also because I respect you as a fellow truth-seeker, and would like to persuade you of the truth as I see it. I don't intend to harm or ot humiliate you; I simply want you to see how important this is." It is worth mentioning that the Gandhian model does not resolve conflicts in any final or settled sense, for it is truth-seeking—rather than settled convictions in Absolute Truth—that is allowed into the political arena. This means that all political actions and decisions on the Gandhian view are seen as provisional and always subject to revision. If granted credibility, they are judged as the best available policy, action, or decision for the moment in a given instance rather than for all times and places.

In contrast to a thinker like Rawls who fears the destabilized potential of controversial moral claims and finds ways to avoid such conflict, the Gandhian takes this conflict to be a necessary and, perhaps, even a productive part of political life for it is the inevitable result of the sort of pluralism that characterizes truth-seeking itself. In this way, a Gandhian vision of political life. which allows a plurality of conflicting positions to engage one another rather than close off discussions about truth, provides for a far richer and more complex kind of politics—a kind of politics that understands the likelihood and even the necessity of political convictions that are fused often indissoludly and in complicated ways, with moral or religious views. Given the current backlash in many countries against models of politics that attempt to banish truth from the political arena, the Gandhian model may, in fact, be a more constructive way to engage those who wish to see political life reinfused with truth-seeking.

There are serveral other ways in which Gandhi's vision of political praxis provides a more realistic understanding of political life than its Rawlsian counterpart. For instance, Gandhi's emphasis on the necessity of suffering as a tool of political action suggests he is deeply attentive to the harsh reality that violence is a constant possibility in politics. Despite his insistence on the merging of politics and morality, Gandhi's vision suggests that he is simultaneously able to see the dark, conflictive, and often imperfect nature of the political world. This is, perhaps, why he insists so strongly on non-violent suffering as a tool to mitigate these recurring features, by structuring the requirements of political action accordingly—an understanding of politics that may be more pragmatic than one in which we assume that political conflict can altogeher be avoided by institutionalizing a kind of informed agreement in which the most controversial views of citizens are taken off the table.

Gandhi's vision recognizes another key feature of the political world. Inherent in all political action is always the possibility that one may have thrown the weight of one's moral and political effort behind an action or project that turns out to be wrong. We often seek, for instance, to reassure ourselves that the cost of political confict is worth it. Did we risk ourselves for the right cause? Embedded in such questions is the possibility, always lurking underneath, that our cause may not be right or our understanding of a matter misguided. The Gandhian requirements of episemological humility and non-violent suffering recognize and attempt to correct for this intrinsic risk to political action, instead of eliminating it altogether.

How, then does the Gandhian avoid the most violent and divisive turmoil that pluralists such as Rawls fear, given how willing he is to admit conflicting truth claims into the public arena? In the Gandhian view, the genuine pursuit of truth, if moderated by procedural requirements, need not necessarily lead to turmoil and violence. Another distinguishing feature of the Gandhian model is the priority of dispositional conditions over substantive commitments within the process of engagement. The dispositional requirement of the civic virtue of non-violence—that is, the sort of disposition that those engaging in non-violent action are expected to have—mitigate any potentially violent conflict among the underlying substantive commitments of the participants to the conflict. The public pursuit of truth about justice need not threaten the security of anyone in a pluralist society as long as guidelines exist for the interaction among people in their respective pursuits of the truth a commitment to pursuing relative rather than absolute truth, mutual respect, toleration of difference, the commitment to reasoned debate, and the disavowal of violence. A society should have nothing to fear from people who are earnestly committed to working out what is true—on a piecemeal, case-by-case basis, rather than in an absolutist way—and who are respectful of one another's attempts to formulate answers, even when the fundamental metaphysical commitments of each party are at stake. Anyone committed to the genuine pursuit of truth should do so on the basis of mutual respect and toleration and should therefore, not be likely to engage in the sort of violent conflict that pluralists, like Rawls, fear.

Certainly, in a pluralist society, reasonable disagreement may exist among well-intentioned persons exercising conscientiously their powers of reason and judgment in the course of political life. However, to take seriously the requirement of epistemological humility, for instance, causes one to think more deeply about one's stand than if one were simply staking out a position based on self-interest or convention. It also allows for a more reasonable and humble kind of disagreement among conscientious individual, a kind of disagreement that may, in the end, be more productive than destructive to political life. For example, I may take a stand based on the disciplined call of my conscience in any given instance. But let one say I do so while realizing that my adversary is worthy of respect as a fellow truth-seeker, and that his ideas should be accorded some presumptive respect, since they could potentially be more in tune with the truth than my own. Meanwhile, I scrutinize my own position and subject it to much rigorous examination. If reasonable people take such an approach, then the resulting disagreement, we may say, need not be all that disagreeable. In fact, if combined with the requirement of rational persuasion, it may produce a useful dialogue of philosophical depth, which forces the parties to articulate their own moral position and argue in the clearest possible terms. In the Gandhian view, the problem of conflict has less to do with substantive commitments to diverse truth claims than with the conditions under which debate over their convictions might occur.

This it might initially appear, to mirror the view of contemporary pluralists who call for rigorous engagement of conflicting view points through dialogue. What distinguishes the Gandhian position is that it provides for a final, active step-that of conscious self-suffering that dramatically brings one's position into relief, allowing the political actor to argue on the basis of an absolute conviction yet to do so without harming others.Conscious self-suffering adhers to presumptions about fellow human beings that are inherent in dialogical models of action and discourse, such as equal respect and toleration of difference, allowing this dialogical process to serve as the background or foundation for arbitration. However, it distinguishes itself in providing a non-violent step beyond such dialogue. The standard problem we encounter in dialogical models of political interaction pertains to the very shortcoming of dialogue itself. That is, when dialogue fails, we arrive at a deadlock in which each party digs their heels in. The only options we have traditionally been left with are power imbalances (one party decides to overwhelm the other through force and impose its own truth), cognitive apartheid (both parties simply ignore one another), or consensus-building (restricting ourselves to that about which we can agree, rather than arguing about the truth). The civic virtue of non-violence allows us to take a step further than all these alternatives in the confrontation of truth claims.

We have argued, therefore, that Gandhigiri serves as an alternative to contemporary understandings of arbitration and justification in cases of political conflict. It provides as more realistic understanding of political life and a more productive approach towards such conflict. In contrast to Rawls who tries to avoid the encounter of controversial claims and focuses on the pursuit of agreement, Gandhi allows for a non-violent way in which confliciting moral claims can engage one another, offering a realistic vision of politics that accounts for the strong connection between moral belief and political action. We want to end by suggesting that this contrast has certain implications for the project that we might call comparative political thought. As we creatively engage in a genuine comparison of models of political action emerging from diverse traditions, we enlarge and which our understanding of political thought beyond the narrow boundaries of the Anglo-American world.

9

Gandhi and Gandhigiri

> There is no such thing as 'Gandhism', and I do not want to leave any sect after me. I do not claim to have originated any new principle or doctrine; I have simply tried in my own way to apply the eternal truths to our daily life and problems. The opinions I have formed and the conclusions I have arrived at are not final. I may change them tomorrow.

Language in its communicative and playful functions, its literary formations and its shifting meanings – is a perennially fascinating topic. All of us know that words constantly take on new meanings since they do not necessarily, not even usually obliterate the old ones, we should picture this process not on the analogy of an insect undergoing metamorphoses but rather on that of a tree throwing out new branches, which themselves throw out subordinate branches in fact, as ramification. The new branches sometimes may overshadow and kill the old ones but by no means always. We shall again and again find the earlier sense of a word flourishing for centuries despite a vast overgrowth of later sense which might have been expected to obliterate them.

The philologist's dream is to deconstruct all the meaning of a word so as to have a perfect semantic tree of its every twig traced to its branch, every branch traced back to the trunk. But there is apparently some real danger of forgetting that overwhelming majority of those who use the word neither know nor care anything about the tree.

It is an important principle that enables this speaker to give half a dozen different meanings to a single word with very little danger of confusion. What is certain is that in ordinary language the sense of a word is governed by the context and this sense normally excludes all others from the mind. The proof of this is that the sudden intrusion of any irrelevant sense in other words – the voluntary or involuntary pun – is funny. It is funny because it is unexpected. There is a semantic explosion because the two meanings rush together from a great distance; one of them was not in our consciousness at all till that moment. When a word has several meanings, historical circumstances often make one of them dominant during a particular period. The dominant sense of any word lies uppermost in our mind.

It will be diagnosed by man as a symptom of the inveterate snobbery of the human race; and certainly the implication of language is hardly ever egalitarian. A word like nobility begins to take on its social and ethical meaning when its refers not simply to a man's status but to the manners and character which are thought to be appropriate to that status.

In recent years many words have entered into popular imagination, media vocabulary and public discourses. Words like 'netagiri', 'dadagiri', 'goondagiri', 'babagiri', 'votegiri' and recently 'Gandhigiri' have become buzz words. In the post-*Lage Raho Munnabhai* period, Gandhigiri is swiftly catching the imagination of the people. Gandhigiri based on the simple weapons of truth and non-violence, unleashed an indomitable moral force which not only aroused Indians to free themselves from colonial oppression and social injustice, but inspired millions of people all over the world in their quest for freedom, justice and a life of dignity. It continues to do so to this day.

All his life Mahatma Gandhi pursued one thing: spiritualism. He was ever in quest of God. Whatever he did, or advocated, was based on that one single factor. And he was convinced about it. For him, Truth is God.

Gandhi was a unique phenomenon, a man of many parts. He combined political shrewdness with religious and moral ideals—a rare feat indeed. He took politics to India's villages and created a potent political force based on ahimsa and spirituality. As the British historian Arnold Toynbee pertinently noted, "After Gandhi, humankind would expect its prophets to live in the slum of politics."

Gandhi could have chosen to seek 'moksha' for himself and leave the struggle for independence to others. But he would have none of it. His goal was to change society and use his own spiritual power for the good of humanity. He was as much in politics as he was in pursuit of God and there was no way of saying how to separate the two Gandhis. Rightly Bhikhu Parekh writes: "He [Gandhi] was a man of action desperately anxious to acquire the enormous power he needed to change his society. It was, therefore, not enough for him to possess the powers naturally resulting from self-realisation. He had to be sure he had them, he had to transform them into political power, and he had to deploy them consciously to secure the desired political and social objectives."

The search for God was, however, the mainspring of all his actions. Gandhi once wrote:

> What I want to achieve, what I have been striving and pining to achieve these thirty years [this he was writing in 1925] is to see God face to face, to attain *moksha*. I live and move and have my being in pursuit of this goal. All that I do by way of speaking and writing, and all my ventures in the political field, are directed to this same end.

Given the circumstances, one wonders whether, if there was no Gandhi in the first quarter of the 20th century, there would have been need to invent one. What is true and has seldom been contradicted is that the times proclaim the man. In 1940, Britain needed Winston Churchill, not Neville Chamberlain. In 1920, India needed someone other than Bal Gangadhar Tilak and that was Gandhi. Given India's long and painful history, would anybody, apart from a Gandhi, have been able to successfully combat the British?

Many questions remain unanswered. Could Gandhi have internalised his quest after the Supreme and led the Congress in secular terms? Then he would not have been a Gandhi. Could he have stuck to his quest but remained outside politics like latter day Sant Tukarama or Kabir? Then India would have been deprived of a titanic leader. Perhaps Indian society would have changed even without a Gandhi because of the onset of technology and globalisation. All these issues may be highly speculative and debatable but what cannot be denied is the impact that Gandhi has had on people all over the world and the legacy he has left behind. It is a validation of Gandhi's philosophy that across the world social activists and leaders have chosen to follow his principle of militant non-violence. Martin Luther King Jr. was greatly influenced by

Gandhi's ideology of non-violent social protest. The Dalai Lama has acknowledged the inspiration he has received from Gandhi's teachings. Nelson Mandela and Aung San Suu Kyi have fought oppressive regimes drawing upon Gandhi's legacy.

Gandhi had no intention of founding a new cult or establishing a following to preach his doctrine. In fact, he professed to a "horror of *'isms'*." He believed in the unifying nature of ahimsa and its power to create unity in diversity. A new cult would go against the very definition of ahimsa by further dividing people. He, therefore, discouraged people from deifying him in any way.

> There is no such thing as 'Gandhism', and I do not want to leave any sect after me. I do not claim to have originated any new principle or doctrine; I have simply tried in my own way to apply the eternal truths to our daily life and problems. The opinions I have formed and the conclusions I have arrived at are not final. 1 may change them tomorrow.

Gandhi never encouraged blind faith, insisting that every doctrine had first to be tested with reason before it was accepted. If "Gandhism" was anathema to him, how would Gandhi have reacted to "Gandhigiri", the phenomenon that has recently swept the country thanks to Bollywood's *Lage Raho Munnabhai.* It is astounding that almost sixty years after the Mahatma's death his ideology has been brought back to life by making it applicable to our changing times. The film brings Gandhi and his ideals to the masses in a contemporary, acceptable format. It presents him, not as the grim, dour, to-be-revered personage of our history books, but as a cool, practical, sympathetic man of exemplary stature whose philosophy has much to offer to today's young generation.

Gandhi always emphasised, satyagraha is not of the weak. Force is essential to overcome any wrong, except that the nature of the force has to be non-violent. And to be able to exert such force, as Gandhi did, one has to first rid oneself of all vestiges of violence. Gandhigiri, too, is about such a force—a moral force. It implies persuading the opponent to stop his wrong-doing or oppression by changing his very attitude. It is a fundamental, positive transformation of a person, which can only be accomplished through peaceful, non-violent means. Instances of people using Gandhigiri to redress difficult situations in their day-to-day lives have been reported from all over the country and foreign lands.

Whether Gandhigiri has come to stay, and how much it will succeed, only time will tell. Whether militant non-violence can become a successful weapon in combating the ills of a world greatly changed since Gandhi's times, remains a question mark. But the Mahatma would surely be happy to know that Indians have woken up to his philosophy and are assimilating it into their lives in whatever measure they can. After all, it was the dedicated, non-violent pursuit of the goal that mattered to Gandhi. Truth shall always remain truth, and what the Gandhigiri phenomenon clearly points to is the adaptability and relevance of Gandhi's ideas for all times. In the words of M.V. Kamath, "Gandhi's thought is visionary; his approach rational; his ideals universal; and his philosophy of truth and non-violence, manna for our troubled world." To quote the irreverently delightful words of Munnabhai: *Bande mein tha dum* (the man had guts),

The satyagraha movement changed the course of history. It first won respect, though limited, for Indians living in racist South Africa. It then brought freedom to India from the mightiest colonial power of the day. It went on to serve as a guiding spirit to some remarkable personalities in their own struggles. Badshah Khan, Nelson Mandela and Martin Luther King Jr. come readily to mind.

September 11 in our own times has become a nightmare in our collective memory. Ironically, it was also on the 11th day of September in 1906 in Johannesburg that a young lawyer, dissatisfied with the idea of mere passive resistance, unveiled the concept of "Satyagraha". The lawyer Mohandas Karamchand Gandhi described satyagraha as a "force which is born of truth and love of non-violence." He insisted that non-violence is the greatest force at the disposal of mankind. It is mightier than the mightiest weapon of destruction devised by the ingenuity of man.

In his design of satyagraha, the empowerment of the weakest was fundamental and means were as crucial as ends. He did not claim to have originated any new principle or doctrine. He was always at pains to point out that, in his own way, he was trying only to apply the eternal truths to daily life and its problems. Satyagraha and all that it entailed was a completely novel mode of mass mobilization and non-violent action. Over the years, it was used with dramatic effect. It showed how the individual can bring about social and political change.

Respect for tradition was combined with bold iconoclasm. A life of contemplation was lived with galvanic energy and titanic spirit. A personality unyielding in principle was also flexible in praxis. Austerity was his hallmark, Ahimsa his creed. Everything he thought, everything he did was open to public scrutiny. Never has there been a man who was so merciless in self-criticism and self-reproach. Never has there been a man more unremitting in self-analysis and self-healing. He once remarked that self-purification was fundamental to satyagraha. Thus, while we reflect on what he taught us, we should not forget how he lived. It is this coming together of thought, word and deed that is unique to Gandhigiri. .

I have not written this book to celebrate Mahatma Gandhi once more, or to simply add to the Gandhian bibliography, so to speak. I have written this book not just to recall what Mahatma Gandhi said and did yesterday but to explore what he might say and do today. We must engage in public debates and discourses to learn from each other, to share our experience, to reignite the spark of hope amidst the indifference and cynicism that afflict us. Although much of what he did has to be seen in the specific context of his times, the core of his philosophy reverberates even more strongly today.

Gandhigiri has four specific but interrelated themes. First, a non-violent approach to conflict resolution and peace building. Second, for poverty eradication, education and people's empowerment. Third, dialogue among people and cultures. Foruth, towards a nuclear weapons- free and non-violent world order.

The end of the Cold War has not seen a worldwide resurgence of peace as we might have hoped. Democracy has certainly spread. But sometimes democratic forms can mask and mystify undemocratic practices. There has certainly been a growth of nationalism. But too often, this nationalism, in the guise of chauvinism and jingoism, is stoking prejudice with horrifying consequences. We continue to witness outbreaks of large-scale violence across the world targeting innocent men, women and children. Millions have been killed and displaced from their homes.

We are today faced with the scourge of terrorism fuelled by religious, political, ethnic or sectarian conflict. In too many parts of the globe, societies are in discord, nations are at war, human security at risk. In a number of cases, violence is the cry of the oppressed and the exploited. It is a sad reality that in many instances violence has to be romanticized in order to be heard.

In the immediate aftermath of Hiroshima, Gandhi has said that the moral to be legitimately drawn from the supreme tragedy of the bomb is that it will not be destroyed by counter-bombs, even as violence cannot be destroyed by counter-violence. Humankind has to get out of violence only through non-violence. Since then, nuclear weapons have become more of a terrifying reality. They have become the very currency of power. The world's nuclear weapon states have more than adequate atomic arsenal to destroy humanity many times over. And it is not just nuclear weapons. We also confront the spectre of chemical and biological weapons.

Yes, India has nuclear weapons. This becomes India's strategic compulsion born out of the failure to persuade the world to abolish nuclear weapons. But the commitment to comprehensive, universal nuclear disarmament remains Indias' profound conviction and commitment which we intend to carry forward.

While the underlying causes of conflict have to be understood, we should not rationalize, justify, let alone glorify violence in any way. It provides no lasting solutions. It leads to untold suffering and atrocities. Gandhi was decidedly against the idea that violence is the only answer to violence. He philosophically remarked: "An eye for an eye only ends up making the whole world blind."

Globalization is a double-edged sword. It has had both positive and negative effects. It has offered both hopes and fears. It has certainly expanded opportunities and possibilities for many in the developing world but it has also left many poor countries behind with uncertainties. Moreover, even in the countries that have reaped the fruits of economic expansion, there are regions and communities that have become poorer, at least in the relative sense. Our own country, for instance, has made spectacular gains over the past decades and is being rapidly transformed. But destitution, poverty, malnutrition and illiteracy are still widespread. Inequality is very much visible.

We live in an age of incredible scientific achievement and awesome technological innovation and advance. But are not the fruits of this achievement and advance still inequitably distributed? Is it not the case that a few enjoy the gains, while many bear the pains? We must accelerate economic growth. But should we not be mindful of possible adverse consequences of that progress and take steps to deal with them? Can we not have development with a human face? Can we not satisfy material wants and aspirations without threatening ecological security and planetary survival?

Does economic progress have to be necessarily accompanied by the spread of social bigotry, as we see in many places? Must gender and disadvantage continue to be synonymous? To be equitable, economic growth has to be sustainable. To be sustainable, economic growth has, in turn, to be all-inclusive. The 'mantra' will no longer be the Benthamite doctrine of the "greatest good of the greatest number". It is actually "sarvodaya", or "the rise of all". This idea is captured by Gandhi's statement that "the earth provides enough to satisfy every man's need, but not every man's greed." In this simple statement on sustainable development Gandhi showed us the value of high thinking and simple living. The concern for our environment that now envelops civil society across the globe is best articulated by this simple statement. We do sincerely believe that the world cannot sustain the vulgar lifestyles of the affluent. We need a new development paradigm that caters to everyone's need and can tame human greed.

Gandhigiri has equally great relevance to our world today, because this idea can foster peace between peoples, cultures, nations and civilizations. Gandhi proclaims "I do not want to stay in a house with all its windows and doors shut. I want a house with all its windows and doors open where the cultural breezes of all lands and nations blow through my house. But I refuse to be blow off my feet by any." This pluralism, this liberalism, this commitment to an open society, an open polity, and an open economy, is what shaped our national movement under Gandhi's leadership. These wise words must guide us all in this era of globalization

The essence of Gandhigiri is the empowerment of every individual, irrespective of caste, class, race, creed or community. Representative democracy is the institutional form in which modern societies have sought to empower individuals. Democracy is not just about periodic elections. Democracy is not just about keeping alive democratic institutions. Democracy is about tolerance. Democracy is about asserting the right to dissent. Democracy is about protecting the dignity, autonomy and self-respect of every human being. We must respect the value of dissent. But those who dissent must also respect the value of building a viable consensus. We must foster tolerance for the other point of view. Every one has a right to be heard, and must be heard. We must learn to listen to the other point of view. Violent conflict never allows this. Violence deafens us. Non-violence helps us to hear. A civilized society must offer space for discussion and dialogue. All human progress must be based on the firm foundation of social consensus. But in a modern democracy, we must respect the role of institutions that seek to create and translate the consensus into policy action.

While Samuel P. Huntigton is surly wrong to advance the idea of a "clash of civilizations," a civilization of clashes is today's reality. That is what makes dialogue among cultures and peoples urgent. Dialogue to be meaningful has to be infused with a sprit of accommodation, compromise, reconciliation, respect and humility. Gandhi once declared that intolerance is the worst form of violence. Without genuine tolerance, without that tolerance that springs from within, no dialogue can have an enduring impact. Of course dialogue is between peoples and among cultures. But Gandhi did more than this. His external engagement proceeded from a ruthless internal interrogation of himself. That is what made Gandhigiri unique. He was not always successful, as he himself admitted more than once. But he never abandoned his pursuit. For us to follow in his footsteps, we need to rid our minds of stereotypes that condition us to act with hostility and hatred towards others. We divide the world as 'we' and 'they'.

Gandhigiri is based on universal ideals. Many "isms" battle for colonizing our minds, but few succeed in touching our hearts. Many political ideologies have come and gone over the past century, some with doubtful legacies and others with tragic consequence. The only political philosophy that will remain relevant for us as long as humankind seeks peace—peace in our societies, peace between nations and peace with nature—will be the ideas and values we associate with Gandhi. These ideas and values are today remembered not just when we gather to celebrate the life and teachings of Gandhi. They are remembered across the world when his disciples—like Martin Luther King Jr., Nelson Mandela, Bishop Desmkond Tutu, Vaclav Havel, Lech Walesa, and scores of others have opted for the path of non-violence in the struggle for purposeful social change.

If there is one message India should be remembered for, and identified with, it is the message of the Gandhi the message of tolerance, of pluralism, of the need to "live and let live". Every civilized society must respect human freedom, must care for the poorest of the poor and must enable the coexistence of all religions, all languages, all castes, all races, all classes, all colours and all creeds.

Our pluralism is our biggest and most enduring tribute to Gandhi. As long as the 'idea of India' lives in our hearts and minds, the legacy of the Mahatma will live on. This 'idea of India' is the idea of 'unity in diversity'. The idea of pluralism, the idea that there need be no 'clash of civilizations', the idea that it is possible for us to facilitate and work for a 'confluence of civilizations is essence of Gandhigiri.' These ideas have a universal, a truly global relevance. The non-violent resistance movements in Hungary, Poland, Czechoslavakia from the late 1950s to the late 1960s, were all met by brute force. But in the late 1980s and the early 1990s, the moment had clearly come in these movements which could actually bring in independence and self-determination.

Writing about Gandhi in the year 2000, Nelson Mandela called him a 'sacred warrior' and he pointed out—a point that Mr. Rutelli made as well—that Gandhi's real political brilliance lay in going against the prevalent wisdom of any particular moment in time. And this is what Mandela said: "At a time when Freud was liberating sex, Gandhi was reining it in; when the dominant European thought had dropped God and soul out of the social reckoning, he was centralizing society in God and soul; at a time when the colonized had ceased to think and control, he dared to think and control; and when the ideologies of the colonized had virtually disappeared, he revived them and empowered them with a potency that liberated and redeemed."

In Union Square in New York, there is a very beautiful statue of Gandhi that was built by the trade unions of America. Everyday there must have been 500 or 600 bouquets around that statue. People went to Union square and to Gandhi statue to somehow seek a way of dealing with the violence of 9/11 that would not be retaliatory or vengeful in any way. Something else we should recall is that in the aftermath of 9/11—and this is not to do with the US Administration, it is to do with perhaps different collections of American people—six states in America introduced Gandhian teachings into their textbooks, which is something astounding.

The point that Gandhi made are so relevant to us even today. In 1947, talking about India, Gandhi said: "If India takes up the doctrine of the sword, she may gain momentary victory. But then India will cease to be the pride of my heart. What policy the National Government will adopt, I cannot say, I may not even survive it, much as I would love to." This is, of course, just about nine months before he was assassinated. "If I do, I would advise the adoption of non-violence to the utmost extent possible, and that will be India's great contribution to the peace of the world and the establishment of the new world order." He added: "Democracies face a problem that obviously dictatorships do not. Violence and democracy do not co-exist well".

It would be very interesting to know that in 1942, somebody asked Mahatma Gandhi, "What are you talking about? Why don't you talk about socialism? Look at what is happening in the Soviet Union. It would be good if you look at the socialist experiment and talk about socialism rather than what you are talking about." This was in 1942. And he said, "Let the Soviet example live at least 50 years. If it survives 50 years, then we must give a thought to it, then we will think about it." Now look at the fate. Almost to prove Mahatma Gandhi right, exactly after 50th year of this statement, the Soviet empire collapsed. So, how do we reconcile justice and freedom? This is what Mahatma Gandhi wrote. This is his dialogue on Swaraj: "Where truth is not only the truth of the material self but truth also of the spiritual self of an individual."

He further said, "An India reduced in size but purged in spirit may still be the necessity of the non-violence of the brave." Finally, he averred: "If I can have nothing to do with the organized violence of the Government, I can have less to do with the unorganized violence of the people. For me, popular violence is as much an obstruction in our path as Government violence. Indeed, I can combat government violence more successfully than popular violence. For one thing, in combating the latter, I will not have the same support as in the former." This is, of course, something we know very well. Governments really look at the short end of the stick when it comes to the issues of violence. Mandela pointed out how valid Gandhi's ideas on the decentralized or the small-scale society were for today's globalized world. Again, Gandhi very strongly and earnestly argued that centralization as a system is inconsistent with the democratic and non-violent society. This, of course, is a great experiment for the European Union today, faced with the riddle of how to build a really democratic and non-violent Europe without appearing to be weak and divided as they were on the Iraq war.

The most corrosive crisis that our society is facing, is often not manifested as a dramatic political episode. It rather reveals itself in periodic outbreaks of senseless violence or grim reminders of society losing its moral compass. Just the random perusal of news for a couple of days, rioting in Agra, violence in Dohna, inhumane torture of a petty offender in Bhagalpur, road range, a child dead because of petty street clashes, increasing crime, the sordid goings-on in a Delhi school, were all reminders of just how fragile a social order can be. Given the dramatic character of political violence in India—terrorism, naxalism, communalism—should we really worry about outbursts of violence that traffic accidents occasion? And in each instance don't we have a ready structural explanation for violence, a master narrative that explains it all? When the sate has no outlet for legitimate grievance, violence will erupt. The surprise is not that we often have senseless violence without an object; the surprise is that we don't have more of it.

After the now already forgotten Nithari can any news of an insidious sickness creeping on Indian society really surprise us? But we focus on side issues: the fundamental question: why is India becoming a society with a reputation of preying on its own children in the most appealing ways one can imagine? Rightly a social scientist, Pratap Bhanu Mehta says: "There is an unspoken dread enveloping urban India; a new freedom producing new vulnerability, a new sophistication accompanied by a loss of innocence, a new sense of aspiration accompanied by a greater sense of danger."

Different types of violence have their own psychology and sociology. But there is a thread that connects seemingly disparate forms of violence that lurk under the surface of our existence. The first is our attitudes to them. The minute we encounter such violence a kind of containment strategy sets in. We control the meaning of these events, by explaining them in terms of some master narrative: the omissions of the state, the inherited inequalities of society or the depravations of tradition. But the ease and frequency with which these are invoked suggests not so much a diagnosis but an avoidance strategy. We oscillate between thinking that this is a violence that always happens elsewhere on the one hand, and it is over-determined and inevitable on the other. Either way this violence becomes something that does not demand our intervention.

The second thing this violence draws our attention to is just how attenuated our conceptions of social order have become. Societies are complex entities, held together not so much by a state but by an amalgam of attributes: mores, traditions, sensibilities, sympathies, taboos, reciprocities, even an aesthetic. In a society that is rapidly changing, these are all coming under immense stress. When a democratic country take to violence, it may undermine the very nature and fundamentals of that democratic polity. That, of course, is not the case with dictatorships.

Hindu psyche has an ambivalent attitude towards violence. It has not condemned violence outright. On many occasions, it has condoned violence and authorized the rulers to use violence for the sake of 'rashtra'. Our scriptures, shastras and epics even have justified and legitimized the use of violence. In *Ramayana*, *Mahabharata* and other *Purans* we have ample evidence of glorifying violence. This justificatory attitude towards violence has reflected in the speeches and writings of nationalist leaders during the freedom struggle.

As part of its celebration of the 60th anniversary of Independence, a leading newspaper ran a series of exhortations from nationalist leaders of the past. One came from Subhas Chandra Bose. Addressing a rally in Burma in July 1944, Bose said that "men, money and materials cannot by themselves bring victory or freedom". All patriots, he continued, "should have but one desire today – the desire to die so that India should live—the desire to face a martyr's blood". Bose ended his speech with these stirring words:

> "Friends! My comrades in the War of Liberation! Today I demand of you one thing, above all. I demand of you blood. It is blood alone that can avenge the blood that the enemy has split. It is blood alone that can pay the price of freedom. Give me blood and I promise you freedom."

It was once the conventional wisdom that Indian Independence was achieved through a popular mass movement led by Mahatma Gandhi. This freedom struggle was celebrated precisely because it was on satyagraha and ahimsa, on a morally robust, truthful, and non-violent means of collective protest. While that wisdom is endorsed by most historians, some scholars have argued that the British might have quit India much earlier had they been faced with a well organized armed struggle. Some others have claimed that the British quit India when they did not because of Gandhi or the Congress or the official discussions on the transfer of power, but because they had succumbed to fear and panic in the wake of the popular support for the returning soldiers of the Indian National Army. The nervousness of the British was reinforced by the revolt of the naval ratings in 1946. And so they left, before being forced to leave.

This historical revisionism is both provoked and reinforced by a strong current of public opinion. Gandhi is held to be the Father of the Indian Nation. But many Indians would rather argue that India had placed someone else on that pedestal. The prime candidate on the right is Vinayak Damodar Savarkar, a hero to the RSS and the BJP who, between them, were successful in installing his portrait opposite Gandhi's in the halls of Parliament. The prime candidate on the left is Bhagat Singh who, since his death at the hands of the British in 1931, has become a hero to leftists and Marxists of all shades and stripes. The latest to claim him are the Naxalites, who, to stave off the accusation in their icons are all foreigners—as in the notorious slogan 'China's Chairman is our Chairman' – have now started speaking reverentially of the martyred Sikh.

Beyond Left and Right, there is the fascinating, intriguing, figure of Subhas Bose. Although he was stoutly secular and by no means a card-carrying communist, both the BJP and the CPI(M) have sought at various times to claim him. But his popularity is not confined to political parties or programmes. Many ordinary Indians also admire him, as witness his presence on posters and calendars in middle-class homes across the land. Bose's appeal is enhanced by the fact that for the bulk of his career he operated within the mainstream of, indeed at the very top of, the national movement. He was twice elected President of the Indian National Congress. That he then broke away from Gandhi and company and forged an alternative path of his own places him in a different category from Savarkar and Bahgat Singh.

However, despite these differences in personality and philosophy, from the historian's point of view, Savarkar, Bhagat Singh and Bose are akin in two crucial respects—namely, that both opposed Gandhi, and that both opposed him on the question of non-violence. It is in this that their continuing appeal lies. For many Indians believe that had freedom came at the price of our collective blood, it would have come sooner, and it would have been more comprehensive. What India needed, these Indians believe, was a real revolution—a revolution that would have swept away the cobwebs of colonialism, allowing the new nation to lay its foundations on principles altogether different from what the British bequeathed us. For the Right, the correct national principles would have been drawn from the classical or mythical Hindu past; for the Left, on the models already provide by the Russian and Chinese revolutions. What we got instead—so the argument runs—was a derivative political system, borrowed uncritically from our erstwhile colonizers.

In the eyes of these critics, a real, that is to say violent, revolution, would have restored to the Indian people a sense of self-confidence, so cruelly dented by the rulers who had crushed and oppressed them. The Right principally identify the rulers with alien religions—hence the Hindutva claim that the Hindus had suffered for a thousand years at the hands of first Muslim and then Christian invaders. On the other hand, from the perspective of the Left, the rulers were representative of exploitative economic forces. It was not that the Mughals were Muslims—it was that they were feudal. And the Christian faith of the British was irrelevant—what mattered was that their regime was capitalist and imperialist.

Savarkar and Bhagat Singh, and their followers and epigones, represent political tendencies that can be clearly identified. These are a religion-based nationalism in the one case, and a class-based socialism in the other. These political trends, of course, are not restricted to India. In different shapes and guises, they have emerged and re-emerged in other parts of the world. The politics of Subhas Bose in his last phase was a more curious amalgam, a mixture unique to himself, a mish-mash of ideologies both Western and Indian. He certainly favored an assertive and interventionist state. His admiration for a strong state, however, was ecumenical. He began by praising Soviet Russia, but ended by allying with Nazi Germany and Fascist Italy. In his worldview there are also traces of Indian or more especially Bengali influence—the call for blood sacrifice, for example, must come from the traditions of Kali worship in his native province.

In the end, though, these varying traditions and ideologies are united precisely by that call for blood. Blood must be spilled, and plenty of it: whether to build a Hindu Rashtra, a Socialist Utopia, or a Boseian India. One's own blood, and the blood of one's enemies. As it happened, India won Independence chiefly through the means of non-violence, and India consolidated its Independence through multi-party democracy rather than by a single-party dictatorship or Left or Right.

As it happens, those who lost the political argument continue to have millions of followers and admires. The chief architect of Indian freedom was Gandhi; the chief architect of Indian democracy, Jawaharlal Nehru. However, were a poll taken among middle-class men, Savarkar, Bhagat Singh and Bose would all garner more votes than Nehru and in some states and among certain communities and classes – even more votes than Gandhi.

But Gandhi strongly neutralised this public opinion in favour of violence. He ruthlessly condemned violence in any form. This is what he said about terrorism: "I do not regard killing or assassination or terrorism as good in any circumstances whatsoever. This includes revolutionary terrorism. I do believe that ideas ripen quickly when nourished by the blood of martyrs." We would like to stress that sentence because it shows what clear political understanding Gandhi had of how mass ideologies and mass force works. "But a man who dies slowly of jungle fever in service, bleeds as certainly as the one of the gallows, and if the one who dies on the gallows is not innocent of another's blood, he never had ideas that deserve to ripen." In conclusion, while about terrorism, he also says, "The only way to deal with violence is to understand what is the root cause of that violence'.

Modern civilization is grappling with one very intrinsic problem—the inability to reconcile justice and freedom—the two governed by political and spiritual needs of human beings. In Swaraj he showed how these harmonies. When Western civilization upholds freedom, it brutally violates justice; and when from its own womb socialism came up with promise of justice, it brutally violated human freedom.

Every human being, of whatever colour, creed, class or nationality, is naturally born with two most fundamental quests. One is the quest for freedom. We can see the most of human history is replete with wars for freedom. Another similar quest which is more powerfully explosive is the quest to be loved and to love someone, to be selfless, to make sacrifice. The quest for justice is only the other side of the same coin of the quest for love and sacrifice. These are the two quests and in modern times we do see that when some nations have tried to maximize freedom, they did it through employing human reason to its best ability. The West did this. The Western civilization, the modern civilization is one of the best examples probably in the human history of exhausting human reason in order to find the truth about the material world. Right in the beginning, perhaps during the ancient Greek times, they decided that they cannot find the truth of the creation. What the West has achieved since is a marvel. They have finally reached the ultimate indivisible constituent of matter. Human reason thus employed only looked at the material side of the world and not at the spiritual side. So the spiritual side, the other truth of human existence, was unknown to Western civilization because the Western civilization was born out of this quest of reason in the middle centuries when the liberation of intellect demanded that everything that could put shackles on human reason must be rejected. So they rejected God, divinity, they rejected sacredness; they rejected everything that could not be perceived by the human senses. All those things which could not be perceived by human senses were thus declared untruth and all those things which could be perceived only by human senses, which today we call the 'infrastructure of modern science' were the only truth in the terms of modern civilization.

Mahatma Gandhi dialogued on the true spiritual culture of human beings. Spirituality to him does not have a separate compartment of its own. What is a human being? Human being by nature is non-violent. Non-violence is a human being's culture. There are different stimulates and therefore our other attributes are conflagrated and the attributes of non-violence are repressed. But in the most violent cultures, in the most violent person, if the right attributes are stimulated, you can grow non-violence in them. Mahatma Gandhi proved it and Badshah Khan is the greatest example. Pathans are known to be aggressive people, but what must be the great magic of that man who turned this most violent race into the best soldiers of non-violence. Similarly in Africa, this was proved, where manhood was attained only when one killed a lion. That Africa also showed us the great example of non-violence. Our problem in India, with Hinduism and with Islam is that we have lost the track of reasoned faith. Godless reason and reasonless religion are two curses of modern times.

Mahatma Gandhi's dialogue acquires a very great significance in today's times because those who have mastered human reason were earlier driven by the quest of freedom. They put human reason and rationality to the service of seeking freedom. But after 9/11 things have changed radically. The West is now driven, not by the quest for freedom. It is driven by fear. It has become fearful out of its own deeds. The same excellence of human reason is no more in the service of refining the meaning of human freedom. It is now hinged to fear, it is now employed entirely in the service of fear. Do we realize that this is the most deadly combination! Do we understand the meaning of this radical shift that the world has arrived at today? There can be no deadlier combination than the most excellent human reason being in the service of fear. And it has happened after 9/11. Where is a dialogue on human culture and civilization that can match this challenge? This 'is' the time therefore for a serious global dialogue on the paradigm Swaraj, the culture of non-violence.

When somebody asked Mahatma Gandhi the reason why he was talking about God and spirituality, he said: "Look reason is like

King of England, guided and controlled solely by its council of ministers, the senses." Our human reason is not pure. It is impure because it is captive of our self-interest, of desires, of our ego, our fears therefore. How to liberate human reason so that reason becomes purer and it does not become the weapon of exploitation, domination and of violence is the problem all peoples, cultures and nations have to face.

The force of love, the force of truth exists everywhere. Somewhere it manifests in certain higher levels, somewhere it manifests in certain lower levels, but it is never absent. Therefore, to paint anyone as just dark or to paint someone else as just the enlightened would be very wrong on the anvil of truth. Therefore, Gandhi's dialogue is on truth, the truth that combines the reason of the spiritual self and reason of the secular self.

Gandhigiri is now practiced by many people. But we shall keep in mind that it is a serious enterprise. Gandhi did provide a criterion which is sometimes forgotten. In conditions where cowardice and violence are the only alternatives, then violence is the lesser evil. In spite of giving the impression at times of seeing things in black and cons of a situation, and no decision was taken without thorough inquiry into the factors concerned, especially the human element, as was possible in the circumstances. That self-suffering will eventually move the heart of the opponent was an article of faith with him. But even if it did not, he believed it was better to be killed than to kill. He used the weapon of self-suffering over a period of many decades, beginning with the South African period of his life. He showed it could be used to alter economic, social and political situations, and the very movements he led of his life he confessed that the weapon was a new one, yet to be perfected, a technique which was still in an experimental form. Without the preliminary self-purification on which he laid such stress, the method, 'Gandhigiri' could degenerate into a form of blackmail or sheer coercion-'dadagiri'.

Mahatma Gandhi's courage of conviction, his all-encompassing compassion and spirit of service to humankind, his renunciation of power and its worldly trappings, and his unwavering self-discipline in practicing what he preached, imbued all his words and actions with a compelling moral authority. In a world riven with ethnic and religious conflict, terrorism, and growing emphasis on economic prosperity and the cost of human, social and environmental factors, Gandhigiri will provide tangible answers to many of the dilemmas and problems of modern society.

Great leaders leave behind a rich inheritance for posterity, making their indelible mark on the annals of world history. In this respect, Mahatma Gandhi was surely the towering figure of our times, whose philosophy of Satyagraha was a supreme example of the invincibility of the human spirit. His message is universal, timeless and eternal. His philosophy embraced all human kind, and was never confined by the narrow divides of national boundaries or barriers of religion or culture.

This volume is an attempt to bring together the essence of Satyagraha to the challenges confronting the world today, we believe it is imperative for the leaders of today, and especially for youth, to nurture and sustain Gandhian values for the generations to follow, so that Mahatma Gandhi's legacy continues to be our guiding light through the 21st century.

It is only natural to ask the question: is Gandhigiri feasible at all today? Can it prevail against terrorism and extremism? It would be a grave error to dismiss Gandhigiri as irrelevant to our age. There are individuals and groups who are trying to adapt and adopt Gandhigiri to deal with changing circumstances and situations. The challenge for us now is to find creative inspiration form Gandhigiri to evolve a Satyagraha appropriate to our times.

The relevance of Gandhigiri is not the real issue. Our preparedness for him is. The question is not whether Gandhigiri is relevant for us. Instead, it is whether we are ready to embrace it once again. It is not a question of going back to Gandhi as much as it is of going forward with him.

This is not as simple as it sounds. While he fascinates and enchants, we have to admit that it is difficult to emulate him. It is easy to make him an icon. But it is infinitely more exacting to make him our beacon. He did not provide us with final answers. He wanted us to find our own and make our own experiments with truth. The task before us is how we, individually and collectively, lunch as organized, disciplined mass movement for peace, non-violence and empowerment, which is the very essence of Gandhigiri.

A Fresh Look at Gandhigiri

Interestingly, Gandhi was an ordinary person like everybody in his times, except that he was sincere, rational, self-righteous, receptive to new ideas, obedient, and god-fearing. This ordinary person, who set out to become a barrister in search of success and prosperity, gradually became a rebel, due to perpetual attacks he faced on his personality, his existence as an independent, rational, moral and self-righteous individual. Particularly, the hostile racial, social, political, and economic conditions he faced in South Africa, made him a stubborn rebel. Up to this, the evolution of the personality of Gandhi was quite normal. But the path he had chosen to stand up against the state, society, and the civilization which he denounced as irreligious, devoid of any moral or spiritual foundation made him an extraordinary person rare to be found in several generations.

On the basis of his experiences, observations of the society, and experiments he made with his life, Gandhi developed an integrated approach and perspective to the concept of life itself. All this he did as an experiment for himself, was a continuous process of experimenting and perfection of ideas. He never claimed that his ideas were completely perfect or what he believed and preached was the only truth or the correct thing. Yet he firmly believed that what he preached and professed after careful experimenting and meticulous practice was the truth which could be relied on. His ideas, which came to be known as his philosophy, doctrines, principles, or ideas, were, in fact, as he himself admitted several times, part of his relentless search for the truth. Gandhigiri is a part of that relentless search for truth.

The concept of Gandhigiri therefore, is related to the social, political, cultural, economic, and psychological conditions which influenced the life and personality of Gandhi. Gandhigiri, thus, includes social, political, and moral and all other aspects of the life and struggles of Gandhi. The relevance, scope and application of this concept is essentially linked to the evolution, growth and perfection of the personality of Gandhi as an individual. Any attempt to trace the relevance of this concept necessitates a realistic riview of the circumstances and conditions that have paved the way for its evolution in the life of Gandhi.

The origins of the concept of Gandhigiri have been traced to the evolution of Gandhi as an individual trying to establish himself in severely trying, hostile socio-economic and political conditions. Though lie was greantly influenced by the epic characters like Prahlad, Buddha, and Jesus Christ about whom he studied when he was a child, he realized their importance and significance when he went through the socio-economic and racial repression during his early years in South Africa. As is known from his autobiography and other source, Gandhi was a meek, self-righteous and moral and yet a stubborn person from his childhood. Besides these qualities, the influence of mythological heroes like Rama, Harishichandra, etc. and the writings of Tolstoy, Thoreau, and Ruskin he came across when he grew up, provoked and inspired him to launch his relentless campaign of search for his own identity, which he did in his own unique way.

He adopted the non-violent approach to resist all the forces that exerted pressure on him physically and psychologically. He chose this method to assert his own existence, his beliefs, ideas, and what he thought was true or right. He did not use violence in his search for self-assertion and truth. He believed that violence was not necessary to support the cause of truth, as it is inherently strong and capable of supporting itself. He did not think it necessary or as justified to use violence in case what he believed and adopted was not true. According to him, on both counts non-violence was the appropriate course.

Holding on to the truth in a non-violent way requires inflicting or inviting suffering on oneself. Gandhi understood this, taking the examples of Prahlad and Jesus Christ. He maintained that this requires a sense of love for all and hence the satyagrahi should bear troubles and sufferings without any ill-will towards the opponent. Even if the opponent adopts violent methods and causes pain and injuris to him, it should be borne willingly without any grudge or hatred towards the perpetrator. Suffering for the cause of the truth, according to Gandhi, is the process of self-purification. In this process, the satyagraha will emerge stronger at the end of that particular non-violent resistance.

Gandhi, if we can try to understand and analyze his non-violent approach, appears to be very practical and realistic in his given circumstances. For a person, living in an alien land and among enemies and facing a mighty force as the opponent with his back to the wall, there could be no honourable alternative other than this non-violent resistance. The type of resistance he had chosen reflects his personality, his will and the intensity of his self-assertion.

Spiritual influence and belief in the religion also had a profound role in the evolution of the doctrine of Gandhigiri. The experiments Gandhi made with truth and non-violence, which are the main pillars of Gandhigiri, were inspired by his faith in and commitment to the religion. He believed that the supreme law that governs the whole living things and the universe is nothing but love and non-violence. He argued that Gita implicitly carried the message of non-violence. It was Gandhi's firm belief that the basis of all religions of the world was the law of love. Moral and spiritual principles, for Gandhi, were not different from the social or political principles. The very purpose of non-violent resistance and upholding the principles of truth was nothing but the process of self-realization and realization of life itself, which from an individualist point of view is none other than asserting the freedom of one self over his mind and body. Satyagraha, which Gandhi designated as the "soul force," and rightly so, was basically his own soul force, meant for the self-realisation of Gandhi himself. Though Gandhi declared it to be of universal application, it was designed, developed, and perfected according to the inner strength (soul force) of Gandhi himself. Therefore the evolution and practice of Gandhigiri was individualistic but he sought to apply it universally because he had the confidence that the Indian masses would accept it as a means of their salvation, which in the immediate sense was freedom from foreign rule.

The origins and evaluation of Gandhigiri had something to do with the personality of its architect. Gandhi, self-conscious, morally bound and self-righteous person, never allowed any external force or authority to dominate him. He believed that he was subjected to the law of morality and as he started experimenting with truth and non-violence, it was strengthened on a firm basis. The external conditions and socio-political restrictions confronted him challenging his personality, conscience, and freedom, which he did not want to compromise. Thus he resisted the external authority at every stage in his life as it clashed with his personality and character. Holding on to truth and following the law of morality and non-violence, and which he believed as the underlying principle of human existence, he developed this technique of conflict resolution-Satyagraha. As he started to gain success in his experiments with Satyagraha in South Africa, he designated it as a weapon of non-violence and soul-force. It was recognized as a weapon to resist, in a non-violent manner, oppression or unwanted pressure on one's mind or body. For Gandhi, Satyagraha emerged as the highest manifestation of his individual moral freedom.

Mamata Banerjee's fast unto death has opened the debate on the meaning and content of Gandhigiri. There was sympathy for Mamata Banerjee because her "fast unto death "over the issue of the Tata car factory at Singur in West Bengal and many people argued that in its fourth week, it had started taking a toll of her health. But this is a purely self-inflicted ordeal that she would be well advised to end as soon as possible. For, in a democracy where lawful methods are available for resolving every issue or dispute, there cannot be any room for the kind of technique she is using to achieve her political and personal objectives. To call what is going on blackmail would be no exaggeration.

Her supporters are bound to shout and scream that what the Trinamool leader is using is a potent 'instrument against injustice' devised by none other than Gandhi, and therefore she is only following the Mahatma to defend the rights of Singur farmers. To put it bluntly, such an argument is nothing short of an insult to the memory of the father of the nation. Gandhi was fighting a mighty empire on which the sun was supposed never to set. For six decades India has been independent and a functioning democracy through this period except the 19 dark months of the Emergency. This fact may have escaped those who are inclined to threaten a 'fast unto death' or sit on an indefinite dharna at the drop of a hat.

Moreover, those who use history selectively need to be told that the Mahatma usually fixed a time limit for his fasts though he did undertake a few 'fasts undo death' when the stakes were very high. One such occasion arose because of Babasaheb Ambedkar's demand for separate electorates for the Scheduled Castes. Eventually, Gandhi won his point. Ambedkar agreed to what is known as the Poona Pact. (Incidentally, long, long before Gandhi thought of a fast unto death, an Irish freedom fighter, Terence MacSweeny, had starved himself to death in a prison. But that is a different story.)

In independent India, Potti Sriramulu was the first individual to under take fast unto death in 1953. His cause was the separation of Andhra from what was then the Madras Presidency. Jawaharlal Nehru refused to succumb to this pressure because he realised that to do so would open the floodgate for similar blackmail. In fact, the first time the Mahatma undertook a 'fast unto death' in the thirties, Nehru was "shocked" by what he described as "primitive and irrational tactics" but his enormous love and reverence for Gandhi prevented him from voicing his critiusm publicly. The state of Andhra was formed, of course, but some months after Sriramulu's death, and this became the prelude to the redrawing of the country's political map along linguistic lines.

Nearly a decade before Pheruman, the much taller Akali leader —indeed the tallest at that time — Master Tara Singh had also undertaken a 'fast unto death' demanding that a Punjabi Suba be formed at once. It became something of a joke. As Nehru remarked in Parliament, "What kind of a fast it is that goes on and on?" The House laughed because most people knew that Masterji was taking care quietly to consume enough calories every night. Consequently, Tara Singh lost not only face but also the Akali leadership to Sant Singh.

Like her father, Indira Gandhi also looked the other way when an Akali member of the Rajya Sabha, Darshan Singh Pheruman, followed Sriramulu's example on the issue of transfer of Chandigarh to the Punjabi Suba she had conceded a few years earlier. The prolonged and farcical was the subsequent fast of the Shankaracharya of Puri who wanted a complete ban on cow slaughter. He did not save the cow and its progeny but lived a long and healthy life himself.

In a different class was the fast, also 'unto death', that Moraji Desai embarked upon in the spring of 1975. The Gujarat state assembly had been dissolved at the start of the year because of the famous Nav Nirman agitation. Desai was not alone in believing that Indira Gandhi was deliberately delaying the fresh poll, and demanded that it be held immediately. This time around her reaction was entirely different. She asked her confidant, Uma Shankar Dikshit, to fly to Ahmedabad. His brief: "Settle with Morajibhai whichever way you can."

Against this rather bizarre backdrop isn't it time to end not only the mounting crisis in Kolkata but also the unacceptably crass use of the weapon of fast unto death? Especially because compared with what Sriramulu, Pheruman and Moraji were seeking, the problem in Singur is simpler and relatively minor.

Both sides are agreed that half the land acquired at Singur is kosher. The dispute is about the other half (roughly 50,000 acres). Mamata and her followers assert that this land was acquired forcibly, not 'surrendered' voluntarily. To this Chief Minister Budhadeb Bhattacharjee's answer is that he is willing to discuss the problem and find a way out by consensus. However, the Trinamool leader characteristically insists that the state government should first cancel the allotment of land to the Tatas and that she would give up her fast and agree to talk only after this was done.

Understandably, the chief minister too has dug in his heels. There is no way he would say no to the Tatas because this is the surest way to block all private investment in West Bengal. It is the proverbial situation involving irresistible force and immovable object.

To resolve this deadlock, Prime Minister Manmohan Singh, former Prime Minister V.P. Singh, West Bengal Governor Gopal Gandhi and several others have earnestly appealed to Mamataji to give up her fast and hold talks with the state government. At the same time, the BJP, which has its own fish to fry, has joined the fray primarily to reinforce her obstinacy. This just shows how bereft of principles Indian politics has become.

Gandhigiri has become global

There are news that an Italian party has Gandhi on its flag and the Mahatma has become popular in Palestine

While in the centenary year of Satyagraha, Gandhi thrives in India under J.J. colonies of bacteria and on soiled rupee notes, he is in political currency in much of Europe, Palestine, South Africa and America.

Radicali Italiani is a political party that was part of the coalition running Italy till a few days ago, before it was brought down by the volatile politics of that country The flag of this organisation bears an image of Mahatma Gandhi. Emma Bonino, leader of Radicali Italiani (Italian Radicals), a 59-year-old single woman who is known to be a smoker, minister for international trade and European affairs in the previous Italian government, and a former European commissioner, has for almost 30 years been a "rigorous" practitioner of Gandhism.

"Gandhi's name has instant recognition in Italy," says Bonino. "He is there in great detail in school textbooks and we take him very seriously." While the greatest of 20th century polltical icons have fallen, been commoditised or been retired, Gandhi's political legacy is being perpetuated, albeit away from home. A giant graffiti depiction of Gandhi on the Israel-imposed separation barrier with Palestine, in a village that lies between Jerusalem and Ramallah. His statues still stand in New York, London and Pieterburg. In the last week of January, he was brought alive by peace crusaders like Desmond Tutu, Kenneth Kaunda and Ahmed Kathrada in New Delhi at the Satyagraha centenary celebrations.

"In Europe, we don't consider the mystical elements in Gandhi's writings relevant. But we follow his political methods. We believe in passive resistance," says Bonino, who was recently in Mumbai as part of an Italian trade delegation. "For us Gandhi is a political leader first."

"Active non-violence" is the creed of a pan-European alliance — the Transnational Radical Party—to which Bonino's party belongs. Gandhi's image has adorned Radicali Italiani's flag for 20 years. Its members frequently participate in hunger and thirst strikes, and its main political campaigns have been accompanied with acts of civil disobedience.

In America, in the run-up to the March 2003 invasion of Iraq, there were posters in university campuses asking, "What Would Gandhi Do?" And, when it was announced, before President George Bush's visit to India, that he would lay a wreath in honour of Gandhi, anti-war intellectuals across the US denounced the gesture as cynical, disrespectful and symbolic.

Three years ago when Hillary Clinton, campaigning for a Senate candidate, said in jest that Mahatma Gandhi used to run a gas sintation St Louis, the public reaction was so strong that she had to apologise immediately "No, Mahatma Gandhi was a great leader of the 20th century" she said. Going further, she quoted Gandhi, in the context of the candidate's underdog status, "First they ignore you, then they laugh at you, then they fight you, then you win."

In Palestine, Gandhi is providing a political alternative to people fighting the increasing territorial transgressions of Israel. Realising that little has been achieved through violence, a network of NGOs has launched a programme called the *Gandhi Project* to propagate the merits of non-violence and passive resistance in waging a struggle.

Gandhi has special appeal in Palestine. While he was sympathetic to the plight of European Jews persecuted by Hitler, he never gave in to endorsing Zionist territorial designs in the Middle East, and opposed the formation of Israel.

The Gandhi Project promotes his philosophy by hosting screenings of Richard Attenborough's film (dubbed in Arabic) in cities, villages and refugee camps throughout the Palestinian territories. There have been hundreds of screenings in Bethlehem, Jerusalem, Ramallah, Hebron, Nablus, on the separation wall at the Kalandia checkpoint and other places.

Bonino is optimistic about Gandhi's legacy: "Look at Europe. It's only through the last 50 years that we have lived in peace. Otherwise, the history of our continent is a series of bloody battles, of long and devastating wars. Some oi us try very hard to maintain peace."

Gandhigiri in the Twenty-first Century

Is Gandhigiri relevant to the present-day society or, so to say, to the twenty-first century? The answer is both "no" and "yes." Rather, it is not even simple yes or no.

When we try to decide whether it is relevant to the present-day society, the fundamental point we have to consider is the nature of the present-day individual. It is also necessary to consider the nature and characterstics of the present civilization in comparison with that civilization which Gandhi thought to be right. It is quite uncertain whether it suits the present-day individual, who wants to do things and get things done instantaneously, effectively, and emphatically. Self is the predominant preoccupation of the individual of the present generation, and everything that concerns this "self" is related to wealth or material well-being of the individual. Wealth, material prosperity, and power are final objectives of the present-day individual. Today's individual, who lives in atomized families, is more inward looking than the individual of any previous generation. Spiritual, moral, and civic virtues, which are essential qualities of a satyagrahi, do not have any significance in the modern society. The present-day individual is shrewd enough to use all of them according to necessity but at the same time does not attach any specific importance to them. In the present society, in the present socio-economic and political scenario, there is no place for Gandhigiri in its true sense. But, it is used as a means of achieving the desired objective depending on the circumstances. Generally the objectives are of pecuniary nature or related to power, position, or material benefits. While Gandhi advocated good means for good ends, for the individual of today, in general, Machiavellian means is acceptable only if it is capable of achieving the desired objectives, which also may not be good or rational.

Gandhi was well aware of the increasing influence of materialistic and hedonistic considerations on the modern society and individual. He wanted the satyagrahi to be away from the influence of wealth and other worldly desires. The discourse of the modern civilization is acquisition of wealth and comforts or luxuries as much as possible. Poverty which is a virtue to the satyagrahi, is a vice for the modern individual. Gandhian satyagrahi who is an uncompromising seeker of the truth and non-violence, who resorts to satyagraha not for his personal benefits but for the general welfare of the society or for assertion of the individual self as a moral and spiritual entity may not fit in the present-day social system. Following all the principles and conditions of satyagraha for the modern individual is not only very difficult but also almost impossible. It seeks too much of human nature. Satyagraha is no simple matter and that too for the individual in the fast changing socio-economic and political world, it is not possible to say about the legitimacy or efficacy of satyagraha. A true satyagrahi, dedicated to the principles of truth and non-violence and all that which it stands for, remains, to a large extent, unfulfilled like the Plato's *Republic*. As an integrated concept, satyagraha aimed at the spiritual and moral realization of the individual self. It was developed by Gandhi in the course of his own search for identity and self-realization. His experiences and experiments were carried out in an ambience which characterized racial discrimination, political oppression and economic exploitation by the alien people and external forces. His struggles opposed the basic character, policies, laws and actions of the state both in South Africa and in India, which negated his basic existence as an free, moral, and spiritual individual. The situation changed drastically in the post-independence India. It cannot be claimed by anybody that there was no oppression or exploitation in the preset socio-political set-up. Yet, it has to be said that the perception of the individual about the social and political values and issues has changed; the methods and approaches to tackle the problems have changed. Neither the individual nor the state has time and patience for the ideals like simplicity, morality, spirituality, bread labour, chastity, poverty etc. Laegitimacy of the state is based on the legality which is determined by the majority in the legislature, thus, rendering morality and rationality relatively less important. In the circumstances, the state itself resorts to violence to assert its legitimacy and authority. For the individual of today values and morality are not very much relevant, a share in the power and wealth has become a more important consideration for his allegiance to the state. Only when his share is denied, he resorts to some kind of struggles which need not be satyagraha of Gandhian type. Non-violence is a necessity but not a value or principle. Everything in the present civilization and political system, throughout the world, is judged on the basis of publicity and not on the basis of facts i.e., truth. Thus, *Satya* in the twenty-first century is a myth at the least and a relative concept at the most.

So much is the negative for satyagraha in the twenty-first century. It is so, if we take the principles and qualifications of satyagraha as postulated by Gandhi as static and unalterable. But that will be quite rigid and it restricts the use of this practice to a miniscule minority, if not altogether none. Revelance of any particular thing can be safeguarded and perpetuated when it is adapted to the changing circumstances and conditions. If we can accept the limitation and predicaments of the human beings and allow the practice of satyagraha with minimum restrictions, but of course, with the strict adherence of non-violence and the principle of love, then it can be relevant and useful for many many years to come.

It can be reminded, that according to Gandhi, the main objective of satyagraha was to eradicate the evil or to reform the opponent. In the present socio-economic-political system there is a dire necessity to wean away the individual from the influence of wealth, luxuries, and power. As the violence, strife into fevance and hatred are increasing, the social and political values are getting perverted. Lawlessness, corruption, greed, malice, and selfishness are contaminating the society and state making the individual devoid of rationality and the sense of right or wrong. Multiplicity of wants and craze for worldly pleasures are increasing the competition and rivalry among the people, relegating the ideals of simple living, charity, and integrity to the background. All these developments would not have pleased Gandhi. He wanted the self-realization of the individual, his freedom, and spiritual well-being. He would have advocated satyagraha as a panacea for all the maladies afflicting the twenty-first century society. But how far would he have been successful, is anybody's guess. Still, at least some modest change can be brought in thinking and activities of the people at large, if the concept of Gandhigiri is given proper publicity and people are made to practice the basic principles of non-violence, love, mutual respect, social responsibility and spiritual values.

As a political activist, social reformer, and a philosopher Gandhi's Satyagraha offers a highly original theory of social change. It may be accepted, if not in toto in practice, but at least as a theory aiming at the reformation of the individual and society, it is sound and plausible.

Relevance or irrelevance of a particular concept theory or idea is generally considered to find out as to what extent changes have taken place in the historical setting or socio-economic-cultural-political conditions. It is generally agreed that with the changes in the physical and psychological conditions pervading that particular concept, its applicability and efficacy diminishes gradually. This is true of all great things also. That is how, with the passage of time and the practice, applicability, and, efficacy of or the basic character and nature of society, culture and religion have changed beyond recognition. While the original idea retains its practice, application may assume new method and approach depending on the nature and spirit of the times. The idea or the main creator of the idea is remembered, revered, and deified but the idea itself corrodes in its actual practice in different places and times.

Gandhigiri is such an idea. It is remembered, admired, respected, and eulogized by the people of succeeding generations. Gandhigiri has become global. On 15th June, 2007 the United Nations General Assambly unanimously resolved to observe October 2, the birth anniversary of Mahatma Gandhi as the International Day of Non-violence. Gandhigiri is always the idea, it is the original, it can never be reproduced as original. However, as long as the idea is respected, emulated, and practised sincerely, there is always a chance to achieve some tangible results rather than giving it up as unpracticable and idealistic.

Appendix

Story of a Soldier of Truth [-1]

The heroic Socrates, *an* extraordinary person with a fine moral character, was born in 471 B.C. A Greek, he lived a virtuous and benevolent life. Unable to bear his moral excellence and his virtue, some envious persons made false accusations against him. Socrates lived in fear of God[1]and cared little for the obloquy of men. He had no fear of death. A reformer, he strove to cleanse Athens, the capital of Greece of the evil which had entered its political life and thus came in contact with a large number of persons. He made a powerful impression on the minds of the young who followed him about in crowds.

Socrates teaching had the result of putting an end to the unconscionable gains made by persons with predatory tendencies. It came in the way of those who lived by exploiting others.

In Athens it was an offence to disregard the traditional religion of the *polis* or encourage others t.o do so. The offence, if proved, was punishable with death. Socrates adhered to the traditional religion, but called upon the people to fight the corrupt elements associated with its observance. He himself would have nothing lo do with them.

Under the law of Athens, such offences were tried before a popular assembly. Socrates was charged with violating the religion of the state and teaching others to do likewise and was tried before an assembly of eliders. Many members of the assembly had suffered as a result of Socrates' teaching. Because of this, they bore him a grudge. They wrongfully declared him guilty and condemned him to die by taking poison. A prisoner sentenced might be put to death in any one of a number of ways. Socrates was condemned to death by poisoning.

This brave man took poison by his own hand and died. On the day of his death he discoursed to his friend and companion on the perishable nature of the human body and the immortality of the soul. It is said that up to the very last moment Socrates showed no fear, and that he look the poison smilingly. As he finished the last sentence of his discourse, he drank the poison from the cup as eagerly as we might drink sherbet from a glass.

Today the world cherishes Socrates' memory. His teaching has benefited millions. His accusers and his judges stand condemned by the world. Socrates has gained immortality and Greece stands in high esteem because of him and others like him.

Socrates' speech in his own defence was committed to writing by his companion, the celebrated Plato. It has been translated into many languages. The defence is excellent and imbued with moral fervour. We, therefore, wish to translate it, but rather than render it literally, we print only a summary of it.

We have much to struggle for, not only in South Africa but in India as well. Only when we succeed in these tasks can India be rid of its many afflictions. We must learn to live and die like Socrates. He was, moreover, a great satyagrahi. He adopted satyagraha against his own people. As a result the Greeks became a great people. If, through cowardice or fear of dishonour or death, we fail to realize or examine our shortcomings and fail to draw the people's attention to them, we shall do no good to India's cause, notwithstanding the number of external remedies we may adopt, notwithstanding the Congress sessions we may hold], not even by becoming extremists. India's good does not lie along that direction.

When the disease is diagnosed and its true nature revealed in public, and when, through suitable remedies, the body politic of India is cured and cleansed both within and without, it will become immune to the germs of the disease, that is, to the oppression by the British and the others. If, however, the body itself is in a state of decay, then if we destroy one kind of germs, it will be attacked by another, and this will ruin the body politic—India herself.

We argued thus and saw in the words of a great soul like Socrates the qualities of an elixir. We wanted our readers, therefore, to imbibe a deep draught of it, so that they might be able to fight-and to help others fight-the disease. It is with this objective in mind that we summarize Socrates's speech.

Indian Opinion, 4-4-1908

Story of a Soldier of Truth [-II]

"I cannot tell, O Athenians, how far you have been carried away by my accusers' words. For my own part, they nearly made me forget who I was, so plausible were they. But I say that their arguments are a lie. Among their falsehoods there was one which astonished me most. They asked you not to be misled by my eloquence. It is they who are rhetorical. I have no skill in the art of speaking. If by rhetoric they mean truth, I admit that I possess it. However, if they allow that I am a truthful person, I am not an orator in their sense of the word. For they have spoken with dazzling effect, but there is nothing of truth in their words. For my part, I shall place before you the whole truth and nothing but the truth. I have not come to you with a prepared speech, I am an old man. It is not for me to speak before you eloquently or in brilliant words. Do not be surprised, therefore, if I speak as simply as I am used to. I am now more than seventy years old, and this is my first experience of a law court. I am thus a stranger to the dignified ways of a court and to the manner of speech appropriate to it. Do not therefore mind my style. As judges, your duty is to consider whether or not what I say is just. My duty is to place before you nothing but the truth.

"My accusers are many in number. One of the charges is that I inquire into all things and make the worse appear the better reason, and so mislead the people. Those who accuse me thus are powerful persons. They say that I do not adhere to the religion of our forefathers. Moreover, they made these accusations when I was not there and it was therefore impossible for me to defend myself. I hope that your hearts will be freed from the bias created by their malicious or cunning reports. Nevertheless, I know that my task is a difficult one. I shall say what is needful, be the issue as God wills it.

"I mentioned a while ago the substance of their charge against me. They also lampoon me in plays and show me as trying to walk on air. I have not even thought about these things. I do not mean to suggest that it is impossible to walk on air. If anyone can do so, let him try by all means. For rny part I have no knowledge of these matters, yet Meletus has made a charge against me to that effect. Many of you here in this assembly have known me for a long time. You may consult among yourselves and find out whether I have ever talked to anyone on these matters. If all of you agree that I have not, you will see that the other charges against me must be equally false.

"My accusers say, moreover, that I undertake to educate men and demand payment of money in return, This, again, is false. Even if it were true, I see nothing wrong in it. There are many teachers among us who ask to be paid for their work. If they do their teaching well and are paid for it, I sec no dishonour in that. If we owned an animal, we would engage a man to train it and pay him. for his work. Why then should we not teach our children to be good, to do their duty as citizens? And if we found a teacher who might lead them along the right path, why should we not pay him? But, speaking for myself, I have not had the opportunity to be such a teacher.

"You may well ask me, 'If you have no faults, why is it that so many accusations are brought against you? If you have done nothing to mislead the people why are these accusations made against you and not against someone else ?' This would not be an unfair question to ask. I shall endeavour to show why these charges have been brought against me. Perhaps you think that I am jesting. Be assured, however, that I speak nothing but the truth. The reason for their accusations is that I possess a certain wisdom. If you ask, 'What kind of wisdom?' I can only say that, although it be but human wisdom, even the oracle has said that I have more of it than others.

"Though these are the words of the oracle, I did not readily believe them. Accordingly, I went to one reputed to be the wisest among us. I asked him a few questions and discovered that his was only a pretence to knowledge. I make no such claim. To that extent, therefore, I must be wiser than he is. For he who knows the extent of his own ignorance is wiser than another who does not. But when I proved his ignorance to that learned man, he came to bear me a grudge. Then I went to another person of learning. He also laid claim to knowledge which was only a cover for his ignorance. I proved the truth to him and thus made an enemy of him. I approached a large number of men in this manner, and all of them tried to shield their ignorance. I showed to each one of them how ignorant he was and so incurred his displeasure. I observed that the greater the pretence to knowledge the greater in fact the darkness. I also came to realize that true knowledge consists in being aware of how utterly ignorant one is.

"I went to many a poet and many an artisan. I found that a large number of poets could not explain the meaning of their compositions. The artisans were certainly superior to me in virtue of their skill, but out of pride in their skill, they assumed themselves to be wiser than others in other matters as well. All of them are really steeped in ignorance without knowing it. I learnt that I was more fully aware than any of them of the true state of our ignorance."

Indian Opinion, 11-4-1908.

Story of a Soldier of Truth [-III]

"You will now understand why I have so many accusers. I have been so busy bringing home to the people how ignorant we are and how very limited our knowledge is that I have taken no part in other public affairs. I have neglected my own affairs and have remained very poor. But I thought that I was serving God by opening the eyes of men to their own ignorance. It is because I chose to do this that people are enraged."

"Some young men who have little work to do follow me about and imitate me in cross-examining half-baked persons. The persons who are thus cross-examined and exposed as frauds become angry with me. Being unable to bring any other charge against me, they say that I look into things far too closely, that I disbelieve in the gods and make the worse appear the better reason. Intent on covering up their own ignorance, they fill your ears with calumnies against me. Such are Meletus and a few others. Meletus says that I corrupt the youth of Athens. I shall now examine Meletus himself."

socrates: Melctus, do you not think that young men should be trained to be virtuous in every possible manner?

Meletus. I do.

S: Who is it then who makes them virtuous?

M: The laws.

S: That is not the answer to my question. What I asked was, 'Which man improves them?'

M: It is the judges who do so.

S: Do you mean to say that those who occupy the seats of justice are able to teach them virtue ?

M: Certainly.

S: All of them? Or only some of them?

M: All of them.

S: That is well said. Now I ask you whether the listeners here can also improve the young or not.

M: They can, too.

S: You mean then that all the Athenians can instruct them in virtue while I alone corrupt them.

M: Most certainly, you do. Yes, that is what I mean.

S: You have made a serious charge against me. What you say probably holds good in the case of horses, too. Will you say that one man does them harm and everyone else improves them? On the contrary, is it not that only a very few are skilled in the art of training horses and the rest are ignorant? Surely you will admit that the same rule applies in the case of other animals? I think you cannot help doing so, for, of course, it does. And in saying that the case stands differently with men, you have given no thought, as far as I can see, to your charge against me. Besides, won't you admit that those who spend much time in the company of bad persons come under their evil influence?

M: I must admit that it is true.

S: Would you then say that anyone would want to injure himself intentionally? .

M: That I cannot say.

S: Now tell me, do I corrupt the young intentionally or unintentionally?

M: I say you corrupt them intentionally.

S: How can you say that? You are young. I am an old man. Do you really believe that I do not realize how, by corrupting others, I would myself become the worse for it? You have yourself admitted that this is what would happen. For we saw that those who keep company with the bad themselves become bad. No one will believe it likely that I want to be hurt. If my argument is correct, your charge that I corrupt the young intentionally falls to the ground. Now let us suppose that I corrupt them unintentionally. In that case, it was your duty to show me how I did this. You have not even tried to correct my error. You would have nothing to do with me. You only brought me up here for punishment.[1] It *is* thus clear from what Meletus has said that he has never given the slightest thought to any serious matter. Now let us consider how I corrupt the young. Meletus, you say that I corrupt them by teaching them not to believe in the gods of the city?

M: Yes, most certainly, I mean that.

S: What do you imply by that? Do I teach them to disbelieve in the gods.of the city, or to believe in some other gods?

M: I mean that you do not believe in any gods at all.

S: Bravo Meletus! You say that I believe neither the sun nor the moon to be a god, as the rest of the city docs.

M: Yes, I do say that you believe the sun to be stone and the moon to be earth.

S: Who will believe you? No one will believe your charge. If I tried to teach any such thing, everyone would know that there was nothing new in that. These are others' ideas. I myself do not believe in what they say. However, since you accuse me thus about the sun and the moon, you will also say, I suppose, that I wholly disbelieve in the existence of God.

M: I do most certainly assert that you deny the existence of God.

S: You are then deliberately asserting something impossible. How can I say that there is no God? Can anyone assert the existence of man's attributes but deny the existence of man? Or assert the existence of things pertaining to horses but deny the existence of horses? Or assert the existence of things pertaining to angels but deny the existence of angels?

M: The existence of what pertains to a thing implies the existence of the thing itself.

S: You admit that I talk of things pertaining to gods; you must admit therefore that I grant the existence of gods.

Indian Opinion, 18-4-1908

Story of a Soldier of Truth [-IV]

"I have nothing more to say about Mcletus's charge. I believe, moreover, that most of the people here are opposed to me. You will condemn me not on the basis of what Meletus and others say, but because of the prejudice and suspicion of the multitude. But many a good man has suffered in this way and many more will suffer thus in future.

"Someone may well ask: 'Are you not ashamed, Socrates, of pursuing studies which are likely to lead to your death?' I should answer such a man with perfect justice: 'You are wrong. Even a man of slight worth must be prepared for death. He must think only of one thing when embarking on any course of action, namely, whether he is acting rightly or wrongly, whether the action is worthy of a good man or not. If, as you imply, an act which involves the risk of death is a bad act, all the great warriors who fell in the battle at Troy, while doing their duty, must be deemed very bad men indeed. Patroclus was warned by his mother that, if he killed Hector, his own death would follow close upon Hector's. Patroclus replied that it was a thousand times to be preferred that he should die for killing Hector ro that he should live on as a coward. Patroclus was not frightened of death. The right thing for a man is not to desert his post, even if he has to run the risk of being killed or any other risk, whether he has chosen the post of his own will or has been put there by a superior.

"Consider, moreover, that when I was in the service of this State, I remained at the post where my commander had placed me and ran the risk of death. How strange would it be if, when my heart bade me seek a certain wisdom, I did not follow is bidding or failed to speak out for fear of death ? If I should fear death, that would be contrary to my belief that I am an ignorant man. If I think myself wise, without being wise, I would certainly deserve to be brought to trial. To fear death is to presume knowledge. For who has discovered for certain that death is a thing to be afraid of? Why should we not believe that death is the greatest good that can happen to men? Men fear it as though they knew very well that it was the greatest of evils! What greater ignorance can there be than this, of assuming that we know what we do not know? On these matters I think differently from others. If I have any wisdom, it is this: I claim to know nothing about death, and therefore make no attempt to conceal my ignorance. But I do well know that it is evil to do wrong and to disobey my superior. I will therefore never shrink in fear from what I hold to be right. If you were, therefore, to say to me without listening to my accusers' argument, 'Socrates, this time we will spare you, but on the condition that you cease this quest of yours; if you are found engaged in these pursuits again, you shall die, I should say in reply, 'Athenians, I hold you in the highest regard and love; but I will obey God rather than you. As long as I have breath and strength, I will not give up philosophy, or exhorting everyone I meet and those who would listen to me, saying, "O excellent Athenians! You are citizens of a famous city. You are known to be men of strength and wisdom. Yet you are so keen on making money that you give little thought to the means you employ for the purpose. You are eager for positions of honour and for reputation. Are you not ashamed of these things? You show little concern for your soul, for wisdom and truth. You take no thought for the perfection of your soul."' If, in reply, someone were to say that he did care for his soul and sought truth, I would not let it go at that. I would ask him in what way he cared for all these things. I would test him before I let him go. If in the course of the enquiry I found that he had no truth in him, I would reproach him with setting the lower value on the more important things and the higher value on those that are of less account. This I should do with everyone—citizen or stranger, young or old—but more especially with you, since I am better known among you and more nearly akin to you. Be assured that it is the command of God that I should speak thus. I even go so far as to claim that the commands of God are very dear to me and that this fact is in itself conducive to the highest good of the city. I have only one interest. To all, the young and the old, I say only one thing, namely, that you should care less for wealth and more for the soul; that you should strive for its perfection. Virtue does not come from wealth, but wealth, and all other things of this world, will come to you if you have virtue. If anyone says that I corrupt the people of this city by teaching them this, it would mean that virtue is vice. But if any man says that I teach anything else, he is trying to mislead you."

Indian Opinion, 25-4-1908

Story of a Soldier of Truth'[-V]

"And therefore I say to you: whether or not you believe the accusation, whether or not you acquit me, be sure that I will not forsake the path I have chosen for myself even if I have to die for it many times."

"Please do not be angry with me for what I say. Pay heed to my words. I think you will profit by them. What I am about to say now will perhaps make you angry. But listen carefully without anger. Since I am what I am, if you put me to death, you will do more harm to yourselves than to me. Meletus and others can do me no harm for it is not in their power to do so. It is impossible that a good man can be injured by a lesser person. As a consequence of his charge against me, I may be put to death, or exiled", or deprived of my rights as a citizen.

"You imagine that these things will be a great punishment for me. But I do not think of them as such. Rather, a person who tries to put another to death unjustly only harms himself. Do not therefore feel that I am arguing in my defence. I stand here to tell you what is in your own interest. I want to save you from the wrong of violating the divine command. If you put me to death, you will not easily find another man to fill my place. It is, of course, not for me to say this, but I cannot help pointing it out. As a strong horse needs reins, you need reins. Since you are also strong, I think it is the will of God that I should serve as your reins, and if you take my advice, you will spare me. But it is likely that you will thoughtlessly order my death, being vexed with me as . one sleeping is vexed with another who wakes him from his sleep and rushes at him ready to strike. And then you will drop off to sleep again, unless you have another man to fill my place. I strive for your good, having been sent by God for that purpose. You can see that I have neglected my own affairs, busying myself unceasingly for your good, counselling each one of you like a father or an elder brother and striving to lead you along the right path. You would have had some reason to doubt me if I had asked to be paid for what I was doing or made money thereby. But my accusers have not charged me with demanding money. And I have, in my poverty, the most convincing evidence that I have not accepted or demanded any payment of money.

"Perhaps you will ask me, why, if I go on exhorting people to virtue, moving from house to house, I do not take part in the political affairs of the city and strive for its welfare. I have often given my reason for that. I think I hear a divine voice whispering into my ear, telling me not to take part in politics. And I think it well that this has been so. If I had attempted to take part in politics, I should have perished long ago, without doing either you or myself any good. Do not be angry with me for speaking the truth. No man would be free from danger to his life, if he opposed the misrule prevailing in the city and tried to prevent injustice. He who would approach every question from the standpoint of justice had better stay out of the bother and bustle of politics. Let me give examples to prove this. You will see then that even the fear of death cannot force me to do what I consider to be wrong. But you will also see from them that, if I had busied myself in political affairs, I would have perished long ago. You may perhaps find that what I am about to tell you interests you but little. Nevertheless, it is true. I was at one time a member of our Assembly. It happened once that you resolved to sentence ten generals to death. I alone of all the members opposed the proposal. All of you then cried out for my death. But I stood firm; I thought that I ought to face death or imprisonment rather than join you in your unjust proposal. This happened in the days of democracy.

"When democracy had yielded place to oligarchy in this city, a person named Lyson was ordered to be brought over, so that he could be put to death as sentenced. I was among those who received this order. I knew that the sentence of death against Lyson had been passed unjustly. I ran the risk of death if I refused to go and bring him over. I did not fear death; I refused to go. If that Government had not been overthrown soon afterwards, I would certainly have been put to death.

"You will now see that if I had taken part in public affairs and had always upheld the cause of justice, (Justice being the breath of my life, I could not have done otherwise.) I could not have remained alive all these years. Throughout my whole life I have done no one an injustice, in private or in public; I have never acted in violation of justice. I have never presumed to be a teacher. But I never refused to answer anyone's questions, if he sought me out to learn from me. Moreover, I pay the same attention to the questions of both the poor and the rich, answering each one to the best of my ability. If, in spite of this, anyone has failed to learn goodness from my words, I am not to be blamed. If anyone among you asserts that I taught one thing to one man and something else to another, be sure he does not speak the truth.

"It has been asked why so many persons want to spend their time in my company; you know the reason why. If there are persons who think that they are wise while they are not, other persons delight to hear them cross-examined. It is certainly very amusing to listen to that. I think it is a duty enjoined upon me by a god that I should examine people, I .have done nothing wrong thereby. If it is true that I have corrupted the young by my teaching, those of them who are now grown up and are in a position to understand their true interests would have come forward to accuse me in your presence. Or even if they did not do so, their kinsmen would have come forward to do so. I see some of these young men and their kinsmen here in this assembly. Why has Meletus not called any of them as witnesses? If he and my other accusers have forgotten to summon them, I would permit them to do so even now. Let their evidence be taken. Instead of deposing against me, they will testify that their children have benefited by my company. They will have no reason, save a love of justice, to speak in my favour, and they have nothing to gain by so doing.

"I have said most of what I had to say in my defence. It generally happens that the relatives of the accused come to the Court and entreat the judges for mercy, and the prisoner himself sheds tears. I have done none of these things, neither have I any intention of doing them. This again will perhaps make some of you angry. I have kinsmen too. I have three sons—one of them is grown up and the other two arc still small. But I do not want to bring any of them before you. If I refrain from doing so, it is not because I mean to slight you. Do not impute it to my arrogance either. Let us also put on one side the fact that I have no fear of death. But I think it would be a discredit to me, and to you, if, at this age and with my reputation, such as it is, I had my kinsmen to shed tears before you. It would be unworthy of me. Everyone admits that in some way Socrates is different from the mass of mankind. If there should be among you any persons who excel the others and if they were to be prosecuted as I am being prosecuted, it would be shameful of them, from fear of death, to make anyone cry before you. If death were a misfortune, or if it were true that having once escaped death one would become immortal, an appeal to the sentiments of pity through one's relatives could possibly be justified. When our eminent men, although virtuous, begin to entertain such fear of death, foreigners are bound to scoff at us. They will say: 'Even those Athenians who are chosen for high office because of their superior virtue behave no better than women. How poor in spirit then must the other Athenians be!' I believe therefore that no good man should enact such a farce. If anyone attempts it, you ought to disallow it for the sake of the city's reputation. Whatever your sentence, it is the duty of the persons concerned to endure it in patience. And your duty is to despise those who give way to such pitiful melodrama.

"But, leaving aside all talk of credit or discredit, I do not think it is proper for the accused to plead for mercy. His duty is to ask for justice and to do so by stating facts and arguing from them. The duty of the judge is not to show favour but to dispense justice impartially. And therefore it behoves you and us that we should none of us forswear ourselves.

"If I were to entreat you to break your oath, it would amount to proving Meletus's charge against me, namely, that I do not believe in God. If anyone who believes in God teaches someone to violate his oath, then that will amount to teaching him to disobey God. Such a person does not believe in God. But I believe in God more firmly than anyone among you is ever likely *to*, 'and therefore, trusting in Him, I leave my case in your hands without fear."

Indian Opinion, 2-5-1908

Story of a Soldier of Truth [-VI]

It was by mistake, we [the editer] announced last week that this series was concluded. Socrates ended his defence. He was then found guilty by a majority vote. Socrates spoke as follows on the question of the punishment to be awarded to him:

"I am not vexed at your finding me guilty. Your decision is not an unexpected one. I am surprised rather at the large number of votes in my favour. I had thought the majority against me would be an overwhelming one. Instead, I find the margin is narrow. If three more had voted in my favour, I would have escaped punishment. I find, moreover, that I have been absolved of the charge of not believing in the gods.

"You can now sentence me to death. What can I say about it? What do I deserve to pay or suffer for having given up offices and political appointments and gone from house to house to teach virtue? If in the gymnasium someone keeps you amused and gives you the illusion of happiness, you will maintain him at public expense. I taught you the way to real happiness, not merely to the semblance of it. If, therefore, I am entitled to ask for anything, it is that in my old age you should maintain me at public expense.

"Perhaps you will think me arrogant for talking in this way after having been pronounced guilty, for demanding a reward instead of punishment. But it would not be true. Though you have found me guilty, I believe myself innocent. I have wronged no one. You have not been able to understand this, for my examination lasted only a day. How much can I explain to you in so short a time? If I had had more time with you, perhaps, I could have persuaded you to better effect. Since I am innocent, I do not propose any penalty for myself. Shall I propose imprisonment ? That will not be right. Shall I pay a fine ? I do not have the money for it. Shall I propose exile? How can I do that? I do not hold my life so dear as to want to pass the rest of my days wandering from place to place, continually haunted by fear.

"Someone may well suggest that I should retire into solitude and hold my peace. I cannot do that either. I believe I am commanded by the gods to discourse to people on what I hold to be virtue. I am also commanded by the gods to look unceasingly for principles of moral conduct. I do not think these are matters which you understand. But that is no reason why I should hold my peace.

Socrates was then awarded the death penalty by the Court. Unperturbed, the great Socrates immediately addressed the assembly as follows:

In any case, I have only a few years left to live. You could not be troubled to wait and you have earned an evil name for yourselves by condemning an innocent man to "death. If you had waited a while, I would have died in the course of nature, for I am an old man, far advanced in years. If I had used ignoble arguments before you and adopted the course common on such occasions, I would have escaped the death penalty. But that would have been inconsistent with my duty. I am sure a free man will never do anything unworthy of himself to save himself from death or other danger. One ought not to try to save oneself from death by any and every means. In battle, a man can save himself by laying down his arms and surrendering to the enemy. But we think such a man a coward. In the same way, anyone who resorts to unscrupulous means to save himself from death is an unworthy person. I think it is more difficult to save oneself from wickedness than from death, for wickcdncss is swifter than death. Being impatient and rash, you have taken a step which spells wickedness—wickedness which is so swift in its advance. You have sentenced me to death. I shall now leave this world. My opponents will be looked upon as men who betrayed truth and perpetrated an injustice. I will suffer my punishment. But they will also suffer the penalty for their evil deeds. This sssis what always happens. Perhaps it is just as well that it should be so.

And now, before I die, I wish to address a few words to you.

I am sure that after I die you will come to suffer greatly. You must not believe that, by getting rid of me, you will be able to go your wicked ways undisturbed. Do not assume that there will be no one to reproach you. Before I am taken to the place of execution, I shall address a few remarks to those who trust my words. So, those who wish to hear what I have to say may please stay on. I want to explain to you the meaning of death as I see it. Believe that what has happened to me is a good thing and that those who believe that death is an evil must be mistaken. Death may mean one of two things. Either the dead man wholly ceases to be and loses all sensation or the soul migrates to another abode. If the first belief is true and there is an end to all sensation, death is but the highest form of sleep. We look upon sleep as a blessing. If that is so, death, being the highest kind of sleep, must be a still greater blessing. If, on the other hand, we believe that death is a journey to another place, I shall only join those who have preceded me. In their presence, I shall get pure justice. There is no evil in this. If I have to go where Homer has gone, and other great souls with him, I shall deem it a great good fortune. I count it a high honour that I should join the souls of those who were victims of unjust punishment.

Believe it as a truth that no good man can come by evil either in life or after death. Such a man is never forsaken by God. And you may be sure that the man of truth is always happy. Therefore I am not unhappy that I am to die today and be released from these mortal coils. And so I am not angry with the judges or with my accusers. If they have wanted to do me evil, they deserve to be censured for that, but their intention can have no evil effect on me.

Now my last request: if, when my sons grow up, they begin to care for riches or for any other thing before virtue, if they think they are something when they are nothing at all, warn them, censure them, punish them just in the same manner as I have warned you against these things and reproached you with the love of them. If you can do this, I shall consider that you have been kind to me and my sons.

Now the time has come, and we must go hence: I to die, and you to live. God alone can tell which is the better state, mine or yours.

This is a historical event, that is, an event that actually occurred. We pray to God, and want our readers also to pray, that they, and we too, may have the moral strength which enabled Socrates to follow virtue to the end and to embrace death as if it were his beloved. We advise everyone to turn his mind again and again to Socrates's words and conduct.

Indian Opinion, 9-5-1908

Bibliography

Ambedkar, B.R. *What Congress and Gandhi Have Done to the Untouchables*? Bombay: Thacker and Co., 1946.

Andrew, Charles. *Mahatma Gandhi's Ideas.* New York: Macmillan, 1930.

Ananthanathan, A.K. "The Significance of Gandhi's Interpretation of the Gita." *Gandhi Marg*, 13, 3 (October 1991) : 302-15.

Ashe, Geoffrey. *Gandhi*. New York: Stein and Day, 1980.

— *Gandhi – A Biography*. Cooper Square Press, 2006.

Baker, J.I. "Gandhi and the Gita: Sanskrit and Satyagraha." *Gandhi Marg*, 15, 1 (April 1993): 39-61.

Bandyopadhyaya, Jayantanuja. *Social and Political Thought of Gandhi.* Bombay: Allied Publishers, 1969.

Bhattaharya, Buddhadeva. *Evolution of the Political Philosophy of Gandhi*. Calcutta: Calcutta Book House, 1969.

Bhattacharyya, Sailendra. *Mahatma Gandhi: The Journalist*. Bombay: Times of India Press, 1962.

Bondurant, Joan V. *Conquest of Violence*. Berkeley: University of California Press, 1967.

Bose, Nirmal Kumar. *My Days with Gandhi*. Calcutta: Nishana, 1953.

— *Studies in Gandhianism*. Calcutta: India Associated Publishing Company, 1962.

Brown, Judith. *Gandhi's Rise to Power: Indian Politics 1915-1922.* Cambridge: Cambridge University Press, 1972.

— *Gandhi: Prisoner of Hope*. New Haven: Yale University Press, 1989.

— *Gandhi and Civil Disobedience: The Mahatma in Indian Politics 1928-1934*. Cambridge: Cambridge University Press, 1977.

Buber, Martin. *The Writings of Martin Buber*, ed. By Will Herberg. New York: Meridian Books, 1958.

Buck, Lucien. "Gandhi and Jefferson on Democracy and Humanism," *Gandhi Marg* (July 1995): 175-92.

Chakravarty, Bidyut, *M.K. Gandhi*. New Delhi : Rolli Books, 2007.

Chatterjee, Margaret. *Gandhi's Religious Thought*. Notre Dame: University of Notre Dame Press, 1983.

Chatterjee, Partha. *Nationalist Thought and the Colonial World. A Derivative Discourse*. New Delhi : Oxford University Press, 1966.

Copley, Antony. *Gandhi: Against The Tide*. New Delhi: Oxford University Press, 1993.

Copley, Antony, and George Paxton, eds. *Gandhi and the Contemporary World*. Chennai: Indo-British Historical Society, 1997.

Dadhich, Naresh. *Gandhi and Existentialism*. Jaipur: Rawat, 1993.

Dalal, CB, *Hanilal Gandhi—A Life*. New Delhi: Orient Longman, 2007.

Dalton, Dennis. *Mahatma Gandhi: Non-Violent Power in Action*. New York. Columbia University Press, 1993.

— "The Ideology of Sarvodaya: Concepts of Politics and Power in Indian Political Thought." In *Political Thought in Modern India*, ed. By Thomas Pantham and Kenneth Deutsch. New Delhi: Sage, 1986.

— *The Indian Idea of Freedom*. Gurgaon: Academic Press, 1982.

Dhawan, G.N. *The Political Philosophy of Gandhi*. Bombay: Popular Books Depot, 1946.

Diwan, Romesh and Mark Lutz, eds. *Essays in Gandhian Economics*. New Delhi: Gandhi Peace Foundation, 1985.

Dworkin, Ronald. *Taking Rights Seriously*. Cambridge: Cambridge University Press, 1988.

Embree, Ainslie. *Source of Indian Tradition*. New York: Columbia University Press, 1988.

Erikson, Erik H. *Gandhi's Truth: On the Origins of Militant Non-Violence*. New York: Norton, 1969.

Fisher, Louis. *Gandhi: His Life and Message for the World*. New York: New American Library, 1982.

— *The Life of Mahatma Gandhi*. New York: Harper and Row, 1981.

Fox, Richard. *Gandhian Utopia: Experiments with Culture*. Boston: Beacon Press, 1989.

Gandhi, Rajmohan. *The Good Boatman: A Portrait of Gandhi*. New Delhi: Viking, 1985.

— *Mohandas – A True Story of a Man, His People and an Empire*. Penguin, New Delhi, 2006.

Gandhi, Tushar A. *Let's Kill Gandhi*, Rupa, New Delhi, 2007.

Gandhi, M.K. *All Men are Brothers*, ed. By Krishna Kripalani. New York: Cambridge University Press, 1988.

— *An Autobiography or the Story of My Experiments with Truth*. Ahmedabad: Navajivan Publishing House, 1972.

— *Constructive Programme*. Ahmedabhad: Navajivan Publishing House, 1941.

— *Hind Swaraj*. Ahmedabad: Navajivan Publishing House, 1938.

— *India of My Dreams*. Ahmedabad: Navajivan Publishing House, 1959.

— *My Religion, ed*. By B. Kumarappa. Ahmedabad: Navajivan Publishing House, 1955.

— *Panchayat Raj*. Ahmedabad: Navajivan Publishing House, 1959.

— *Rebuilding our Village*. Ahmedabad: Navajivan Publishing House, 1952.

— *Satyagraha in South Africa*. Ahmedabad: Navajivan Publishing House, 1950.

— *Socialism of My Conception*. Bombay: Bharatiya vidya Bhavan, 1957.

— *Trusteeship*. Ahmedabad: Navajivan Publishing House, 1960.

— *Truth Is God*. Ahmedabad: Navajivan Publishing House, 1990.

Gier, Nicholas. "Gandhi, Ahimsa, and the Self. *Gandhi Marg* 15, 1 (April 1993) 24-38.

— "Gandhi" Pre-Modern, Modern, or Post-Modern?" *Gandhi Marg* 18, 3 (October 1996) 261-281.

Glendon, Marg. *Rights Talk: The Impoverishment of Political Discourse*. Cambridge: Harvard University Press, 1991.

Green, Martin. *Gandhi: Voice of a New Age Revolution*. New York: Continuum, 1993.

— *Tolstoy and Gandhi*, New York. Basic Books, 1983.

Girija Kumar. *Gandhi, Brahmacharya and His Female Associates*, Bitastar Publication, 2006.

Guha, Ramchandra. *India After Gandhi*, Picador, 2007.

Haksar, Vinit. *Rights, Communities and Disobedience*. New Delhi, Oxford University Press, 2001.

Hendrick, George. 'The Influence of Thoreau's Civil Disobedience' on Gandhi's Satyagraha. *New England Quarterly*, Vol. 29, 1956.

— 'Influence of Thoreau and Emerson on Gandhi's Satyagraha, *Gandhi Marg*, 1959.

Henry, Garojini. "Social Ethics of Mahatma Gandhi and Martin Buber" *Journal of Dharma* 16,4 (1991): 375-386.

Hunt. D., 'Thoreau and Gandhi: A Re-evaluation of the Legacy', *Gandhi Marg*, 1970.

Hick, John, and Lamont Hemple. *Gandhi's Significance for Today*. New York: St. Martin's Press, 1989.

Iyer, Raghavan. *The Moral and Political Thought of Mahatma Gandhi*. Oxford: Clarendon Press, 1973.

Joshi, Dinkar. *Mahatma vs. Gandhi*, Delhi: Jaico Publishing House, 2007.

Kakar, Sudhir. *Mira and the Mahatma*. Penguin Books, New Delhi, 2004.

Kamath, MV. *Gandhi: A Spiritual Journey*: Indus Source Books, 2007.

Karunakaran, K.P. *New Perspectives on Gandhi*. Shimla: Indian Institute of Advanced Study, 1969.

Kothari, Rajni. 'Thinking of Gandhi As if He Were Still Around us' *Gandhi Marg*, Volume 27, 2005.

King, Martin Luther. "More than Any Other Person in History." *Peace News*, (January 1, 1958.)

King, Martin Luther. *Stride: Towards Freedom*. New York: Harper and Row, 1958.

Mehta, V.R. *Foundations of Indian Political Thought*. New Delhi: Manonhar, 1992.

Merton, Thomas, ed. *Gandhi on Non-Violence*. New York: New Directions Paperback, 1964.

Naes, Arne. *Gandhi and the Nuclear Age*. Totowa, N.J.: Bedminster Press, 1965.

Nanda, B.R. *Mahatma Gandhi: A Biography*. New Delhi: Oxford University Press, 1958

— *Gandhi and His Critics*. New Delhi: Oxford University Press, 1985.

— "Gandhi and Religion." *Gandhi Marg*, 121 (April 1990) : 5-23.

— *In Gandhi's Footsteps: The Life and Times of Jamnalal Bajaj*. New Delhi: Oxford University Press, 1990.

Nandy, Ashis. *At the edge of Psychology: Essays in Politics and Culture*. New Delhi: Oxford University Press, 1980.

Panter-Brick, Simone. *Gandhi against Machiavellism: Non-Violence in Politics*. London: Asia Publishing House, 1964.

Pantham, Thomas. "Gandhi's Intervention in Modern Moral Political Discourse." *In Gandhi and the Present Global Crisis*. Shimla: Indian Institute of Advanced Study, 1996.

— "Gandhi, Nehru, and Modernity." *In Crisis and Change in Contemporary India*, ed. By Upendra Baxi and Bhikhu Parekh. New Delhi, Sage, 1995.

— "Indian Secularism and its Critics." *Review of Politics* 59, 3 (Summer 1997): 523-40.

— "On Modernity, Rationality, and Morality: Habermas and Gandhi." *Indian Journal of Social Science* 1, 2 (1988): 187-208.

Parekh, Bhikhu. *Colonialism, Tradition and Reform*. New Delhi: Sage, 1989.

— *Gandhi's Political Philosophy*. Notre Dame: Notre Dame University Press, 1989.

— *Gandhi*. Oxford: Oxford University Press, 1997.

Parel, Anthony J., ed. *Gandhi: Hind Swaraj and Other Writings*. Cambridge: Cambridge University Press, 1997.

— "Gandhian Satyagraha and Machiavellian Virtue." In *The Meanings of Gandhi, ed*. Paul Power. Honolulu: University Pres of Hawaii, 1971.

— "Gandhi's Idea of Nation in Hind Swaraj." *Gandhi Marg* 13, 3 (October 1991): 261-81.

Power, Paul F. ed. *The Meanings of Gandhi*. Honolulu: University Press of Hawaii, 1971.

Prabhu R.K. and U.R. Rao. *The Mind of Mahatma Gandhi*. Oxford: Oxford University Press, 1945.

Prasad, Nagashwar, ed. *Hind Swaraj: A Fresh Look*. New Delhi: Gandhi Peace Foundation, 1985.

Rolland, Romain, *The Life of Vivekananda and the Universal Gospel*. Almora, India: Advaita Ashrama, (1931), 1965.

Rao, M.B. *The Mahatma: A Marxist Symposium*. Bombay: People's Publishing House, 1969.

Rawls, John. A *Theory of Justice*. Cambridge: Harvard University Press, 1971.

Ray, B.N. *Reading Gandhi*. New Delhi, Authors Press, 2008.

Roy, Ramashray. *Self and Society: A Study in Gandhian Thought*. New Delhi: Sage, 1985.

Rudolph, Loloyd, and Suysanne Hoeber Rudolph. *The Modernity of Tradition*. Chicago: University of Chicago Press, 1967.

— *Gandhi: The Traditional Roots of Charisma*. Chicago: University of Chicago Press, 1983.

— "Contesting Civilizations." *Gandhi Marg* 13, 4 (January 1992) 419-31.

Ruskin, John. *Unto This Last and Other Writings*, ed. Clive Wilmer. London: Penguin, 1985.

Savarkar, V.D. *Hindutva: Who Is a Hindu*? Bombay: Veer Savarkar Prakashan, (1923) 1989.

Sharma, Anand (ed) *Gandhian Way*. New Delhi, Academic Foundation, 2007.

Sharp, Gene. *Gandhi Wields the Weapon of Moral Power*. Ahmedabad: Navajivan, 1960.

— *Gandhi as a Political Strategist*. Boston: Porter Sergeant, 1979.

Singh Ajai, and Shakuntala Singh. "The Tagore-Gandhi Controversy Revisited," *Indian Philosophical Quarterly* 19, 4 (October 1992) : 265-82.

Southard, Barbara. "The Feminism of Mahatam Gandhi." *In New Dimensions and Perspectives in Gandhism*, ed. By V.T. Patil. New Delhi: Inter-India Publications, 1989.

Sudhakar K. 'A Fresh Look at Satyagraha'. *Gandhi Marg*, Volume 27, 2005

Terchek, Ronald J. *Gandhi: Struggling for Autonomy*. New York: Rowman and Littlefield, 1998.

— "Gandhi and Moral Autonomy." *Gandhi Marg*, 13, 4 (March 1992): 454-65.

— "The Psychoanalytic Basis of Gandhi's Politics." *The Psychoanalytic Review*, 62, 2 (Summer 1975).

Thoreau, Henry David. *Walden and Civil Disobedience*. ed. Owen Thomas. New York: Norton Critical Editions, 1966.

Tidrick, Kathryn . *Gandhi: A Political and Spiritual Life*. *IB*. Tauris, London, 2006.

Tolstoy, Leo. *The Kingdom of God is Within You*, trans. Constance Garnett. University of Nebraska Press, 1984.

Weber, Thomas. 'Claiming Credit for Gandhi'. *Gandhi Marg*, Volume 27 Number, 2005.

Woodock, George. *Gandhi*. London: Fontana Modern Masters, 1972.

Wong, Huiyun, "Gandhi's Contesting Discourse." *Gandhi Marg*, 17, 3 (October 1995): 261-85.

Wolfenstein, E. Victor. *The Revolutionary Personality: Lenin, Trotsky, Gandhi*. Princeton: Princeton University Press, 1971.

Index

❑❑❑